IF WE COULD CHANGE THE WORLD

. . . .

if we could change the world

YOUNG PEOPLE AND AMERICA'S

LONG STRUGGLE FOR RACIAL EQUALITY

Rebecca de Schweinitz

THE UNIVERSITY OF
NORTH CAROLINA PRESS
CHAPEL HILL

. . . .

Designed by
Courtney Leigh Baker
Set in Whitman and
Vitrina by Tseng Infor-
mation Systems, Inc.

The paper in this book meets the
guidelines for permanence and durability
of the Committee on Production
Guidelines for Book Longevity of the
Council on Library Resources.

The University of
North Carolina Press has
been a member of the
Green Press Initiative
since 2003.

. . .

The following works have been reprinted in this book: excerpts from *Uncle Tom's Children*, by Richard Wright, © 1936, 1937, 1938 by Richard Wright, copyright renewed 1991 by Ellen Wright, reprinted by permission of HarperCollins Publishers Inc.; "Strange Fruit" (song), by Lewis Allen, reprinted by permission of Edward B. Marks Music Company, © 1939 (renewed) by Music Sales Corporation (ASCAP), international copyright secured, all rights reserved; "Ella's Song," words and music by Bernice Reagon, © 1991 by Songtalk Publishing Company, Washington D.C., used by permission; excerpts from *Native Son*, by Richard Wright, © 1940 by Richard Wright, copyright renewed 1993 by Ellen Wright, reprinted by permission of Harper-Collins Publishers Inc.; excerpts from *Strange Fruit*, by Lillian Smith, © 1944 by Lillian Smith, copyright renewed 1972 by Paula Snelling, reprinted by permission of Harcourt, Inc., and Mc-Intosh and Otis, Inc.; and Rebecca de Schweinitz, "The 'Shame of America': African American Civil Rights and the Politics of Childhood," in *The Politics of Childhood: International Perspectives, Contemporary Developments*, edited by Jim Goddard, Sally McNamee, Adrian James, and Allison James (London: Palgrave Macmillan, 2005), reprinted by permission of Palgrave Macmillan.

Library of Congress Cataloging-in-Publication Data
De Schweinitz, Rebecca.
If we could change the world : young people and America's long
struggle for racial equality / Rebecca de Schweinitz.
p. cm.
Includes bibliographical references and index.
ISBN 978-0-8078-3235-6 (cloth : alk. paper)
1. African Americans — Civil rights — History — 20th century.
2. Civil rights movements — United States — History — 20th century.
3. Youth — United States — History — 20th century. 4. Children —
United States — History — 20th century. 5. Youth — United States —
Attitudes. 6. Children — United States — Attitudes.
7. United States — Race relations. I. Title.
E185.61.D39 2009
323.1196073 — dc22
2008053302
13 12 11 10 09   5 4 3 2 1

FOR

BENJAMIN DERSU,

GRACE MING LU,

AND OTHERS

WHO WILL CHANGE

THE WORLD

. . . .

The virtues of one generation are not sufficient for the next.

—JANE ADDAMS, "A Modern Lear" (1912)

. . . .

The child-mind has what your tired soul may have lost faith in.

—W. E. B. DU BOIS, *Darkwater: Voices from within the Veil* (1917)

. . . .

We may have different stories, but we hold common hopes. . . .

We all want to move in the same direction—towards a

better future for our children and our grandchildren. . . .

The children of America are not those kids, they are our kids.

—BARACK OBAMA, "A More Perfect Union" (2008)

CONTENTS

ILLUSTRATIONS

ACKNOWLEDGMENTS

Thanks go first to Peter, whose love, faith, encouragement, and questions have been as crucial to this endeavor as the long hours spent in libraries and at my computer. It seems fitting that he is in Ghana working with local villagers on a public health project as we close this chapter in our lives. Ben and Ming Lu have taught me firsthand (whether or not I liked it) about the agency of children and the ways they influence adults and shape the world around them. This book—and all of life—are more meaningful because of them. My parents, Bryant and Shauna Christensen, have provided ongoing moral support and much more. Their care for my children has enabled me to research and write about young people in history.

Cindy Aron's astute advice, reassuring criticism, and friendship strengthened both me and this book. Thanks also to Grace Elizabeth Hale, Brian Balogh, and Steven Nock at the University of Virginia for their encouragement and advice. The indefatigable Ed Ayers got this girl from Fairbanks, Alaska, excited about southern history and responded so enthusiastically to my first foray into children's history that I figured I must be onto something.

I thank Lori Gates Schuyler and her husband, Ridge; Jolene and Sam Bodily; Megan and Matt Clawson; and Anne Hyder for providing room and board, sometimes transportation, and always good company on what would otherwise have been lonely and expensive research trips.

Thank you to my colleagues at Brigham Young University. Fellow history department writing groupies Jay Buckley, Brian Cannon, Karen Carter, Mark Choate, Kathryn Daynes, Jessie Embry, Ignacio Garcia, Amy Harris, Christopher Hodson, Paul Kerry, Matt Mason, Jenny Pulsipher, Susan Rugh, Brett Rushforth, Aaron Skabelund, and particularly Richard Kimball deserve special thanks for reading multiple (long) chapters and offering valuable (if not always taken) suggestions. Kendall Brown, Arnold

Green, Craig Harline, Shawn Miller, Julie Radle, and Neil York may not have commented on the manuscript, but I appreciate and recognize their support of my work in other ways. Ellen Goldlust-Gingrich, Lisa Hawkins, Megan Olsen, and James Phillips provided fabulous research and editorial assistance.

I appreciate the insights of Joseph Hawes, James Marten, and the third, anonymous, reviewer for the University of North Carolina Press. This book is much better because of their perceptive readings and recommendations. Thanks also go to my editors at UNC Press. Charles Grench in particular supported me through the process and allowed me to stick to my vision for this book. He and everyone else at Chapel Hill have been a pleasure to work with.

I began work on this project at an auspicious time. A group of scholars (including a quiet graduate student) gathered in Washington, D.C., in August 2000; from that meeting emerged the Society for the History of Children and Youth. I have benefited greatly from SHCY's biennial conferences and the ongoing encouragement and insight of many people associated with this organization — it has been a great environment in which to grow up intellectually, so to speak. Every scholar should be lucky enough to be part of such an invigorating and just plain fun group of people.

I am grateful for the opportunities I've had to present portions of this work at conferences, including those sponsored by the Southern Historical Association, the Organization of American Historians, the American Historical Association, Stillman College, the Birmingham Civil Rights Institute, the University of Tours, and the Centre for the Social Study of Childhood at the University of Hull. Thank you to all who commented on and raised questions about my research and analysis. Many of you will see that your feedback has improved this project.

Thanks go to the University of Virginia Graduate School of Arts and Sciences and Corcoran Department of History for financial support. Generous grants from Brigham Young University's College of Family, Home, and Social Sciences as well as BYU's Family Studies Research Center made possible many research trips, student assistance, and the inclusion of illustrations in the pages that follow. The Women's Research Institute at BYU also supported this project. And a postdoctoral fellowship (for another project on race and childhood) at Yale's Gilder Lehrman Center gave me a chance to check out some great collections at the Yale Divinity Library.

Among the numerous research librarians who have contributed to this book, I particularly thank the archivists and staff at the University of North Carolina's Southern Historical Collection; the Special Collections Department at the Robert W. Woodruff Library at Emory University; the McCain Library and Archives at the University of Southern Mississippi; the Schomburg Center for Research in Black Culture at the New York Public Library; the Rockefeller Archive Center; the National Archives II; the Library of Congress; the Archives Department at the Birmingham Public Library; the Special Collections Department, the J. Edgar and Louise S. Monroe Library at Loyola University–New Orleans; the Amistad Research Center at Tulane University; the Yale Divinity Library; the Martin Luther King Jr. Center; the Hoover Institution Library and Archives at Stanford University; the University of Michigan's Bentley Historical Library; and the Virginia Historical Society. Clarence Hunter at the Mississippi Department of Archives and History made unprocessed collections available to me, while Ti'ata Sorenson and other staff at BYU's interlibrary loan office kept the microfilm and other materials coming.

In the spring of 2008, I spent a couple of days at a conference sponsored by the Birmingham Civil Rights Institute. I was delighted to talk with other scholars, activists, community leaders, and local people interested in exploring (and in doing something about) a range of human rights issues. I was also delighted to meet two of my heroes, Carolyn McKinstry and Bob Zellner, who, as ever, are doing their part to change the world.

I hope that this book does some justice to the experiences and contributions of Carolyn and Bob and other young activists who did so much to make America a more just place. I hope that their stories and my story about children, youth, and America's long freedom struggle will help inspire a new generation of young people to overcome the challenges that remain.

IF WE COULD CHANGE THE WORLD

. . . .

INTRODUCTION

In the late 1960s, researchers asked black children at St. Cecilia School in Chicago, "If you could change the world in any way you wanted, what change would you make?" With all of the decade's youth protests, it was the type of question that increasingly interested sociologists and political scientists who wanted to understand better the political socialization of children and how to control or predict young people's political activism.[1]

I am under no illusions that even the most enlightened scholars (or parents) can control or accurately predict what young people might do, say, or believe. This volume, however, asks a similar question about youth activism during a similar time period: How did young people and popular conceptions of children and youth influence the black freedom struggle and help to change America's racial landscape? On one level, this book adds to our understanding of childhood as a social construct. Specifically, it explores when and why the nation's sentimentalized construction of childhood began to include African American children, both rhetorically and in reality. It looks at how shifting ideas about childhood and youth influenced political struggles over black Americans' place in the nation's sociopolitical order. Social constructions of childhood and public discussions about youth have had a significant impact on America's racial politics. Building on the work of children's historians, this book also recognizes children and youth as important agents of change. It examines the ways that young people contributed to the civil rights movement and explains why so many young Americans joined the struggle for racial equality in the late 1950s and early 1960s.[2]

Young people and ideas about them lie at the center of this study. But it is a history of the civil rights movement — the kind that recognizes the long history of the movement — as much as a history of children, youth, and our ideas about them. This book begins in the early twentieth century, a time of heightened interest in the welfare of children but also a time in which white southerners—and even white liberals sympathetic to the plight of blacks—generally accepted the pickaninny descriptions of black children commonly encountered in books and advertisements that defined African Americans as a child race in need of white guidance and incapable of assuming the full rights of citizenship. Black leaders challenged such stereotypes, often drawing on ideas about childhood to prove the respectability of the race. W. E. B. Du Bois and the National Association for the Advancement of Colored People (NAACP) frequently used images and stories of young blacks who perfectly embodied conceptions of the ideal white middle-class child to challenge negative stereotypes of blacks and demonstrate the political fitness of their parents (or at least their fathers) and the race. This strategy for racial progress, however, had a downside: by focusing on images of young African Americans who reflected childhood ideals, race leaders in some ways obscured the problems that most black children faced. Indeed, such a focus may well have perpetuated notions of the undeserving black, since childhood ideals were all but impossible for most African Americans to achieve.

By the 1930s, ideas about childhood had shifted, influencing perceptions of black Americans and their struggle for greater civil and political rights. Scholars generally identify 1930 as marking the triumph of sentimental over economic conceptions of childhood in America—as the beginning of the historical period in which American children from all classes became "priceless."[3] The same year, the White House issued the Children's Charter (appendix A), a document that identified nineteen "rights of childhood" that the nation pledged to help all of its children, including black children, achieve. Childhood became in some respects a political as well as an emotional category, a developmental stage that carried with it certain rights and that obligated certain protections from the state. Childhood also became, at least to some people (and in official American discourse), a racially inclusive category.

Armed with ideas about children's rights in a democracy, race leaders, reformers, and civic and educational leaders increasingly emphasized the discrepancies between childhood ideals and the plight of young underprivileged blacks. Scholars have shown that during the Great Depression, blacks pressured the Justice Department and the NAACP to address local concerns, working-class African Americans made a place for themselves in labor unions, various organizations campaigned against lynching, and Washington-based activists pushed for African Americans' equal inclusion in New Deal programs and government employment.[4] At the same time, black and white scholars, reformers, educators, and organizations interested in America's young people began to forge a youth-centered racial liberalism that would at least indirectly influence the course of the civil rights movement. Historians have identified the importance of the 1930s to the struggle for racial equality. This book adds to that scholarship by suggesting another reason why that decade is crucial to understanding the civil rights movement. The rise of youth subcultures and the exigencies of the Great Depression fueled interest in the problems of youth, especially the problems of rural and black youth. Reformers and influential government and private agencies who addressed youth issues increasingly criticized Jim Crow's effects on young people and suggested that all of the problems of all of America's youth—including its most destitute—could best be alleviated through a system of universal and equal education.

In the 1940s and early 1950s, ideas about education, rhetoric about the rights of childhood, and national security concerns converged with ideas about African American civil rights to influence the Supreme Court decision in the *Brown* case. Scholars of the civil rights movement have debated both the reasons for the Court's 1954 ruling and its significance (or lack thereof) to the movement. They have detailed important local struggles that influenced civil rights strategies, including the push for desegregated schools. They have outlined the ideas and vision of NAACP lawyers and the work of the U.S. Department of Justice, Civil Rights Section. They have looked at the influence of social scientists, judges, international sentiment, World War II, the cold war, New Deal liberals, and unions. Indeed, a considerable body of scholarship tells us much about the context of *Brown* and about how America began to dismantle legal segregation and build a mass movement dedicated to racial and economic justice.[5] This book builds on that work, adding another layer to the complex history of *Brown* and the fight for African American civil rights. Like many other studies of the black freedom struggle, this volume identifies *Brown* as a watershed in movement history. But *Brown*'s significance cannot be fully understood without looking at it in the context of widespread beliefs about childhood and the rights of childhood and in relation to the public debates about childhood, youth, education, and national security that occurred in the years leading up to the ruling. These debates linked ideas about childhood, youth, and the rights of young people in America with the future of democracy and the role of public schools.[6]

Brown was pivotal to the movement partly because ideas about childhood, youth, and the rights of young Americans influenced both the Supreme Court ruling and the subsequent presentation of the black freedom struggle to the American public. Whether it was *Life* magazine talking about students who wanted to integrate and suffered because of closed schools, Martin Luther King Jr. giving speeches about his daughter's feelings of inferiority, or activists from the Student Non-Violent Coordinating Committee using propaganda photos and stories that illustrated the effects of racism on black children, the national press and African American leaders and organizations argued for desegregation and for racial equality by calling on ideas about childhood, youth, and children's rights, ideas on which the Supreme Court also called to explain its 1954 ruling against segregated public schools.

Not surprisingly, those ideas influenced public perceptions of the movement. In the domestic-centered decades after World War II, linking African American civil rights to ideas about childhood and to images of young people helped make the movement meaningful, even compelling, to blacks as well as to a white American public not yet committed to the idea of racial equality. Ideas about childhood help to explain *Brown* as well as answer one of the other central questions that scholars have asked about the civil rights movement: Why did the movement achieve a level of success for that short period of time in the 1950s and 1960s? One reason, this book suggests, is that connections between the struggle for racial equality and ideas about childhood brought sympathy and a measure of support for the black freedom struggle at a time when ideals about home and family, parents and children, strongly influenced the nation's political culture. It is no coincidence that the Supreme Court ruled against segregated and decidedly unequal schools and that the South was widely criticized for physically and mentally attacking young blacks during the so-called golden age of the American family. Despite the inaccuracies of popular historical memory of the era and regardless of whether or not the ideals expressed in popular television shows such as *Father Knows Best* (which first aired in 1954) reflected reality, the 1950s and early 1960s were a time in which the nation glorified domestic life and Americans had clear conceptions about what constituted a proper childhood.[7]

The same connections between ideas about childhood and the struggle for racial equality that helped make possible some of the black freedom movement's success, however, ultimately limited support for African American civil rights.[8] White America was willing to come to the aid of young blacks and childlike adult civil rights protesters but was less willing to address the economic concerns of the black community or to support more radical black strategists.

Ideas about childhood and youth were not alone in influencing the struggle for racial equality. Equally important were young people themselves, who have indeed changed the world; they have been significant, often autonomous, political actors. Ideas about childhood and assumptions about the relative lack of value of young people to the movement have often obscured the extent of youth participation and influence. Nonetheless, young people played crucial roles in the black freedom struggle. In fact, children and youth who participated in the sit-ins and other protest demonstrations of the early 1960s built on a militant youth organizing tradition that began in the 1930s. During that decade, the NAACP, in response to youth activism and fears about potential youth radicalism, developed (with the help of and pressure from young members) a strong youth program that officially encouraged the use of direct-action techniques. Moreover, from the time the NAACP organized youth councils and college chapters in the 1930s, young people pushed the association and thus the movement in more militant directions.

Looking at young people and youth organizing in the civil rights movement helps us to better understand youth influence on the movement. It helps us to see more clearly the nature and dynamics of the NAACP and it reveals the importance of the pre-*Brown* period of the movement's history. Placing young people at the center of the movement also helps to explain the most militant and studied period of civil rights protest—that is, it helps to clarify why many Americans supported the struggle for racial equality and why young people engaged in widespread protest against Jim Crow and for the expansion of black civil rights in the late 1950s and early 1960s. This focus also gives voice to people we rarely consider in the stories we tell about the civil rights movement.

If looking at notions of childhood and young people themselves in the African American freedom struggle markedly changes the way we understand that struggle, then it is less certain that we can clearly define—or, rather, set age limits on—children and youth. This book suggests that childhood and race were (and are) shifting social constructs with considerable political meaning; childhood and youth have never been fixed categories. To be sure, significant differences exist among six-, fifteen-, and twenty-four-year-olds. But ideas about childhood and the term "child" were often applied to young people of all those ages. Indeed, the age and developmental differences between little girls trying to integrate elementary schools in New Orleans, teenagers marching in the streets of Birmingham, and college-age activists organizing voter registration drives in the Mississippi Delta were usually lost as activists and the media presented the story of the civil rights movement to the American public. This book's use of childhood, children, and youth, its inclusion of the experiences, perspectives, and contributions of elementary school–age children, adolescents, and young adults, reflects the indistinctness with which words such as "child" and "youth" were often (and still are) used. The ambiguity of those terms has not diminished their influence or made the young people who have moved in and out of socially constructed categories of childhood and youth (or other names we have assigned them) any less significant as historical and political actors.

One

· · · · · · ·

THE SHAME OF AMERICA

THE RIGHTS OF CHILDHOOD, THE YOUTH

PROBLEM, & RACE IN THE GREAT DEPRESSION

In the spring of 1931, word spread around the South that the black "brutes" responsible for ravaging two white women on a train near Scottsboro, Alabama, had been convicted of their unspeakable crimes and sentenced to die in the electric chair. Many white southerners believed that justice was finally at hand. After all, the *Chattanooga News* reported, the difference was like "night and day" between "the nine men who perpetrated those frightful deeds, and [a] normal, kind-hearted man who guards his little family and toils through the day, going home to loved ones at night with a song in his heart."[1]

The difference between the way the white South and those defending the accused presented the Scottsboro case was also like night and day. Prosecutors and the white southern press described the nine defendants as men, savage and sexual, unquestionably capable and so probably guilty of heinous crimes against southern womanhood. But defenders highlighted what came to be one of the more compelling aspects of the case: the nine accused were not men at all, but children—the youngest only thirteen at the time, the oldest not yet twenty. These were not men predisposed to perform "frightful deeds" or even men with families to guard, although the depression had forced them, as it had other youth, to seek work. These were boys, with mothers who worried when they did not return home and cried when they learned that the Alabama penal system held their sons. As William Pickens, a field secretary for the National Association for the Advancement of Colored People (NAACP), wrote in an editorial, "Newspapers . . . refer to these colored children as negroes, saying nothing about their being mere children and leaving the impression on the ignorant public that they are men. That is part of their scheme to get them murdered without waking up public sympathy."[2]

As Pickens and other defenders of the nine knew, in the 1930s South, black *men*, regardless of their innocence, had little hope of eliciting public sympathy and less hope of finding justice. But race leaders hoped that black *children*, at least if they could be thought of as children first, might bring public pressure to bear on a southern court system dedicated to racial prejudice. White northerners shared many of the South's racial beliefs but were also invested in ideas about the sanctity of childhood. For them, childhood had become a sacred state, protected by legal codes, cultural ideals, and even certain rights. By the time the nine Scottsboro youth went to trial, reformers had curbed industrial child labor and established child protection and welfare services. Moreover, the 1930 presidential Children's Charter (appendix A), created at the third decennial White House Conference on Children and Youth, had established guidelines for American childhood that reflected the nation's middle-class ideals. It even attached specific rights to notions of childhood and insisted on a racially inclusive definition of childhood. The document specified that "the first rights of citizenship" belonged to all American children, including rural children and "every child . . . wherever he may live under the protection of the American flag . . . regardless of race, or color, or situation." Those rights included a child's right to "health protection" and "an education which . . . will yield him the maximum satisfaction." They also included the right to "grow up in a family with an adequate standard of living" and "protection against labor that stunts growth, either physical or mental, that limits education, that deprives children of the right of comradeship, of play, and of joy."

Most white southerners might not have thought that black youth, especially poor black youth riding the rails, deserved such rights. They quickly found, however, that widespread beliefs about childhood and a growing consensus that the federal government should act to protect young people undermined efforts to enforce a racialized judicial system. Perhaps for the first time since Reconstruction, the region's ability to manage its racial affairs was extensively called into question as the story of the Scottsboro Boys was told and retold over the course of the decade (as the case dragged on) in the national and international media and even in some moderate southern papers not as a story of crimes against white womanhood, as the white South insisted, but instead as a story of crimes against childhood.[3]

In what the Scottsboro Defense Committee hailed as the "*real* story of Scottsboro," each of the defendants was like "puny" Eugene Williams, who did not "look a day over his thirteen-and-a-half years" and who grew up the oldest of six children in a leaky two-room hut on a muddy alley. The ninety cents his mother made taking in washing and ironing each week bought little food, so Williams decided he would have a better chance of helping his family if he took to the rails. He might find a job down the line, and at least there would be one less mouth to feed at home. Williams and the other boys were admittedly "poor and ignorant," and most of them probably would never amount to much, but they were ordinary boys, trying to do right by their families under the most deplorable of circumstances.[4]

Just a few years after Williams and the other boys began their nightmarish quest for justice, the newly formed American Youth Commission (AYC) would bring increased attention to the problems of young Americans, including young black Americans. In many ways, the Scottsboro Boys epitomized the young people whose appalling plight would soon become more widely known to the American public through the commission's work as well as through that of reformers and New Deal agencies. Like those who later publicized America's depression-era "youth problem," defenders of the nine boys juxtaposed the rights of childhood with the problems of poverty, unemployment, and lack of education. They were not bad boys. Like other underprivileged rural youth, they were just making every "effort to escape the toils of poverty." Moreover, like other poor young Americans, their rights to childhood had gone unrealized. Instead of finding state protection during their innocent and vulnerable years, the Scottsboro Boys found themselves living in dire circumstances, suffering from precisely the ills against which America was supposed to guard its young. Even worse, the state, which should have been taking care of them—protecting them from conditions that led to youth transience and delinquency—had turned against them. Police harassed them; the courts, as civil rights groups charged, legally lynched them; and jailers beat them. These "nine negro children grow[ing] to young manhood in jail," defenders argued, represented the "shame of America."[5]

One paper's description of the scene in Alabama in July 1931 exemplified the ways defenders elicited public opinion in favor of the boys by calling on widespread beliefs about childhood: "Down in Kilby prison tonight

there sit in death row eight negro boys . . . the youngest a slender strip-
ling of fourteen. Unless the Alabama Supreme Court intervenes this mere
child, who looks as though at any minute he might fling himself on his
mother's breast and cry over a lost top or broken toy, will march with his
seven fellows to the electric chair which sits grimly awaiting his hundred
pounds of flesh just beyond the green door fifty feet from his cell . . . [t]he
image of forlorn youth."[6]

Many of the boys' advocates supposed that as images of the innocent,
suffering children continued to be broadcast around the nation and the
world, the "boys will be saved . . . because America cannot afford to be
held up to the civilized world as such a savage nation." One observer later
compared the Scottsboro case to Birmingham police chief "Bull Conner
turning the hoses and dogs on young black protesters" in the 1960s. From
his perspective, both incidents came as "a great shock to a large number
of people and made [them] face up to a situation which they would have
not faced up to before." The black community was especially moved, and
while "most blacks had tended to stay away from black people in trouble
. . . they joined in the fight for the Scottsboro Boys."[7]

But it was the 1930s, not the 1960s. And although defenders of the boys
marshaled public opinion to their cause and eventually freed some of the
boys (the younger ones, not incidentally, first), black childhood, at least in
the South, was not sacred in the same way as middle-class white childhood
and all white womanhood. White southerners believed that upholding the
virtue of white women was more important than respecting the nation's
ideas about childhood—at least when it came to applying those ideas to
black children. And that belief held true even when white women came in
the form of male-attired girl tramps with loose language and sexual repu-
tations. Many white southerners considered the idea of a separate state of
childhood for blacks impossible, since, according to racist philosophies,
blacks lived in a perpetual state of childhood. As W. E. B. Du Bois put it,
"They cannot conceive [of] Negroes as men." It was sadly ironic that black
men could attain the status of men only when they seemed to threaten
white womanhood and that under such conditions, black boys were denied their true status as children.[8]

The Scottsboro Boys case certainly did not represent a complete victory
for civil rights advocates or for racially inclusive ideas about childhood.
But it did help awaken the public to the severe and unjust presumptions
against black youth. Moreover, since the Communist Party quickly came

to the boys' defense and used their plight as evidence of the corrupt nature of America's capitalist democracy, the case indicated that discrepancies between childhood ideals and realities could be closely tied to national security issues. The Scottsboro Boys case and the Communist Party's involvement also pushed the NAACP, which initially refused to defend the nine less-than-respectable black youth, to take up the cause, partly because the organization's leaders saw that cultural beliefs about childhood led to public support rather than condemnation of the Scottsboro Boys.[9]

The case of the Scottsboro Boys offers a fitting starting point for a book about young people and the civil rights movement and a chapter primarily about youth in the 1930s. The incident provides a gripping example of how stories about civil rights were often told and understood in a way that connected ideas about childhood and youth to the black freedom struggle. It intimates connections between national security—the future of democracy—and the experiences of young people. It exposes the severe economic, social, and political constraints young blacks often faced, reveals that many Americans held racially specific ideas about childhood and youth, and shows that race leaders hesitated to associate their cause with young people who embodied the problems of young blacks in America. Most of this chapter considers how the Great Depression and ideas about childhood and youth—and the rights of childhood—brought attention to the problems of America's young blacks, largely through the work of the AYC, which helped create a racial liberalism focused on young people, education, and personality development. But the chapter first examines how the NAACP, in its early years, also drew on ideas about childhood and youth to promote racial uplift.

CHILDHOOD, RACE, AND THE POLITICS OF RESPECTABILITY

"All human problems . . . center in the immortal child," Du Bois declared in *Darkwater: Voices from within the Veil*, his 1920 polemic against Jim Crow. Scores of contemporary reformers and even everyday Americans, not otherwise inclined to give much thought to America's racial problems, might have agreed with this statement. In the first decades of the twentieth century, optimistically labeled "the century of the child" by child welfare advocates, America had taken steps to protect its young. By 1920, state, local, and (less frequently) federal statutes limited child labor, created separate juvenile courts, extended public schooling opportunities, provided for infant and maternal health benefits, and funded parks and recreation programs as well as research on mothers and children. With all of these efforts to "save childhood," Du Bois's credo, "I believe in the Training of Children, black even as white, the leading out of little souls into the green pastures and beside the still waters . . . for life lit by some large vision of beauty and goodness and truth," seemed to reflect the currents of the era at the same time it challenged their racialized limitations.[10]

Darkwater was not Du Bois's first attempt to expand the nation's ideas about childhood to further the aims of the African American struggle for racial equality. Nor was it the first time he used black children as a means to help whites see the respectability and humanity of his race. Throughout the early twentieth century, white southerners justified Jim Crow laws and the continued economic exploitation of black Americans with prejudicial racial theories that defined blacks as helpless and dependent children. In contrast, Du Bois drew on qualities associated with middle-class white childhood to call attention to racial injustice and to create a positive and sympathetic portrait of African Americans. Indeed, in his most famous work, *The Souls of Black Folk* (1903), Du Bois contrasted notions of childhood innocence with the inability of black teachers and parents, especially black fathers, to shield their children from the physical and psychological effects of the color line. Through stories about his and others' lives, Du Bois poignantly illustrated how "the shadow of the Veil" shaped the lives of black youth. The nation's doctrines and practices surrounding race made young African Americans—his own or those he taught in rural Tennessee—seem less like the children the nation increasingly idealized, full of energy and promise, and more like prisoners, "half hopelessly" watching "the streak of blue above." In one especially moving chapter, Du Bois described his feelings as a new father. Looking at his "beautiful . . . olive-tinted" child for the first time, Du Bois experienced both joy and anguish. His helpless infant's bluish eyes, "dark gold ringlets," and "perfect little limbs" clearly resembled those of idealized white children. Such features could easily, Du Bois implied, win praise from eugenicists who normally scorned blacks for their inherent biological inferiority. As Du Bois told readers, however, his child's yet "uncolored" world and sense of himself would soon change, "like the sky from sparkling laughter to darkening frowns." Du Bois further suggested that because the color line so tragically distorted childhood, the baby's death a few days later was a "blessing," an "escape."[11]

In his descriptions of black parents' helplessness to protect their children, the "shadow" of Jim Crow, and death as a welcome alternative to life in racist America, Du Bois was making arguments similar to those antislavery advocates had made more than half a century earlier. In the years before emancipation, abolitionists, black and white, called attention to the evils of slavery with what were then new sentimentalized views of families and children. "Put yourself in the place of a slave parent," they urged; think of the "tender" slave child "robbed" of "parental care and attention . . . thrown upon the world without the benefit of its natural guardians . . . without hope, shelter, comfort, or instruction." In her best-selling and widely read novel, *Uncle Tom's Cabin* (1852), Harriet Beecher Stowe repeatedly showed slave parents struggling to protect their children and suffering when they could not keep their families together. One character in the book was so distraught by the realities of slave life that she poisoned her youngest child rather then let him grow up under such conditions. Stowe portrayed this mother's actions as tragically heroic. "O, that child!—how I loved it!," Cassy said, continuing, "I am not sorry, to this day [that I killed him]; he, at least, is out of pain." Escaped slave Harriet Jacobs similarly explained in her autobiography that it was "mockery for a slave mother to pray back her dying child to life! Death is better than slavery." And sounding very much like Jacobs, Louisa J. Hall, in her 1849 poem "Birth in the Slave Hut," contrasted the effects of the shadows of slavery with the "instinct of joy" that usually accompanies the birth of a child. The middle-class white abolitionist considered it perfectly understandable that a new slave mother would wish to "feel myself childless again / Or dare with my own hand to tear / The life from this creature of pain!"[12]

Freedom from slavery brought black Americans more hope than they had possessed in the antebellum period. And Du Bois did not condone infanticide or necessarily see it as an act of defiance against an unjust society, as it may have been in the slave South. But he and his readers would certainly have been familiar with this compelling literary tradition, a tradition that drew on sentimental notions of childhood, often punctuated by stories of child death, to illustrate the truly unconscionable plight of blacks under slavery. By appropriating this literary convention to the early-twentieth-century struggle for racial justice, Du Bois no doubt hoped, like his predecessors, to foster sympathy for his people. At a time when interest in the welfare of children heightened and when theories of racial difference continued to question the full humanity of blacks, he also hoped to convince white Americans that racism hurt children and that African Americans shared with their white counterparts the strongest and noblest of human emotions.

Booker T. Washington's turn-of-the-century autobiography similarly linked earlier abolitionist literary traditions and strategies to the post-emancipation struggle for civil rights. Washington explained that as a slave child he had never gone to school, slept in a bed, or even sat down for a meal with his family. He recalled that there had been "no period of [his] life . . . devoted to play," that his mother "had little time in which to give attention to the training of her children," and that even as a young boy he spent every day "occupied in some kind of labour." His description of slave childhood sharply contrasted with American ideals. Like antislavery advocates, he reminded readers who might not have known firsthand its horrors that slavery effectively stole the childhood of black Americans. More important, his account made the realization of middle-class childhood ideals a central part of the meaning of freedom. It also explained that although black children had many more opportunities to enjoy the kind of childhood Americans increasingly idealized, even in freedom, "the Negro youth starts out with the presumption against him."[13]

Washington clearly lamented the obstacles African American youth encountered; however, he also believed that they offered a starting point for racial progress. After all, if young blacks began life with so much working against them, any success they achieved would have to be considered all the more remarkable. His life offered proof that blacks could rise, even "up from slavery," as his autobiography was titled, to achieve greatness. For all their differences, Du Bois and Washington could agree to at least some extent on this point and this strategy. Du Bois became more critical of Jim Crow and its incumbent racial theories than Washington. And unlike the more conciliatory Washington, Du Bois ultimately refused to accept a racial reconciliation based on the idea that blacks were something of a child race, destined to occupy a separate and subordinate position in American economic and political life. In fact, again employing child-centered rhetoric, Du Bois warned that the type of compromise Washington supported would bring only "a harvest of disaster to our children, black and white." But both leaders believed that one of the best ways to help uplift the race was to prove that black youth, despite the presumptions against them, could rise above white stereotypes of blacks and embody white middle-class conceptions of childhood.[14]

To this end, Du Bois wrote sentimental vignettes, stories of black youth whose "soft eyes," "so poignant with beauty . . . so hard with sorrow," know that their parents are lying when they tell them they trust white people, stories of black children with "the same eagerness, the same joy of life, the same brains as in New England, France, and Germany," who faced the "thundering wave," the "black eddies," the "meanness and smallness" of the white world. He balanced such sketches with inspirational stories of young blacks who overcame society's low expectations. In telling about his life, for example, Du Bois, like Washington, chose not to emphasize the prejudices working against him but instead how such prejudices "spurred [him] to tireless effort," so that he felt "not so much disowned and rejected as rather drawn up into higher spaces and made part of a mightier mission." Du Bois knew that other young blacks would, as he had, shed "secret tears" over manifestations of racial prejudice. He hoped, however, that they, too, would become determined to prove themselves and their race.[15]

Historians have suggested that "the idea of home and family" as important sites of racial progress and respectability was central to the racial uplift ideologies espoused by many (especially male) black leaders in the early twentieth century. As Kevin Gaines explains, "Elite blacks celebrated [and race leaders championed] the home and patriarchal family as institutions that symbolized . . . freedom, power, and security." These institutions, as defined and idealized by the white middle class, stood "at the heart of blacks' visions of oppression, liberation, and citizenship."[16]

Scholars who have addressed the relationship between "respectable" black family life and notions of racial progress have focused on issues of gender—on the patriarchal nature of idealized family life and on how black leaders' acceptance of idealized white gender roles often limited their critiques of the nation's sociopolitical order.[17] "Respectable" family life, however, depended on middle-class notions of childhood (and girlhood and boyhood) as much as on middle-class notions of manhood and womanhood, of fatherhood and motherhood.

In the nineteenth century, abolitionists used sentimental ideas about families and children to argue for the humanity of blacks and against the tyranny of slavery. After the Civil War, black leaders drew on similar ideas to argue for racial equality. For them, blacks' ability to re-create the family patterns and roles idealized by the white middle class, especially black parents' ability and determination to provide well for their children, demonstrated the race's moral and political virtue.

Du Bois was among those who drew on this compelling theme. His writings repeatedly demonstrated black America's commitment to middle-class childhood ideals and black children's potential to equal or even surpass their white peers. In *The Souls of Black Folk*, Du Bois presented himself as the model middle-class father, dedicated to protecting and nurturing his children through the hazards of life, which included the added and unjust hazards of racial prejudice. In *Darkwater*, he again highlighted childhood themes, describing how his mother, who as a single woman might easily have "preferred a steady income from [his] child labor rather than bank on the precarious dividend of [his] higher training," instead committed herself to the ideals of the middle class. In the early twentieth century, Progressive reformers criticized working-class and immigrant families who sent their children to factories rather than schools. Du Bois's autobiographical account similarly denounced black parents who sacrificed their children's education for financial gain. But *Darkwater* was not just an advice book for black Americans. Ever the propagandist, Du Bois also intended that it demonstrate to whites the virtue of the black race. For the benefit of both audiences, Du Bois emphasized that even with a limited income and an absent father, his childhood home had been neat and tidy, a place of music, education, and morals where a child—even a black child—could live the way American children were meant to live. And indeed, young Du Bois grew up, as he recalled, "perfectly happy . . . very much one of . . . the town gang of boys," every bit as good as and often better than his white classmates despite their growing sense of racial superiority.[18]

As editor, Du Bois similarly filled the pages of the NAACP's *The Crisis*, especially its annual "education number," and the association's short-lived periodical for youth, the *Brownies' Book*, with thousands of examples of young blacks who honored their race and challenged white supremacy by winning academic awards and athletic events, by graduating from high school and college, and by succeeding in professional pursuits. Feature articles also highlighted young blacks' accomplishments and African American parents' commitment to middle-class values and racial uplift. In "The Education of the Bond Family," for example, the family's patriarch detailed the activities of his five college-educated children (some of whom had postgraduate training as well). Bond explained that his family's com-

mitment to education had begun with his slave-born mother, who overcame considerable obstacles to make sure her children went to college.
Like Du Bois, Bond hoped his story would "inspire young parents to dedicate their lives" to creating a home atmosphere that taught the importance of "knowledge . . . training for life work [and] the setting of up of proper ideals."[19]

Photographs of black children and youth who embodied middle-class values were another regular feature of NAACP publications. *The Crisis* published pictures of individual blacks who graduated from northern universities and class photos from southern institutions. The magazine also ran countless photographs of black children and babies (some of them winners of NAACP-sponsored contests). In early-twentieth-century America, baby contests became a popular means for encouraging infant health and other childhood ideals as well as nativist prejudices. Shortly after its founding in 1909, the NAACP began holding "beautiful baby" contests. These contests raised significant amounts of money and countered one of the aims of white baby contests by promoting positive perceptions of African Americans. Black children, they showed, could be flawless specimens (to use the era's science-infused language) of the human race, too.

Like the writings of Du Bois and others, such contests served a second purpose, urging black families to embrace and work toward white middle-class family ideals. Du Bois published photographs of contest winners and other black children who perfectly expressed the nation's idealized conceptions of childhood. Healthy, well-dressed, and happy, the children who graced the pages and covers of *The Crisis* countered prevailing stereotypes of young blacks as half-savage and proved the respectability of their parents and their race. Babies might appear in photographs wearing white gowns, which implied their parents' Christian faith and upstanding character. Girls were often pictured in frilly dresses with ribbons in their hair, posed with books or musical instruments. These images demonstrated affluence and black parents' determination to raise cultured and feminine daughters. Boys might be dressed in sailor outfits, which were indicative of discipline and future military service, or suits, suggesting their parents' and their own future monetary success and respectability. Such photographs confirmed the African American community's dedication to an assortment of middle-class ideals, including sentimental childhood and traditional gender roles. They also raised questions about strict racial categories (as Du Bois did in his written work as well), since they

Simmie Johnson, 1927. This photograph appeared in *The Crisis* with a brief article praising Johnson, a thirteen-year-old Los Angeles girl who "sacrificed her lunch money for five days to be able to put one dollar of her own money into the [local NAACP] baby contest," which raised more than four thousand dollars. This photograph is representative of the type of idealized images of children and youth that the NAACP used to challenge negative stereotypes of blacks and prove the respectability of the race. (From *The Crisis*, March 1927, 10; courtesy William Pickens Photograph Collection, Photographs and Prints Division, Schomburg Center for Research in Black Culture, New York Public Library, Astor, Lenox, and Tilden Foundations)

revealed a range of skin colors and other physical characteristics among black Americans. Pictures of Tuskegee or Hampton students hard at work in laboratories or sewing classes and family portraits of the black middle class similarly upheld black youth as models of health, industry, morality, and cleanliness.

As historians have shown, better-class blacks regarded the excellent appearance and upright behavior of their children as directly relevant to the struggle for racial equality. Du Bois explained that "our baby pictures" show that there is "a class of well-nourished, healthy, beautiful children among the colored people." They also, he wrote, reveal "the fiction of the physical degeneracy of the American Negroes" and prove that the idea of poor health and physique as an "inescapable hereditary ill [is] arrant nonsense." Through idealized stories and images of children and youth, black Americans challenged racism and projected a positive future for the race. Indeed, the NAACP consciously used sentimentalized images of children to, as historian Susan Bragg puts it, "market the modern Negro" to the American public. Proving that young black girls and boys could overcome the white (and often upper-class black) public's negative perceptions of black children, that they could look and act like proper, even ideal, American youth, despite the color of their skin and "presumptions against them," was central to proving that at least some black adults merited full citizenship rights.[20]

At a time when most white Americans equated black children with the stylized pickaninny images common in books and advertisements, images of robust black children with hair ribbons, white bonnets, suits, and patent leather shoes and stories of them winning spelling bees, track events, and scholarships truly challenged negative stereotypes. This was definitely not the way that young African Americans were usually portrayed. And if their children did not fit racist stereotypes, then black adults certainly could not be as incompetent as white southerners claimed. By focusing attention on young blacks who embodied middle-class ideals about childhood and youth, Du Bois, the NAACP, and others questioned the racial classifications and stereotypes that justified the politics of the day. Moreover, even if that attention did little to convince most whites that blacks deserved greater equality, it encouraged African Americans to work toward middle-class family ideals. And Du Bois and other early-twentieth-century race leaders considered the growth of the black middle class—the "talented tenth"—an essential first step toward racial equality.[21]

THE LIMITS OF IDEALIZED CHILDHOOD
AND RESPECTABILITY

As potentially revolutionary as it was, this racial uplift strategy had its limitations. Sounding very much like Du Bois, a white mother wrote an article for *The Nation* that solicited sympathy for black Americans by contrasting the experiences of black childhood with idealized childhood. "Primarily the problem of my [black] neighbors," she wrote, "concerns their children." Those young ones could not experience "the freedom and unconsciousness of normal, happy childhood" that her children enjoyed. Instead, racial discrimination often made playing with friends and going to school awkward and hurtful activities. Moreover, she lamented, her neighbors could not even take their children to concerts or plan other similarly respectable outings. Because of a slight difference in skin color, the author explained, her African American neighbors, however honorable, would never be able to "shield" their children from the "shapes of shame and terror" that all young blacks in America invariably faced.[22]

As this example attests, reformers used sentimental ideas about childhood to criticize America's racialized sociopolitical order and to elicit white sympathy for African American civil rights. Notwithstanding such intentionally heart-wrenching attempts to challenge racism by evoking ideas about childhood, civil rights advocates in the early decades of the twentieth century more often used notions of childhood to demonstrate that black Americans deserved political rights than to highlight the unjust constraints that black children and families faced. Tellingly, even this example dealt with better-class black children whose plight seemed appalling because of their class and relatively light complexions as well as because of their young ages. Instead of criticizing societal ideals that were nearly impossible for most blacks to achieve, early-twentieth-century proponents of racial progress frequently suggested that the more enlightened members of the black race lived according to cultural ideals about children and families.[23]

On one level, stereotype-defying stories and images in the pages of *The Crisis* and other publications merely presented a cleaner, middle-class version of the smiling, watermelon-eating pickaninny. According to both kinds of images, African American children were perfectly content; the nation had no visible racial problems. In the early twentieth century, photographs of black children with torn clothes, "kinky" hair, and bare feet, playing in the dirt or standing next to broken-down shacks, may have helped to justify racial hierarchies. But photographs of young blacks who fit sentimentalized images of American childhood gave no visual clues about the racialized constraints that those children likely encountered. And tales of young blacks who achieved academic success did little to indict the Jim Crow conditions under which most black children struggled. Such images and stories certainly undermined prevailing stereotypes and eugenicists' arguments about "natural" racial hierarchies. They did not, however, fully call into question America's racialized economic, political, and social order.

Southern white reformer Edgar Murphy called "true families and real homes [the] most honorable and hopeful aspect of Negro life." Murphy and contemporary race leaders alike lamented that such respectable homes were an aspect of African American life of which "the white community . . . knows practically nothing." And that was especially true when compared to what it "hears through the press and police court . . . of the destructive factors in Negro life." Idealized images of black children helped to make visible this "honorable aspect" of African American life and directly contradicted racial theories that defined blacks as innately incapable of achieving the level of civilization represented by the white middle class and deemed essential for full political participation.[24]

Such images not only challenged but also perpetuated notions of undeserving blacks. Race leaders no doubt recognized the racial component of the severe economic, social, educational, and health problems that the majority of black children in America experienced. But they often did not seem to recognize that in celebrating black youth who were models of middle-class childhood, they were also indicting or ignoring those who did not fit ideal conceptions of childhood. As a result, African American leaders may have directed attention away from racial solutions.

Black leaders intent on demonstrating that black children and their families did or could embody middle-class ideals may have missed opportunities to address the needs of young blacks and to challenge American racism. When images of poor, disheveled black children appeared in racial uplift publications of the 1920s, they were juxtaposed with "after" photos of the same children transformed into model young Americans. While such images demonstrated the importance of idealized childhood to racial progress and the impermanence of racial stereotypes, they also reinforced the idea that the problems blacks faced were individual rather than social, requiring behavior modification and a commitment to middle-class norms, not political remedies. The NAACP similarly tended to blame individuals and poor black families for many of their problems. It urged African Americans, for example, to limit family size to two or three children so that parents would be able to provide their offspring with the physical and spiritual benefits that parents "owe their children." In *Darkwater*, Du Bois pointedly asked, "Ought children be born to us? Have we any right to make human souls face what we face today?" His answer to this question revealed his class biases along with his vision for racial progress: "It is our duty . . . to bring not aimless rafts of children to the world, but as many as with reasonable sacrifice we can train to largest manhood." A few years later, he likewise suggested that there were "not enough children in families of the better classes" and that well-to-do blacks might want to consider adopting less fortunate "colored folk." Du Bois meant to inspire a generation of educated, militant race leaders rather than to condemn the mass of African American parents. Yet not unlike contemporary white reformers who criticized those they sought to help, Du Bois and the NAACP sometimes scorned those outside the talented tenth rather than directly addressing the racial constraints that all black parents—especially poor black parents—faced as they tried to provide for their children.[25]

While judgmental middle-class white reformers regularly talked about what society owed its children at the same time that they found fault with working-class parents and cultures, this was not a strategy that race leaders commonly embraced. In 1909, at the first decennial White House Conference on Children, Washington characteristically minimized the needs of poor black children and society's responsibility to them. During his address to the assembled child-welfare reform advocates and public officials (many of whom had already proved sympathetic to the needs of poor black children), he cited relatively low numbers of African American youth living in institutions and explained that "this [favorable] condition exists because . . . the Negro . . . has had trained into him the idea that he must take care of his own dependents." As historian Kriste Lindenmeyer suggests, Washington could have pointed out that the low percentage of black children in institutions reflected discrimination rather than need.[26] From Washington's perspective, however, insisting that African Ameri-

cans took care of their dependent children challenged negative stereotypes of blacks and promoted the idea that members of his race fulfilled
their parental and hence societal obligations. That black children reflected
white middle-class ideals proved African Americans made good citizens.

Scholars who have looked at child welfare and labor reform in the early
twentieth century have noted its "whiteness." They generally attribute the
lack of attention to the welfare needs of black children to the racism of
white reformers or the white public whose support reformers required.
They also suggest that early child-labor reforms targeted industries that
rarely employed black workers, let alone black child workers, and that
early maternal and child health studies, such as those conducted by the
U.S. Children's Bureau, focused on urban populations with high concen-
trations of white immigrants instead of on locations with high percent-
ages of poor blacks. Most white reformers were indeed racist and, as historian Shelley Sallee shows, child labor and other child-welfare-related
reforms gained acceptance in the early twentieth century, especially in
the South, by using expressly racist arguments. Southern white reformers
forthrightly described their work, for example, in terms of the "redemption of the [Anglo-Saxon] race." Moreover, most black children worked in
agriculture, which received little public scrutiny until the 1930s. But in the
first decades of the twentieth century, black leaders also seemed reluctant
to dwell on images of poor, unhealthy, and uneducated black children.
White Progressive reformers used images, such as those captured by Jacob
Riis and Lewis Hine, of sickly, unkempt children in the disturbing environments in which they lived and worked to elicit support for industrial
child-labor reforms, infant and maternal health programs, juvenile courts,
foster care, compulsory education laws, and public intervention in cases
of child neglect. Race leaders, conversely, preferred to highlight black children who embodied middle-class ideals.[27]

African Americans would have been understandably wary about asking
for state (which meant white) help for their children. After all, the pre-
sumed inability of black parents to adequately care for their young had
been used to justify slavery and, following the Civil War, the termination
of black parental rights and the apprenticeship of black children to their
former masters.[28] But drawing attention to the plight of poor black children would also have undermined black leaders' efforts to counter negative
racial stereotypes. Moreover, in the minds of many early-twentieth-century

African American leaders, the struggle for middle-class respectability, perhaps best represented by images of idealized children, was indistinguishable from the struggle for racial equality.

African American leaders had to make difficult choices about the most effective strategies for securing greater civil rights at a time when better-off whites often blamed all victims of poverty (especially the parents of poor children) for their condition and when few whites of any class questioned ideas about the racial inferiority of blacks. Regardless of the intricacies of their dilemma, race leaders' choices contributed to the lack of attention to the problems of poor black children and the tendency to frame their problems, when such discussions did arise, in terms of the pathology of poor black families. Black educator and scholar Horace Mann Bond was certainly right when he noted in 1934 that "the Negro child of our Nation . . . is the forgotten child." Three decades earlier, John Spargo, Edgar Murphy, Florence Kelley, Lillian Wald, and a host of other reformers had said the same about America's poor white children. And while in the mid-1930s it was still debatable whether the twentieth century really would be "the century of the child," the U.S. Children's Bureau, created in 1912 in response to increased attention primarily to the plight of underprivileged white children, could boast that at least some progress had been made on important issues related to the welfare of young Americans.[29]

REMEMBERING BLACK CHILDREN
AND YOUTH IN THE 1930S

Until the 1930s, progress for American children usually meant progress for white American children. The country's poor black children were all but forgotten. Given the pervasive disfranchisement and economic exploitation of blacks and the general state of American race relations, this is perhaps less surprising than the fact that young blacks were remembered during the Great Depression. Bond's study, which condemned America for forgetting its black children and detailed the history, economics, and current problems of black education, was only one of a number of significant studies published or initiated during the 1930s that dealt specifically with the experiences and needs of black children and youth. These studies made clear that although one out of a hundred young African Americans might come from a home that fit the middle-class ideals the NAACP emphasized, most came from impoverished southern tenant-farm families. Moreover, at the same time that Bond and those involved in similar research began to emphasize the constraints that most black children faced, black civil rights leaders also began to talk more about the distance between the lives of African American children and the childhood Americans idealized.[30]

The nation became increasingly committed to its black children, and race leaders became concerned not only with proving the respectability of black youth but also with exposing the gap between idealized notions of childhood and the real lives of young blacks. Those shifts can at least partly be explained by the success of child welfare reformers in the early twentieth century and the nation's increasing commitment to sentimental childhood and to what, by the 1930s, many considered to be "the rights of childhood."[31] The rise of "youth" as a significant developmental and social (and potentially political) category also influenced attention to the problems of young blacks in the 1930s. Widespread unemployment and the threat of political extremism during the Great Depression further motivated public and private officials to consider more carefully the experiences and problems of all of America's youth, including black youth. In addition, the depression encouraged agencies and reformers to focus attention on the plight of rural youth, agricultural child laborers, and migrants—groups that included significant numbers of young blacks. In his description of "the Negro child of our Nation" as "the forgotten child," Bond deliberately adapted the phrase that earlier reformers had used to talk about rural whites and that Franklin D. Roosevelt appropriated to solicit support for the New Deal—"the forgotten man." Bond's allusion was fitting, for young African Americans were remembered only as the nation began to remember other forgotten groups during the depression years.[32]

A number of scholars have explored the successes and failures of child-welfare reformers and the increasing sentimentalization of childhood in early-twentieth-century America.[33] But as sociologist Viviana Zelizer points out in her seminal work, *Pricing the Priceless Child: The Changing Social Value of Children*, despite dissent and some uncertainty regarding the "proper economic roles for children," notions of the sacred child prevailed by the 1930s. By then, even working-class and immigrant children "occupied a special and separate world, regulated by affection and education." Zelizer does not address issues of race. Sallee, however, suggests that after child-welfare reform was widely accepted, reformers could focus "less on whiteness and more on the intrinsic value of childhood." In other words, only after the "sacralization" of childhood and the legitimization of child-protection would public opinion permit child-welfare advocates to look more closely at the plight of poor black children. Not until the 1930s, when reformers had "rehabilitated" the image of poor white children (meaning that "cracker" children came to be thought of in the same sentimental terms as white middle-class children), did race leaders and child-welfare reformers turn public attention to the experiences of poor, unclean, unhealthy, and uneducated black children. Only then did they believe that attention to the problems of African American children would do something besides lend credence to white southern tales of the beneficence of slavery, prejudicial racial theories, and Jim Crow practices.[34]

Moreover, as historian Lorraine Gates Schuyler shows, although federal funding for child and maternal-health programs (the Sheppard-Towner Act) lapsed in 1929, the nation's recently enfranchised women used their votes to insist that states and local governments fund a range of child-welfare services. Throughout the 1920s and into the 1930s, women voters used their newly won political leverage to advance solutions to children's issues and to advance the idea that America's children had a right to a certain type of childhood, which women realized could only be guaranteed through publicly financed programs. In addition, Schuyler finds that southern white women sometimes used their electoral clout to push for programs and institutions that specifically benefited young blacks. Not coincidentally, then, sustained public attention to the conditions in which poor black children and youth lived began after women won the right to vote and at the same historical moment that Zelizer and others say marked the triumph of sentimental constructions of childhood.[35]

President Herbert Hoover's racially inclusive Children's Charter and the rights it outlined offer yet another important indicator that the 1930s marked a significant turning point in how Americans thought about childhood generally and African American childhood specifically. The charter reflected many of the concerns of the almost twenty-year-old U.S. Children's Bureau. It reflected enfranchised women's legislative priorities. And it reflected the president's interest in protecting childhood. Hoover had headed relief efforts to European refugee children during World War I, had served as president of the American Child Health Association in the early 1920s, had issued a widely circulated 1922 statement on "The Child's Rights," and had investigated community child-health resources during that decade. Moreover, the League of Nations embraced his expressed beliefs about children's rights in 1924 when it instituted its Children's Welfare Committee and approved the Geneva Declaration on the Rights of the Child (appendix B). Later, in 1946, as the world emerged from war, the former president helped found the United Nations International Children's Emergency Fund (UNICEF).[36]

For Hoover and many others, including women voters, safeguarding childhood was intimately connected to safeguarding democracy and promoting peace. Although it contained no enforcement mechanisms, the charter's call for specific rights for all American children signaled a growing national commitment to protecting childhood and democratic ideals. It also provided a standard for measuring America's successes and failures regarding children. That the charter defined childhood as a distinct political category and suggested that the country's first citizenship rights, which began at birth and included the right to an education and good physical and psychological health, could not be denied to black children would have important consequences for the black freedom movement. White southerners continued to deny young blacks—and black adults—their rights as citizens. But the charter indicated that attention to the conditions of black childhood might raise questions about the state of the entire nation instead of about the respectability of African Americans. Moreover, the charter implicitly gave the federal government responsibility for the well-being of the nation's children. The charter and the ideals on which it was based offered reformers, scholars, civil rights activists, and individual African Americans a culturally and politically powerful rights-based rhetoric that they could and did use to demonstrate the appalling state of black childhood and to press for action on behalf of young blacks.

During the 1930s, the Children's Bureau, which had long been interested in serving the "whole child," began to talk more explicitly about the rights of childhood and to make clear that those rights belonged to all American children. Its publications explained that federal programs were open to young people of all races and featured photographs of poor black and other minority children, often interspersed with photographs of poor white children. In an article for *The Crisis*, Children's Bureau chief Grace Abbott explicitly discussed the problems of young blacks, noting higher infant and maternal death rates among African Americans and the fact that "the delinquency rate among Negro children . . . is higher than among white children." Abbott also promoted "equalizing opportunities for Negro children" and suggested that any statistics showing that black families needed mothers' pensions or other types of public aid less than white families undoubtedly revealed that "their needs have not been fully considered." Abbott no doubt hoped that her article would encourage communities and black families to do more to safeguard the physical and mental health of young blacks, but they could only do so, she recognized, if they first acknowledged the problems.[37]

The NAACP similarly though cautiously pointed out the less-than-ideal state of black childhood and encouraged support for civil rights by highlighting the discrepancies between the rights of children and the experiences of typical African American children. The association's publication, *The Crisis*, continued to note academic, cultural, and athletic accomplishments of black youth, sponsor "beautiful child" contests, and run articles on topics such as "Gifted Negro Children." It also, however, included NAACP membership advertisements that asked readers to consider the "*extra* hard times" experienced by America's black children and whether the country provided the kind of schools, housing, neighborhoods, recreation, and hope for the future supposedly guaranteed all American children. In 1931, *The Crisis* took an unprecedented step when it published a photograph that showed a group of poor black children receiving aid from the Red Cross. "A generation of American citizens denied education and a fair chance to earn a living," read the caption. Two years later, at the urging of a recent college graduate, Du Bois admitted that that the association had not recently published anything "concerning the present problems of the Negro." He further recognized that "there is both need and widespread demand for a re-examination of . . . present Negro problems." Du Bois went on to outline some of those problems, identifying health, education, discrimination, race pride, and recreation, among other difficulties. He also questioned the NAACP's current "class-building technique," whereby "the educated, the rich, the well-to-do and the moral . . . separate themselves from the poor, the ignorant and the criminal." And he asked, "Should we regard the development of lower masses among our people as inevitable, and if so, what should be our attitude toward these masses?" Although Du Bois clearly retained what he called "bourgeois" ideas about what African Americans "should" aspire to, he also acknowledged the need to address the problems of the race, including those of the masses.[38]

Du Bois and the association did not altogether neglect the problems of black youth before the Great Depression. In the 1920s, *The Crisis* published a series of articles that vividly outlined the discrepancies between white

and black schools in a variety of states. But despite attention to the problems of black *schools*, *The Crisis* couched attention to youth themselves in
positive, idealized terms. Du Bois explained the association's reluctance to
talk about failing black youth when he explained the NAACP's hesitation to
take up the Scottsboro Boys case. "The NAACP is not an organization to defend black criminals. . . . We did not know whether [the Scottsboro Boys]
were guilty or not." Although the association's caution bothered some
readers and at least one member later complained that *The Crisis* did not
devote enough space to the case, given the magazine's previous avoidance
of young people such as the Scottsboro Boys, it is perhaps significant that
it devoted as much space as it did to their story—including a cover photograph of the boys. In the early 1930s, *The Crisis* also published articles that
dealt more generally with poor young blacks. In "Wandering Negro Boys,"
Carlena Alexander told the story of a "gaunt, ragged" black youth who was
nevertheless willing to work hard. The harsh conditions of his life, however, seemed likely to lead him to vice and skepticism—to become "an
habitual bum, if not a criminal." Such young people, the author warned,
were merely representative of "thousands of other homeless Negro boys
wandering about the country today, who will also be the prey of vicious old
men and women; who will also suffer years of mal-nutrition, and lack even
the rudiments of an education." That the association discussed "illiterate
in mind, diseased in body, destitute" youth and that it took up the cause of
the Scottsboro Boys—young people who exemplified the myriad problems
faced by young African Americans rather than the idealized image of black
youth that usually received all of the organization's attention—in some
ways reflected a potentially significant shift in how the NAACP looked at
underprivileged youth and the black freedom struggle.[39]

THE RISE OF "YOUTH"

Increased and sympathetic attention to the plight of young blacks was influenced by beliefs about childhood and the rights of childhood and by the
rise of "youth" as a meaningful category for analysis. In the first decade of
the twentieth century, psychologist G. Stanley Hall and others described
the period between childhood and adulthood as developmentally and socially significant.[40] But notwithstanding the efforts of Progressive-era reformers, religious groups, and social scientists to address the unique chal-

lenges of youth, not until the 1930s did the government begin seriously to consider young people in their teens and early twenties as a significant social category deserving of special attention.

The ascendance of sentimental constructions of childhood and ideas about the rights of childhood contributed to the growing recognition of the importance of youth. After all, only if childhood was a special and separate period of life would a similarly special and separate transitional stage between childhood and adulthood be necessary. In some ways, youth did not substantially differ from idealized childhood. Indeed, the rise of youth as a meaningful category occurred because ideas about the rights of childhood had become so influential that they could be extended to an older cohort. Even the differences between ideas about childhood and ideas about youth reflected the influence of sentimental constructions of childhood. For example, the main difference between the two stages— that youth was considered a period of development in which adult concerns about work might begin to have a legitimate place — only became necessary with the complete shift from economic to emotional valuations of childhood. The ascendance of notions of childhood innocence also perhaps necessitated a distinct category of development wherein traditional fears about children could be projected. And in fact, by the 1930s, youth had assumed, in popular culture and public debates, some of the negative qualities and fears once associated with childhood.[41]

That youth was a period during which noneconomic children would make the transition into the economic world of work was another reason why youth became an important category, meriting concern and investigation. Not surprisingly, young people shared with their elders greatly increased rates of unemployment during the Great Depression. Researchers in the 1930s estimated that youth between the ages of sixteen and twenty-four constituted "a third of all unemployed" and expressed concern that young people suffered from high rates of unemployment, low wages, and limited employment opportunities. Young people themselves regarded unemployment as their most pressing problem. And New Deal programs attempted to address youth employment needs through the National Youth Administration and Civilian Conservation Corps, agencies that assisted a total of close to 7.6 million young people.[42]

But New Dealers were somewhat ambivalent about youth employment and advocated recreational and educational opportunities more than youth employment opportunities. As Kriste Lindenmeyer notes, one of the National Youth Administration's aims was to keep young people "in school at least through high school graduation," and federal spending on youth recreational programs rose to $750 million during the decade of the Great Depression. The New Deal also tried to restrict the labor of youth between the ages of sixteen and eighteen (rather than just children) through the short-lived National Recovery Act codes. Economic and employment realities undoubtedly motivated ambivalence about youth employment. But that ambivalence was also influenced by notions of childhood as a sacred period of development and by the strong and growing belief that older young people as well as children should be guaranteed certain rights, including the right to healthful recreation, education, and protection from labor.[43]

The growth of a recognizable and significant youth culture, along with fears about the autonomy and potential radicalism or criminality of young people, also motivated greater public and private interest in the problems of youth during the Great Depression. By the 1920s, young people formed recognizable subcultures characterized by distinct language, dress, and status-hierarchy patterns. More time spent with others their age in high schools and colleges as well as in recreational pursuits encouraged youth to look to each other instead of their parents as they developed opinions about a variety of cultural as well as political topics. In the 1930s, despite the depression, youth subcultures flourished, high school and college attendance rates increased, and student organizations proliferated. By the middle of the decade, the term "teenager" entered the American vocabulary, and researchers began to explore and write about what would later be called the "generation gap" between youth and their elders.[44]

The economic and potential political instability of the period made young people's autonomy and reluctance to follow traditional authority figures especially disconcerting to an array of adult leaders. Public officials complained that "youth of today more than ever questions the schools. . . . Youth senses a crumbling of the religious doctrines of his parents. . . . He has little respect for the stern virtues of his grandparents." Fears of communism, student radicalism, and delinquency fueled attention to and concerns about young people. The cynicism of youth and their "latent potentialities for political evil," brought on by the "dark days of depression discontent," seemed especially threatening because of communist organizing efforts among youth and radical youth political movements overseas. Young people seemed so threatening in 1935 that, with funds from the Rockefeller Foundation's General Education Board, noted civic and educational leaders from the American Council on Education created the AYC, which began to examine the needs and problems of youth between the ages of twelve and twenty-five. "Youth is unusually skeptical today and holds a questioning, suspicious attitude of disillusionment," commission studies cautioned. Privately, the group's executive committee members wondered how to "train citizens who will be propaganda-proof" and "arm youth" against leftist "governmental coercion." And the commission's director charged, "Youth must be led to believe [in American democracy]. There must be no widening gap between youth and society."[45]

THE AYC AND THE PROBLEMS OF YOUTH

The AYC was not the only organization to take up the problems of youth during the 1930s. One commission publication listed and described hundreds of governmental and nongovernmental "youth-serving organizations." Many student clubs and programs such as Boys State and the NAACP youth councils that began or expanded in the 1930s (see chapter 4) were at least partly designed to steer young people away from communist and other leftist groups and toward less radical reform movements or more conservative American values.[46] The need for such programs seemed especially acute in the 1930s both because of the depression and because communists and fascists commonly recruited youth, attracting them with camps and training workshops as well as with militant ideologies. While the proliferation of youth organizations in the 1930s was a remarkable phenomenon in itself, the AYC was especially significant. Although it lacked the official authority of a federal agency, the commission as well as the U.S. Children's Bureau effectively defined the problems of young people in America and encouraged the implementation of solutions to such problems. The commission was also significant because it reflected the nation's—including the federal government's—increasing interest in youth, acted as a clearinghouse for information on youth, promoted further interest in youth, and sponsored important research on youth, including black youth.[47]

The problems of youth boiled down to, in the words of one commission-sponsored publication, "the ever widening period between the time when schools are through with [youth] and jobs are ready for them." The commission lamented and detailed the difficulties youth, primarily males, faced in securing adequate, fulfilling, and nonexploitative employment but also explained the genesis of the youth problem in a way that celebrated the "widening period" between noneconomic childhood and economic adulthood. Moreover, the report advocated "nation-wide action . . . to abolish the evil of child labor." The youth problem, commission director Homer P. Rainey wrote, went "back to the days when the more or less indiscriminate employment of children in business and industry was generally accepted with casual indifference." Rainey explained that below a minimum age (which he did not specify, although others on the commission mentioned age twenty), the employment of youth might be socially unjustifiable. Beyond that age, he was dedicated to seeing that youth "have a chance to work and earn a livelihood." But as much as he and the commission expressed concern about youth unemployment, they seemed even more dedicated to ensuring that young people be protected as long as possible from the economic anxieties that, according to widespread beliefs about childhood, should belong only to adults. And of course if young people could be protected from labor and economic concerns, they were less likely to identify with and be attracted to communism.[48]

In addition to employment, the commission studied the youth problems of health and medical care, personality development, home life, leisure-time activities, and education. Youth problems, it seems, coincided with all of the fundamental rights of childhood as outlined in the Children's Charter. The commission stressed the importance of preventive health measures and health education for youth. Moreover, building on an early-twentieth-century (sometimes racist) concern with "mental hygiene" as well as with what historians have labeled "the psychologizing of childrearing," the AYC helped to popularize and stimulate research on young people's personality development. Commission publications especially promoted two themes that had less significance in the 1930s than they would come to have in the 1940s and 1950s (see chapter 2): the idea that unnecessary illnesses and fatalities among youth "handicapped" the nation, and the need for youth to develop "effective and healthy personality and individuality." Young people, the commission asserted, needed to "find a satisfying place among fellow youth" and to "experience personal achievement." Such assertions sounded very much like those of contemporary child-rearing literature. The commission, however, also identified conditions likely to produce "maladjustments among young people," which, in turn, would threaten American democracy. And according to these studies, neither the depression nor the nation's racialized sociopolitical order was good for

America's youth. Indeed, the conditions AYC researchers found most likely to "arouse despair, resentment, and horror" in youth included "overstimulation," "economic insecurity," "feelings of being uprooted," "competition," and the frustrations that develop from "belonging to a racial minority." The final factor received sustained attention from the commission and became a prominent theme in public debates about youth and national security during World War II and the cold war.[49]

In addition to stimulating public concern regarding and research on the personality development of young Americans, the commission worried that youth faced difficulties as they tried "to establish and enjoy a happy home." Poverty was not a new condition for many depression-era families. During the 1930s, however, those conditions spread and became more visible as thousands of previously middle- and working-class families began to suffer from the effects of the depression. Public officials and agencies feared the disintegration of American family life as they watched rates of desertion and the custodial care of children rise, living standards fall, and men and women delay marriage and postpone parenthood.[50] Many officials and agencies explained and justified New Deal programs in terms of families because of the very real difficulties families faced and because they knew it would be hard to argue against social welfare programs whose main object was to save American families. Works Progress Administration and Farm Security Administration photographers, among others, captured images of destitute parents and children walking along roads, playing in dirt, and living in tar-paper shacks (or worse) to explain the meaning of the depression and to elicit support for New Deal programs. These images included Carl Mydans's "Slum Children at Play in Their Backyard," Arthur Rothstein's Gee's Bend photos, and most famously Dorothea Lange's images of migrant mothers and children. And advocates deemed programs such as Social Security essential expressly for "the protection of the family life of wage earners," helping to protect American families and especially children. Moreover, they promoted notions of children's rights and established the government's responsibility for securing those rights. Through programs ranging from free school lunches and nursery schools to work-study opportunities, school construction, and Aid to Dependent Children, the New Deal marked the first time that "the federal government intervened in children's lives on a significant scale." In effect, the New Deal helped many young people realize the rights of childhood and codified "childhood dependency from birth to age eighteen."[51]

Child of former tenant farmer, Ellis County, Texas, June 1937. The most famous images from the depression showed white children and their families, but New Deal photographers also documented the plight of poor black families. This image, by Dorothea Lange, one of the era's best-known photographers, uses childhood innocence and vulnerability to suggest that the circumstances of tenant farmers demanded government action. (Courtesy Farm Security Administration–Office of War Information Collection, Library of Congress, Prints and Photographs Division, LC-USF34–07102-C)

The AYC helped to promote the notion of public responsibility for the nation's young and basic standards of what young people's lives should look like. It suggested that the disintegration of stable home life, which its researchers regarded as especially detrimental to the country's dependent and vulnerable youth, necessitated action. AYC officials insisted that "youth was experiencing as great a change in home life as in Russia." And commission publications expressed concern about weak families' inability to care physically for their young, teach them good habits, and provide the feelings of security, "enduring affection," and "healthful emotional life" considered indispensable for good "mental health and happiness" and regarded as one of the rights of young people in a democracy.[52]

Home life had become so disrupted by the depression that not just unemployed men but "boys and girls, flesh-and-blood youngsters who should be in high schools and homes . . . were in box cars and [hobo] jungles. [Girls] looking, except for their dirt and rags, like a Girl Scout club on an outing [had to] sell their bodies for bread. . . . Boys in need of shoes had to steal to get them." The Youth Commission admitted that youth "of the road . . . are quite definitely a minority," and it hoped to keep it that way. But to keep young people from becoming interested in "social and political structures that ardent lovers of democracy deplore," the nation needed to recognize its "responsibility to the youth in families whose incomes are too low to provide opportunities for such growth and development as is fundamental to a healthy and enduring democracy." The depression had made clear that individual families should not simply be criticized for the unmet needs of their children, nor should they be left to care for children on their own. Those children were the nation's children, too. It was therefore in the best interests of America to secure the rights of childhood for all of its young.[53]

The commission, like many other groups, expressed concern about home life because it thought of youth as a period in which young people began to shift from a stage of sexual innocence to a stage of sexual activity. Disturbing accounts explained the open sexual culture of transient youth and the prevalence of adult sexual predators among those young people. The commission worried that even the sexual innocence of more typical young people was not adequately protected and that America's youth did not receive information about sex from "accurate" or "mature" sources. In addition, the problems of unemployment and poverty, especially when combined with the "relaxation of . . . moral and religious taboos" about premarital sexual intimacy, seemed to negatively influence youth perceptions of marriage. While adult uneasiness about the sexuality of young people was not especially new, the growth of youth cultures, declining marriage rates, and general feelings of economic and political insecurity troubled commission researchers. They worried that in such a climate young people would continue to choose "heavy petting" and premarital sexual relations over stable marriages. Increased sexual activity among "immature" and "uninformed" youth, they cautioned, would lead to higher rates of venereal disease, prostitution, illegitimacy, and abortion. And low marriage rates, they intimated, might even lead to political radicalism.[54]

But commission spokesmen optimistically maintained that despite such trends, youth really were eager to form families and make wise decisions about their sexual behavior (which usually meant reserving sexual relations for marriage). According to the commission, youth merely needed to be better educated about home life. Teaching youth skills such as budgeting, giving them "instruction on the subject of choosing a mate," being more accepting of the sexual impulses of youth, and providing more information "about the sex aspects of marriage," commission studies suggested, would help young people overcome the difficulties of home life, including their apprehensions about forming families. Commission studies also frankly recognized that most youth would no longer be able to find fulfilling work and become economically secure "through mere effort and industry." But they suggested, somewhat ironically given the supposedly precarious state of American families, that young people could perhaps be directed to look to "happiness within the family as their chief source of enduring satisfaction." As in the cold war period, public officials in the 1930s hoped that family life might be able to "contain," to use historian Elaine Tyler May's apt term, many of the economic, political, and cultural insecurities and dangers of the time.[55]

The AYC hoped that some of the insecurities and dangers of the period might also be contained by recreational activities. The Children's Charter declared that young people in America had a right to healthful recreation. The commission confirmed that recreation, or the "re-creating of the vital energies of man," was "as essential to [young people's] well being as food, sleep, and work." But increasing concern regarding youth unemployment and what one writer called the "age curve of American crime" also stimulated increased interest in youth leisure-time activities during the 1930s. Despite what appeared to be relatively high rates of crime among youth, re-

THE SHAME OF AMERICA

searchers maintained that there was nothing "peculiarly 'criminal'" about that age group. They did suggest, however, that the "physical and nervous energies" young people naturally experienced, youth unemployment, and the lag between the time youth finished school and began jobs required more "programs of constructive activity." They also insisted that if public officials hoped to curb rising delinquency rates, youth needed more recreational facilities and more opportunities to attend secondary schools and colleges. Commission research revealed what many at the time feared— that young people spent an inordinate amount of time milling about. But AYC research also indicated that youth wanted more opportunities for "wholesome . . . social" recreation. According to youth surveys, young people especially hoped for "parks and playgrounds, community centers, swimming pools, dances, supervised activities, educational classes, clubs, and movies." And New Dealers responded to the call for improved recreational programs for youth. Works Progress Administration workers made toys and started toy-lending programs, taught young people to dance and ski, built swimming pools and athletic fields, and supervised city streets and playgrounds. Over the course of the decade, not only did federal funding for recreation reach $750 million, but the number of local communities with recreation programs doubled and public expenditures for recreation almost doubled as well.[56]

As these programs and figures suggest, many people agreed with the AYC's general proposals regarding recreation. But the commission also insisted that recreational facilities and opportunities were particularly desired and needed in rural and black communities, where the relative lack of constructive outlets for youth energy led to higher rates of "loafing." AYC studies additionally showed that educational levels positively affected the ways that young people used their spare time: the higher the grade level achieved, the less time youth spent, as one young person put it, "piddling around" and the more time they spent reading and in organized club activities. One of the best ways to solve the problems of both recreation (which was really the problem of delinquency) and unemployment apparently was to make secondary schooling available to all young people in America. As the commission pointed out, when young people left school early, they either got jobs, which "displaced adults and aggravated the national problem of unemployment," or were "forced to dawdle through a period of wasted years. In either case," the commission argued, society stood to lose.[57]

The commission's obvious bias for educational solutions was hardly surprising since the commission was part of the American Council on Education and many of its members were respected educational leaders. Its tendency to define youth and youth problems (except when it came to home life and sex) in primarily male terms was not surprising either, given the gendered nature of ideas about citizenship, work, and sexual misbehavior. But notwithstanding its biases, the commission's findings and recommendations were significant. Even if they did not immediately "move people to action," as some commission members hoped, AYC publications helped shape public perceptions of America's youth problem and its solutions. And if educational and gender biases in the AYC's publications were not surprising, the commission's relative racial liberalism perhaps was. At a time in which other authoritative groups paid little or no attention to African Americans and theories of racial difference commonly shaped private impressions of blacks as well as public policy and legal codes, AYC researchers concentrated on African Americans from a variety of backgrounds and repeatedly asserted that lack of opportunity rather than racial characteristics was responsible for black youth's behaviors and experiences.[58]

In an essay for *Social Trends* (a 1933 study President Hoover commissioned in hopes of bringing social science data into the political decision-making process), T. J. Woofter Jr., who came to the project with considerable research experience on black Americans, noted that recent social science research lessened prejudice by substituting truth for "popular misconceptions as to the health, morality, and mentality of the Negro." AYC members recognized that commission-sponsored studies stood at the forefront of social science research on African American youth and fully expected their findings to help break down racist assumptions. Indeed, in the years leading up to the 1954 *Brown v. Board of Education* ruling, which declared the notion of "separate but equal" in public schools unconstitutional, the AYC paid close attention to inequalities among youth and especially to the ways that race, region, and segregation affected young people's experiences, opportunities, and personality development. In just a few years, AYC researchers helped to shift America's understanding of race and human development as they systematically studied and explained what it was like to grow up in rural areas and what it was like to grow up black in America. Earlier indications of problems and inequalities had certainly existed, and the work of scholars and reformers including Bond and Du Bois, both of whom had published work on the discrepancies between black and white schools, undoubtedly influenced commission research. But studies sponsored by the commission showed that severe inequalities of opportunity existed and that rural and black youth, especially in the segregated South, suffered most from those inequalities.[59]

The commission's research on African American youth drew on popular beliefs about childhood and stressed the ways that racism negatively affected young blacks. Noted studies by both black and white authors, including Allison Davis and John Dollard's *Children of Bondage*, Charles S. Johnson's *Growing Up in the Black Belt*, E. Franklin Frazier's *Negro Youth at the Crossways*, Ira D. Reid's *In a Minor Key*, and Robert L. Sutherland's *Color, Class, and Personality*, were sponsored by the AYC and published in the early 1940s by the American Council on Education. These studies influenced scholarly debates and public policy on black youth and families for the rest of the century.[60] They also reflect the AYC's relative racial liberalism and suggest that ideas about the rights of childhood encouraged attention to the plight of poor black youth and influenced the ways that it was presented and likely perceived. For example, in his summary volume designed for a popular audience, Reid emphasized the "disadvantages that have been attached to the condition of being a Negro in the United States" and discussed specific disadvantages that contrasted with the rights of childhood that the nation aimed to provide all American children. "Negro youth," Reid pointed out, "is a group that exists in a world separate from American youth's common experiences." Americans might consider childhood a separate and special period of development, but from the "very beginning of their story," he ruefully observed, black youth occupied a separate world by virtue of their race, not by virtue of their age. Moreover, the world of black children was clearly not very special. "Their mothers are more apt to die in childbirth. . . . More than half of them attend the poorest schools." Black youth had poor health and high mortality rates. And, as homicide, lynching, arrest, and conviction rates attested, young blacks "in conflict with society" were not being "dealt with intelligently," as the Children's Charter pledged, but, in direct opposition to the charter, as "society's outcasts." Reid stressed that "like other youth," black children started out "with ambitions, hopes. . . . But, more so than other youth, their way of life is roughened and obstructed, from birth to death, by the factor of race."[61]

In *Color, Class, and Personality*, Sutherland also stressed the gap between American childhood ideals and the situation of most young blacks. "The world of youth, white and black, is inconsistent," he wrote. Sounding very much like Du Bois, Sutherland argued that young blacks surrounded by the same "incentives, opportunities, and rewards" as white middle-class children proved that black youth were just as capable as their white counterparts. But, he explained, "the mass of Negro youth are isolated from the American Dream." Sutherland condemned the differences in the lives of white and black children. He also asserted that the distance between the encouragement and opportunities white children in the United States could take for granted and the reality of what most young blacks experienced and could hope to attain threatened everyone's future. The "insecurity" of black youth, he warned, contributed to "inferiority complexes, personal frustration, compensatory behavior, and even anti-social conduct" of the Hitler/Mussolini variety.[62]

Others who conducted research for the commission on black youth came to similarly bleak conclusions about the consequences of America's racialized childhood. Many of the AYC's researchers took a case-study approach that offered an especially intimate glimpse into the deprivations and frustrations experienced by young blacks. This work made clear that many African American youth, especially those from rural areas, the South, and poor families, lived in desperate physical conditions, had few appropriate moral or cultural influences, and did not share white youth's opportunities or incentives to learn and work hard. Black youth had little motivation to "strive," since they only found "the rewards taken away." Because of racism, even black youth from northern states, urban areas, and middle- and upper-class families did not lead the kind of lives Americans wanted for their children. "Ellen," from *Children of Bondage*, for example, was deeply aware that her white counterparts had better schools and access to "new and modern . . . beautiful" recreation facilities. According to Davis and Dollard, that resentment distorted her personality and made her hostile to whites. Researchers who wrote about black youth for the AYC in the 1930s and early 1940s may or may not have purposely contrasted the experiences of black youth with the rights of childhood as outlined in the Children's Charter but drew on similar assumptions about the rights of childhood, arguing that such rights should apply to African American children and that inequalities and discrepancies between national ideals and the realities of young African Americans' lives demonstrated the failures of the nation, not those of blacks as a race or as individuals.[63]

RURAL YOUTH, EDUCATION, AND RACIAL INEQUALITY

The AYC's focus on the mental health and personality development of black youth as well as on their educational deficiencies was significant. This seems especially true from the perspective of the mid-1950s, when NAACP lawyers persuaded the U.S. Supreme Court to define separate schools as inherently unequal by drawing on social science studies that pointed to the psychological impact of segregation on young people. But the AYC also—and perhaps more effectively in the context of the 1930s— brought attention to racial inequalities and challenged those inequalities as it confronted the problems of rural youth, white and black. In *How Fare American Youth?*, Rainey, who had grown up on a poor farm in rural Texas, explained that the "mass character of the rural youth problem was catapulted in the arena of public consciousness by the Depression." He noted that before the 1930s, "research on the conditions of youth, especially rural youth, had been . . . scattered and fragmentary." While earlier reform movements focused primarily on urban areas and the problems of industrial labor, the Great Depression brought widespread attention to agricultural sectors of the economy and to those who lived and worked in rural America. Even though census data revealed that most Americans in the 1930s lived in urban areas, the poorest citizens and most of the nation's children and youth still lived in rural areas. Racial prejudice and many middle-class blacks' desire to highlight the accomplishments of the race might have continued to mask the problems of poor black children and youth. Attention to the experiences and problems of rural America and especially to rural youth—to farm tenancy, to the poverty of rural families, to agricultural child labor, to the conditions of rural schools—necessarily brought attention to the plight of black youth. As researchers pointed out, despite movement to the North and urban areas, most young blacks remained in southern rural communities, and most came from tenant-farm families.[64]

With a director sensitive to the problems of rural youth and a U.S. government and public increasingly aware of those problems as well, the AYC

was especially forthright in pointing out the deficiencies of rural education. Rural education, it explained, was marked by short school terms because of the use of children's labor in agriculture and high dropout rates
because of the economic need among farm families for the labor of sometimes even very young children. Lower teacher salaries and inferior facilities and programs also characterized rural schools, especially in the South,
where high fertility and farm tenancy rates combined to give the poorest
areas of the country the greatest educational costs. Inequalities and deficiencies in American education seemed especially alarming since commission research showed that the other problems of youth, including health,
recreation, home life, and child labor, were related to education. "Rural
youth are handicapped educationally in comparison with urban youth,"
commission studies asserted. "In urban areas one school child in four was
attending high school, while in rural areas only one in seven of the school
population was in high school." And according to AYC research, this handicap had nothing to do with "native ability" and everything to do with differences in opportunity. One study even indicated that at least 40 percent
of youth would choose to go further in school if given the opportunity.[65]

The same was true for black youth. Studies charged that "equality of
opportunity does not exist for Negro youth in northern cities" and that
"southern segregated schools are pitifully inadequate by modern standards." According to commission calculations, the median grade level at-
tained for white youth was 10.8, while for black youth it was only 7.5,
and that number was significantly lower for black male youth. Moreover,
surveys indicated that the "probability that a Negro youth will *not* have
gone beyond the eighth grade is twice as high as it is for the white youth."
AYC research also countered southern white propaganda that excused the
absence of black high schools by charging that black youth were generally
incapable of secondary-level work or that black parents and their children
did not want the schools. According to the commission, black youth did
"not attend secondary schools in nearly so large a proportion as [did] white
boys and girls" primarily because school districts failed to provide secondary education for African Americans. In addition, Rainey challenged
negative stereotypes of black youth and pseudoscientific theories about
racial difference. He argued, for example, that while the "hasty scanning"
of school records might seem to indicate a "dull level" of ability, closer
examination revealed that those records were a better "measure of environmental handicap . . . than of inherent ability."[66]

It was hard to argue with commission findings, especially when other contemporary sources confirmed them. Independent writers, scholars, and government investigators described appalling conditions among the nation's rural poor, black and white, especially in the South. They commonly noted that rural school terms were almost two months shorter than those in urban areas and that school terms for black schools were shorter still, often singling out Mississippi and Alabama for particular criticism.[67] Federal Emergency Relief grants had already proved essential to keeping rural schools open; those grants had helped build and improve schools and playgrounds, pay teacher's salaries, and feed children who otherwise would have been too hungry to learn. Moreover, the extreme need for emergency educational aid to blacks in southern states during the depression indicated that even in better economic times, southern black schools were unlikely to receive adequate funding.[68]

Ideas about the rights of childhood and the exigencies of the Great Depression gave the AYC compelling arguments that the nation needed a system of universal secondary education. As one commission study suggested, "The right of the child to the most favorable protection and guidance" and the "promotion of national welfare," or the solving of America's youth problems, made the extension of secondary schooling to all American youth both "justifiable [and] indispensable." The state of rural and black schools and the inability of local communities, even with the help of state aid, to pay for adequate much less equal school opportunities for rural and black youth made federal educational aid and regulation attractive solutions. The commission generally criticized the current state of education in the South; statistics detailing comparative expenditures per student, school term lengths, compulsory attendance laws, and the monetary value of educational facilities repeatedly demonstrated the extreme inadequacy of southern schools.

The AYC directly acknowledged that local districts could do more to distribute present resources equally. But, unlike Progressive-era reformers who sharply criticized the South for its lax child-labor and educational standards, the commission also suggested that the region was not wholly to blame for its failures, insisting that "regional variations in . . . economic resources" made it difficult if not impossible for states to meet their "social responsibility" to educate America's youth. Research indicated that Mississippi, for example, "could not support a school system equal to those of half a dozen of our most fortunate states even if all revenues were devoted to schools, to the exclusion of all other public services." And because the localities least able financially to educate the nation's youth carried a "disproportionately heavy burden" of America's educational costs, the AYC and other agencies and educators insisted that the burden should be shared, since improving education was in the nation's best interests.[69]

Increased attention to the problems of agricultural child labor and especially migrant child labor also supported the commission's findings on the less-than-ideal state of rural and black schools and gave weight to its recommendation that the federal government work toward (and help fund) equalization and a "program of universal secondary schooling." The U.S. Department of Labor, the National Child Labor Committee, and the Consumer's League had investigated agricultural child labor as early as the first decade of the century. The National Council of Churches began building centers and programs to aid agricultural migrant children and their families in 1919. Economist Paul S. Taylor documented the plight of agricultural laborers in the 1920s. And during that decade, a few national periodicals, including *Survey Graphic* and even the mainstream *Good Housekeeping*, published articles on "young nomads" and "children who work on farms." But America's commitment to the family farm ideal and beliefs about the "natural" and healthful quality of agricultural labor limited public attention to the problems of agricultural child labor until the 1930s. During the depression, however, the factory-like conditions of American agriculture and the poverty and poverty-inspired migration of families who depended on the land for their livelihood received widespread attention. And so, too, did the plight of agricultural and migrant child workers.[70]

Gertrude Binder of the National Child Labor Committee explained that "in the minds of most people a childhood spent on the farm is associated with sunshine, green fields, and pleasant outdoor work carried on under the supervision of parents." But as research and publicity during the depression made clear, "the actual picture" looked much different. American agriculture had become "industrialized." And since it remained virtually unregulated, reformers warned that it "consumed [the] fresh energies" of children, many of them under ten years old, as they labored long hours "sitting in a cramped position . . . or crawling along endlessly on hands and knees." "Youngsters who, in our own homes would be considered babies," the Child Welfare League of America asserted, "work a 'sun-up, sun-down' day" — and at a time, no less, "when jobs are scarce [for] men and women . . . who are able without harm to themselves to contribute to the world's work." Public and private agency officials as well as reformers were horrified by stories and photographs of children who picked cotton, beans, or strawberries; bunched carrots; or cut broccoli for ten to twelve or more hours and were "so keyed up" from picking crops that they could not sleep at night. Such accounts were used to elicit support for child-labor legislation that would cover children in agriculture. It was time, advocates argued, that "children's rights [receive] priority over states' rights." The president had affirmed the rights of childhood with the Children's Charter. Now Congress needed what some promoters called "the power to protect childhood."[71]

The living conditions of children who worked with their families in agriculture defied ideas about the rights of childhood. Twelve-year-old Tom, an Alabama sharecropper's son, worked the land with his parents and three and sometimes four of his five siblings. (Five-year-old Jenny sometimes stayed home to care for the baby.) The family lived in a two-room cabin with two window holes and a leaky roof. Water for drinking and washing came from a nearby creek; a hole in the ground served as an outhouse. Tom's black skin did not deter advocates from insisting that his plight was unconscionable. Children whose families moved with the crops often lived in even worse conditions despite the Farm Security Administration's attempts to establish migrant labor camps. Investigators found most migrant shelters "unfit for human habitation." "Dirty, torn tents and makeshift shacks in a sea of mud" were not the homes in which Americans envisioned sheltering their children. And those "homes" apparently did little sheltering, especially from influenza, typhoid fever, infantile paralysis, diarrhea, and other "'filth-born' diseases."[72]

Agencies and individual reformers who were concerned that agricultural labor and migration "robbed" young people "of essential advantages" were often most concerned that books had to compete with beans. Statistics on rural schools indicated that agricultural child labor interfered with education. Studies on migrant children revealed alarming dropout and attendance rates as well as high levels of "retardation" or age-grade deficiency that had nothing to do with native ability and everything to do with opportunity. Research also revealed that schools did not always welcome migrant children of any race and that African American and Hispanic schoolchildren often faced the additional challenge of segregated schooling, which research increasingly indicated meant substandard schooling.[73]

THE SHAME OF AMERICA

Moreover, because migrant children might attend several schools in different areas of the country, attention to the educational problems of mi- grant children highlighted the deficiencies of southern and rural schools and the need for a more uniform system of education. That school districts in the North and West had to accommodate students who had previously attended inferior southern schools helped make the conditions of those schools of national concern and educational inequality a national issue. To be sure, few white Americans could be accused of being racial liberals. And in fact, widespread attention to educational inequalities and the other problems of minority and migrant children came only as everyday white folks and their children — people like the Joads from John Steinbeck's *The Grapes of Wrath* and Dorothea Lange's famous (white) "Migrant Mother" — took to the road in large numbers. But perhaps the reasons for widespread attention to educational inequalities were less important than the results of that attention.[74]

THE REVOLUTIONARY POTENTIAL OF EDUCATION

Many people believed that education held the greatest potential to solve all of the problems of all of America's young people, including its most destitute. The AYC and others argued that "social isolation," "backwardness," "lack of cultural stimulation," and "the social and psychological effects of [an] itinerant existence" could be combated by good public schools. So, too, could poor health and hygiene and the lack of recreational outlets, since schools at least ostensibly employed nurses, made available physical exams and vaccinations, and included health and physical education instruction in their curricula. Improved educational opportunities and expanded and enforced compulsory education laws would also do away with the evils of child labor, help check the national unemployment crisis, lower crime rates, and lessen the appeal of radical politics. Universal secondary schooling and equal educational opportunities for youth promised to assimilate (or indoctrinate) America's underclass, to prevent future social and economic problems, and to meet most of the immediate needs of the nation's youth. It was, as one advocate put it, "a form of social action," and a form that seemed particularly suited to the problems of the time, especially in the context of ideas about the rights of childhood.[75]

Not everyone agreed that educational solutions were the best or only possible way to address America's youth problems. And despite its relative racial liberalism, the AYC likely did not intend to overthrow the South's or the nation's racialized sociopolitical order. Indeed, its solutions may well have aimed to prevent significant challenges to America's power structure. Some of the AYC's members did, however, hope to at least indirectly promote the cause of racial equality. They also fully expected their studies on black youth "to have effects on Negro education and on the attitudes of white opinion-makers toward Negroes," even if ten years would pass before those ideas would "be assimilated by enough people to make their educational implications felt." The AYC's research on young African Americans as well as its publications on the problems of rural youth ultimately led to sustained interest in educational inequalities, especially as manifest in the segregated South. That attention encouraged white southerners, with prodding from local blacks, to improve African American schooling opportunities in the 1940s to forestall federal action: between 1940 and the mid-1950s, the salaries of black teachers doubled, facilities and equipment for black children increased 300 percent, and high school enrollment for black youth "skyrocketed" to nearly four hundred thousand students. Perhaps most important, however, that attention focused the nation on the one problem that would eventually convince the Supreme Court to outlaw segregation.[76]

If it was not yet clear that the struggle for African American civil rights would coincide with ideas about the rights of childhood, especially young people's right to equal education, the AYC had some sense of the revolutionary potential of its work on black youth. "It is my opinion that we have written a new chapter in the interpretation of race relations in America, and have developed a new approach to the study of its problems," commented Dr. Will Alexander at a 1941 AYC Executive Committee meeting. "And I think," he went on to say, "we have laid the foundation here for a new approach to Negro education." Alexander was well known as a racial liberal, but other members of the commission agreed, with one even wondering "if in the long run this [work on African American youth and education] isn't the most permanent contribution we have made."[77]

It was also clear that both blacks and white southerners had some sense of the revolutionary potential of education. Du Bois regarded the education of children as "the problem of problems." In other words, he believed that solving the problem of black education would help African Americans solve their other problems since education was inexorably linked to economic, social, and political advancement. Researchers in the 1930s noted the tremendous faith that many other African Americans placed in education. Black sociologist and AYC researcher Charles S. Johnson recognized both the meager state of African American schools and "the interest which some pupils and parents continue . . . to maintain in education and the faith which they have in the power of education to confer prestige and to facilitate racial and occupational escape." Johnson saw this as the "most hopeful aspect of the present school situation." White anthropologist Hortense Powdermaker also found scores of black Americans convinced that "education will solve the race problem." She and other observers of black life were not surprised that African Americans had looked to education for political and economic salvation directly following the Civil War. That blacks still believed in education in the 1930s, despite the persistence of Jim Crow schools, seemed surprising, however. "Almost every [black] mother was ardent in her wish that her child should receive more education than she did, and thus gain the prospect of an easier and a happier life," Powdermaker noted. White southerners had a different perspective on the race problem but came to the same basic conclusion about the role of education in the region's racialized caste system. For typical southern whites, compulsory, let alone equal, education for blacks "was a dangerous thing. . . . [Y]ou make a Negro dissatisfied with his position."[78]

Because of such divergent views on the race problem, commission researcher Howard Bell may have been prematurely optimistic to suggest in the 1930s that a "decent social conscience demands that equality of opportunity be made more real." But in the context of the nation's growing concern for youth and commitment to the rights of childhood, America's conscience seemed to be becoming more attuned to the plight of young blacks. The AYC had indeed laid an important foundation. In effect, it had promoted a racial liberalism centered on youth and youth problems that would influence the trajectory of the civil rights movement. And though it was not certain in the 1930s that ideas about the rights of childhood would help defeat Jim Crow, the Scottsboro Boys case suggests that ideas about childhood and continued attention to the problems of all black youth, rather than just to the success of a minority of young blacks, might move the nation's social conscience toward the side of civil rights activists.[79]

In 1896, the same year the U.S. Supreme Court upheld the "separate but equal" doctrine in *Plessy v. Ferguson*, Du Bois wondered how long America could "teach its black children that the road to success is to have a white face? How long," he asked, could the United States "escape the inevitable penalty?" Many others began to ask the same question during the 1930s, and even more people asked it during the next two decades, which were marked by physical and ideological war. Over the next twenty years, America would decide that the rights of childhood indeed belonged to black children and that the federal government should act to protect those rights. In the context of World War II and the cold war, linking the rights of childhood to African American civil rights became an even more powerful and effective way of challenging the legitimacy of segregation and eliciting public and political support for racial equality.[80]

Two

. . . .

A CRUSADE FOR CHILDREN

SAVING DEMOCRACY, THE RIGHTS OF CHILDHOOD, & THE *BROWN* DECISION

At the beginning of the twentieth century, many reformers believed that in the next hundred years, notions of childhood would "form the point of view from which all other questions will be judged, all other regulations made." Advocates were undoubtedly disappointed that child-welfare-related reforms were not as forthcoming as they had hoped. But they were right that ideas about childhood would have a profound influence on other issues, including what W. E. B. Du Bois called "the problem of the Twentieth Century . . . the problem of the color line." During World War II and the cold war, widespread beliefs about childhood became linked to issues of political legitimacy and national security. And the connections between childhood and the future of the nation helped to "form the point of view from which" the Supreme Court and the public saw the struggle for African American civil rights. Indeed, the 1954 *Brown* ruling, which made school segregation unconstitutional and ostensibly answered the question of the color line, was a judgment based on cultural beliefs about the rights of childhood in a democracy as well as on ideas about racial equality.[1]

CHILDHOOD, POLITICS, AND THE CHILDREN'S CRUSADE FOR CHILDREN

"You can't hear much about suffering without wanting to do something about it. At least children can't." That is what writer Dorothy Canfield Fisher thought when she heard about a group of school-age children from

Perkinsville, Vermont, who had donated the money they earned picking wild strawberries to children displaced by Hitler's advancing armies in Europe. As a writer of children's books, a longtime advocate of inventive teaching methods, a former committee member of the Women's International League for Peace and Freedom, and an adviser to the American Youth Commission (AYC), Fisher recognized both the humanitarian and educational possibilities of initiating a project based on these children's actions. And so in 1939, with the encouragement of friends and professional associates, she organized the nationwide Children's Crusade for Children, drawing on images of the A.D. 1212 crusade in which thousands of French and German children, armed with pure hearts and Christian faith, set out to "free" the Holy Land. But instead of attempting to save religious "infidels," as did the original children's crusade, Fisher's campaign meant to capture what organizers called the "pity in the unspoiled hearts of children" to save Europe's refugee children.[2]

Press releases, radio addresses, and poems and stories written for the crusade drew on ideas about children's rights and young people's innocence to describe the refugees. "Hungry and afraid . . . robbed of birthright, of sunlight, of playtime, robbed of security . . . prematurely old," these young victims of war, whose eyes had "seen things which no child's eyes should ever look upon," became striking symbols of Hitler's malevolence. And as crusade materials melodramatically explained, other equally innocent children could hold "the lamp to help light the way" and "ignite the spark of better understanding and rekindle in the hearts of adults" a desire to help war-torn Europe. Fisher and other organizers recognized that Americans were reluctant to get involved in another war across the Atlantic — or, as crusade propaganda not-so-subtly put it, many Americans were "hardened by ancient hatred and hoary prejudices, by base ingratitude and ignoble selfishness." But given popular beliefs about childhood, crusaders expected that the country's adults would be inspired by the "simple and uncalculating generosity" of children and, "out of [their] love for a child," would open their hearts and pocketbooks.[3]

Like the humanitarian campaigns Herbert Hoover organized for children left destitute by World War I, the Children's Crusade for Children reassured the public that monetary gifts would make a difference and be well-used, that every penny collected would go directly to aid suffering children in Europe. But collecting "mites" from "mites" on behalf of young "victims of war, famine and persecution" was not the primary objective of the campaign or the real reason for its widespread appeal. Organizers intended that this children's crusade save *American* children as well as children in far-off countries. Specifically, they hoped it would keep the nation's youngest citizens from lapsing into complacency and selfishness, keep them from becoming "infidels" themselves — in this case, political infidels of the undemocratic, Hitler-like variety. Other attempts to aid Europe's refugees in the 1930s, including innocent children, garnered little support, most notably the case in which immigration authorities turned a ship filled with Jewish children away from American shores. The Children's Crusade for Children, however, quickly became a nationwide cause célèbre, championed by famous artists and writers such as Norman Rockwell and Nobel Prize winner Pearl Buck, by prominent educators and child-centered institutions and organizations such as the Children's Bureau, and by notable leaders including First Lady Eleanor and President Franklin D. Roosevelt and Supreme Court justice Felix Frankfurter.[4]

This crusade appealed to Americans by describing how wartime conditions destroyed European childhood and by linking the plight of young foreign victims of war directly to America's children and the future of democracy. In one radio address, for example, an advocate related, "I saw and felt all the devastating ravages of war on the children, children who were aged before they blossomed. They lost their teeth and their hair. Hunger ate the flesh off their bones, stunted their growth and left marks on them that would freeze the blood in your veins." She then urged "young Americans, you who are heirs of this precious heritage of American democracy . . . not [to] forget as you enjoy the blessings of this peaceful land that there are millions of children in the old world today who are hungry, cold, terrorized and tormented." Similarly, a nationally syndicated cartoon pictured a young American boy at a drugstore counter trying to decide whether to spend his money on a piece of candy or to place it into a crusade mite box, while ghostly looking children loom in the background. Such promotional materials implied that if American children did not "prove that democracy understands and is willing to help others to find justice, liberty, and happiness," they might someday meet the same fate.[5]

Crusade sponsors and educators asked schoolchildren across the country to promote democracy both at home and abroad by saving their pennies, learning about the customs and daily lives of their foreign counterparts, and reflecting on the benefits of American democracy. Young people were to inspire public sympathy and support for Europe's most tragic victims

"Helping Hand from Uncle Sam's Children," 1940. These Rochester, New York, public school children show their patriotism and world-mindedness by supporting the Children's Crusade for Children. One child is dressed like a refugee, and another holds a crusade collection can. (From *Rochester Times Union*, 25 April 1940; courtesy *Rochester Democrat and Chronicle*)

through patriotic school festivals and plays. They were to better understand and appreciate the blessings of living in a democracy by writing and reciting poems that insisted that whether they were "yellow and brown [or] black and white," children in the United States enjoyed unparalleled opportunities.[6]

And indeed, organizers were pleased to find that young people across the country enthusiastically gave up going to Shirley Temple movies, decorated tin cans for collection, and wrote about the meaning of the crusade. After discussing the crusade and events taking place in Europe, one young participant wrote that a democracy is "a place where there is justice for everybody and where everybody can be friends no matter what their religion is or what country they or their parents came from. Where we can read whatever books we want to, or hear whatever music we like, and where no one can take our mothers and fathers away from us." Another child wrote that the "nation-wide crusade shows what a kind and wide-awake country America is." At least for some children, the crusade evidently succeeded in its efforts to promote "the brotherhood of youth." Or,

Children's Crusade for
Children collection can,
1940. (Photograph by
Kendall Brown; from
author's collection)

55
.
.
.

as a crusade advocate explained its objectives, to "train children in the old-fashioned, decent American way of generosity in helping those in need . . . and to dramatize the importance of the democratic way of life, too often taken for granted by adults as well as by youngsters."[7]

Such lessons in generosity, "world friendship," and democracy seemed especially important in a world threatened by war and rising dictators. Like many reformers, crusade organizers expressed a paternalistic sense of noblesse oblige. They wanted young Americans to learn about other countries (a trend in children's literature of the time as well) and to demonstrate compassion toward their less fortunate counterparts around the world—to develop mercy, a quality considered "an essential element in American civilization." Crusade promoters warned that "the only essential difference between tyranny and democracy after the war, will be that in one there will be persecution, and in the other there will not," suggesting that if children did not learn to live by America's professed values in their youth, they might later choose a "path that ends against a wall of hate and prejudice and cruelty." Quoting Abraham Lincoln, one crusade press release insisted that "if America is destroyed, its destruction will come from within. . . . [R]emember that the measure of a nation is not its extent or its wealth; but the character of its people." And one crusade advocate pointedly cautioned, "How can men [like Hitler] do such frightful things to children! . . . Those men were once children too . . . and perhaps they do evil now because they did not learn then, to know and to prize what is good in this life."[8]

Possibly drawing on the success of World War I–era propaganda that sometimes juxtaposed helpless children with the Allies' brutal enemies, the Children's Crusade gained nationwide support by contrasting notions of childhood innocence and children's rights with the harsh realities faced by European children. Probably even more effective, however, were the crusade's efforts to contrast the future of a truly democratic United States with that of a United States whose citizens did not learn at a young age to appreciate and put into practice the values of a democracy, especially fairness, tolerance, and compassion.

In portraying such contrasts and possibilities, the campaign reflected, legitimized, and perhaps intensified the fears of the American public and its politicians as they faced the prospect of a second world war. At the time, a wide range of experts, reformers, and public figures noted that children were "the only ones who can save us in the future." And the crusade explained in distinct terms popular as well as scientific beliefs about the choices that confronted American children. Either schoolchildren, through programs such as the Children's Crusade for Children, would learn "the principles of fair play set forth in our bill of rights" and "the enormous advantage of human liberty" and "feel vividly the suffering and loneliness experienced by the children who are victims of a racial and religious intolerance," or they would grow "into the kinds of people who can make war on children." As well-known writer Robert Nathan told American children in a verse written expressly for the crusade, "This is your world, your broad and furrowed fields / Here what you plough will bear its fruit in time / . . . You shall declare the future of this place."[9]

Historians have suggested that America's post–World War II domestic ideology reflected the political ideology of the time. Rather than being separate from politics, parental roles and family centeredness were deeply connected to the fears and aspirations of the cold war and in fact were meant to contain the disturbing political and social forces at work in that era.[10] The Children's Crusade for Children provides evidence that even before the cold war, ideologies of childhood were directly tied to political ideologies. It also exemplifies the ways that the personal experiences of childhood were connected, in the public mind and political thinking, to anxieties and hopes about the future of the nation and the world. The crusade clearly suggested that the suffering of European children signified disturbing political developments. It also promoted the idea that if American children were taught to have compassion for others and gratitude for democracy, they could keep in check the alarming political developments that threatened world peace.

Children had long been connected to politics in Western thought — most notably in relation to education. Plato saw education as central to politics. The nature of civic training, he believed, determined the stability of a body politic. Aristotle believed that "the legislator should make the education of the young his chief and foremost concern." The newly formed United States took up childhood training as the best way to ensure the future of the new republic. And in the early twentieth century, Progressive reformers extended compulsory childhood education to protect the future of the country by properly assimilating immigrants and Native Americans.[11] In these examples and many others, the connections between children and politics primarily related to their status as future citizens. Children were potentially political — when they grew up, they would vote, hold office, and play an integral part in the functioning of their towns, states, and the nation — at least if they were boys. If they were girls (especially before women's suffrage), they would become mothers of voters and leaders.[12]

In some ways, the Children's Crusade for Children reflected this type of thinking; children needed to learn to appreciate democratic values so that they would grow into responsible American and world citizens. But the crusade promoted a definition of childhood that encompassed more than the concept of young people's future worth to the nation. During her tenure with the AYC, Fisher criticized other executive committee members for talking about childhood and youth as "passive" periods of development. Instead, she insisted, the commission and America needed to call "upon youth to be active in the service of their country," especially since totalitarian countries were doing the same. Through her work with the crusade,

Fisher likewise acknowledged young people as significant political actors, asking them to participate in international politics and to promote democracy among adults in their local communities.[13]

In addition to empowering young people, the crusade explicitly linked a nation's treatment of children to its political fitness and even its legitimacy. Like the 1930 Children's Charter, crusade rhetoric intimated that the realization of the rights of childhood offered one measure of an enlightened political state. Conversely, that Hitler's actions betrayed European childhood made his Nazi regime obviously tyrannical and politically indefensible. The crusade, however, came at the end of a decade that had shown that many young Americans, especially young African Americans, hardly enjoyed the so-called blessings or rights of childhood in a democracy. As a result, the crusade raised questions about the state of American democracy itself. During the depression, reformers, AYC research, and the Scottsboro case had exposed the gap between the nation's childhood ideals and realities. The crusade's lofty rhetoric about childhood, when juxtaposed with that gap, indicted American democracy as well as Hitler. The crusade — or at least its ideals — questioned both the legitimacy and the stability of nations that championed one set of values about childhood and practiced another.

Fisher and other crusade organizers were certainly aware of the contrasts between the ideal and real American childhoods. As a member of the AYC's executive committee, Fisher had been among those who urged the group to focus on the plight of black youth. Yet crusade propaganda promoted a view of American childhood and democracy that fit only the experiences of the mostly white middle and upper classes. Crusade advocates of course never mentioned that in the original thirteenth-century Children's Crusade, many young crusaders became disillusioned and abandoned the cause or that the French and German youth who continued their quest either died at sea or became slaves. Not surprisingly, organizers also chose to whitewash the twentieth-century campaign, talking unabashedly about the goodness of American democracy and claiming that "even the poorest American child" was far more fortunate than Europe's refugees. Crusade propaganda, for example, stressed the poverty of the Vermont children who inspired the crusade and highlighted a group of black orphans in Harlem, "moppets" who nobly sacrificed their Sunday ice cream so that they would have money to put in their mite box.[14]

Although they sought to save American as well as European children, crusade organizers remained silent when it came to the considerable problems of poverty and racism that many of those children faced. Rather, they portrayed all American children as living in a world "of dreams . . . and fairy tale endings." New York City might have black orphans, but organizers ignored the racial and economic problems that likely contributed to that status. In some ways, the crusade's use of Harlem's "moppets" can be seen as a type of modern blackface minstrelsy. But instead of darkening their own faces and taking to the stage, whites in this case played with real-life images of blackness in the media to uphold cultural myths about American childhood. The fact that poor and parentless black children could be heralded as positive symbols of American childhood—that crusade organizers could wage a popular campaign based on ideals that were not realized fully in America itself—reveals something of the power of idealized notions of childhood and democracy.[15]

The crusade's propaganda also suggests that despite the efforts of civil rights advocates and public and private agencies such as the Children's Bureau and the AYC and despite the racial inclusiveness of the 1930 Children's Charter, the racial and economic problems of many American children often remained hidden and the nation continued to define itself and American childhood as white.[16] In a 1931 study, scholars asked children to rank and describe different racial and nationality groups. They found that the sixth-graders they interviewed ranked "American" as number 1, "Negro" as 34, and "mulatto" in last place at 39. When asked to describe members of each group, the children talked about Americans as "well-educated" and America as a "free country" belonging to the white race. Their comments about "Negroes" included "were slaves," "from Africa," "black, brown, colored race," and "some are nice." And when asked about "mulattoes," many replied, "don't know them," while others said, "half Negro, half white."[17]

Researchers collecting the data argued that their findings showed how young children readily absorbed society's negative racial concepts and stereotypes. These data also show that children equated being American with being white. To be Negro was to have a history, an origin, a skin color that separated one from America; for many people, to be mulatto was not to exist at all. Later in the 1930s, thanks in part to the AYC's work, society developed a much greater awareness of the needs of black children and youth. Yet for all the commission's efforts to uncover and publicize the problems of young African Americans, the June 1938 issue of *Life* magazine, which featured the commission's work on the nation's youth problem, included no examples of black youth or discussions of their difficulties and concerns. The article's omissions are only partly explained by the fact that it came out before most of the AYC's work focusing on black youth was published. Both the *Life* issue and crusade rhetoric and images indicate that most mainstream ideas and representations of American childhood continued to encompass only the experiences of white children.[18]

In many ways, then, the Children's Crusade for Children supported the racial status quo. The specific qualities crusade organizers insisted American children needed to learn to save the nation and the world, however, challenged America's racial hierarchies. If children were really "exactly alike everywhere," if intolerance was a "contagious disease" that threatened the "minds and characters" of children, if "hatred and persecutions . . . prejudice and cruelty" were really the antithesis of democracy, as the crusade insisted, then America appeared to be in grave danger. Previous connections between children and politics had usually stressed the importance of socializing children into an existing order in hopes of maintaining social norms. The Children's Crusade for Children, however, promoted values that stood in stark contrast to the sociopolitical order. It also suggested that children would lead the way in establishing a world based on those values. Crusade organizers did not highlight the gaps between their rhetoric and real American childhood and democracy. But the values organizers emphasized—the points they made about the need to teach children, in practical terms, such democratic values—would soon come to dominate discussions about how to ensure peace and stability on a domestic and world stage. So, too, would their arguments about children's natural ability to create a more democratic world. Over the next decade and a half, those ideas would also encourage legal, social, and political change.[19]

Moreover, not all contemporary observers and participants kept silent about the contrasts between the rhetoric of the crusade and the realities of life for many American children. One woman captured much of the irony and hypocrisy of the campaign in a letter to the editor of her local Tennessee paper. "Strange things," she wrote,

> have been done in the name of freedom, democracy, and patriotism, but the most subtle yet is the organization of the Children's Crusade for Children. They say "it is well devised to teach patriotism . . . and to

show children the advantages of free government" [while] everywhere in the United States children are suffering for want of the barest necessities of life. . . . And these children are ours . . . on whom the future of this country depends. . . . This is American patriotism which we teach our children—the 1940 variety . . . when we hide the filth, the poverty, the injustice, the despotism that are ours under a scented, embroidered cloak labeled "democracy."

She then went on to "challenge the women of this country to crusade for the rights of OUR OWN hungry, shivering, frightened, and shamefully wronged children!" Others, including children, expressed the same idea. Seventh-graders at Cheney Junior High School in Washington state, for example, wrote to crusade headquarters that they "supported the Children's Crusade for the children of foreign countries and we would like your support in helping us start a crusade for the less fortunate children of our own country. . . . We think we should have a crusade in our own country. . . . We also feel that we have problems confronting our own people. . . . We thought it would be a good thing if there was a drive for the children of America."[20]

In fact, there was such a drive designed to close the gap between the ideals and the realities of American childhood and democracy, a drive that even sought to extend childhood ideals to America's young blacks. While Children's Bureau chief Katharine Lenroot avoided calling direct attention to the discrepancies between crusade rhetoric and the real lives of American children, she concluded a radio address on the objectives of the crusade with a discussion of the report of the "White House Conference dealing with minority groups." The report, she stated, showed that children in America who were "subject to prejudice and discrimination" enjoyed "less sense of security, as well as less opportunity for education, recreation, and vocational preparation" than other children. Sounding very much like crusade advocates worried about the possible political repercussions if American children did not learn to appreciate the advantages of democracy, Lenroot quoted White House Conference officials as saying, "We need to give thought to the possible results in the future of our country, of permitting from five to ten million children to grow up under conditions in which they not only lack the ordinary material advantages of life, but are made to feel that they do not have the same right to life as others, and that they are 'different' and 'inferior' and must fight their way against unreasonable obstacles merely to gain that equality of opportunity which in a democracy should be assured them." She also noted that the conference "calls upon all citizens to work continuously for the elimination of discrimination and prejudice in all their forms" and to recognize that "children are born without prejudice." While not a formal children's crusade, the White House Conference's call for citizens to act and its suggestion that children were naturally inclined toward brotherly love certainly suggested a campaign similar to the one being waged on behalf of European refugees.[21]

CRUSADING FOR AMERICAN CHILDREN: THE RIGHTS OF
CHILDHOOD AND THE FUTURE OF DEMOCRACY

In the first decade of the century, Progressive reformers began a concerted drive for American children by campaigning against child labor and pushing for the creation of a government agency to address the needs of young Americans. That drive expanded on the state level after women won the right to vote and on the federal level during the Great Depression. The Children's Bureau, the AYC, the National Association for the Advancement of Colored People (NAACP), and other organizations as well as individual reformers certainly did much to bring public attention to the problems of young Americans, including racial minorities. Their studies showed that whatever white children suffered, black children suffered more. Despite the words of the 1930 Children's Charter, at the end of the decade, childhood in America remained as segregated as the schools and drinking fountains of the South and the neighborhoods of the North. As a result, discrimination and prejudice became important themes at the 1940 White House Conference on Children in a Democracy, which included special sessions dedicated to minority children. Moreover, in his conference address, President Roosevelt asserted, "We are concerned about the children of minority groups in our population, who, confronted with discrimination and prejudice, must find it difficult to believe in the just ordering of life or the ability of the adults in their world to deal with life's problems. . . . We are concerned about the children who are not in schools or who attend schools poorly equipped to meet their needs. . . . We are concerned about the future of our democracy when children cannot make the assumptions that mean security and happiness." Others in attendance likewise stressed that although reformers had been concerned about "children in this country for the past hundred and fifty years," the 1940 conference represented

something new in its emphasis on "every child." For many conference attendees, being concerned about every child meant doing "something to
decrease the inequalities of opportunity" and to help Americans "develop
a nation-mindedness concerning the problems of children." No longer,
they insisted, could factors such as race and region be allowed to limit the
rights of American children.[22]

All of these comments revealed a growing concern about the plight of
black children as well as the fundamental reason for that concern—"the
future of our democracy." The title of the conference testified to its organizers' focus and anxieties. Previous decennial conferences had concentrated on child health and labor. In contrast, organizers of the 1940 conference hoped that the meeting would "result in practical suggestions as to
ways in which we may give greater security to childhood [in a democracy]
and thus strengthen the foundations of our national life."[23]

After a decade of economic instability that at times threatened the nation's political stability and with the rising specter of dictators and world
war, political leaders and child welfare specialists alike unsurprisingly
turned to traditional connections between children and politics to argue for increased attention to children's issues. More than ever, children
seemed to need the opportunity to grow "into the kind of persons who
justify and cherish freedom." And as President Roosevelt and the conference attendees recognized, black children had only limited opportunities
to do so. The conference, like the Children's Crusade for Children, also
suggested that the current state of childhood mattered as much as training children for their future roles as citizens. Conference speakers, for
example, argued that "it is incompatible with the principles of our democracy that children should be without decent homes or nourishing food,
without protection for health or opportunities for education." In addition,
the conference pointed specifically to the material disadvantages of black
children and to the roots of those disadvantages—to the ways that discrimination and prejudice kept African American children from enjoying
the kind of childhood compatible with democracy. Following the conference, the Children's Bureau published a series of eleven pamphlets, all
titled *Children Bear the Promise of a Better World*, that reiterated conference themes. Those tracts specifically insisted that "every American child"
needed "fair educational opportunity" "to feel pride and patriotism" and
that the "rights of our children" should be "unhampered by political, sec-
tarian, or racial theories."[24]

Both the Children's Crusade for Children and the White House Conference on Children in a Democracy captured and reinforced Americans'
anxieties. But while the crusade in some ways reflected the hypocrisy of
American democracy, the conference signaled a growing belief that extending the rights of childhood to all American children would solve the
country's problems, current or anticipated.

Many historians agree that World War II and the cold war contributed
to African Americans' growing expectations for civil rights and to a general
climate that required the U.S. government to curb racism's most blatant
manifestations. The international political environment also stimulated
increasing concern for America's children and gave child advocates compelling ways to argue for greater protections for all children. Extending
the rights of childhood to all of America's children also meant extending
civil rights to all Americans, as the two causes, at least for a time, became
inextricably linked. In highlighting the discrepancies between American
ideals and the less-than-ideal state of black childhood, the 1940 White
House Conference on Children in a Democracy served as one indicator
that the rights of African Americans would become intimately connected
to the rights of childhood.[25]

Both the White House Conference and the Children's Crusade raised
questions that would become significant during and after World War II
and that would help link the rights of African Americans to the rights of
childhood: How could we safeguard our country from Hitler-like despots?
How could we keep democracy secure here and ensure its triumph on the
world stage? How could we avoid the horrors of war in the future and live
in peace?

As crusade rhetoric suggested, the answers to these questions centered
on children. Simply put, children needed to understand and appreciate
what it meant to live in a democracy. And as the White House Conference
indicated, the answers to these questions involved extending the rights
of childhood to every child; all American children needed to enjoy the
benefits of living in a truly democratic society. In his May 1940 address
to Congress requesting defense appropriations, President Roosevelt asserted, "Our security is not a matter of weapons alone. The arm that wields
them must be strong, the eye that guides them clear, the will that directs
them indomitable. These are the characteristics of a free people, a people
devoted to the institutions they themselves have built, a people willing
to defend a way of life that is precious to them all." In the years following

World War II, many Americans came to understand that strong arms, clear eyes, and indomitable wills could be assured only if all American children enjoyed the rights of childhood in a democracy. People began more clearly to see the significance of the Children's Bureau's assertion that "the kind of vision we have in regard to children will largely determine the future of the world."[26]

PERSONALITY DEVELOPMENT, RACISM, AND NATIONAL SECURITY

During the 1930s, researchers and agencies such as the AYC directed attention to the importance of personality development. The AYC had been especially forthright in suggesting that studies on personality development could serve as "a gateway to an understanding of human problems" and especially of the problems of young minorities, which "we don't get any other way." And the Children's Bureau had long been interested in protecting the "whole child," including young people's emotional security. The 1940 White House Conference, however, may have marked the first time that considerations of children's emotional health and research on personality development and race were directly applied in an official and influential political forum to the issue of children's rights and the safety of democracy. In the years after the conference, American child welfare advisers, educators, and scholars increasingly turned to new research on personality development to better understand how to keep the nation free from political despots. And although other factors influenced the direction of the civil rights movement, the research to which these experts looked and that they promoted helped to shape the black freedom struggle and people's understanding of that struggle.[27]

Reflecting a fairly new interest among social scientists in "the dignity and worth of human personality" and perhaps the AYC's success in defining the problems of young Americans and the solutions to those problems, experts on childhood at the conference suggested that their research on personality development was particularly appropriate for addressing issues of emotional health among white children as well as the constraints under which black children lived. These studies also seemed to promise insights into how the nation might better protect itself against antidemocratic tendencies. Conference participants, for example, deemed it just as significant to the state of American democracy that black children grew up feeling "different" and "inferior" as that those children lacked the material conditions of ideal childhood. As the United States entered World War II and anxieties about the future intensified, social scientists and child advocates began to make even more explicit arguments about the connections between personality development, American childhood, and national security. Discussions about just those themes, in fact, dominated sessions at the 1950 Mid-Century White House Conference on Children and Youth.[28]

Experts at that conference and new research published during the 1940s (and in the wake of the 1950 conference) defined the "healthy personality" as "one who is free to operate at somewhere near top mental and physical capacity; who can open his heart and mind to all the experiences of human companionship; who . . . can accept with respect and dignity those who differ from him; and who can accord to his peers these same strengths and freedoms and capacities which he experiences and values within himself." If American children needed those qualities to "be well prepared in body and mind for the tasks of today and tomorrow," then the country was evidently in trouble. Like the study conducted in 1931 that revealed that white children harbored great prejudices toward African Americans, research more than a decade later showed similar sentiments among the nation's young. In a study published in 1943, white eighth-graders described Negroes as lazy, dishonest, and violent. Another study released during the war revealed that twelve-year-old whites thought more highly of Germans than of Negroes and mulattoes. Participants ranked America's other World War II enemy, the Japanese, only slightly below Negroes and mulattoes. A third study, conducted after the war, compared the attitudes of male university students toward Jews, Negroes, and the Japanese, and found that even among upper-class (and educated) young people, prejudices abounded, with the "highest index of discrimination . . . directed at Negroes." All of the prejudices these studies revealed were considered alarming. One group of researchers explained that even a study that showed racial prejudice in as little as 1 percent of the population or "attitudes of neutrality and indifference" would be "significant when attempting to gauge social pathology." In the 1940s and 1950s, prejudice was no longer just an indication of opinions, preferences, or even social realities but a disease with disturbing implications for the future.[29]

During this period, studies also linked prejudice to certain personality types that exhibited ego weakness, fear, irrationality, emotionalism, irresponsibility, extreme egocentrism, compulsive behaviors, a lack of creativity, an inability to deal with anxiety, and a tendency to follow authoritarian figures—in short, not qualities that make ideal citizens. In fact, studies warned, such "neurotic symptoms" had "killed more men in battle and destroyed more property than all mankind before." Researchers made clear that minorities were not the only ones harmed by such "neuroses." The work of these researchers defined prejudice as a personality disorder that hurt both prejudiced persons and their victims. Experts labeled the prejudiced child the "disturbed child," a being consumed with fear, "insecure, maladjusted, unhappy; unconsciously seeking a scapegoat on whom to project his distressed feelings." "Subject to feelings of superiority," such children, scholars warned, were "no safer than members of the minority group in situations where prejudice and discrimination are involved" and could "easily become victims of personality arrests." While this increasingly common contention that whites suffered just as deeply from racism as blacks may have been misguided, the insistence that racism was a white as well as a black problem certainly helped redirect attention to the issue.[30]

Similar assertions about racism's effects on whites also appeared in popular culture. Published in 1944, Lillian Smith's controversial and instantly best-selling novel, *Strange Fruit*, depicted with horrifying detail the personality damage and societal violence caused by racism. Just returned from fighting overseas in World War I, one of Smith's main characters, Tracy Deen, "knew for the first time who [he] was and what he was after. . . . [T]here was nothing pulling—no confusion, no two ways, no three ways." What he wanted, the only life he could imagine for himself, was to be with Nonnie, his black lover. But the clarity and sense of himself that he had felt in France, where he saw no color barriers, was destroyed when he returned to Georgia. At home, Tracy was forced to remember "his white feelings," which brought back the confusion, pulled at him, made him lose his sense of direction and reality. He loved and respected "every inch" of a "colored girl," but the white world in which he lived told him it could not be true, and so, torn and hurting, he started "on a road whose map had been drawn long ago." That road, the road of racism, led him to hurt the woman he loved and ultimately led to his own death as well as to the lynching of his loyal black boyhood friend at the hands of poor whites.[31]

Smith took the title for her book from a blues song she had heard Billie Holiday sing.

A CRUSADE FOR CHILDREN

Southern trees bear a strange fruit.
Blood on the leaves and blood at the root.
Black body swinging in the southern breeze.
Strange fruit hanging from the poplar trees.

Civil rights activists had long called attention to the suffering of African Americans—to the "strange fruit" of racism—by focusing on the socially approved lynching of blacks in the South. In her book, Smith showed that lynching and racism were white as well as black problems, that racial prejudice created an unnatural and disturbing sense of "twoness," to use Du Bois's famous term, in whites as well as in blacks. The racism that led to the lynching of a black man killed a white man first. Furthermore, Smith intimated that before Tracy was killed, he psychologically killed himself by choosing to accept the prejudices of the white world. Smith described the lynching in only four sentences, and although it is perhaps the most obviously horrific result of racism in the book, it was just one of the many "strange fruits" produced by the American racial order that she depicted. The book really told the story of all the strangeness, the confusion, that both whites and blacks experienced, of the double lives that whites as well as blacks lived because of white supremacy. Tracy, Ed (the black man who murdered him), and the poor whites who lynched Henry were all insecure, all "afraid to be free." They and many of the other characters in Smith's book became for the American public vivid examples of the kind of personality and ego weakness, the kind of individual pathologies discussed by contemporary social scientists. Smith's story forcefully portrayed to a wide audience the social violence and disregard for human life that the strangeness of racism created.[32]

If the assertions of social scientists and writers such as Smith were true, then it seemed clear that America could either bring "first aid to the personalities injured by our present world's madness" or "cast the dark shadow of unhappiness over the future." Unchecked, racism would continue to bring untold suffering to all its victims, black and white. The "price of prejudice," experts insisted, was the "price of peace" for both individuals and for the nation. Racism, they argued, jeopardized the future of the world since prejudiced people, already prone to "crooked thinking" and lynchings, were more likely than healthy, tolerant people to turn to fascist-like rulers. As one writer charged, racism apparently could be "more dangerous to world peace than the atom bomb."[33]

In *Strange Fruit*, Nonnie's sister, Bess, explains that some words make you cry yourself to sleep—words that could never be forgotten because they were "smeared on you to the bone," such as your mother saying, "Folks our color walks slow" or white children calling you "chocolate drop." The white southerners in *Strange Fruit*, like whites in the nonfictional South, liked to think that blacks preferred segregation, that they did not have negative emotional reactions to the strictures of white supremacy. Blacks were, after all, like dogs. But at the same time that researchers directed attention to the effects of racism on the emotional and mental development of white children, they also highlighted the emotional damage that segregation and discrimination fostered in black children. In their famous "Doll Study," for example, Kenneth B. Clark and Mamie P. Clark found that the majority of black children they tested showed a marked preference for white dolls over "colored" dolls. When asked which doll they liked best, which one they would like to play with, or which doll was "nice," two-thirds of the children chose the white doll, while 59 percent of them described the colored doll as "bad." Another oft-quoted study of black children similarly found that "among kindergarten, first, and second grade [black] children, there is much evidence of negative self-feelings and personal conflict concerning group belonging. . . . Many children experience serious ego threats as a result of group prejudices. Negro children reveal most vividly and often the feelings of insecurity resulting from anticipated rejection or insult from white children."[34]

Such findings, child advocates warned, represented a serious "harvest of neglect." If children, as social science research testified, needed to be "infused with a proper and wholesome self-esteem," then black children, "hemmed in at every turn," were hardly receiving a "fair chance to achieve a healthy personality." Child experts worried about the "precarious . . . psychic condition" of children and the psychological damage that resulted when a child was "reproved and punished for being what he is by nature and what he cannot help being." In other words, their research indicated that significant psychological harm came to children who faced harassment and humiliation because of the color of their skin. Inevitably, therefore, the "daily toll" of racism would create in young African Americans an "excessive number" of "personality defects." Social science researchers insisted that greater care for the development of young blacks was essential; otherwise, such damaged young people could not help but turn in frustration to crime, moral cynicism, and other antidemocratic ways. As Bess's

"Grandchildren of Mrs. Ella Watson, a government charwoman, Washington, D.C.," 1942. African American photographer Gordon Parks captured something of the effects of poverty and racism on African American children with this Farm Security Administration image, which he took long before the Clarks' doll studies helped convince the Supreme Court to rule against segregated public schools. (Courtesy Farm Security Administration–Office of War Information Collection, Library of Congress, Prints and Photographs Division, LC-USF34–013426-C)

friend, Dr. Sam Perry, in *Strange Fruit* explains, "There're other things . . . that hurt worse than poverty [that] drive us crazy . . . the little things . . . that work through the skin . . . to your heart. . . . [Y]ou take it and take it and take it . . . day comes you can't take any more. . . . And you turn on somebody. . . . You go crazy as hell."[35]

Youth who did not conform to middle-class behavioral ideals had long inspired distress among reformers. But in the 1940s and 1950s, anxieties about war and cultural change led to widespread attention to the problem of juvenile delinquency, a term that by then encompassed everything from wearing flashy clothing, hanging out on street corners, and having sex to stealing cars and committing murder. Historians have explored this heightened concern over teen crime, which, as they note, was based on broad definitions of illegal behavior for minors and led to the indictment of the music, comic book, and film industries for their corrupting influence on young people. Not everyone, however, agreed that the media were to blame for rising delinquency rates. Sociologist Robert Merton, for example, and others argued that delinquency was caused by the frustration young people experienced when their lives did not match American ideals. In Merton's view, "Delinquency depended on the reaction of society almost as much as it did the action of an adolescent." Members of New York City's Committee on Juvenile Delinquency similarly believed that much of the "antisocial" behavior of children, especially black children, could be prevented if communities showed more concern for children's psychological well-being. The U.S. Children's Bureau also resisted the trend to blame the media for delinquency and used experts to put forward a more complex understanding of the problem. The AYC similarly pointed to environmental, educational, and psychosocial explanations for delinquency. And Gunnar Myrdal's influential 1944 *An American Dilemma*, which drew from the AYC's work and outlined to the world America's racial problems, supported the arguments of social scientists and child welfare advocates who saw individual pathology within the context of social pathology. It, like many other studies of the era, regarded individual pathology—the maladjusted personalities with which both white and black children struggled—as an especially tragic (and potentially dangerous) result of prejudice.[36]

As early as the 1930s, but increasingly in the postwar period, debates about delinquency and the findings of social science researchers intersected with discussions about the rights of childhood and attempts to extend those rights to all young Americans. Advocates argued, "We cannot have a healthy society without healthy personalities." Child welfare reformers and educational experts sometimes sounded very much like Federal Bureau of Investigation director J. Edgar Hoover, psychiatrist Fredric Wertham, and other alarmists of the era. For example, one cautioned that "negro juvenile delinquency is today the most important crime problem in New York." Unlike those alarmists, however, many reformers eschewed simple explanations and solutions for juvenile crime. One reformer, for example, insisted that "Children's Court records indicate a striking relationship between delinquency among negro children and neglect of such children" and that "we cannot prevent crime among negroes unless we fight race discrimination." Child welfare reformers and social science researchers were not surprised by the possibility that black youth were becoming "vigorous rebel[s] against society and against its hypocritical morals."[37]

But these reformers rejected more sensationalized explanations of the problem of delinquency. Instead of blaming the media, they regarded racism as the primary culprit. Racial prejudice, they insisted, was the factor most severely limiting young people's "avenues of democratic expression." Denied the "fundamental drives" of American children and unable to develop a sense of security, a sense of belonging, or proper self-respect, black children were "ready object[s] of such frustration drives," "Frankensteins which we have stupidly created." In the early 1930s, segregationists had argued that giving black children the same educational opportunities as white children led African Americans to develop an inferiority complex. Segregationists' answer was to enforce Jim Crow; otherwise, they warned, black students would likely resort to violence after realizing that they were mentally incapable of competing with white children. But in the years after World War II, many observers came to believe that the racism behind such statements was really the problem. Experts argued that if "a growing number of young people cannot come to terms with our social order, perhaps there is something wrong with the social order itself." Even Wertham, the most vocal champion of the mass media explanation of delinquency, acknowledged the relationship between racism and delinquent behavior, such as when he founded a free psychiatric clinic in Harlem in the 1940s with his friend, African American writer Richard Wright.[38]

In his 1940 novel, *Native Son*, Wright explains just how racism creates "Frankensteins." His main character, Bigger Thomas, "just can't get used to it. . . . Every time I think about it I feel like somebody's poking a red-hot iron down my throat. . . . We live here and they live there. We black and they white. They got things and we ain't. They do things and we can't. It's just like living in jail. Half the time I feel like I'm on the outside of the world peeping in through a knot-hole in the fence." But Bigger does not allow himself to feel the fullness of the shame and misery of his life, for he "knew that the moment he allowed what his life meant to enter fully into his consciousness, he would either kill himself or someone else." Bigger kills someone accidentally but does not see the death as an accident: "He had killed many times before, only on those other times there had been no handy victim or circumstance to make visible or dramatic his will to kill." Most disturbing, Bigger is proud of what he has done. He admires Hitler and Mussolini "running the Jews to the ground . . . invading Spain. [Bigger] was not concerned with whether these acts were right or wrong; they simply appealed to him as possible avenues of escape." Killing gave him "a sense of wholeness." And he killed again.[39]

Writer and child advocate Pearl Buck took a tack that Du Bois often used and that Martin Luther King Jr. later frequently employed when she asked Americans in the 1940s to consider "the moment that faces every colored mother and father, the moment when their child has to know that he is doomed to eternal handicaps because of his color." She suggested that "colored children . . . born under the shadow . . . cannot hope for escape even for their children." In her introduction to the first edition of *Native Son*, Fisher similarly wrote, "Our American society creates around all youth . . . ideals . . . but our society puts Negro youth in the situation of the animal in the psychology lab in which a neurosis is to be caused, by making it impossible for him to try to live up to those never-to-be questioned national ideals, as other young Americans do." In Wright's story, all Bigger wants is "to merge himself with others and be a part of this world . . . to be allowed a chance to live like others, even though he was black." But, as the boy's lawyer explains, this "native son," this "American product . . . is a dispossessed and disinherited man" who exhibits the same "emotional state, the intensity, the ache for violent action, the emotional and cultural hunger" that characterizes those willing to "follow some gaudy, hysterical leader." In *Native Son*, Wright, born a Mississippi sharecropper and conditioned to the streets of Chicago as a young man, gave America what appeared to be an authentic and disturbing example of the only escape many African American youth could imagine because of the shadow of racism. In fact, the AYC recognized that Wright's novel simply exposed "in dramatic form the problems with which our Negro personality studies are concerned."[40]

BACK TO CHILDHOOD: UNMAKING RACIAL
PREJUDICE AND THE NATION'S SCHOOLS

The current state of race relations certainly did not bode well for the well-being of the nation or its citizens. But the good news, researchers reported, was that "race prejudice is not instinctive." Advocates and scholars agreed that there was time before children were "corrupted, by what [English poet Percy Bysshe] Shelley calls 'the world's slow stain.'" In fact, "if boys and girls could grow up in a friendly atmosphere, they probably would not become aware of differences until middle childhood." Child experts and sociologists alike stressed the influence of "the external environment" on racial attitudes and behavior patterns and insisted that children are "blissfully unconscious of differences in color, race, wealth, or social position" and "can get along together if their elders do not set barriers and influence their thinking and behavior." They offered advice to interested parties on "how to keep . . . children free from prejudice" and "understand that to be different does not necessarily mean to be better or worse."[41]

Anthropologists also contributed to the discourse on tolerance and the reassessment of prejudice. In the early twentieth century, Franz Boas undermined evolutionary assumptions about race by describing the industriousness of African peoples and emphasizing their military, political, judicial, agricultural, artistic, and scientific accomplishments. He also portrayed "social groups as historically constructed" and asserted that "the contact of peoples and diffusion of ideas" produced human variation and made racial identity contingent. Within a few decades, Boas, who both influenced and was influenced by black scholars such as Du Bois, further challenged assumptions about essentialist racial types and instinctive attitudes toward different races, arguing that culture and environment were more important than biology or heredity in shaping individuals and that a society's dominant ideas and categorizations (such as race) were "subject to change and drift." In the 1930s, 1940s, and 1950s, other anthropologists such as Boas's students, Ruth Benedict and Margaret Mead, published ethnographic evidence that further challenged American value systems, supported cultural relativity, and bolstered calls for greater tolerance. Their work revealed that diverse people form diverse opinions on topics such as race and suggested that the malleability of human thought meant that different cultural beliefs and socialization processes could produce very different norms and behaviors. In a book she coauthored with fellow anthropologist Gregory Bateson, Mead argued that childhood experiences "predispose" individuals to "maladjustments" and hence could be "culturally handled." And Benedict critically wrote that "contempt for the alien is not the only possible solution of our present contact of races and nationalities. Traditional Anglo-Saxon intolerance is a local and temporal culture-trait like any other. . . . The recognition of the cultural basis of race prejudice is a desperate need in present Western civilization."[42]

Ideas about the social construction of race and the need to change America's understandings of race were also supported by the 1947 report submitted by President Harry S. Truman's Commission on Civil Rights. *To Secure These Rights* affirmed both the dangers of prejudice — in a democracy it could be regarded only as an "outlaw attitude" that might lead to "violent murderous impulses" — and the idea that "most prejudice is learned." Personal stories told by both blacks and whites made similar claims as well. After watching children display "no feelings about 'difference' of any sort" as they played at a park, one father of a mixed-race family wrote to the Children's Bureau that he believed from "the bottom of my heart" that the "path to a better America" was through the children. Others made similar conclusions based on their own lives. In the 1940s, when educator John Rice wrote about his childhood in South Carolina, he stressed the barriers between white and black worlds and how he had often overcome those barriers as a boy. Rice explained that on their own, black and white children played together. He and his childhood friends had "a polity of our own, governed by and governing ourselves." Only when they crossed over into adult spaces did walls go up between the races. On late summer afternoons, Rice and his black and white friends might be playing "Sir Arthur" or "Noah and his ark" when they caught a glimpse of the "watermelon wagon." The children would then race one another "to the tables under the great oak at the back of the house." There they divided, "the Negro children to sit at the table by the smokehouse," the white children "at the longer table in the yard."[43]

According to Rice and others who wrote about growing up in the Jim Crow South, the strict rules of segregation did not always apply to young children. In the 1950s, historian C. Vann Woodward described a window of time from the 1880s through the mid-1890s when southern race relations appeared to be more fluid and Jim Crow was not a foregone conclusion. Child advocates agreed. Memoirs such as Rice's supported the contention that a season of alternatives was truly available to every generation and not just to a brief historical period. As scholars at the time noted, children's worlds were more fluid, shaped by but not precisely modeled after the adult world. Jim Crow, and the racism that created it, might disappear if children were brought up "wisely," enabling them to "be happier . . . live more successfully with one another" and "be relatively free of . . . intolerance."[44]

The *Negro Digest* ran a regular column entitled "My Most Humiliating Jim Crow Experience," and authors frequently wrote about their first experience with Jim Crow. Ann Petry, for example, wrote about her racial coming of age at a Sunday school picnic when a large white child pointed at her and asked their racially mixed group, "What's she doing on our beach? She's a nigger." Her white friends rallied to her support, but Petry had still felt the shame that blackness brought to an American child. "Here in America," she concluded, perhaps thinking about her attacker as well as herself, "they teach us [what race means] when we are very young."[45]

Frank Coggins called his contribution to *Negro Digest* "I Hate Negroes." His essay, like so many others, traced his awareness of race to a particular moment in childhood. He remembered "bringing home a colored playmate. . . . I liked him . . . and I wanted my mother and father to meet him as they did my other friends." But Coggins's father "took pains to ignore the child," and young Coggins sensed that "something was wrong." He began to question himself. "The boy was nice — or was he? Had I been deceived somehow? . . . Hurt and bitter," and unable to "direct the emotional reaction toward my parent, where it belonged," Coggins "dropped the blame on a little pair of black shoulders" and began to repeat the cycle of hate. That looking back on their lives both black and white adults would often choose their first experience with Jim Crow as their most humiliating suggests something of the shock children felt when introduced to racism; the idea of racial difference seemed to a child an arbitrary and unnatural distinction between people, and thus perhaps one that could be unmade in childhood as well. At the very least, such accounts suggest that many adults actively promoted the idea of childhood as a period of racial innocence and believed childhood to be a time of possibility.[46]

Lillian Smith was one of the more articulate proponents of childhood innocence and race as a social construct. The famous author once said that she wrote *Strange Fruit* because of her childhood experiences. Like other young southerners, as a child she "began to feel an invisible wall between human beings," a wall that divided whites from blacks and separated "a child and the people she loved." For her, segregation had "something to do with white and black people," but it also had to do "with childhood, and with mothers and their children, and . . . with the heart's deepest fears and the child's earliest dreams." The book, she said, was a journey "back to childhood," back to what was "left there, so long ago."[47]

In one of the most moving passages from *Strange Fruit*, a passage that appeared in the *Negro Digest* before the book's publication, Smith describes the racial awakening of young Tracy and his black boyhood companion, Henry. The boys, seven and eight years old, are playing outside when a little white girl races toward Henry on her bicycle. "'Move, move, move!' she shrieked. And Henry . . . shrieked back, 'Move, move, move, yourself!'" The two collided, and the boys, "knowing nothing else to do," laughed. Henry's mother saw the accident and regarded it as "something she had to tend to. . . . Mamie whipped her boy. She whipped him, saying, 'I got to learn it to you, you heah! I got to. You can't look at a white gal like dat, you can't tech one, you can't speak to one cept to say yes mam and thanky mam' . . . and Henry, squalling and catching his breath in strangling gasps, said it after her, word for word, three times, as she urged him on, tapping his legs with the tip of the switch as he said it. Then black legs whitened by the lash of his lesson, snuffling and dazed, he ran into the cabin and like a shamed dog crawled under the bed."[48]

To Tracy, Mamie says, "Go to your own folks!" And Tracy begins to "wander, a lost thing . . . until he ached all over, to fill the empty dimensions of a life he had not chosen and did not know the size of and into which her words told him he must go and stay forever." Eventually going back to Mamie and his friend, he feels "a distance great between them, terrifying and strange and measureless between them. A floor that would not bear their weight to cross it." And then Tracy and Henry hear Mamie and Ten, Henry's father, arguing over the "lesson." "'So you beats yo boy half to death cause you thinks white folks like dat.' 'I learn him how to behave.' . . . 'You beat da sperrit outn him. He won't be a man fit fo nothin.' . . . 'He got to learn there's white folks and colored folks and things you can't do ef you want to live. . . . He ain good as white folks. I got to learn him dat.'" The boys listen, wondering, "Do skin color make the diffunce?"[49]

Tracy tries to force the incident from his mind, but it remains, bringing him out of his dreams of a life with his black lover and into his own, white world, a racialized reality that makes no more sense to him as an adult than it does as a child, a reality that causes both his and Henry's deaths. But, as child advocates argued, Tracy's tragic life and all the tragic lives that fill the pages of Strange Fruit did not have to be relived by the next generation. America could make a journey, as Smith suggested, "back to childhood," back to what she and others defined as a period of purity and natural affections. And this time, they could avoid erecting those "invisible walls between human beings," between children and the people they loved, avoid strangling "the free mind" and tying "a moral and spiritual millstone around the necks" of its children. In her 1949 nonfiction work, Killers of the Dream, Smith even more explicitly explained that racism was one of the

cruel things that young white southerners "learned so casually" in childhood. Others agreed that "southerners didn't ask to be brought up feeling
the way they do about Negroes. They didn't look up from their bassinets
and say 'mother please teach me a legend about Negroes that is going to
make me nervous.'" But as Smith urged, precisely because racism "began
. . . not only in the history books but in our childhood," the next generation
might not grow up haunted by its lessons or warped by its effects. As experts on childhood argued, "Community attitudes are not static. . . . [T]hey
are dynamic, can be directed, and do change" if special care is taken to
help all children develop healthy personalities and keep them from learning unhealthy prejudices.[50]

Extant child-centered institutions were perfectly fitted for that task.
Since its founding, America had regarded schools as the institutions responsible for inculcating desirable qualities in its future citizens. Educational experts in the 1940s and 1950s reiterated these long-standing ideas
about schools, arguing that "human beings are peculiarly susceptible to
environment" and that "the indoctrination of youth with loyalty to democratic ideals is the first duty of free schools in a democracy." Child advocates likewise insisted that "schools . . . are in a strategic position to influence the health of the nation." Next to the family, schools did the most to
arm America's children with inner strengths, prevent mental illness, and
help children overcome "prejudices, irresponsibility, and other antisocial
attitudes" in an "ever-changing society." As one white southerner, a future
editor of two prominent North Carolina newspapers, told his classmates
in his rather prescient 1940s high school valedictory address, "Our schools
can do more than any other influence to break down the wall of prejudice.
If schools have a world-wide mission, it is to clear up the idea that some
are born superior to others in human rights."[51]

This undertaking constituted an altogether different mission than
merely re-creating the status quo among children, for the qualities deemed
desirable in the 1940s and 1950s challenged rather than reinforced the current social and political order. The racism that governed American life was
increasingly described as a "mental phobia . . . more contagious than physical disease." Social science experts and child advocates alike argued that
"since the public school is the institution designated by our democracy as
the center where the formal preparation of the children for participation
in society is focused, the school should accept leadership" in dealing with
"the problems of minority groups and intercultural relationships." Schools,

they said, could "prove an effective means for changing the mores, values, and attitudes of a people" and should, in fact, "build a new social order." In the late 1930s, AYC director Homer Rainey had argued that "education creates economic opportunity, conquers disease, and softens prejudice." By the 1940s, many others considered schools the most "important or potentially powerful agency" not just "in promoting assimilation" but also "in substituting reason for prejudice, [and] knowledge for misunderstanding," in encouraging "critical social action," in teaching "techniques for co-operative living," and in helping to extend the rights of childhood to all Americans. Advocates argued that "better public education for both races" would be the means by which prejudice would be "conquered, economic opportunity created . . . and tolerance built up." As Myrdal affirmed in *An American Dilemma*, education was "the best way—and the way most compatible with American individual ideals—to improve society."[52]

Not coincidentally, the U.S. Children's Bureau first emphasized educational issues at the 1940 White House Conference on Children in a Democracy. The bureau previously had left childhood education to be addressed by the Office of Education. But the AYC's work during the Great Depression and the mounting international tensions led many Americans, like those who championed the Children's Crusade for Children, increasingly to see schools as an important place to counter threats to American democracy. Growing attention to issues of personality development, to the rights of black and other minority children, and to the idea of children as agents (or potential agents) of social change inspired child welfare specialists and many others to see public schools as the best place to realize their goals. If the Children's Bureau really wanted to extend the rights of childhood to all children, that process would occur through the schools.[53]

Schools, advocates asserted, could remake America as they met the emotional and mental health needs of all children and fought prejudice. This task seemed vital to the personality development of individual children and hence to the security of democracy. However, World War II also revealed that an alarming number of Americans had grown up without even basic literacy skills, which disqualified them from military service and kept them from fully contributing to what was commonly called the "American way of life." Child advocates and politicians alike cited military rejection statistics as alarming evidence of the kind of gross inequalities in American education that made the country vulnerable to its enemies. "Negroes represented 11 percent of the first million draftees," they quoted, "but they represented 60 percent of those rejected on account of a lack of functional literacy." Such figures, both during World War II and as the cold war developed, brought sustained attention to child advocates and education experts who insisted that the educational inequalities so evident in rural and Negro schools be addressed. America might not want to increase spending on education, but investing in education seemed an increasingly favorable alternative to "the lack of national wealth and strength" and "the expense of the ignorance, inefficiency, and unsocial conduct" that occurred when educational provisions were ignored. Because of the tense international situation, experts warned that even "the dullest mind" could not be neglected "in one part of the country without penalties to the entire Nation."[54]

In the 1920s, Du Bois had used the pages of *The Crisis* to publish statistics detailing the inequalities of segregated education. During the 1930s, the AYC and other child-centered agencies and advocates had also tried to alert the public and the federal government to the nation's serious educational inequalities. In the following decade, Myrdal's *An American Dilemma* reaffirmed such findings. In one black school he inspected, students could not tell him the name of the president of the United States and thought the constitution "was a 'newspaper in Atlanta.'" Their teacher, described as a "sickly girl . . . full of fear," had only high school training, and all the students, whose ages spanned from six to twenty, met in the same room in a dilapidated building. Other experts reported similar findings. Responding to white southerners who claimed that recent progress in black education proved the adequacy of the South's dual school system, one researcher pointed out that at the "current rate of progress," it would "still take thirteen years" for teachers' salaries to equalize, "twenty-nine years to equal expenditures for actual instruction . . . one-hundred twenty nine years to equal the value of school property . . . and . . . two hundred and thirty years to equalize the per capita transportation costs of Negro and white children." This scholar, like other social science experts, child advocates, and child welfare specialists at the time, stressed "the cost in unhappy, inefficient, poorly trained workers which results from denial to the Jew or Negro of his right to the kind of education he desires and deserves . . . the loss in sheer ignorance which in turn causes people to behave unintelligently as consumers, voters, parents [and] the loss in . . . still other ways from which the majority populations also suffer because of their own interdependence with minorities." Such horror stories, as Myrdal called them, might have elicited only a limited response during the 1930s, but even isolated cases of unequal educational conditions signified disturbing possibilities in the 1940s. As the U.S. commissioner of education explained, "We live in epic times. We are participants in a dramatic clash between two opposing sets of ideas." Such times demanded that America sustain a "high general level of education throughout the country," improve the "physical and mental health" of all its children, and develop its "full potential manpower resources."[55]

Child advocates argued that inequalities in education wasted America's most precious resources—its children—and even turned them against America. Scholars asserted that low literacy rates among underprivileged (often black) children "cost us much in maladjustment, in crime, poverty, social conflicts, and disorganization" and that "conditions resulting from the war have emphasized the direct relationship between the increasing problem of juvenile delinquency and the absence of adequate school facilities." Experts looked at schools as potential "bulwarks against delinquency." To serve such a function, however, the nation needed more adequately equipped schools with qualified teachers open "throughout the school year . . . with full day . . . sessions." America could choose, they warned, either to "add inestimable wealth both materially and culturally to the Nation" by improving educational opportunities for rural and minority children or to create "unhappy, unproductive, and maladjusted" individuals. "Unsocial phenomena" such as "delinquency [and] crime" and the necessity of poor relief, experts insisted, were the costs of America's unequal schools. Children denied educational opportunities in the most democratic nation on earth might even turn against democracy. In any case, it was a choice, as the Children's Bureau put it, "between education and catastrophe."[56]

Experts also argued that severe educational inequalities weakened America internationally. "As long as our house is in disorder our actions will speak so loudly that others cannot hear what we say," education leaders asserted. And, as they pointed out, studies that compared schools throughout the nation revealed much disorder, or, in Lenroot's words, "uncovered conditions unworthy of a democracy." In fact, in contrast to Children's Crusade for Children propaganda, some observers described the conditions in the poor South or in places such as Harlem as similar to those under which refugee children in World War II Europe lived. The state of rural and black schools, they insisted, stood out as a "blight on our national life," revealing to the world that democracy in the richest nation of the world had much "unfinished business." Because black children's educational disadvantages affected not only their own futures but also those of the nation and the world, experts argued, America needed a truly democratic public school system both "as an example to the world and for our own domestic well-being."[57]

Scholars have explored the ways that national security concerns intersected with the push for civil rights for African Americans and directly influenced the Supreme Court ruling in *Brown*.[58] America's concern for its image abroad influenced civil rights reforms. And as the Scottsboro case revealed in the 1930s and other images that received widespread play in the international press in the 1950s and 1960s continued to reveal, images of children suffering from American racism generated the most intense criticism from outside as well as inside the country. Secretary of State Dean Acheson commented that school segregation was "singled out for hostile foreign comment in the United Nations and elsewhere." If racial discrimination was an obvious defect of American democracy, if it was "America's number one domestic failure and her number one international handicap," then racial discrimination against children seemed an even more perverse affront to democratic ideals. Lenroot's comment that "child welfare and national security are inseparable" seemed true in more ways than one.[59]

Racism toward American children elicited intense international criticism largely because of a burgeoning worldwide sense that childhood was a sacred state that needed to be protected and that racial discrimination obviously violated. America's efforts to extend the "rights of childhood" to all children reflected a larger trend throughout much of the world. The 1946 creation of the United Nations International Children's Emergency Fund (UNICEF), for example, suggested a consensus on the need to watch over the world's children. Article 25 of the 1948 *United Nations Universal Declaration of Human Rights* further put the weight of the international community behind the idea that "motherhood and childhood are entitled to special care and assistance." That declaration also insisted that "everyone is entitled to all the rights and freedoms set forth in this declaration, without distinction of any kind, such as race." Moreover, in 1959, just a few years after *Brown*, the United Nations reaffirmed a worldwide commitment to children's rights in *The Declaration of the Rights of the Child* (appendix C). It was, therefore, bad enough that many Americans were not

fully incorporated into the American "democratic way of life," but it was
an even greater offense to international values that many Americans did
not enjoy the "birthright of every child." In the years leading up to *Brown*,
debates about America's image abroad and African American civil rights
issues intersected with each other as well as with a growing sense of the
need to extend the rights of childhood to all young people and with a growing awareness within America of the multiple roles that schools played in
safeguarding both childhood and democracy. These multiple intersecting
debates help explain why "equality of opportunity for education" became
a rallying cry for civil rights activists and the myriad political and child
welfare experts who saw it as the "cornerstone of democracy" and the key
to its survival.[60]

For education to be the cornerstone of democracy, however, schools
had to give all children equal opportunities. Just as important, schools had
to be an "experience in democratic living." Du Bois had long argued that
integrated education "provided the intellectual basis for real democracy"
and would help foster the kind of widespread human contact needed for
full human development. Now the U.S. commissioner of education similarly counseled that schools "will not move democracy forward by merely
teaching courses of study" but instead would do so by becoming "a place
where democracy is practiced." Educational experts noted that past efforts
"to develop good citizenship [were] largely restricted to learning the structure and history of democratic organization, while actual democratic behavior was practically ignored with little or no attention paid to the spirit
of the democratic person-to-person relationship." But, they asserted, because of current world circumstances, every school "must become a laboratory and nursery for citizenship," teaching not only what democracy is
but also "to love it, and to live it." "Funds of facts," they warned, are merely
"fragments" that "do not deepen understanding or create acceptance."[61]

If children could be "freed from ignorance, prejudice, suspicion and
fear [and] educated for justice, liberty, and peace" only through the "experience of democratic living," it was unlikely that America's children
would learn their lessons. A 1949 checklist to determine "How Democratic
Is Your School?" encouraged students to ask themselves questions that included, "Are members of minority groups in your classes accepted by other
students without condescension or aloofness?" If such was the measure of
a democratic school, then southern schools "for whites only" or northern
schools in racially segregated neighborhoods obviously did not qualify as

laboratories for good citizenship. And it hardly seemed possible that dilapidated schools composed entirely of black students would inspire those children to understand and appreciate the virtues of American democracy. As scholars increasingly pointed out, children asked to recite the Pledge of Allegiance and salute the flag in racially segregated schools, whether black or white, had every reason to "distrust authority" and "rebel against society and against its hypocritical morals."[62]

Moreover, black and white children in segregated schools lacked the "actual face-to-face" experiences with different groups that experts deemed essential to the development of healthy personalities and good American and world citizens. Researchers argued that segregation "narrowed and distorted" vision and "cultural learning," while integration led to new discoveries, inventions, and a flourishing of the arts. According to educational experts, teaching children good interpersonal relations and "brotherly love" were fundamental strategies for safeguarding democracy and achieving world peace. Such skills, however, required "fellowship in the friendly contacts of personalities across racial lines." To achieve peace, it seemed critical that children not be "walled off" but instead receive opportunities to "run, in close and continued contact, [with] persons from an Other, or They—or Out group." Education leaders stressed that character training is "*caught* rather than *taught*" and asserted that "to have Negroes . . . sit in our lunchrooms, sit in our classes, play on our teams, without making any fuss about it, does far more good than making children conscious of a 'Negro problem.'" Such comments reflected the underlying assumption that in 1940s America "our children" meant white schools and white children and that "Other," "They," or "Out group" meant blacks. More important, however, those comments also revealed a growing awareness that only in racially integrated schools could children learn democratic values and good "intercultural relations." One literary critic captured this viewpoint when he wrote, "Whatever lies beyond the horizon of close personal contacts becomes an abstraction [that] no amount of education or personal cleverness can overcome." Reflecting America's fears at the time, he went on to explain the importance of direct relationships between members of different groups. To him as well as to many of his contemporaries, the absence of those kinds of relationships explained "the psychology of fascists, who are certainly neither stupid or illiterate." If America was to keep from becoming a totalitarian state, it would have to do more to encourage positive associations between the races.[63]

Not all public schools, however, were failing the nation or its children. In the 1940s, school districts in the North and Midwest, plainly influenced by expert debate, determined to make their schools "laboratories in education for democracy." Springfield, Massachusetts, for example, instituted a program, widely praised by social scientists and adopted by schools across the country, that purportedly gave students a realistic rather than idealized picture of American democracy, provided them with "opportunities for democratic living," and taught them "tolerance of all religions, races, and economic classes not through preachment but through contacts." Gary, Indiana, and Kalamazoo, Michigan, integrated their schools principally so that, just as experts recommended, children would have "the opportunity to develop an understanding and respect for democratic ideals by practicing in day to day living . . . principles of cooperation, fair play . . . and respect for the rights . . . of others." News stories about these desegregation efforts also reflected and supported the arguments of social scientists. In Gary, for example, the press pointed out that earlier attempts to integrate schools had resulted in student strikes and violence. In the 1940s, however, despite some community resistance, the members of the football squad voted to support integration, and none of the integrating black children or their families "were molested in the slightest." One writer suggested that "this contrast can be interpreted as proof of progress toward more democratic attitudes" among the younger generation. Newspaper reporters also liked to retell "amusing" incidents associated with these integration efforts that highlighted "the absurdity of racial prejudice" and not inadvertently the lack of true racial prejudice in children. At one elementary school, two first-grade boys, "one white, the other Negro, approached their principal, hand in hand saying, 'We wanted you to know we're leaving school. We don't want to go to school with those coloreds.'" And at another school, a little white boy complained to his principal about going to class with blacks but then walked home with an African American boy from his apartment building, "as great friends as ever."[64]

RESHAPING AMERICA, RESHAPING THE WORLD: CHILDHOOD AND THE *BROWN* RULING

Such stories reinforced social science research and clearly made it seem that if prejudice, negative stereotypes, and the lack of personal relationships between different people were responsible for the problems of the world, then, as the Children's Bureau's Lenroot explained, children were the "key with which to unlock the paradox of history." If the nation could just "reshape the life of one generation," it "could reshape the world." Describing his initiation into adulthood, Rice explained, "A boy . . . had to become a man, whatever that might mean. . . . It was as if he stood, not at the fork of the roads—that figure is too simple—but on the depot platform of any Southern city, surrounded by bawling hack drivers inviting him to perfect destinations." There is a certain amount of regret in reminiscences such as Rice's, a sense not only of lost youth but also of lost opportunities—of choosing the wrong destinations. Smith's novel left a similar impression. After the lynching in *Strange Fruit*, southern white "liberal" Tom Harris tells his son, Charlie, that his generation is "too old to figure out things like this. . . . I hope some day you young folks will find the answer." Young Charlie has ideas about racial equality, but he tells his father, "If I stay here twenty years, I won't have [the answers]. Now I see things without color getting in the way—I won't be able to, then. It'll get me. It gets us all. Like quicksand." Underlying Charlie's comment is the belief, which the book's author shared with contemporary child advocates and education experts, that America could help children choose the right destinations, that the next generation did not have to get caught in the quicksand. Children held all the keys; they could change the world if their worlds were changed a little so that every child enjoyed the rights of childhood. As Du Bois had suggested years earlier, "There is but one patent way, proved and inescapable, Education. . . . The whole generation must be trained and guided and out of it as out of a huge reservoir must be lifted all genius, talent, and intelligence to serve all the world."[65]

In this context, the U.S. Supreme Court made its historic decision in *Brown v. Board of Education*. Legal scholar Robert Mnookin suggests that it was no accident that the decision that effectively dismantled Jim Crow was a children's case.[66] The Court had ruled in earlier segregation cases and could have chosen another with which to overturn the 1896 *Plessy v. Ferguson* ruling that provided the legal basis for the South's system of racial segregation. But the *Brown* case was more compelling than any pertaining to black adults. While the nation was willing to sit by and watch black men and women suffer under Jim Crow, it was less willing to accept children encountering the same discrimination and hostility. Moreover, both the wording of the decision and the cases involved in *Brown* suggest that the justices did not just integrate (or call for the desegregation of) America's

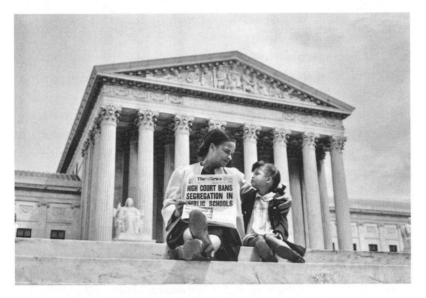

Nettie Hunt, sitting on the steps of the U.S. Supreme Court, explains to her daughter, Nikie, the meaning of the Supreme Court's 1954 decision banning school segregation. Since ideas about children's rights, including their right to an equal education and to a healthy psychological development, were central to the Court's ruling, this oft-reproduced image was a fitting way to announce the *Brown* ruling. Moreover, because of the historic decision, young people soon occupied center stage in the struggle for racial equality. (© Corbis)

schools and invalidate the legal foundation for Jim Crow policies. They also extended the rights of childhood to all young Americans. The decision specifically upheld children's "right" to the "opportunity of an education . . . on equal terms" and through that the right to healthy mental development. The underlying ideas expressed in *Brown* closely resembled those of child welfare advocates and education experts of the time and the 1930 Children's Charter. The appendix to the appellants' brief to the Supreme Court even included many of the research findings previously mentioned. While another decade would pass before Congress addressed equal employment and voting rights for blacks, the Court was willing to grant black Americans in the mid-1950s what amounted to "the first right of citizenship in a democracy . . . to grow throughout childhood in good . . . emotional and social health and security." Popular ideas about childhood and public discussions that linked the rights of children to a stronger democracy and world peace as well as widespread beliefs (backed by contemporary research) that young people could effect significant social change had made it difficult not to make what was quickly deemed "a morally right decision" in the *Brown* case.[67]

As scholars have suggested, "contextuality of thought" was significant to the Court's decision.[68] In the international context, evidence of America's racism violated worldwide sensibilities about human rights—specifically, beliefs about the rights of childhood. In addition, the United Nations, in Article 26 of the *Universal Declaration of Human Rights*, determined that "everyone has a right to education" and that education should "be directed to the full development of the human personality and to the strengthening of respect for human rights and fundamental freedoms. It shall promote understanding, tolerance, and friendship among all nations, racial or religious groups, and shall further . . . the maintenance of peace." Participants in a 1947 radio discussion sponsored by the University of Chicago confirmed that "in recent years," the international community had come to recognize the right to education as a "fundamental human right which is to be enjoyed by all without distinction as to race." Making the cold war context of equal educational opportunity even more explicit, one speaker additionally warned that since this right, "early enunciated in the United States of America has become a principle of international co-operation . . . the failure of the United States to realize its own principle within its own borders can then hardly be a matter for Americans to ignore."[69]

In the domestic context, discussions of national security were often linked to ideas about personality development, the role of the schools in building democracy, the permeability of racial concepts in childhood, and the rights of childhood. The NAACP used these ideas to argue its case, and the justices cited those concepts in their opinion. In some of their first assaults against educational inequalities, NAACP lawyers had stressed the "psychological aspect to white children being transported to school in busses while Negro children plod along the road. An inferiority complex is installed in the Negro children without one word being said." By the 1950s, such arguments carried even more weight. Robert L. Carter, a member of the NAACP's legal team, later recalled that social science research showing the psychological effects of segregation on young blacks provided "the key," the "ingredient" needed "to prevail" in the *Brown* case. And indeed, the justices' opinion considered "public education in the light of its full development and its present place in American life throughout the nation," relied on social science research showing the negative effects of prejudice on both black and white children, and specifically ruled "that in the field of public education the doctrine of separate but equal has no place." Not incidentally, the Southern Regional Council stressed the same points when it reported on the ruling: "Education has become a vastly greater force in preparing our children for their responsibilities as citizens in the world's leading democracy. Virtually all modern authorities agree that setting Negro children apart in separate schools promotes feelings of inferiority, interferes with healthy emotional development, and retards the ability to learn." And of course white segregationists liked to point out the influence of social science on the ruling. As one white woman wrote to the *Atlanta Constitution*, "The greatest unchristian and illegal act of this era is the 1954 decision of the Supreme Court of the United States which declared, for sociological and not legal reasons, that the separate but equal public school facilities were unconstitutional."[70]

However white citizens regarded the data or spun the ruling, the federal government in general was clearly taking seriously the arguments of education, social science, and child welfare experts. Congress had already created the National Institute of Mental Health, and just a few months before the *Brown* ruling, legislation established a new federal Department of Health, Education, and Welfare with cabinet status as well as a commission to study the federal government's role in relation to the states, including issues of education. In declaring segregation unconstitutional in an education case involving young children, the Court had not just made an important symbolic decision that would improve America's image abroad. Rather, if the arguments of child advocates, education experts, and social science researchers were correct, the Court had made the decision that had the greatest potential for making American ideals a reality, protecting American democracy at home, and even promoting the American way of life abroad. As in the Children's Crusade for Children, young people armed with the nation's ideals as expressed in *Brown* were going to save more than an isolated group of suffering people. They were going to save the nation itself and perhaps even the world.[71]

Both segregationists and desegregationists noted at the time of the *Brown* decision that getting rid of Jim Crow was not simply a matter of changing laws. Hearts, too, had to change, which was precisely why America's children had been given the responsibility. For more than ten years, advocates had insisted "that the solution of racial problems lies with the growing generation." And all the best research indicated that young people were more than capable of the task. Indeed, leading experts believed that it would be fairly easy for America's children to end both racial segregation and the disease of racism. As an article in *School Life* magazine issued just before the Supreme Court decision suggested, "If desegregation can take place among adults in the armed services . . . it should be even easier in education where younger persons, with less rigid attitudes and fewer prejudices than adults, are involved."[72]

White parents, however, suffering from the disease of racism and stuck in their "inflexible . . . maladjusted personalities," resisted, just as social science research predicted. The *Brown* decision, in fact, galvanized white southern opposition to civil rights. The specter of white and black children sitting side by side in classrooms prompted many southern communities to organize White Citizens' Councils and to launch "massive resistance" campaigns. Segregationist whites insisted that they were inspired by the very noble intention of "saving their children." They too seemed to believe at least some of the findings of social science researchers. Many were apparently convinced that if all children enjoyed the rights of childhood, if black and white children studied together in an environment that strengthened their personalities, encouraged them to realize their "potentialities," fostered good "interpersonal relations," and gave them experiences in democratic living, then the whole sociopolitical order could be remade. In declaring segregated schools unconstitutional, the U.S. Supreme Court had broken America's long-standing racialized conceptions of childhood and extended the "first rights of citizenship" to young blacks. In so doing, the Court had also signaled the breakdown of racialized conceptions of manhood and womanhood and of adult citizenship. But with many whites determined to deny black children their rights as children in a democracy—to save American childhood for white children—civil rights activists had to continue to fight, often turning to ideas about children, as in the Children's Crusade for Children and the Scottsboro case, to try to turn America's hearts.[73]

Three

· · · · · · ·

NO PLACE FOR CHILDREN

CHILDHOOD, *BROWN*, & STORIES ABOUT THE

SOUTHERN STRUGGLE FOR RACIAL EQUALITY

In 1964, the Student Non-Violent Coordinating Committee (SNCC) published a pictorial documentary, *The Movement*. Opposite the title page is a photo of a young black girl, eyes looking directly into the camera, face sullen and serious, arms cradling a sign: "Justice." The book ends with a similar image: Hattiesburg, Mississippi, a boy, maybe ten years old, dripping wet, mouth open, wide eyes staring, expectant. The caption reads, "They stand in the hose fire at Birmingham; they stand in the rain at Hattiesburg. They are young, they are beautiful, they are determined. It is for us to create, now, an America that deserves them."[1]

Scholars have often criticized the way the media presented the struggle for African American civil rights. And, indeed, the press certainly did not capture the complexities of the movement or movement organizing. Nonetheless, the media and civil rights activists, including SNCC, frequently presented the black freedom struggle in strikingly similar ways. Like the national news media, African American activists often focused on ideas about childhood and images of children to explain the meaning of the movement and to elicit public support for civil rights politics. Questioning the way the story of the civil rights movement was told in the press and remembered by everyday Americans has helped us understand better the movement. This chapter suggests that looking more closely at how and why the story was told the way it was can also deepen our understanding of the black freedom struggle. The chapter considers why particular narratives about the movement arose and what those narratives meant for the movement.²

Ten years before the publication of SNCC's book, the U.S. Supreme Court issued its decision in *Brown v. Board of Education*, putting its weight on the side of civil rights activists and affirming black children's rights to some of the fundamental rights of childhood. If the *Brown* decision indicated that America, or at least some of America, including its highest court, was willing to grant black children the "first rights of citizenship" in a democracy, then it seems fitting that the images civil rights organizers used to communicate the meaning of the movement to the public often centered on children as well. SNCC's pictorial featured boys and girls, barefoot, in torn, ill-fitting clothes, turned away from local pools or surrounded by men with guns, bayonets, and gas masks. It pictured them being strangled by cops and hosed down by belligerent city officials, kneeling in prayer, lying in coffins. Such images emphasized that in addition to keeping African Americans from realizing their basic constitutional rights, Jim Crow politics betrayed America's children. A decade after *Brown*, black children continued to be denied the rights of childhood.

Stories of children suffering under America's racist sociopolitical structure were all too familiar by the time SNCC published its documentary. Depression-era studies and the Scottsboro Boys case had thrust the less-than-ideal state of black childhood into public consciousness decades earlier. In the years following the *Brown* ruling, however, such images captured widespread media and public attention and brought sustained support for civil rights. The *Brown* decision heightened public awareness not just of racial inequalities and the struggle for African American civil rights, as legal scholar Michael Klarman suggests, but more specifically of the effects of those inequalities on children and on their struggle to secure the rights of childhood. Moreover, with its decision, the Supreme Court enlisted public schools, one of the most important "symbols which control the community" and certainly the most important public institution affecting the lives of America's children, in the struggle for racial equality. That ruling also, at least legally, "institutionalized" black children's rights to childhood. Scholars have dismantled much of Philippe Ariès's thesis in *Centuries of Childhood* but generally support his contention that the institutionalization of childhood through formal education marks a crucial turning point in the history of childhood in any society. In the decades leading up to *Brown*, child welfare advocates and other reformers, including African American leaders, used ideas about childhood in their campaigns for social and political change. But only with *Brown* did the United States formally recognize black children's rights to the same education as white children — in effect, to the same childhood as white children. And, not incidentally, only after the justices ruled against segregated public schools did evidence of the unequal and precarious state of black childhood motivate significant numbers of white Americans and their representatives in Congress to support the larger black freedom struggle.[3]

School desegregation became what *Life* magazine and others quickly labeled a "moral" battle, both because *Brown* extended America's democratic ideals to black citizens and especially because the 1954 ruling extended the rights of childhood to all of America's children. Southern school districts that violated the Court's decision or white citizens who thwarted attempts to comply with integration orders by harassing black students were also violating cultural beliefs in the sanctity of childhood. Images of black schoolchildren attacked by white adults disturbed an American public that was not yet unequivocally committed to the idea of African American equality. As civil rights historian Harvard Sitkoff notes, northern whites who otherwise considered civil rights organizations too radical "were shocked at the news headlines of schools being dynamite-bombed and the televised scenes of hate-filled white mobs." Those images made clear that racism threatened American childhood as much as it threatened the civil and political rights of black Americans.[4] And just one year after the *Brown* decision, the murder of fourteen-year-old Emmett Till showed America and the world how necessary that protection really was.

WHAT KIND OF BOY WAS EMMETT TILL?:
BLACK CHILDHOOD ON TRIAL

While some of the details of the incident are lost to history, journalists and scholars have outlined the basics of Emmett Louis Till's murder.[5] While visiting family in Mississippi in August 1955, the boy ventured with relatives and friends into a local store. Young Till bought some gum and perhaps said a few words to or whistled at the young and pretty white woman behind the counter. A few days later, the woman's husband and his half brother tracked the boy to his great-uncle's home and forced him into their truck. Likely with the help of others, they drove Till to a country barn, where they harassed, beat, and killed him. The murderers dumped the boy's mutilated body in the Tallahatchie River. The cotton gin fan they used to weigh it down, however, did not do its job, and a seventeen-year-old who was fishing soon discovered Till's remains. J. W. Milam and Roy Bryant went to trial, but the all-white southern jury quickly determined, despite overwhelming evidence to the contrary, that the men were not guilty. Happy and smiling, the two men kissed their wives and children, smoked cigars, and went home.

Historians have noted that the Till incident marked a decided shift from earlier lynching cases in which whites murdered blacks who supposedly transgressed racial boundaries or otherwise posed a threat to the white community. Earlier in the century, white southern communities celebrated such atrocities, and the perpetrators of such acts harbored no fear of punishment. But Till's killers tried to hide their deed, and the white community at least went through the motions of seeking justice.[6] Scholars and activists have also labeled Till a martyr and suggested that his murder stands out as a defining moment in the history of the black freedom movement for the ways it brought attention to the depths of southern racism and injustice and motivated a new generation of black protesters.[7]

Till's murder stood out in large part because his mother turned her private grief into a public spectacle. "I wanted the whole world to see what I had seen," she said, opening her boy's casket to Chicago's mourners and the nation's photographers.[8] Mamie Till Bradley exposed America's racism by showing her son's body to the world, but Till's youth exposed the depths of that racism. While other racially motivated murders that year received little or no public attention, the media treated the Till case as big news, and civil rights organizations, Black Muslim groups, and the Communist Party frequently referred to the case in speeches and promotional materials. Because of Till Bradley, millions saw not merely the effects of southern racism but more specifically its effects on children. The public wondered, "How could they do that to him? He's only a young boy!" and realized, as Myrlie Evers, who would later lose her husband to Mississippi's racism, observed, "that even a child was not safe from racism, bigotry, and death." Since the 1940s, social science researchers and child advocates had insisted that racism severely damaged both black and white children; this "brutal senseless crime" "took racism out of the textbooks and editorials and showed it to the world in its true dimensions."[9]

At the time of Till's lynching, attention was already directed at whether the white South would uphold the rights of black children. As news of the fourteen-year-old boy's disappearance and death broke, the head of the National Association for the Advancement of Colored People (NAACP), Roy Wilkins, charged, "It would appear from this lynching that the state of Mississippi has decided to maintain white supremacy by murdering children." Wilkins saw Till's murder as involving more than the death of one boy: it involved all black children suffering the consequences of the destructive and even murderous tendencies of America's racist social and political structure. Social scientists and child welfare experts had testified to the Supreme Court that white supremacy and segregation hurt children. Till's murder offered tangible evidence that racism did not merely damage children's personalities, it destroyed their bodies. Historian Ruth Feldstein suggests that Till's murder reveals contested meanings of motherhood in 1950s America. In seeking justice for her son, Bradley drew on popular ideals about motherhood and womanhood, ideals that were often elusive and problematic for black women. But the case also reveals contested meanings of childhood and the significance to the civil rights movement of racially inclusive ideas about childhood.[10]

Northern newsmen were struck by the irony of a sign posted just east of the town that tried and freed Bryant and Milam: Sumner was "a good place to raise a boy." As Till's murder made clear, the residents of Sumner meant a good place to raise a *white* boy. Articles about the incident explained that it had started when Till and his "chums" drove "to the nearby hamlet of Money to buy 2 cents' worth of bubble gum," an innocent enough adventure, as the media pointed out, for a group of young people. Till, however, transgressed the South's racial boundaries and in so doing lost his innocence, at least from the perspective of many white southerners. He may have whistled or spoken to attractive, young, white Carolyn Bryant, an act that observers at the time and later feminist scholars recognized would normally have been considered a perfectly acceptable expression of boyhood bravado. But white southerners did not see Till as a normal boy, and since Carolyn Bryant was a white woman, his behavior produced a sense of fear instead of laughs and cheers from his locally bred peers.[11]

News accounts provided contradictory answers to the question, "What kind of boy was Emmett Till?" The importance of this question both at the trial and in the press suggests the contested nature of black childhood in America and especially in the 1950s South. Two white men were not the only ones on trial in Sumner—Till was also on trial.[12]

Till's defenders described him in terms that echoed sentimental ideas about childhood. To them he was a "little boy," "a stuttering child not old enough to realize the tenseness of the race situation . . . in Mississippi." Mose Wright, the boy's great-uncle, stressed Till's innocence and naïveté, telling his killers and later the public, "This boy ain't got good sense." Sympathetic reporters told stories of how the happy-go-lucky youth almost missed the train that took him to Mississippi. They talked about his trip south as a "vacation"—a city boy going to the country for a couple of weeks. Those who knew Till likewise "insisted that he was polite and mild mannered," "a nice kid, just as obedient as you would want to see." "He was a Little League ball player. He was religious, with a near-perfect attendance at Sunday School." He had a nickname, Bo. He had a dog. Till seemed to be an all-American boy.[13]

Sympathetic journalists described the black youth who testified against Till's murderers at the trial in similar terms. Wheeler Parker, Till's sixteen-year-old cousin, narrated the scene at the corner store and the kidnapping. Retelling "young" Parker's story, the press stressed his youth and powerlessness. "Helplessly," they said, the "young negro" watched "while three white men and a woman roused his friend, fourteen-year-old Emmett Till from bed, dragged him to an auto, and drove away." News accounts depicted twelve-year-old witness Simeon Wright as "neatly dressed" and William Reed, eighteen, as "a gangling youth." Moreover, the press not only repeated Reed's eyewitness account—that he saw Till in a truck with white men, Milam with a gun, and heard "licks and hollering" coming from a nearby barn—but also reported that after Reed heard the whipping, he "went home and got ready to go to Sunday School." To make a case against the two white men, Till and the other black boys involved in the trial had to embody white middle-class ideas about childhood. By 1955, black children allegedly enjoyed the rights of childhood, but they still had to prove they were worthy of those rights.[14]

Questions about the "kind of boy" Till was also figured prominently in the defense's side of the story. Bryant and Milam's lawyers and white southern papers suggested that Till was "feeble minded," describing him as "a husky Negro lad" who had "molested" or made "indecent advances" toward a white woman. Articles also warned white Americans about the latent criminality and immorality of black youth with tales of white girls raped by gangs of young blacks in Chicago and Memphis. On the first day of the trial, Carolyn Bryant supported inflammatory rumors about

Till circulating in the press by testifying, as one reporter put it, that "she was molested by a wolf whistling negro." Pitting the sacredness of white womanhood against negative black stereotypes, the southern press reported that the "young Mississippi white mother" said that Till "caught her hand" when she put it out to take his money, asked her for a date, and then put both of his hands around her waist and "addressed her in terms too unprintable to relate, ending with the sentence, 'with white women before.'" Although the judge ruled Carolyn Bryant's testimony "unrelated in time and substance" and therefore inadmissible, the members of the all-white, all-male jury knew enough about "the kind of boy" Till was. In their minds, the "fresh, impertinent" Till was hardly an innocent victim, a child who needed protection or at this point at least deserved justice. Rather, he was a sexual predator, a black "man" who merited no sympathy and in fact deserved exactly what he got.[15]

This was how Bryant and Milam saw Till, and it was how they wanted America to see him. In their confession to *Look* magazine reporter William Bradford Huie, they asserted that the boy "looked like a man." Till was "muscular" and "stocky." Yet he hardly could have seemed physically imposing to "Big Milam," who Huie said measured 6′2″ and weighed 235 pounds. What turned Till into a man to his killers was his failure to bow to accepted racial boundaries. In 1931, white southerners had talked about nine black boys, the youngest only twelve, as "brutes," "men" responsible for "frightful deeds." Those black boys, whom most whites, both North and South, would have seen as "boys" all their lives, became men only when they seemed to threaten white womanhood. Bryant and Milam described Till as a "man" in the same way that countless southern whites before them had transformed black males of all ages into men to justify their harsh and barbaric treatment. According to the doctrines of white supremacy, blacks were generally like children, helpless and dependent, ruled by emotion, and stuck in a perpetual state of relative stupidity. As "children," they relied on whites for guidance, care, and protection. But blacks who defied the strictures of Jim Crow, who acted decidedly unchildlike by asserting their economic independence, their sexuality, or their dignity, were stripped of the sentimental notions surrounding childhood that guaranteed their safety or at least prompted some measure of white leniency. They became men.[16]

But the America of 1955, including much of the white South, was not so willing to transform an innocent black boy, a "lynched Negro child," into a black man who deserved punishment. Till's murder outraged whites as well as blacks across the nation. Even some white southern newspapers published articles that condemned Bryant and Milam's actions, calling the murder a "stupid, horrible crime" committed by "sick . . . men," "white trash," or "peckerwoods . . . who should be removed from society." The "existence of a state of mind that makes it possible, even easy, for a teen-aged boy to be kidnapped and murdered, whatever his alleged offense may have been," seemed terrible to white as well as black editors. (Other southern papers, equally eager to demonstrate their respect for childhood ideals, expressed pity for Till but blamed his disappearance on the NAACP.) Some white southerners wrote letters to their local papers saying that the pictures of fourteen-year-old Till made them "feel sick within." They likened Till to their own boys. Till might have been black, but like their own sons, he "was born free in America" and had a "right to American freedom." "This is a crime," one white Mississippi father asserted, "that should make every one of us bow our heads in shame." That at least some white southerners, including white supremacist groups, publicly spoke out against Till's murder suggests a significant change in thinking about black childhood since the Scottsboro Boys case had made international head-lines. As much as they resented the *Brown* ruling and were determined to fight it, many white southerners knew that Till was an "ill chosen" symbol of "the white-hot determination of Mississippians" to maintain the status quo. The *Chattanooga Times* called Till "a damaging symbol — an-other skeleton in the South's closet." The paper was literally correct. Till, however, proved to be more than just "another skeleton." In the mid-1950s, black children in the South had at least some claim to America's ideals about childhood.[17]

To be sure, not all whites saw Till's death as a tragedy or agreed that black children had the same right to childhood as their own offspring. As one Sumner local put it, "I've never heard of making such a mountain of a molehill." Some southerners who expressed regret were motivated to criticize the boy's killers primarily because of the case's possible economic and public relations repercussions for the region. Others worried about the nation's credibility abroad. The *Atlanta Constitution*, for example, rec-ognized that "a boy had been killed for an act for which a boy of another color would have been whipped or reprimanded." The paper expressed more concern, however, that the case would be used by communist pro-pagandists in the Soviet Union and China. Yet regardless of their motives, even the least sympathetic whites were required to treat Till's case as tragic because of his youth. Even before Till's body was found, Greenwood, Mississippi, sheriff George W. Smith arrested Bryant and Milam when it became evident that they were connected with the missing boy; at least publicly, Smith expressed fear and remorse that the boy's disappearance suggested foul play. Deputy sheriff John Cothran, whose suggestion that Till had made a mistake in "whistling after looking at a white woman" belied racialized conceptions of boyhood, and who, like Smith, had no intention of bringing Till's murderers to justice, likewise felt compelled to remark that "the white people around here feel pretty mad about the way that poor little boy was treated."[18]

Even if one approaches their interview with Huie with skepticism, Bryant and Milam also seem to have struggled with their racialized conceptions of childhood and manhood before they killed Till. The two white men told Huie that they had intended only to "scare some sense into him," sense that the boy's great-uncle admitted Till lacked. That sense — the sense required of all blacks in the Jim Crow South — was a sense of deference to whites, a sense of the invisible lines between black and white worlds, and the sense to stay behind those lines, behind what W. E. B. Du Bois called "the Veil." Reflecting the practices of many nonfictional black parents of the time, Henry's mother in Lillian Smith's 1944 novel, *Strange Fruit*, had whipped that sense into her boy. Bryant and Milam purportedly had the same idea. Only Till would not learn the lesson they wanted to teach him. "What else could we do?" asked Milam. "He was hopeless." Mose Wright "had talked to his nephew about the 'trouble' . . . had urged that he leave" Mississippi, but ultimately "didn't think they'd kill a boy." The two white men didn't think they would kill a boy either: "I'm no bully," Milam told the reporter. But from their perspective, Till did not act like a boy, at least not like a proper black boy in Jim Crow Mississippi. "I'm not afraid of you. I'm as good as you are." No "yes sirs." He "never hollered, and kept making perfect speeches," complained the murderers. Bryant and Milam wanted Till to be a "boy," to be afraid of them, to bow his head, cry, and beg for mercy, to stay behind the veil. But they could not, in Lillian Smith's words, "learn him how to behave," they could not "beat da sperrit outn him." The Chicago boy insisted on being a man. And a black man asserting his manhood in Mississippi had to be killed, "just so everybody can know how me and my folks stand," said Milam.[19]

But while his killers believed that Till had crossed the line between white and black worlds and hence between childhood and manhood, they and the white southerners who came to their defense, including the jury, knew that Till's status as a child made "two BIG BRAVE white" men's pleas of innocence sound hollow to the ears of the trial's international audience. The disappearance or murder of a black man would have gone (and frequently did go) relatively unnoticed. But beliefs about childhood demanded that the 1955 death of a fourteen-year-old boy, even if he was black, be accounted for—especially if he was a black boy from Chicago whose mother was not afraid to show the world what had happened to her son. So to prove to the world that they understood and respected the sanctity of childhood, Bryant and Milam came to the trial, as one reporter put it, "armed . . . with their wives [and] baby boys."[20]

Scholars have noted that the local white community helped transform the two working-class defendants into models of middle-class respectability.[21] That meant turning them into model husbands and fathers. Before the trial, southern papers featured sympathetic stories about the defendants' families, complemented by idealized family portraits. "They were never into any meanness. . . . I raised them and I'll stand by them," said the half-brothers' mother, who had raised eight sons, seven of whom had served in the military. Milam and Bryant had been good boys, and now they were "ideal" fathers. "The children worship" them, claimed Milam's lovely young wife. Images of Bryant and Milam holding their young sons at the trial made them appear respectable and middle class and, like the images and stories that appeared in southern newspapers, directly countered images of them as child killers. These were family men who loved and would never hurt children. Sumner really was "a good place to raise a boy." Appearing with their sons also raised questions about Till's boyhood. Till, black and fourteen, perhaps sexually active, was technically still a child. But while his age if not his race made him a boy in America, his physical maturity stood in stark contrast to Bryant and Milam's boys, who were white and only two, three, and four years old.[22]

The defendants and the all-white jury ultimately could not argue against widespread notions of childhood. They had to agree with the rest of the world: Till was a child, and the death of a child required retribution. Although unable to separate Till from the emotive qualities associated with childhood, they took advantage of the physical contrast between young Till and the childhood represented by Bryant and Milam's sons. During the trial, Sheriff Smith reported that the body local police had recovered from the Tallahatchie River "looked like a grown man." In the desperate logic of the white South, the size of Till's body provided Bryant and Milam with a viable defense. The manly corpse found in the river simply was not Till's. He, after all, had been a child. Despite Mamie Till Bradley's motherly conviction "that it was her son she buried," the jury freed the two white men. As Feldstein notes, the jury's insistence that the body was not Till's stripped Bradley of a mother's natural authority over and attachment to her child. The jury's decision indeed denied Bradley's claims to motherhood. Significantly, however, it did not deny her son's claims to childhood.[23]

Till's physical stature — that the boy looked like a man — gave Sumner's white jury a way to release the two killers. Their "unconscionable verdict" highlighted the tenuous boundary between physical childhood and adulthood. It also signified the ambiguous position of all black bodies in America. Whether or not Till's body was manlike, to many Americans it became "the quintessential" symbol of black innocence. Myrlie Evers reflected that the Till case "was the story in microcosm of every Negro. . . . For it was the proof that even youth was no defense against the ultimate terror. . . . It was the proof that . . . no Negro's life [even a child's] was really safe." Although the Till case in some ways affirmed black children's right to childhood — even the white South agreed that young Till was a child worthy of concern — it also affirmed the vulnerability of black children and in fact of all blacks in America. Black men, black women, and black children were equally helpless in the face of southern white supremacy. So, too, it seemed, was the federal government. Some observers saw the case as "a symbol of the depravity of the 'white devils' and of the helplessness of the Federal government to provide protection for all of its citizens, or to bring whites who are guilty of crimes against Negroes, to justice." If two white adults could commit such a "sorry and tragic error . . . on an afflicted Negro child" and get away with it, then how, these commentators insisted, "could any black American hope for justice?"[24]

According to Huie's exposé, Bryant and his wife regarded *Shane* as "the best picture they ever saw." Their choice was fitting. The popular 1953 film pitted images of a lawless, individualist Old West, gunslingers full of pride and whiskey, against a moral, law-abiding, family-centered New West. It was the story of a young boy caught in a figurative and literal showdown between these two possible worlds. As in all Hollywood Westerns, good eventually triumphs over evil, and there is the promise of peace and a family-centered civilization. But to make that transition, the boy—the child—must first witness violence and murder.[25]

Bryant and Milam had forced Till to become a victim, not just a witness, and many more black children would get caught in the cross fire between Jim Crow and civil rights. But perhaps ironically and certainly tragically, images of Till and other black children suffering under America's racism encouraged the nation to become more civilized. Most American adults, at least in the 1950s and 1960s, did not like to witness the suffering of innocent children, and Till's lynching indelibly linked white supremacy to such suffering. It showed the world that American racism had "no restraining influence of decency." Evers said that "the Emmett Till case shook the foundations of Mississippi, both black and white." Black congressman Charles Diggs recalled that "the picture in *Jet* magazine showing Emmett Till's mutilation . . . stimulated a lot of interest and anger on the part of blacks all over the country." The Sumner verdict did not surprise him. Rather, it strengthened his "belief that something had to be done about the dispensation of justice." Diggs was not alone. Till's murder and the travesty of justice that followed figured prominently in the testimonies of six witnesses who appeared before the Senate Subcommittee on Civil Rights two years later. Those testimonies helped create the Civil Rights Act of 1957, which included specific provisions for federal involvement in the southern justice system. In the weeks after the Till case, thousands of blacks all over the country joined together in rallies of protest, and the NAACP's fund to "help victims of racial attacks reached record levels." Perhaps most significantly, as historian Stephen Whitfield shows, "Till's death exerted a considerable psychological impact on young Southern blacks." Dozens of future civil rights activists cited the Till case as a turning point in their young lives.[26]

Mamie Till Bradley called her dead son a "little nobody who shook up the world." But the *Brown* decision ensured that Till would not be the only "little nobody" shaking things up. In its 1954 ruling, the Supreme Court determined that young people in America would change the country's racist practices. Growing up and going to school together, black and white children would "reshape the world." The intransigence of Jim Crow and the white adults who would not let it die, however, increasingly thrust images of those children into the press and into America's consciousness. As in the Till case, images, pictures, and newsreels of white adults contesting the rights of black children often motivated support for civil rights.[27]

CIVIL RIGHTS STORIES: CHILDHOOD, *BROWN*, AND THE AMERICAN PRESS

In reporting on the civil rights movement, the news media developed a "formula" that "demanded," as one scholar notes, "that telling facts be woven into a story to make them complete and satisfying" to their middle-class readers. Press coverage of the sit-ins turned civil rights activism into a "morality play, appropriately cast." With their depictions of black students as "studiously polite, orderly, resolute in seeking their rights, but not obnoxious; the white opponents . . . almost Faulknerian in degeneracy," the media made clear where their sympathies lay. The press used a similarly compelling "formula" for telling school desegregation stories. Photos of "neatly dressed, hair-ribboned" black children stood in striking contrast to images of frantic whites, most often adults, abusing those children, yelling obscenities outside America's schoolhouses. The stories the media told readers about such events were so compelling that John Steinbeck noted in *Travels with Charley* that "the incident most reported and pictured in the newspapers [in 1960] was the matriculation of a couple of tiny negro children" in New Orleans. Reporters loved the story, he explained, because of "a group of stout middle-aged women who . . . gathered every day to scream invectives at . . . the small dark mites." The "cheerleaders," as the women came to be known, played their parts in desegregation's morality play perfectly.[28]

Scholars who have looked at the role of the media in the movement have missed the ways that the formula the press used—the stories told—often depended on widespread beliefs about childhood and ideas about children's rights. That young black students embodied qualities associated with childhood, even if they were not actually children, or that it was six-year-olds that New Orleans's "cheerleaders" frightened with their "bestial . . . vomitings," often influenced how the press framed stories and how Americans responded to civil rights events. Media stories about the black freedom struggle purposely drew on cultural beliefs about childhood to elicit public sympathy (and interest). Moreover, like the Supreme Court in the *Brown* decision, the national press linked the struggle for civil rights with the struggle for African American children to realize the rights of childhood. In fact, stories in the press about civil rights echoed the popularized findings of social science researchers, educational experts, and child welfare advocates who had helped convince the Supreme Court to rule in favor of black children. Reporters contrasted images of innocent young people with images of depraved adults, showed the willingness of youth to integrate while their elders resisted, and intimated the dangers that continued segregation posed to children and to the nation.[29]

In July 1955, *Life* magazine ran a story, "An Arkansas School Board Does Some Soul Searching and Negro Children Enter Desegregated Classes." *Life* reported that the school board in Hoxie, Arkansas, a town that ran a midsummer school term to allow children time off to pick cotton, "conscientiously interviewed parents and came to the conclusion that integration was 'morally right in the sight of God.'" The article upheld both the morality of school integration and social scientists' arguments that children could remake racial boundaries. While tense white parents "waited to see whether any misgivings would be justified," their children quickly accepted the new situation.

> The school day . . . began in an atmosphere of self-conscious tension. White children stared curiously and Negroes tended to treat whites with deference. . . . A few white parents accompanied their children and made no secret of their distaste for the new arrangement. . . . But among the children the novelty soon wore off. During noon recess white boys sought out Negro boys and invited them to try out for the school team in basketball. . . . Negro and white girls happily romped together. By the end of the day the children were behaving as if they had gone to school together all their lives.

According to the press, white parents might have feared the demise of Jim Crow and declared it a shame their children "had to sit next to Negroes," but just as expert witnesses had predicted to the Supreme Court, the children took the "problem in stride." Even eight-year-old Peggy Cole, whose mother insisted that her daughter was afraid of Negroes, was pictured strolling "arm in arm" with two black girls soon after her mother's reluctant departure. Like the stories social science researchers told to help convince the Supreme Court to rule against segregation, *Life*'s report pitted open-minded children against fearful adults, the rights of childhood against images of innocent black children being "handicapped by poor standards

Peggy Cole, a white student at the newly integrated elementary school in Hoxie, Arkansas, shows that she has quickly adapted to integration. (From *Life*, 25 July 1955; photograph by Gordon Tenney; courtesy Josh Kaplan)

in their own schools" and of adults who obviously suffered from the kind of "maladjusted" personalities then considered so threatening to national security and the future of democracy.[30]

At the start of one of the country's most famous desegregation battles, involving Central High School in Little Rock, Arkansas, the *Arkansas Gazette* optimistically asserted, "We do not believe any organized group of citizens would under any circumstances undertake to do violence to school children of any race." The paper's editorial board was not alone in assuming that cultural beliefs in the sanctity of childhood, if not the Supreme Court's dictum, would protect the black teenagers. But when white supremacists proved resistant to racially inclusive notions of childhood, the media and others who supported integration used images of white mobs attacking (and National Guardsmen protecting) children to convince the American public that white supremacy endangered not just blacks but childhood itself. Constant reminders that integrating the nation's schools required an armed escort to keep children safe made civil rights issues compelling to many Americans. In their recent study of the press and the civil rights movement, Gene Roberts and Hank Klibanoff note that stories such as Little Rock had a profound "emotional impact" on both reporters and the general public. As one southern editor commented at the time, "There is something so very personal about a school. It involves our children, their happiness, their safety, their dreams, and our dreams for them." It is no coincidence then that one of the most powerful and lasting cultural images of the era was Norman Rockwell's "The Problem We All Live With." Rockwell's painting, which first appeared on the cover of the same mass-circulation magazine that published William Bradford Huie's exposé on Till's murder, portrayed six-year-old Ruby Bridges on her way to William Frantz public school in New Orleans. Ruby, wearing a white dress with matching hair ribbons and carrying her schoolbooks, is surrounded by racist graffiti, rotten fruit, and U.S. marshals who are so much bigger than she that their heads do not fit in the scene. Such images, visual and descriptive, of children under attack and surrounded by military figures might have brought to mind government propaganda used to solicit support for World War II. In any case, as Rockwell and others presented it, and as many Americans came to understand it, "The Problem We All Live With" was more than the problem of segregation or racism, it was the problem of segregation in the nation's schools, the problem of racism directed toward little girls with bows in their hair.[31]

Still, like Emmett Till, America's black children had to be models of middle-class childhood to prove that they deserved the rights of childhood and the sympathies of the nation. As Rockwell later depicted young Ruby, newspaper and television reports on the nine youth chosen to integrate Arkansas's Central High School featured pictures of the "children . . . well scrubbed and greased down," looking, in the words of African American

writer Henry Louis Gates Jr., like "black versions of models out of *Jack &*
Jill magazine" as they patiently endured the verbal and physical abuse of
hysterical white mobs. On her first day of school, a sympathetic white reporter, hoping to help create a favorable public impression, told Elizabeth
Eckford, "Don't let them see you cry" as the girl tried to navigate through
the hostile crowd. As the year went on, the press confirmed the worthiness
of the nine teenagers with stories of how the God-fearing, churchgoing
"children" and their families made the difficult decision to go to school
each day and how, despite the dangers, "they get into the station wagon
laughing like they are going on a picnic." If the black students could ignore
the taunts of segregationists—or even better, if they could appear to be
innocent, carefree children—then the American public would remain
sympathetic. But of course if they did not, they could not expect support
in realizing their rights, as Minnie Jean Brown discovered when Central
High's principal promptly expelled her after she dumped her lunch on
white hecklers.[32]

At the same time as the Little Rock standoff, similar stories and photos
of "twelve carefully chosen little Negro children . . . in neat green dresses,
their hair done up in braids," in Nashville, Tennessee, and of young
Dorothy Counts making her way through white mobs in Charlotte, North
Carolina, attracted national and even international attention. Utilizing an
oft-repeated approach, *Time* ran a story that compared the "quiet" six-year-
olds integrating Nashville's schools to the wild crowds (including tattooed
waitresses) throwing rocks at them. Those who were among the first to
exercise black children's newly granted rights of childhood appeared remarkably like the young people featured in early-twentieth-century edi-
tions of *The Crisis*; they embodied ideals about childhood to show that
they deserved rights. The black students' obvious respectability was also
essential to countering white fears and widespread accusations that black
children would corrupt their white classmates. Counts, for example, was
a top student who regularly attended church. The photo of her that ran
in newspapers all over the world juxtaposed a poised and neatly dressed
girl—a model American child—with jeering protesters, white men and
women intent on keeping blacks, regardless of their age, in their place.
In this, as in many other media stories, racists appeared "stupid, vulgar,
and one-dimensional," partly because of their blatantly racist behavior
but also because they transgressed cultural beliefs in the sanctity of childhood. It was one thing to be racist. These racists, however, were willing

to attack children, even white children, in the name of white supremacy: "If you don't want something to happen to your boy . . . better keep your daughter home," segregationists warned white as well as black parents. The press was also quick to reveal that racists would harm their own children. *Time*'s report on the Nashville situation included a description sure to tug on readers' heartstrings and let them see one of the unintended (but invariable) effects of white supremacy as well as what might finally convince segregationists to stop their protests. There, a local "rabble rouser" seemed to question his actions after his daughter began to cry. Touched by his eight-year-old's distress, "the man . . . smoothed down her blonde bangs, pulled out a handkerchief and began to mop her eyes. [Then] suddenly a look of pain broke across his face. 'I didn't go out there to cause any trouble,' he blurted, [and] he too, burst into tears." Photos and stories of white adults attacking children poignantly confirmed the arguments of social scientists who had warned that the "moral and spiritual millstone" of prejudice kept people from developing complex, healthy personalities and instead encouraged violent, irrational behavior that injured all American children. American racism included or could include little children, perfectly innocent, absolutely vulnerable, trying to get an education, the right of every American child, while white adults — even "pure," southern white women — became "fanatical" and "filthy" in their defense of white supremacy, attacking those children. Such images and stories made clear why the Supreme Court had ruled against segregation.[33]

America and the world watched as young blacks held their heads up despite the maelstrom around them. To many contemporary observers, young people such as Counts became "symbol[s] of freedom." One white columnist wrote an ode to Counts, complimenting her perfect blend of humility and dignity as well as her confidence and pride in the face of a spitting, jeering, and screaming crowd. "The posture of her head was unchanged. That was the remarkable thing," he wrote. "And if her skin was brown you had to admit her courage was royal purple." Such reports not only revealed something of the prejudices of even comparatively liberal white Americans at the time but also confirmed, as did photos of Counts, the social science argument that the *Brown* ruling canonized: If America's children grew up believing that "the chains of prejudice did not have to bind them," they could free the nation as well as themselves.[34]

As the news media sadly reported, however, in Counts's case, after four days of being called names, pushed, spit on, and ignored by teachers as well as more serious acts of intimidation, the girl and her family decided that the situation was too dangerous to continue. In a statement to the press they said,

> It is with compassion for our native land and love for our daughter Dorothy, that we withdraw her as a student at Harding High School. As long as we felt she could be protected from bodily injury and insults within the school's walls and upon the school premises, we were willing to grant her desire to study at Harding. . . . In enrolling Dorothy in Harding High School, we sought for her the highest in educational experience that this tax supported school had to offer a young American. Yet, when a continuous stream of abuses undermines this objective, our purposes are nullified and effects are damaging to ethical and religious training. . . . This step, taken for security and happiness, records in our history a page which no true American can read with pride.

Their statement highlighted their daughter's right, as an American child, to go to a public high school where she could reach her academic potential. But it also stressed that constant exposure to violent manifestations of white supremacy threatened Counts's other rights of childhood—her physical safety and personality development. The social scientists who testified to the Supreme Court were right; racism hurt children, and that, the press release suggested, hurt America.[35]

Looking back on her desegregation experience, one of the Little Rock Nine explained, "It was like being a soldier on a battlefield." The school, she said, "that was meant to nourish us . . . became, instead, a furnace that consumed our youth and forged us into reluctant warriors." Contemporary news accounts of desegregation efforts similarly stressed the ways that racism distorted the lives of America's youth, black and white. A *Life* story on Virginia's desegregation crisis called attention to the "Lost Class of 1959." Instead of attending class proms and struggling with homework, thousands of southern teenagers spent "dreary . . . empty days . . . making small talk in hangouts near schools now closed. . . . The condition of their lives . . . boredom—and rising cynicism at the way their elders have loused things up." Experts (and novelists) had warned that juvenile delinquency, wasted talent, and distrust of authority and democratic ideals were the fruits of white supremacy. Now, as *Life* confirmed, both white and black children in towns all over the South were suffering the consequences. "The

"Dark Laughter. Now I Aint So Sure I Wanna Get Educated," 1963. This cartoon by African American Oliver Harrington suggested the respectability of black youth, the fanaticism of prejudiced white adults, and the understandable fears of African American parents and their children. (From *Pittsburgh Courier*, 21 September 1963; courtesy Dr. Helma Harrington; Library of Congress, Prints and Photographs Division, CD-1-Harrington, no. 94)

South last week got a frightening, meaningful sample of what its massive defiance of the law of the land on school integration could cost in human terms," *Life* asserted. Closed schools meant that "thousands of students" wandered around "bored and restless, a worry to parents and a potential source of mischief."[36]

Such a specter seemed especially alarming when, just a month after integration conflicts began in Arkansas, the Soviet Union launched the world's first artificial satellite. With Sputnik and Little Rock as the two biggest news stories of 1957, the connections between segregation and national security became even more apparent. Harlem's *New York Amsterdam News* pointedly editorialized, "Let the historians' record show that in the week in which the Russians hurled the first living earthly thing into outer space, the Big Story in U.S. newspapers was how and when the people of Little Rock, Arkansas, U.S.A., were going to throw Mrs. Daisy Bates and other NAACP leaders into jail for upholding the right of nine Negro children to develop and cultivate their brains in a school which their parents helped to pay for though blood, sweat, and tears." Black papers were not the only media to link the two events. At the same time it reported on desegregation battles, *Life* ran articles unfavorably comparing the state of U.S. education with Russian schools. "The schools are in terrible shape. What has long been an ignored national problem, Sputnik has made a recognized crisis. The only thing U.S. schools have plenty of is children. There are 33.5 million of these." But if many of the "owners of the nation's future brains and skills" could not attend schools of any kind, what would America's future look like? Lacking scientists and specialists, America would be no match for "The Golden Youth of Communism." The NAACP's Wilkins warned, "As we face a ruthless and skillful adversary bent upon destroying our way of life, we must educate, train and utilize every ounce of manpower and every brain and skill we possess." Southern white liberals agreed. Resistance to *Brown* in the Sputnik Age was madness, they said: "Not only would it guarantee that we have no new scientists coming along, but it would bring down upon America the further hatred and scorn of a world already fed up with Little Rock. We can't afford much more of that. We need scientists like George Washington Carver much more than we need hate-makers like [Arkansas governor Orval] Faubus." Even a member of Louisiana's state legislature complained about resistance to integration (specifically the governor's role) in the midst of cold war tensions, "What are we trying to achieve—a generation of segregated idiots?" he asked.

The nation's press agreed with the NAACP's and others' assessments, implicitly and explicitly reminding readers that America's real enemy was the Soviet Union and that the *Brown* decision was designed, at least partly, to help equip the nation for that struggle.[37]

Like the national media, the *Arkansas Gazette* juxtaposed stories about the Little Rock crisis with news of disturbing world political developments. As school began, the paper reported that Russia ridiculed Western technology. It ran stories about fascism on the same page that it featured editorials calling for citizen cooperation and understanding in carrying out integration. Since the late 1930s, social scientists had warned that race prejudice threatened American democracy, because the same personality types that demonstrated racism tended to follow authoritarian figures. The position of stories about violent resistance to the *Brown* ruling alongside stories about the threat of communist states and fascist ideologies might have encouraged readers to ask questions about the nation's future if school integration did not proceed more peacefully. Such questions were also likely to arise since America's press also made clear that desegregation conflicts undermined the nation's "prestige and influence around the globe." As black poet Langston Hughes noted, "Stories of . . . strangely uncivilized doings directed to children were headlined around the world." *Time* commented on how much attention America's racial battles received in foreign papers. In Italy, it noted, a communist paper reported, "It is hard to imagine a country where the new scholastic year opens in an atmosphere other than serene, where the thought of desks, notebooks and blackboards is mingled with visions of rifles, tear gas, spring knives, and clubs. . . . Such a country does, however, exist, and it bears the high-sounding name of 'United States of America.'" Even southern papers recognized that in the context of the cold war, evidence of racism, especially when directed at innocent children, "alienated," as the *Arkansas Gazette* put it, "half the world" and made it difficult for America to establish itself as the model of "true civilization" and "the champion of democracy." The *Atlanta Constitution* similarly warned, "Violence in Little Rock and Nashville makes it difficult for our friends abroad to believe our claims of democracy for all our citizens." As Ethel James Williams of the National Council of Negro Women testified to a U.S. congressional subcommittee on education and labor, "Often Americans abroad are asked, 'Do you really practice what you preach?' Certainly there can be nothing more basic to equality of treatment than the education of children."[38]

Newspapers and magazines reporting on school integration also intimated that given the opportunity, children would handle the process differently. Reporters claimed that "kids have shown a lot more courage than some adults" and that children's voices, unheard "in all deliberations which led to [school] closings," carried "a sense of tolerance not typical of their intransigent elders." Even Terrence Roberts, one of the Little Rock Nine, reported, "I was pretty well accepted by the white students. . . . Some offered to talk and gave advice." Students in Milford, Delaware, likewise considered all the fuss over the *Brown* decision "much ado about nothing" and felt that "integration could and would work out if it had not been interfered with by adults." The student vice president at Little Rock's Hall High, a football player who hoped to go to West Point after graduation, told the press that he hoped "they'd just let us go to school. . . . I think we'd work it out." Chuck Spencer, a student body president at a white Virginia high school, believed that "the only difference between a white and black man is where their ancestors lived. Skin pigment gets darker as you move toward the equator," he suggested. "If I moved to Africa, my descendants would be black." *Life* quoted another student council member as saying, "I don't care if I'm the only white girl in a whole school of Negroes. I don't care if they're pink, yellow, or whatever, I just want to go to school." Another school leader who also served as secretary for her church youth group told *Look* magazine reporters that "the Negros are entitled to as equal an education as the whites. The prejudices of some parents should not be forced upon their children, thus depriving them of an education for the world in which they live." A Birmingham student council president similarly revealed that he favored "integration as a matter of conscience." Ten white teenagers from Little Rock editorialized in their local paper, "We wouldn't mind going to school with Negroes so why should the parents object? . . . Let's be the democratic and civilized people we are supposed to be." Other students likewise affirmed that "education is more important than segregation." And one white girl exclaimed, "These white folks who complain! They let colored maids raise their children and fix food for them. But they don't let their children come to school and get near colored kids."[39]

Not all the young people reporters interviewed recognized the hypocrisies of segregation or held such progressive opinions. But the national press and sometimes even southern papers clearly intended that their stories about southern massive resistance reflect the arguments of social science experts. Students were able to see the situation "without color getting in the way"—if left on their own, "young folks [would] find the answer," or at least a better answer. *Life* reported, for example, that Front Royal, Virginia, students "voted 53–2 for a resolution asking the Governor to reopen the school even if integrated." Students at Virginia's Granby, Norview, and Maury High Schools likewise disagreed with the inflexible decisions of their adult representatives. As the national and international press reported, student clubs at those schools took out advertisements in local papers and petitioned officials to reopen schools. The *Nashville Tennessean* suggested where young people stood on the issue when the paper wondered "if the city fathers have ever thought of asking [the children] what *they'd* choose." Central High's student editor encouraged her peers to "prove that America's youth has not 'gone to the dogs'" by letting their "knowledge of science help . . . determine [their] action[s]" rather than the "custom, superstition, or tradition" that motivated adult protesters. Student council leaders at Central High even tried to plan an orientation for the Little Rock Nine (which the newly formed segregationist Mothers' League stopped). White students also undertook an organized if short-lived effort to "to make a public show of support" for the black students by sitting with them at lunch. In December 1958, a *Look* magazine article told readers how the fifteen-year-old student council president at Arkansas's Van Buren High School convinced her community to proceed with integration. Angie Evans, a "mature" and "serious-minded" "straight-A student" and active member of the local Methodist congregation, had stood up at a crucial school board meeting and told board members that the majority of current Van Buren students favored letting blacks attend the school. She then denounced segregation as un-Christian and asked those gathered to consider "what you make those negro children feel like, running them out of school." Another article in the same issue described "Dixie's New Rebels," youth leaders in places such as Charlottesville, Virginia, who similarly "took the lead" to reopen and integrate schools. And in contrast to Alabama governor George Wallace's intransigence, *Newsweek* reported that a white Birmingham youth shouted back at protesting crowds, "I'm going in. . . . I came here stupid three years ago and I ain't going away stupid." The way newsmagazines and papers told desegregation stories suggested that the comments and actions of students who supported integration and racial equality reflected the true feelings and beliefs of white youth in general. Whether it was black and white first-

"Dixie's New Rebels," 1958. Student leaders in Charlottesville, Virginia, collect signatures from their peers on a petition to reopen public schools on an integrated basis. (From *Look*, 9 December 1958; © Bob Lerner; *Look* Magazine Photograph Collection, Library of Congress, Prints and Photographs Division, Look-Job 58–8047)

graders happily playing blindman's bluff, singing Elvis Presley songs, and drawing together or white high school seniors insisting that "we're all created equal," the press suggested that America's children were naturally inclined toward integration.[40]

In contrast, the media made negative student actions and comments about integration sound like young people parroting the obviously false or foolish ideas of their elders. As Wilkins explained, "Resistance is the plan of adults, not of young people." In the early 1960s, representatives of the Southern Student Human Relations Project reaffirmed that the child "learns his social behavior primarily by following the modes and models of behavior around him. Indeed, he has little choice." Youth organizations such as the YWCA and YMCA similarly concluded that young people would resist racial equality only if their elders first "prime[d] the pump." That being the case, it seemed crucial to the groups' national leaders that community adults "discipline themselves so that careless talk on their part does not produce thoughtless behavior on the part of teen-agers." White youth in Little Rock likewise declared, "Most kids our age would not have given it a second thought and accepted it if someone's parents hadn't started a commotion. We are just polly parrots after all, reflecting the ideas we get at home or from older people." The *Charlotte Observer* made clear that the teenagers who harassed Counts did so at the bidding of adult conspirators who told them, "It's up to you all to keep her out. . . . Spit on her girls!" The paper also pointed out that the scene was much more peaceful at Charlotte's other newly integrated schools, which, not surprisingly, lacked the same kind of adult interference. Moreover, it let readers know that two of Counts's attackers were later arrested and that one was an eighteen-year-old sophomore. Other news reports similarly described students who protested integration as "hoods, hoodlums, and young punks" or mischief makers from "disturbed" homes. In one such article, *Time* magazine called young people who protested Central High's integration "pool-hall bums led by a beefy-red-faced man." And Pulitzer Prize–winning Atlanta news-paperman Ralph McGill contrasted the "neat, well-mannered, talented Negro children . . . from Christian homes" with the "juveniles . . . who in conduct and action, including the possession of weapons, did not appear as very good advertisements for the Klans and Councils which had poisoned and exploited their youth with a philosophy of hate."[41]

The press repeatedly claimed that young mobs were either composed of "the smelly element" or that white youth who chanted such slogans as "All we want for Christmas is a clean white school" did so because they had little choice in the matter. A *New York Post* reporter explained that in Nashville, white mothers dragged their crying children to picket lines; gave them signs saying, "Keep Our White Schools White" that their children "were not quite large enough to carry"; and taught them to chant "Go home, niggers, go home." The paper suggested that some of the children had learned the words their mothers whispered in their ears but that such lessons were a "horribly ugly" "burden" too heavy for little children to carry. A columnist for the *Atlanta Constitution* similarly drew attention to Klan members who forced little white girls and boys to the front of their rallies, a practice that evidently brought tears and frantic searches for mothers rather than a sense of racial pride. Such stories drew on readers' sympathies and affirmed contemporary social science research findings that young people might "pick up prejudiced talk" without developing the beliefs or behaviors assumed to go along with such talk. The *Atlanta Constitution*'s writer supported notions of children's racial innocence (as well as the ridiculousness of white supremacy) in a more comical way when he acerbically suggested that "just as we are attempting to do with the whoop- ing crane, we should try to preserve a few Klansmen for our children to see. Otherwise [they] will never believe that as late as 1962 grown men stood on the streets of downtown Atlanta wearing bed-sheets." And *Life* hinted that youth sometimes imitated their less-than-respectable elders without understanding the implications of their words. For example, re- porters quoted sophomore Diane Milner, who the magazine also identi- fied as a cheerleader, as flippantly saying, "I'd rather go to no school at all than to an integrated one. I guess I'd just have to be illiterate." The older, more thoughtful student leaders they quoted, conversely, almost always made comments that supported integration and condemned school clo- sures.[42]

To Wilkins, negative student comments were revealing and tragic evi- dence of "the corrosive injury [segregation] has done to white youngsters" and the nation. Using the same arguments that had convinced the Supreme Court to rule against segregation in the *Brown* case, he asserted that a na- tion that continued to teach its children the rules of white supremacy in- stead of "mutual respect and dedication to the ideal of liberty and equality" created "useless citizen[s]" and was "well-nigh suicidal." In cold war America, Wilkins insisted, children had to have "training in democracy that teaches them that people are people regardless of skin color." The press agreed. *Life* called Milner and the rest of the thirteen thousand stu- dents hit by Virginia's massive resistance campaign that year "passive vic- tims in a national tragedy." To be sure, *Life*'s report and other stories in the national press claimed that young people lacked agency only when they ex- hibited negative views toward integration. Whether or not students acted on their own to protest mixed schools, the tendency to make them helpless victims of prejudicial racial ideologies reflected prevailing social science research. Experts, civil rights organizations, and white liberals continually warned that "we need to worry less about" integration and more about negative adult attitudes, "both conscious and unconscious." Programs de- signed to train leaders to help southern communities move toward inte- gration emphasized that "student reactions" would reflect administrative, teacher, and parental attitudes; if adults would "show a willingness to ac- cept the idea . . . it would markedly reduce friction among the students." National news reports generally intimated the same idea. Regardless of their stated views on integration, none of America's children deserved (or really wanted) what their parents and political leaders were doing to them, and probably none of them would resist integration without the coaching of parents and adult officials. Even white southern editors who initially supported resistance to *Brown* were admittedly "sobered" by students who complained that they were "losing our education." Some of those newsmen, like *Lynchburg News* associate editor John Hamilton, thought "poor kids," and wondered, "Is this something we should be doing?"[43]

In covering school desegregation, the media told stories of adults picketing integrated schools while "children, white and colored, were playing happily together in the school yard." Picket lines, at first staged by adults, may have been "taken over" by the students themselves, but as the press pointed out, "adult leaders stood around the corners directing and stimulating the teenagers." In both Hoxie, Arkansas, and Milford, Delaware, integration initially met with only limited resistance, which came, as the media indicated, from reluctant parents. The children "mixed" "in a normal manner." But white adults in those communities, seemingly easily influenced by "outside agitators," began organizing and quickly destroyed the peaceful progress toward integration that the children had achieved. The result, as the press grimly reported, was "children roaming the streets with nothing to do," and hundreds of "seniors [who] have slipped completely from the records."[44]

Closed schools seemed especially tragic when reporters insisted that the social scientists cited in the Supreme Court's 1954 ruling were right. Shortly after the ruling, the Southern Regional Council expressed its faith in children's ability to "adjust to integrated schools." "There is much truth in the saying that if school integration were left to the children there would be no problem. Children are born without prejudice and only acquire it through constant exposure to the attitudes of grownups. . . . [A]ll previous experience indicates children of different races adjust to each other quickly and naturally when given half a chance. Most Southerners can find confirmation of this in their own childhood, when they accepted playmates of the other race without a thought." Schools that sent students from "'protest' high schools to observe integrated classes" reflected a similar faith in the ability of young people to easily achieve integration if they received the proper encouragement. And the stories the press told about desegregation conflicts likewise affirmed that white supremacy wasted the country's most precious resources and that white and black children generally wanted to go to school together and could do so peacefully. Just

"NOW HURRY UP, CHILD — YOU'LL BE LATE FOR SCHOOL."

"Now Hurry Up, Child," 1960, and "I Started a Correspondence Course," 1958. Political cartoonist Bill Mauldin frequently commented on school desegregation struggles in his work. Many of his cartoons drew on popular understandings of childhood and youth and the arguments of social scientists to criticize school closures and resistance to integration. NAACP field secretary Ruby Hurley kept a copy of "Now Hurry Up, Child" taped to a map on the wall in her Atlanta office. The map had pins in it representing NAACP chapters across the South. (Joe Cumming/ Atlanta Bureau to Education [Newsweek], 5 September 1961, Folder: Segregation School Opener 1961, Box 12, Newsweek Atlanta Bureau Records, Special Collections Department, Robert W. Woodruff Library, Emory University, Atlanta, Ga.) (© 1960, 1958 Bill Mauldin; courtesy William Mauldin Estate; Library of Congress, Prints and Photographs Division, CD-1-Mauldin, nos. 659, 1464)

Children attending a desegregated school in St. Louis, Missouri, 1956. Reiterating
beliefs about young people's racial innocence and the need to break down prejudices
in a modern democratic society, *Look* magazine suggested in the caption that appeared
with this photograph that "getting on with others is a talent to learn early. A boy can
acquire the habit easily if prejudice does not get in the way. It will last him a lifetime."
(From *Look*, 3 April 1956; photograph by Bob Sandberg; *Look* Magazine Photograph
Collection, Library of Congress, Prints and Photographs Division, Look Job 56–6443)

like NAACP lawyers in the *Brown* case, the media presented the struggle
for civil rights in terms that highlighted sentimental notions of childhood
and juxtaposed adult anxieties and rigidity with children's ability to act as
agents of democratic social and political change. Indeed, press accounts
about integration supported and perhaps helped to legitimate the historic
ruling and the arguments on which it was based.[45]

FOR THE CHILDREN

Framing stories about the civil rights movement in terms of ideas about
childhood and the rights of childhood not only reflected one of the prem-
ises of the *Brown* ruling but also made the movement especially compelling
to black and white Americans. In addition, such stories captured one of the
reasons that many blacks joined the civil rights struggle. Certainly, as historian Charles Payne suggests, "more mundane activities . . . helped make
[big civil rights confrontations] possible." And as Joseph Crespino has re-

cently argued, tales of "gothic southern racism" run the risk of oversimpli-
fying the struggle for civil rights. Moreover, blacks living in the segregated
South faced myriad problems—jobs and housing issues, a criminal justice
system that was anything but just, disfranchisement, and the daily indigni-
ties of segregation. But without denying the complex ways that the movement developed or that Jim Crow shaped the lives of African Americans,
the dramatic moments featured by the press in many cases represented
one of the central motives for black activism as well as the results of years
of community-based protest. Many African Americans would have agreed
with Juanita Signal, a New Orleans schoolteacher, who told interviewers
in 1949 that "the things most Negroes would like to do cannot be done because they lack the proper education." Indeed, in the decades both before
and after the *Brown* decision, hundreds of black parents petitioned local
school boards to let their children attend all-white schools. Even in Mississippi, more than two hundred families filed petitions in 1955 alone. Historians have shown that such petitions represented a long tradition of black
parental activism specifically directed toward better education for their
children. Yet even with the Supreme Court's backing, black communities
usually faced school boards willing to proceed only with token integration
and local whites determined to prove that "where integration occurs, violence becomes inevitable." Given the Herculean efforts of countless black
families on behalf of their children and the determination of young people
themselves, photographs of violence directed against young blacks as they
tried to exercise their rights as American children fittingly represented
the African American freedom struggle. Moreover, when the NAACP first
began its campaign to end segregation in the 1930s, legal counsel Charles
Houston identified educational discrimination as "symbolic of all the more
drastic discriminations which Negroes suffer in American life." And not
only was education an important symbol of inequality, but schools were
institutions that directly affected the lives of all black Americans.[46]

In *Notes of a Native Son*, James Baldwin explained that every black parent faced an "impossibility": "how to prepare the child for the day when
the child would be despised and how to create in the child . . . a stronger
antidote to this poison than one had found for oneself." Most black parents
recalled with dread the day they had to teach their young children the difference between white and colored drinking fountains, why they ate their
ice cream outside the store instead of at the counter, why they would not
be going to the brand-new school a few blocks away. Melba Pattillo Beals,

one of the Little Rock Nine, recalled that at age four she was "asking questions neither my mother nor grandmother cared to answer, 'Why do the white people write colored on all the ugly drinking fountains, the dingy restrooms, and the back of buses?'" No one, she said, presented her with a handbook when she was teething and explained "Here's how you must behave as a second-class citizen." But, she asserted, those "humiliating expectations and traditions of segregation creep over you, slowly, stealing a teaspoonful of your self-esteem each day."[47]

Many black parents decided that if supporting the movement meant that their children would not have to "burn up inside," that their children could be saved from what Baldwin called "the rage, the fever," "from the insults and the humiliation that were constantly displayed in the community anywhere and anytime," then maybe the struggle would be worth it. SNCC chair James Forman linked his commitment to civil rights to his racial awakening as a child and his hopes for future generations of young blacks: "If my life could make it possible," he resolved, "for future black children not to have that experience, then it was worth living." An old woman who participated in the Montgomery Bus Boycott similarly explained the reasons for her activism: "Children, I ain't got many days left. . . . So I ain't walking for myself. I'm walking for my grandson. I want him to be able to pay his money and take his seat." A Birmingham demonstrator recalled, "I decided that I wanted things better for my children and myself, but mainly for my children. . . . [A]nd my father wanted things better for me." And a Memphis man expressed his desires for his seven-month-old daughter (and capitalized on sentimental views of children) when he pushed her in a baby carriage during a freedom march with a sign that read, "Daddy, I want to be free, too." In the early twentieth century, W. E. B. Du Bois had lamented the "cold and shuddering arms . . . the shadowy, formless thing . . . that hovered between [his child] and the world." He hoped that some day the "veil" would be lifted, that "sad little lives" would be replaced by "little children . . . singing to the sunshine." This hope motivated individual blacks to participate in the movement decades later. Furthermore, this hope also lay at the heart of the NAACP's direct assault on segregation. In 1945, African American leaders gathered to discuss their goals and strategies. They determined, in the words of one participant, that "we were going to have to change directions if our children weren't going to die as black bastards too." Robert L. Carter later recalled that at other 1940s conferences, NAACP lawyers shared "views about what should and could be done with our legal talent to better the lot of black children." And Houston, the head of the association's legal team, was personally and deeply motivated to do whatever he could to ensure that black children got "an equal chance for education." Indeed, at the time of his death in 1950, he wanted his family to remember that he "went down fighting that [his son] might have better and broader opportunities than I had without prejudice."[48]

In 1956, *Life* magazine published a study of one Negro family that tried to communicate to *Life's* mostly white middle-class readers how African American parents felt about segregation. Albert Thornton and his wife, of Mobile, Alabama, had nine children and nineteen grandchildren. The son of a slave, a sharecropper and independent farmer for most of his life, Albert Thornton had worked hard and sent four of his children to college. Yet, as *Life* reported, "when he takes his grandchildren for a walk through the neighborhood, he sees the status of the Negro little better than it was when he was a child himself. In some regards, it is worse." One granddaughter, a mother herself, must still tell her children "that they cannot play in a nearby playground for whites, but must use a separate but equal one for Negroes. The children," just as social scientists anticipated, "do not grasp the logic of this, and view the white playground as a special wonderful place from which they are being deliberately excluded." A photo showed the children watching their white counterparts at play, their black bodies trapped behind a fence. The Thornton family, like many African American families, understood Jim Crow and the struggle against it in terms of its impact on children. How did their lives differ from those of their children? How were they the same? Did their children still live behind the veil?[49]

SAVING WHITE CHILDHOOD

Many white parents had hopes for their children, too, and those hopes did not include any changes to the sociopolitical order. And they explained their resistance to integration in terms of notions of childhood as well. Efforts to block integration, they argued, stemmed from natural parental desires and obligations to protect their children and provide them with the rights of childhood. "I am afraid for my . . . daughter," one white parent told news agencies. "Children are being harmed," some parents protested. Others complained, "What a shame it is that the battle of integration must for fought with our youth as wide-eyed watchers. . . . Why must this happen to our children?" White segregationists formed Mothers' Leagues and Concerned Parents' Associations. They warned "weak-kneed" politicians not to "trade [their] daughter[s] for a mess of nigger votes" and parents to fight desegregation and keep their children away from integrated schools. "Shall we reside in supineness or shall we make ourselves heard in defense of our schools, our children." "Don't wait for your daughter to be raped by these Congolese," they chided. "Don't wait until the burr-heads are forced into your schools." They also charged, "Our children are no longer ours, but now become the property of the federal government." The South's elected leaders often used the same type of child-centered imagery. Mississippi's U.S. senator, James O. Eastland, for example, urged parents to protect "home and fireside, and the welfare of our children" by fighting integration orders. Segregationists insisted that they wanted to save their children from desegregation conflicts, that their children were "helpless pawns in a frightening struggle," "victims of unfortunate political circumstances." They complained that their children or grandchildren had to attend schools with "rifles and bayonets pointed to [their] backs." Many parents, however, brought their children to protest integration, no doubt hoping that white children holding picket signs would help generate public sympathy for southern resistance.[50]

The national news media as well as many African Americans embraced the idea that the *Brown* ruling was at least partly meant to protect all American children and guarantee them the rights of childhood. Emphasizing the same basic values, white southerners suggested that integration would hurt white children and that black children did not qualify for the rights of childhood. Black youth, they asserted, would bring down the educational level of white students: "Both black and white teachers admit there is a definite lowering of standards in the integrated schools, the white children are being pulled down to the intelligence level of the Negroes." Moreover, segregationists insisted, young blacks' innate sexuality, lax moral standards, and tendency toward violence threatened the innocence of southern white children. The National Socialist White People's Party circulated fliers asking if parents were "just going to sit there and let your kids go down the drain, your boys ganged up on, knifed and . . . your girls tormented by hate-filled she-niggers?" The New Orleans school board argued that "our Negro population has little or no sense of morality. . . . [T]o intermingle them with the white children in our public schools could well corrupt the minds and hearts of the white children to their lifelong and perhaps eternal injury." In many southern communities that moved toward integration, white segregationists circulated fictitious rumors of black boys molesting white girls, beating teachers, or drawing weapons on white youth. Others published dire warnings that similarly drew on domestic values and white parents' fears for their children: "A 17 year old White girl was dragged to the boiler room of a high school and raped by 30 Negro students. . . . [S]tudents in junior and senior high schools have been taught gutter language. . . . Beatings, knifing, rapes, extortion, muggings, riots have become a way of life for many of our young people." "What kind of cultural and moral climate do we want [our children] to grow up in?" asked a segregationist pamphlet.[51]

Defenders of segregation warned that the *Brown* ruling would lead to "interracial amalgamation." "The trouble with integration is not nearly so much at the adult level as among teen-agers, and especially in their social activities," one white southern editor explained. Louisiana state senator William Rainach argued that the *Brown* decision was an attempt by "alien forces . . . to herd our white and colored children into mixed schools like so many animals with amalgamation of the races as their objective." Do not "give your children" to "please . . . the world," do not "sell" your "descendants' future," warned Citizens' Council leaders. Evoking stereotypes of the black beast rapist, whites especially expressed concern about their daughters. One father protested that his daughter would "now be compelled by a nigger inspired Supreme Court decision to attend non segregated schools" and urged other white fathers who had "self respect" and wished "to have white grandchildren" to join the fight against "the Black Menace."[52]

Arguments conflating interracial sex with interracial schools revealed white fears, especially about youth sexuality and peer culture, and reflected long-standing excuses for Jim Crow practices. According to the doctrines of white supremacy, segregation and the denial of African American civil and political rights protected white women and the purity of the white race. Segregationists maintained that even without Jim Crow laws, white children would have a natural physical aversion to blacks. But, they argued, "most white parents don't want to take chances." Calling on both traditional rationale and newer sociological theories, they charged, "A white girl might be forced into sexual relations by some colored associate. Or a white child, rejected by its own environment for some reason, might turn to the negro world on close acquaintance." Whites were also willing to admit that an "occasional youngster" might be an "exhibitionist" or want to hurt his or her parents. But white adults had a solemn responsibility to "prevent such [interracial] association," especially "in the years immediately preceding marriage."[53]

Mixed schools seemed especially threatening in the late 1950s and early 1960s because of young people's increasing fascination with popular music, which was more blatantly sexual than the older generation's music and was sometimes performed by black singers and musicians or inspired by African American musical traditions. Segregationists continually decried the "'jive' talk and 'hep-cat' antics of the modern juvenile." Instead of being "taught, tutored and supervised by [their] elders," young people's "minds, morals, social values, and customs and even their language and dress," white supremacists lamented, "are being shaped and molded by a new kind of pied piper . . . the silky voice of the mulatto crooner, the filthy double-entendre of the 'rhythm-in-blues' singer, the vulgar gyrations of the rock-and-roll performer."[54]

Such arguments provide information about white supremacists' fears about waning parental authority, the generation gap, and cultural change as well as about their anxieties about the more obvious sociopolitical changes of the time. These statements may also raise questions about white supremacists' interest in black culture and sexuality or their constructions of it. But arguments linking school desegregation with sexual taboos also reveal that many white southerners wanted notions of childhood to remain racially exclusive. Innocence was a quality that black children either did not possess or possessed only when they remained separate from whites. In the minds of many white southerners, black children who crossed racial boundaries also crossed the boundary between childhood and adulthood. Chicago bishop Louis H. Ford began the services at Till's funeral with a well-known biblical reference: "For as much as ye have done unto one of these my little ones . . . ye have also done unto me." But Till's murder, press reports describing white adults verbally and physically attacking black students, and segregationists' arguments about the sexual dangers of integration suggest that many whites did not see black children as God's innocent "little ones." The most virulent racists even insisted that young blacks were more akin to animals. "There are little dogs and cats and apes and baboons and skunks and there's also little Niggers. But they ain't children," declared a speaker at a Ku Klux Klan meeting. Most southern whites would not have expressed their sense of racial difference in such stark terms, and, unlike Bryant and Milam, most whites did not murder black children who defied racial boundaries. But many still refused to see or treat African American children as they did "real" children. Grace Lorch, the white woman who guided Elizabeth Eckford away from the mob on her first day at Central High in Little Rock, recognized the discrepancy between cultural notions of childhood and the crowd's attack on Eckford. Lorch saw her efforts to protect the girl as natural — "After all," she told reporters and reminded Americans, "she's just a kid."[55]

Although white segregationists often denied black children's claims to childhood or its rights, they sometimes used those claims to argue for the continuation of Jim Crow schools. White Citizens' Council leaders charged that "the most precious possession of true parenthood is children." Parents must be "faithful to their God-given task" to protect the "physical, mental, and spiritual development" of their children, a task that "race mixing," they warned, made impossible. White supremacists insisted that "where parents . . . love their children . . . there will continue to be found true [segregated] education!" And this, they maintained, applied to black as well as white parents. "Think about what you are doing to the children, both white and colored. . . . Don't you know you and your children are only cat's paws for the politicians and the communists?," they told black parents. White southerners insisted that contrary to the expert opinion cited by the Supreme Court ruling, "uncontradicted expert testimony" proved that "integration kills education" and "that Negroes and whites cannot in fact be educated together without psychological injury to *both races*." Noted black leaders such as the NAACP's chief legal counsel, Thurgood Marshall, were products of segregated schools, segregationists pointed out. Such examples offered proof enough, they asserted, that "the field for Negro advancement in the South under our system of segregation is unlimited." Integration, segregationists warned, would produce no such role models but would leave black children "physically and psychologically maimed for life!" Whites insisted that black parents who really loved their children and wanted them to have the best opportunities for intellectual, social, and mental development would keep them out of "places where they are not wanted and where they are unhappy and where they are not inspired." At integrated schools, black children would "never be president of their class . . . never be able to play a part in a class play, nor . . . play in the school band."[56]

These kinds of arguments made sense to at least some members of the black community. If the goal really was to help black children "to grow throughout childhood in good . . . emotional and social health and security," then some African Americans wondered if sending their children to white schools was the best way to realize that goal. An unsigned letter to the editor, ostensibly written by an African American father, explained,

> Maybe I ought to be willing for my children to be martyrs for the sake of complete equality for a future generation. I'm not. I shiver to think that for this happy, fulfilled, wholesome experience where their abilities and their attractive personality get the place to which they are entitled in their own pattern with their own group, there would ever be substituted a situation where they would feel unwanted and at a disadvantage and develop, instead of the happy confidence they now have in their own environment, a defiant attitude of inferiority. . . . I shall fight to the last gasp against having my children attend a white school.

Whether written by a truly concerned black parent, by an "Uncle Tom," or by a white segregationist, this letter demonstrates some of black parents' legitimate fears about integration. Would the harassment and discrimination their children experienced as they attended previously all-white schools be worthwhile? Similar fears had led Counts's parents to withdraw her from a newly integrated school. Even more directly, however, the letter reveals the ways that segregationists drew on notions of childhood and social science research about childhood to make their case against integration. Going to racially mixed schools, whites argued, would make otherwise well-adjusted black children feel inferior and become delinquent. Anticipating the outcome of the *Brown* decision, NAACP leaders suggested that white southerners would comply with the Court ruling because of their concern for their children. "We do not believe that [southern whites] would rather have their children grow up in ignorance than have them taught in the same classrooms with Negro children," an article in *The Crisis* asserted. And indeed, some white southerners, especially mothers, urged parents not to be misled by segregationists "who would make your child suffer" by closing public schools. Mrs. Gordon G. Henderson, the president of Mississippians for Public Education, affirmed, "Every parent wants to do the very best he or she can for his child's welfare. Love, shelter,

good nutrition, health care, and a sound, solid education are essentials. I
find it hard to believe that any American would advise a parent to deny
his child one of them." In the early 1960s, other southern white mothers,
including Brownie Ledbetter, joined with their black counterparts to conduct integration training panels, where participants discussed prejudice
as a disease that affects all children. Ledbetter, for her part, tried to stress
the difficulty of having to explain to her children why they went one direction to school while black kids went another. And in New Orleans, Save
Our Schools organizers led similar discussions that refuted segregationists' inflammatory charges, arguing, for example, that "no Negro child has
ever brought into any of our schools a problem that has not already been
presented somewhere by a white child. . . . It is never possible to explain
a child's behavior simply in terms of his race, or to classify children's problems on a racial basis." For the benefit of white southerners less inclined
to think in racially inclusive terms about either the problems or the rights
of childhood, this group also stressed the need to conserve "our greatest
resource — our children" by keeping public schools open; otherwise, parents could find themselves having to send their children to unaccredited
schools in decaying orphanage buildings with no chemistry laboratories,
cafeterias, or elective classes and taught by retired teachers. Such comments were certainly moving, but white segregationists proved just as
adept at using widespread ideas about childhood to justify their resistance
to the *Brown* decision. Their arguments tried to turn the Supreme Court
ruling on its head by arguing that both black and white children would be
better served by maintaining separate schools.[57]

White supremacists did not always employ social science arguments in
such seemingly altruistic ways. While Wilkins argued that "it is a sick and ill
prepared white child who grows up to believe that just because he is white
he is superior," some whites countered that youth were being "warped and
twisted" by new educational ideas rather than by prejudice. Others went
so far as to suggest that the lack of racial consciousness in childhood made
it even more important for adults to teach their children proper "racial
self-respect. . . . [T]he truth is that young children are equally unprejudiced against dirt, poisonous insects, and a multitude of other harmful or
undesirable things." Teaching children "racial awareness," they insisted,
was akin to teaching them "table manners and personal hygiene." White
segregationists also elicited support and criticized integration efforts by

Children at a Ku Klux Klan rally, Tucker, Georgia, 4 October 1954. Southern white
parents brought their children to KKK rallies to learn proper race pride.
(© Bettmann/Corbis)

arguing that cunning race mixers had chosen southern schools as their
primary target "because there the adolescent and 'unprejudiced' mind
can be REACHED . . . BECAUSE THE ADOLESCENT AND THEREFORE
DEFENSELESS MIND WOULD THERE BE EXPOSED TO BRAIN-WASHING
which it would NOT KNOW HOW to REFUTE." Taking a somewhat different
tack, noted agitator Jim Johnson commended whites who showed their
commitment to segregation by sending their children to schools outside
their hometowns. He pointed out, however, that such solutions presented
a potential danger, not unlike those about which social science experts
had warned the Supreme Court. Undoubtedly influenced by contemporary theories of racial socialization, Johnson cautioned that students "of a
tender age," removed from "parental guidance and a happy home environment," might be exposed "to influences that could be almost as damaging
to their future development of character as would their attendance at an
integrated school." And of course, segregationists publicized President
Dwight Eisenhower's apprehensions about integration, especially the fact
that his grandchildren transferred to a private school after he made Washington schools into a supposed "laboratory to demonstrate to the world
how easily and effectively integration and Democracy would work."[58]

The national media and segregationist whites were not the only ones to use America's ideas about childhood to tell their stories. Black leaders, too, recognized that cultural beliefs in the sanctity and rights of childhood had influenced the *Brown* decision and continued to influence opinion in favor of civil rights for African Americans. In his study of civil rights events in Selma and the Voting Rights Act of 1965, David Garrow relates the impact of American political culture and the media to the success of the Selma campaign. As Garrow explains, Martin Luther King Jr. and protesters at Selma used to their advantage the nation's political culture, or the "set of attitudes, beliefs, and sentiments [that] provide the underlying assumptions and rules that govern behavior in the political system." In the 1960s, Garrow asserts, American political culture championed the democratic ideology espoused by civil rights activists and condemned the aggression of segregationists (such as the violent reaction to protesters on the Edmund Pettus Bridge) as illegitimate political behavior. The violent, unprovoked action of local law enforcement officials elicited overwhelmingly negative public reactions and led, Garrow argues, directly to the passage of the Voting Rights Act of 1965.[59]

But America's "subjective orientation to politics" in the years after World War II also included, as historian Elaine Tyler May shows, a belief in the importance of parenthood and childhood. Men and women were encouraged to focus their energy, attention, and ambitions on their children. Such a domestic focus, government officials indicated, would strengthen America both at home and abroad. The postwar baby boom, as May describes it, reflected America's political orientation as much as it reflected individual family choices and demographic changes.[60]

The struggle for African American civil rights in the years following World War II needs to be understood in the context of this domestic, child-centered political orientation. Evidence of racial inequality in and of itself did not lead to sympathetic interpretations of the civil rights movement or legislative action. However, evidence that the domestic tranquility required by cold war politics and venerated by American culture remained elusive for black families because of racism and Jim Crow did have a positive effect. In the 1950s and early 1960s, the fact that black parents' hopes for their children could not be realized in a society based on notions of white supremacy helped to generate public and political support for African American civil rights.

The stories the press told about children suffering under Jim Crow took on added significance in a political culture that emphasized men's and women's roles as parents, as movement leaders and strategists well understood. In June 1963, one *Jet* magazine cover featured an image that captured as well as promoted a particular meaning of the movement. Young black activists James Bevel and Diane Nash appeared with their baby and the words "Freedom Fighting Family." Two months later, the press sentimentally reported that "the children of the slaves [Abraham Lincoln] emancipated" gathered around the Lincoln Memorial while Joan Baez sang, "Little baby don't you cry, you know your mamma won't die, all your trials will soon be over." And that afternoon, the Reverend Dr. Martin Luther King Jr. gave the most well-known speech of the civil rights movement, announcing, "I have a dream that my four little children will one day live in a nation where they will not be judged by the color of their skin but by the content of their character. . . . I have a dream that . . . little black boys and black girls will be able to join hands with little white boys and white girls and walk together as sisters and brothers. . . . Now is the time to open the doors of opportunity to all of God's children."[61] At the March on Washington, King spoke to America not as a minister, a civil rights activist, or even an African American man who had suffered from the many manifestations of racial prejudice and hatred. Instead, he spoke as a parent, explaining the meaning of the civil rights movement in terms that every American mother and father understood. Whether white Americans agreed with his desires for a new social, economic, and political order, they could at least understand his dream that his children would have better lives. By identifying himself as a parent and calling on widespread beliefs about childhood, King made his politics accessible to everyday Americans. As scholars have noted, "King's dream had no real nay-sayers."[62] Even if some whites did not like the idea of black equality, no one in 1960s America could argue against the sacredness of childhood.

Penned a few months before the march, King's famous "Letter from Birmingham Jail" explained the struggle for racial equality in similar, child-centered terms.

> There comes a time when the cup of endurance runs over . . . when you suddenly find your tongue twisted and your speech stammering

Martin Luther King Jr. with two of his children at an Atlanta park, 1960s. King often drew on ideas about childhood and highlighted his role as a parent when he explained the black freedom struggle to the American public. (© Marvin Koner/Corbis)

as you seek to explain to your six-year-old daughter why she can't go to the public amusement park that has just been advertised on television, and see tears welling up in her eyes when she is told that Funtown is closed to colored children, and see ominous clouds of inferiority beginning to form in her little mental sky, and see her beginning to distort her personality by developing an unconscious bitterness toward white people; when you have to concoct an answer for a five-year-old who is asking: "Daddy, why do white people treat colored people so mean?"

Because of the country's domestic-centered political orientation and the focus of the *Brown* ruling, equating the movement with a black father's dream for his children, with children's ability to dream, made the struggle for black equality understandable, even compelling, to the American public. King and other civil rights leaders and organizations repeatedly drew on America's most important cultural ideals and myths to argue for black equality. And very often, the ideals and myths they highlighted related to childhood.[63]

The March on Washington had initially been conceived as a children's march from Alabama to the nation's capital. Following the Birmingham campaign, Bevel, considered by many observers to have been the best movement strategist, proposed that schoolchildren, eager to be a part of the movement, be taken on a longer march. Bevel knew that because of sentimental ideas about childhood, the country would pay close attention if the march involved young people — "The nation would be enthralled."[64]

Although the march was eventually (at least officially) restricted to those age fourteen and older, Bevel was right about what caught the nation's attention. A few months earlier, the Southern Christian Leadership Conference (SCLC) had asked that Bevel and Andrew Young come to Birmingham to help recruit college students to participate in demonstrations. But hundreds of high school, junior high, and even elementary school children enthusiastically joined the cause as well. Their participation in the Birmingham campaign confirmed that the presence of children and evidence of the ways that racism perverted ideal childhood pushed the public to the side of civil rights activists. Few people, black or white, paid attention to the campaign before schoolchildren began marching on 2 May, and leaders had little hope of realizing any of their demands. But after the children joined in and Bull Conner released his racist fury at them, Birmingham's black adult community and people across the country responded, including President John F. Kennedy's administration and members of Congress. The administration immediately sent Burke Marshall, the head of the Justice Department's Civil Rights Division, to assess the situation. Congressional leaders compared Conner to Nazi storm troopers and called his assaults on schoolchildren a "national disgrace." And "the cries for equality in Birmingham" led Kennedy to voice his support for strong civil rights legislation and to do so in child-centered terms, no less. He told the country via television and radio,

> It ought to be possible . . . for every American to enjoy the privileges of being American without regard to his race or his color. In short, every American ought to have the right to be treated as he would wish to be treated, as one would wish his children to be treated. . . . We face . . . a moral crisis as a country and as a people. . . . It is time to act. . . . We cannot say to 10 percent of the population that . . . your children can't have the chance to develop whatever talents they have; that the only way that they are going to get their rights is to go into

the streets and demonstrate. . . . I am asking for your help in making it easier for us to move ahead and to provide the kind of equality of treatment which we would want ourselves; to give a chance for every child to be educated to the limits of his talents.

Kennedy was not the only person motivated to act boldly. Both blacks and whites who had previously stayed away from the movement experienced such a strong emotional response to the images of children under attack in Birmingham that they began to support the protests. One observer noted that "in a twinkling of an eye, the whole black community was instantaneously consolidated behind King." As Bevel said, "It was time to defend the kids."[65]

King explained that nonviolent protest "dramatized the essential meaning of the conflict and in magnified strokes made clear who was the evildoer and who was the victim." But only when children became the victims did the meaning of the conflict really come through. It was one thing for politicians and the public to see images of black adults being beaten and taken to jail and quite another for them to see dogs and fire hoses unleashed on children. Attorney General Robert Kennedy tried to convince civil rights leaders not to use children, arguing that "an injured, maimed, or dead child is a price that none of us can afford to pay." But that was exactly the point. Not just adults but countless black children had already been injured, maimed, and killed in the name of white supremacy. "The disease of racism," as Bevel explained, was "already shaping the lives of these children and limiting their place." Years earlier, black congressman Adam Clayton Powell Jr. had expressed a similar view. "There is no difference between the young people and the old people," he told delegates to an NAACP Youth Conference. "The heartaches, tears and sufferings of young people are the same as those of adults." But mid-twentieth-century definitions held that children were not supposed to face the same kinds of problems as were adults. They were supposed to remain innocent and carefree. They could be only helpless victims. And they deserved protection. By linking the cause of racial equality to the plight of children, by revealing that novelist Ralph Ellison's "Invisible Man" was sometimes a child, black freedom leaders touched America's consciousness in a manner that would not let it turn away. The Birmingham campaign, combined with the killing of four black children in the bombing of a black church, taught Americans the price of prejudice.[66]

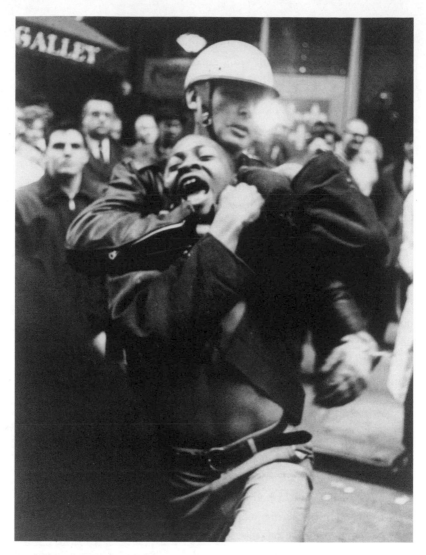

An Atlanta policeman arrests Taylor Washington, a high school honors student who had already been arrested seven times, 1963. This image, which appeared on the cover of the Student Non-Violent Coordinating Committee's *The Movement*, revealed the disturbing results of white supremacy. Children and youth, who should have received protection from the nation's law enforcement personnel, were instead strangled and beaten as they peacefully tried to exercise their rights or protest racial inequalities. (Hansberry, *Movement*, 126.) (© Danny Lyon/Magnum Photos)

As *Newsweek* reported, 15 September started at the Wesley household with that "special quiet hustle that goes with getting the kids to Sunday School." After breakfast, "bubbly, bright eye[d], 14 year old Cynthia" helped her father do the dishes, "got into her Sunday best—a ruffled white dress . . . draped a red sweater over her shoulders . . . fed her cocker spaniel Toots," and went to church. A few hours later, this all-American child was "a headless body," identifiable only "by her ring and dress." Three other innocent girls, one only eleven years old, also died "in the horror and heaps of bricks, wood and glass" at the Sixteenth Street Baptist Church that morning, their Sunday school lesson on "love that forgives" cut short by a terrifying blast. Many others were wounded. It was "Youth Day" at the church.[67]

Children in cold war America were routinely taught to "duck and cover," to take shelter under their desks, in ditches, or in basements. But bombs were supposed to be coming from the Soviets, not fellow Americans. To the nation's press, the black community, and much of America, the death of four girls at church and two black boys in the violent aftermath of the bombing became undeniable evidence of the depravity of southern racism. In the context of an American and world political culture that championed ideas about the rights of childhood, such acts of aggression appeared especially unjust. "The pure horror of what happened in Birmingham Sunday overshadows all else that has transpired in the South in the recent record of racial turmoil," one paper reported. "Now the ultimate has been reached; the last depth of racism has been plumbed." Images of children under attack as they tried to attend integrated schools in communities across the South or march during Birmingham's spring civil rights demonstrations had already shocked a public sensitive to the plight of children. But the murder of four girls in the sanctuary of the church (girls who, as reporters related, were truly innocent because they had not been involved in those protests) and the subsequent shooting of two boys—one by Birmingham police and the other by white teenagers as he rode his bicycle—did "more violence to the tenets of civilization, of Christianity, of common humanity" than any other "crime against the spirit of brotherhood."[68]

The 15 September explosion was only one of more than forty unsolved bombings directed against Birmingham's black homes, businesses, and churches in the years after World War II. Just nine months before the Sunday school tragedy, the Southern Conference Education Fund reported that a sleeping toddler and two children rehearsing a Christmas play were cut by flying glass when a bomb went off. In 1956, the Reverend Fred Shuttlesworth and his family "barely missed" being killed by a bomb that blew up in the city's Bethel Baptist Church. A year later, he spoke to reporters from a stretcher after a group of white men had beaten him, his twelve-year-old daughter, and other black students as they tried to enter Birmingham's all-white Phillips High School. "I guess this is the price you pay for freedom," Shuttlesworth said.[69]

The Sunday school bombing came six years later, just eleven days, as the press pointed out, after local blacks again attempted to desegregate public schools "over the vehement objections of the Governor and segregation organizations." In some ways, the incident constituted just another instance of southern resistance to school integration. But closing schools, verbally intimidating black children, even physically attacking them and their parents, and threatening that schools would never be integrated as long as "I have breath in my body and gun powder will burn" were one thing; dead children were quite another. While Birmingham officials could ignore previous terrorist acts against the black community, ideas about childhood demanded (as they had in the Till case) a sympathetic response to this event. "How shocking it is to a community when innocent children are killed," a prominent white Birmingham citizen remarked. Other white city leaders were likewise quick to express their grief and shock over the "untimely death of innocent children."[70]

But America had seen pictures of Emmett Till. It had seen images of Dorothy Counts, Elizabeth Eckford, Ruby Bridges, and other black children being attacked by white mobs. And because of the tactics civil rights organizations used earlier that spring as well as young people's determination, the public already knew what white supremacy politics were capable of doing to Birmingham's black youth. This was no isolated incident. "We've been expecting this all along, waiting for it, knowing it would come, wondering when," said the Reverend John Cross, minister of the bombed church. "This type of tragedy," black leaders asserted, was "the invariable consequence when hate and bigotry are flaunted so defiantly." The media agreed. While Birmingham's mayor insisted that the city and its white population were also "victims" in this "tragedy," a *Life* magazine article argued that "every person . . . who had in any way contributed to the popularity of hatred is at least as guilty . . . as the demented fool who threw the bomb." A southern paper similarly editorialized that "the hands at the fuse" included all those who supported "the kinds of politics that

Governor Wallace represents." And the *Atlanta Constitution*'s editor wrote a story about the event that focused on a bewildered black mother who aimlessly wandered the streets near the bombed church, carrying the shoe of her dead child. "We broke those children's bodies," he told his fellow white southerners. "We, who know better, created a climate for child-killing. . . . We hold that shoe in our hand, Southerner. Let us see it straight, and look at the blood on it." The Sunday school bombing seemed to prove the conclusions of social science researchers who linked racial prejudice to violent, irrational, self-destructive behavior and who warned that racism was especially injurious to American childhood.[71]

In his 1967 autobiography, *North Toward Home*, Willie Morris shared one of his experiences as a white boy growing up in the Jim Crow South: "One summer morning . . . I sighted a little Negro boy walking with . . . his older sister. . . . I hid in the shrubbery . . . jumped out and pounced upon him. I slapped him across the face, kicked him with my knee, and with a shove sent him sprawling on the concrete." Morris hid, expecting retribution. When none came, he felt "strangely light and giddy. Then later, the more I thought about it," he said, "I could hardly bear my secret shame." As he grew up, Morris came to realize that this experience represented more than "a gratuitous act of childhood cruelty." It was something "infinitely more subtle and contorted." Moreover, it was but one example of the kind of "unthinking sadism" that he, his friends, and the larger white community commonly directed toward blacks.[72]

Martin Luther King Jr., in his "Eulogy for the Martyred Children," suggested that "the death of these little children may lead our whole Southland from the low road of man's inhumanity to man to the high road of peace and brotherhood. [Their] spilled blood . . . may cause the white South to come to terms with its conscience." "God has a way of wringing good out of evil," King assured those gathered for the funeral. The Birmingham children "did not die in vain," he insisted. Through their deaths, these "unoffending, innocent, and beautiful" children would lead "every minister of the gospel," "every politician," and "every Negro" on a "holy crusade for freedom and human dignity," a crusade that would "transform dark and desolate valleys into sunlit paths of inner peace." King hoped that the events in Birmingham would put an end to the "unthinking sadism," the "secret shame." The white South would be redeemed, and African Americans would finally realize the American dream.[73]

King's address turned out to be less prophetic than he hoped. But his words reflected an awareness that although many African American leaders earlier in the century had believed that evidence of black "intellectual parity" and reason would lead the American conscience toward civil rights, evidence of the ways that segregation damaged and destroyed childhood more often brought support for the black freedom struggle. Birmingham revealed the South's "secret shame" in a way that made it difficult for the public and its politicians to remain neutral on civil rights issues. Letters and telegrams to civil rights leaders and stories in the press after the murders testified that the nation and the world had been "aroused" by this "unbelievable tragedy" and could no longer "stand indifferent to the glare of inequality and injustice." In killing innocent children, segregationists had committed "a crime against all the American people," not just against blacks.[74] African American civil rights were not simply, as traditional narratives about the movement have frequently suggested and as many Americans continue to believe, the result of an idea whose time had come.[75] But King and other postwar civil rights leaders recognized that America was devoted to ideas about childhood. Linking the movement to those ideas, as King did in his eulogy for the Birmingham children and in his "I Have a Dream" speech, transforming it into a "children's crusade" or a "holy crusade" conducted in the memory of dead children and on behalf of future generations of children, made it compelling to an otherwise uncommitted white America as well as to blacks reluctant to become involved in the movement.[76]

Shortly after the Sunday school bombing, a slightly inebriated white man approached the chair of the Congress of Racial Equality (CORE), James Farmer, as he sat in an airport coffee shop. The man explained that on his last flight, an Alabama native "spent the whole trip telling me we shouldn't be concerned about the death of those four little girls in their Sunday school down in Birmingham." Was the man in the coffee shop convinced? "Agitated," the man insisted that he did not need to be convinced "because I'm not concerned. This isn't my fight. . . . I will not be involved." Farmer sensed that despite this vehement denial, the man was moved by "the death of those four little girls." But also, like many other Americans, he was "trying hard not to make up [his] mind" about civil rights issues. "You must be involved . . . you can't be neutral," Farmer told him.[77]

Farmer repeated this story at a civil rights rally. Its retelling in that context suggests not only that the Birmingham tragedy forced apathetic

Americans to confront civil rights issues but also that civil rights leaders purposely used ideas about childhood to motivate blacks and whites to join the fight for racial equality. Farmer's message for the white man was his message for his integrated audience: anyone who thought about those girls could not possibly remain neutral in the struggle; their deaths challenged the sanctity of childhood. At the same rally, Farmer told other stories to remind his listeners about the connections between civil rights and childhood. He talked about his father, who had grown up in South Carolina and Georgia, where segregation "burned [him] up inside." Farmer told the audience about his initiation as a four-year-old boy into the brutal world of white supremacy and about the experiences that segregation brought to every black mother's child. As a consequence of such efforts and others, in 1964, Farmer noted, the "big bulk of apathetic people have lashed in our favor."[78]

At a 1944 NAACP youth council conference, workshop leaders told attendees, "The public is a tough nut to crack. . . . Generally the public is apathetic (Negro and White). . . . Your job is to make them sympathetic." They advised participants to use words, symbols, and ideas to attack others and to simplify, "driving your program home, and identifying your fight as justifiable." In the years after World War II, and especially after the *Brown* decision, nothing seemed to "crack" the public, to justify the struggle for civil rights, as much as proving that the social science researchers who testified before the Supreme Court had been right: segregation hurt children.[79]

In Cairo, Illinois, "demonstrations . . . continued this week after the imprisonment of two Negro juveniles in state reformatories." In Mississippi, "two Negro girls [were] shot in [the] home of voter registration workers," "the mayor of Ruleville . . . willfully and maliciously beat a 14 year old Negro youth," and "two Negro children [in Indianola], 8 and 9, were arrested while passing out leaflets." In Albany, Georgia, demonstrations took place "to protest the beating of three Negro boys by police." In Amelia, Virginia, a "bottle filled with fire crackers [was] thrown on [the] driveway of local Negro girls." And again in Mississippi a freedom school in Laurel was bombed.[80] SNCC and other civil rights workers routinely reported such incidents to the press and the FBI. That their reports often included references to attacks on children suggests that children actively participated in the movement and that movement organizers recognized that the public and the federal government were more likely to back civil rights efforts when they saw that white supremacy continued to threaten and harm children. These reports also indicate that the members of the black community responded, taking to the streets when children suffered. Scholars and participants in the movement have shown that black adults who otherwise tried to stay away from the movement found it difficult to maintain that distance when they saw their own or other black children under attack.[81] But scholars have missed the ways that civil rights groups specifically used ideas about childhood to solicit support for the movement. Whether emphasizing acts of aggression against black children or appealing to adults in their roles as parents, civil rights activists knew that linking the fight for black equality to notions about childhood made the movement meaningful to many people.

At mass meetings, organizers such as Farmer told stories of tragic racial awakenings, black children being assaulted, spending their youth in ghettos, or dying in white men's fields. In 1967, SNCC's Forman even used ideas about childhood to motivate potential activists during a stage in the movement dominated by ideas about Black Power. He closed his speech by insisting that his listeners should be "concerned about all the unborn . . . Emmett Tills, and when you are concerned about your own children, then you are ready to take care of business. And," he continued, "you ain't got no business having any children if you ain't gonna fight for their freedom."[82]

Civil rights organizations mounted advertising campaigns that similarly drew on beliefs about childhood and responsible (meaning activist) parenthood. One frequent postwar NAACP advertisement featured a picture of a little black girl and asked, "Will she live in peace and security? Or will she cower behind her silent mother's skirts?" In the sixties, SNCC and other civil rights groups commonly circulated flyers that featured pictures of bombed-out schools and impoverished black youth working in the cotton fields and urged, "Give them a future in Hattiesburg, register to vote," or "Think not of yourself, but of your fellow Negro Brothers and the unborn boys and girls of this city." Organizers promoted civil rights films with advertisements that showed black children sitting on the steps of shacks or drinking from tin cans. "These people tell their story . . . will you listen?" they asked, knowing the country was more likely to listen if those stories centered on children. The titles of such films likewise linked images of children to the civil rights struggle. "The Streets of Greenwood" would have brought to mind images of Till's mutilated body, while "A

Dream Deferred" would have conjured images of black children growing up stigmatized instead of hopeful.[83]

In 1965, SNCC created a pictorial history using the work of photographers who had been commissioned to document the movement and capture images that could be used for publicity and fund-raising purposes. Photographs in that book portrayed the movement's more famous child-centered moments — children in strangleholds, prisons, coffins. But perhaps more significantly, many of the other images chosen to represent the everyday meaning of the movement, the need for racial equality, also involved children — a woman holding a baby outside a New York City tenement, a ragged-looking black girl standing against a brick wall, a child playing on an iron balcony in a ghetto. The publication includes a quotation from John F. Kennedy: "The Negro baby born in America today, regardless of the section or the state in which he is born, has about one-half as much chance of completing high school as a white baby . . . one-third as much chance of completing college . . . of becoming a professional man; twice as much chance of becoming unemployed. . . . [L]ife expectancy . . . is seven years shorter." The book also shows children holding picket signs. "I have 4 books at P.S. 200, 1st grade." "I had NO books at P.S. 282, 4th grade." Their parents protest, "Don't let the board of education kidnap our children," "25% less spent in Chicago to teach a Negro Child." Some pictures have poor black, white, and Hispanic boys together, while another shows black and white children swimming side by side, naked. All of America's children, even those "blissfully unconscious of differences," SNCC's book testified, suffered under Jim Crow.[84]

Other photographs by SNCC workers, some of them used to solicit donations or political support, also told stories about racial struggles that reinforced the links between civil rights and children's rights. Young Georgians marching for "one school system"; black youth bowing with their elders, holding signs protesting "the detention of children"; students marching and singing at Stearns dry goods store in Louisville; police with bats, standing over black youth lying on the ground in Mississippi towns. SNCC staff member Julian Bond used some of the photos in his 1965 campaign for the Georgia House of Representatives, a campaign that otherwise stressed economic issues. In one image, he sits looking out a window, holding a little girl on his knee. In another, he stands by a poster of a poor, grimy white girl. "For Freedom," the poster reads. And one photograph used in a SNCC pamphlet that lauded the public attention that riots in

Dixie Hills, Summerhill, and Watts brought to the problems of black communities shows black children and is captioned, "For the sake of our children."[85]

Other civil rights publications communicated the meaning of freedom in similar terms. According to CORE's pamphlet *Cracking the Color Line*, local protests effectively eliminated segregation in parks, swimming pools, skating rinks, playgrounds, and other youth-centered recreation facilities in many communities. But, the pamphlet suggested, despite those gains and the Supreme Court's ruling, America's black children still did not enjoy the rights of childhood. The booklet includes stories of school desegregation conflicts, young people being arrested and herded into open-air stockades, and photos of black children, their intent yet questioning eyes demanding help.[86]

The cover of another CORE pamphlet, specifically about school integration, featured a photograph focused on a frowning, obviously scared child. As in Rockwell's painting of Ruby Bridges, the girl in this image is surrounded by adults whose faces are not visible. Drawing on contemporary beliefs about childhood to shame adults into supporting integration, the text of the booklet went on to emphasize that children, like six-year-old Barbara Jean Watson, desperately needed community adults to help them integrate their schools. The pamphlet poignantly alludes to ideas about young people's natural innocence and lack of prejudice, suggesting that children involved in integration efforts did not understand why "the people outside make so much noise." They were, however, "beginning to suspect why the mobs had gathered." Reflecting other contemporary social science arguments that connected childhood with civil rights, the publication also quotes *New York Times* writer Robert Alden's comments about integration struggles: "It seemed to me . . . that calling a little girl filthy names or screaming at her . . . was as great a crime as the dynamiting of a school. A school can be repaired, the mind of a child, once scarred, can never be mended."[87]

Juxtaposing the brutality of white supremacy with beliefs about childhood as a protected state, another publication, *Mississippi Eyewitness*, recounted instances in which white Mississippians used "terror to keep Negroes 'in their place.'" Violence, so "basic to the system of slavery," the pamphlet asserts, "was never abandoned." The publication counts the lynchings of Till and nineteen-year-old Mack Parker, the murders of three young civil rights workers the summer of 1964, and the vicious arrest and treatment of fifteen-year-old June Johnson and other teenage activists as especially disturbing evidence of the unrestrained nature of southern violence against blacks. "The federal government forgot its pledge to protect the rights of newly freed slaves in 1876," the pamphlet said. And now, if the killing and torture of young people did not move the government and the public to intervene, "what [would] it take to get America to care?"[88]

An SCLC pamphlet, *The Black Revolution*, similarly implied that even if the government remained unwilling to protect black adults, it could not abandon young people who became victims of racist violence. And, it, too, called on beliefs about children's lack of prejudice and young people's activism to garner support for the movement. The booklet reminded readers that black children had "walked calmly up to the police dogs that lunged at them with a fury capable of tearing their small bodies to pieces." Those children, the pamphlet said, exposed "their bodies to death in order to show God and man that they believed in the just rights of their people." But fearful white men, warped by prejudice, "felt menaced . . . by the clear eyes of children" and attacked them and threw them in jail. The pamphlet also declared that if those men had heard the message of the black children, "they would cease to be the people they were." Of course the message of those children was not just meant for the Birmingham police force. By underscoring violence against innocent children as well as praising young people's courageous commitment to democratic values, the SCLC no doubt meant for the clear eyes and "heroic Christian witness" of young civil rights activists to challenge the rest of America as well.[89]

CHILDHOOD, CIVIL RIGHTS, AND POWER:
THE LIMITS OF AMERICAN SENTIMENTALITY

If linking the movement to ideas about childhood challenged America, if it garnered sympathy and support for the black freedom struggle, it also shaped and limited that support. Many white Americans were willing to come to the aid of black children or at least to protect the ideal of childhood. But they were only willing to do so if it did not affect white children too much, as the controversies surrounding busing and affirmative action revealed. When integration struggles moved north and west and it became clear that achieving racial equality would require more than an abstract belief in democratic principles and the rights of childhood, even some white liberals began sounding very much like southern segregationists.

Northern whites insisted that they remained committed to childhood and civil rights, but, as historian Genna Rae McNeil notes, "space remained for new rationales to buttress white privilege." And indeed, whites began using terms such as "'racial imbalance' to describe the demographic profile" of their school systems and "de facto" or "de jure" segregation to differentiate western and northern segregation from the legally mandated segregation of the South. NAACP legal counsel Robert L. Carter suggested that such terms allowed parents and policymakers to minimize or completely dismiss "the deleterious impact" of segregated schools outside the South on young blacks. In their defense of "neighborhood schools" (which Carter identified as "a euphemism for northern segregation"), white parents made clear that any attempts to correct "racial imbalances" imperiled (white) children. As one ostensibly liberal New York City parent complained about busing, "Of course I understand that Negro and Puerto Rican parents want a decent education for their children, just as I do for mine. . . . We must be prepared to live with them as equals and even to make sacrifices to that end. Just so long as we are not expected to sacrifice children!"[90]

After more than a decade of watching black children suffer as they bravely tried to carry out the *Brown* ruling, many African Americans must have regarded such statements as fairly ironic. But they could hardly have been surprised that white America's concern for black children yielded so easily to fears, prejudices, and self-interest. Even before the struggle for racial equality moved to the cities of the North and West, the Supreme Court, so insistent in 1954 on the importance of public schools and the psychological damage segregation inflicted on the nation's young, stalled in its 1955 follow-up ruling. While the NAACP argued for immediate relief for black children, the Court instead placated white southerners with its "all deliberate speed" decision. After indicating to the nation and the world that it would protect black children from Jim Crow and extend to them the benefits of American childhood, the Court backed down. The justices agreed with segregationists that the best interests of all involved—especially the children—dictated that the federal government should allow southern communities time to adjust to the 1954 ruling. African Americans were also likely not surprised that whites outside the South, like their southern counterparts, justified resistance to integration by calling on ideas about childhood.

Tepid in its commitment to black youth, the country was also reluctant to address the problems of black adults. So while black children were guaranteed the rights of childhood—schools were desegregated at least officially and Head Start programs were funded—the federal government never seriously addressed many of the African American community's other concerns, especially those involving economic issues. Segregation, of course, affected all blacks, not just children, and as numerous scholars have shown, school desegregation was often considered only "part of a broader assault on . . . white supremacy." But black freedom struggles in the late 1950s and early 1960s (and media coverage of them) had focused largely on children and youth. And although the Civil Rights Act of 1964 and the Voting Rights Act of 1965 were certainly not just about children, young people had been on the front lines pushing for those changes, and widespread support for civil rights legislation often directly resulted from youth activism and violence against young people or others who engaged in nonviolent protest that made them seem innocent and vulnerable—like children. Moreover, although whites all along had resisted, sometimes brutally, changes to the racialized sociopolitical order, the nation experienced a massive white backlash in the late 1960s. Even whites who had previously supported the movement abandoned civil rights when blacks began to focus less on children's educational rights and the effects of Jim Crow on young people or on childlike protesters and instead stressed labor and housing issues, Vietnam, and Black Power.[91]

Historians of women and gender have shown the limits of basing pleas for social, political, and economic change on women's special qualities and gender distinctions. Pleas for change based on notions of childhood have proven just as limiting, because childhood, like gender, signifies "relationships of power."[92] In the case of the black freedom movement, linking ideas about childhood to the plight of African Americans required the state, in its role as parent, to protect blacks. But when activists (and the media) stopped linking civil rights to childhood, stopped concentrating on what appeared to be children's issues, and started attacking the state itself, asserting themselves as proud black men and demanding economic independence and equal property rights (long the American determinants of adulthood/manhood), white public support and that of the federal government virtually ended. Many whites believed that decidedly unchildlike blacks neither required nor deserved the state to act, however timidly, as a guardian of the African American community.

Literary theorist Maurice Williams argues that popular images of African Americans have been a means of "demonstrating black humanity and political deservedness"—or perhaps undeservedness, as the case may be. In the years after the *Brown* decision, images of helpless black children or even images of seemingly helpless black adults demonstrated to an otherwise uncommitted white public that African Americans were indeed human and that they deserved greater civil and political rights. But, as Williams suggests, such popular images also tend to "frame" blacks "within a rigid and limited grid of representational possibilities."[93] And indeed, civil rights activists in the late 1960s who stepped outside the accepted boundaries of popular images of deserving blacks lost public support. Journalists and scholars of the civil rights movement have suggested that the movement lost support after 1965 because either the media's "sympathetic picture of the Negro struggle" or "the roles to which the audience now assigned each of the groups" changed.[94] Neither of these interpretations, however, recognizes the agency of black protesters. The media often captured—it did not wholly create—the sympathy-building strategies that movement organizers used. The press may have been telling stories about the movement to the public, but black activists also chose, at least to some extent, the roles they played. Moreover, both of these explanations for the shift in public opinion about civil rights miss the ways that positive interpretations of the struggle for racial equality depended on ideas about childhood. When organizers linked their protests to the rights of childhood, showed how white supremacy hurt children, or represented themselves as innocent and vulnerable—as NAACP lawyers had done in the *Brown* case—they won public sympathy. But not unlike Till's encounter with Bryant and Milam, civil rights activists who refused to fit the country's conceptions of deserving blacks and who, like Till, refused to be "boys" found themselves under attack. All of white America, and not just the white South, insisted that Negroes stay in their place. As James Baldwin wrote in "Fifth Avenue, Uptown," "Neither the southerner nor the northerner is able to look on the Negro simply as a man. It seems to be indispensable to the national self esteem that the Negro be considered either as a kind of ward, or as a victim."[95]

After her husband's murder at the hands of Mississippi segregationists, Rita Schwerner found that despite enormous interest in the case, the news media did not use "her numerous statements and the tapes she had made, because she refused to be maudlin, sentimental, or tearful and had instead tried to discuss the [political] issues involved." Even before Michael

Schwerner and two other young civil rights workers were killed the summer of 1964, the national press was searching for stories to tell about Freedom Summer that linked the struggle for civil rights to beliefs about childhood, especially stories that involved young white participants. As one of those participants wrote home, "*Look* magazine is searching for the ideal naive northern middle class white. . . . And when one of us gets killed, the story will be even bigger." This volunteer thought that the "big story ought to be Life in Mississippi." But it seemed clear that without the presence of young white civil rights activists, the challenges that blacks faced in Mississippi were all but invisible. Organizers agreed. Indeed, in the summer of 1964, they deliberately brought Michael Schwerner, Andrew Goodman, and hundreds of other young whites together with James Chaney and other blacks to capture the interest and hearts of America. With white students—white "children"—up against the violent intransigence of Jim Crow, helping to register voters and teaching young blacks, civil rights groups knew that America would pay attention.[96]

Like Rita Schwerner, however, they were disappointed to find that capturing the nation's attention and gaining public sympathy did not necessarily translate into support for specific civil rights issues. After Goodman, Chaney, and Schwerner disappeared that summer, FBI agents swarmed Mississippi looking for them but did so only because two of them were white. As one Mississippi black reported, "I am sorry about the three fellows is dead. But five of us that we know about have been killed this year and nobody raised any hell about it. . . . Now two white boys is dead and all the world comes running to look and see. They never would have done this had just us been dead." Federal agents in fact discovered the bodies of two young blacks who had participated in protest demonstrations earlier that year before they found the three Freedom Summer volunteers. Even with government investigators on hand, activists and local blacks continued to face the terrorist tactics of white supremacists and to be denied basic civil and human rights. Moreover, in August of that year, the Democratic Party again allowed an all-white Mississippi delegation to represent the state. The murders of Goodman, Schwerner, and Chaney revealed not just the depravity of white supremacy but also the continuing invisibility of the plight of black Americans. Those murders also revealed the limitations of American sentimentality. When Goodman arrived, Schwerner told him that "Mississippi was no place for children." Goodman replied, "I'm no child, I want to get into the thick of the fight." But America seemed unwilling to look at either man as anything but a child or to see what they were really fighting for.[97]

In "Down by the Riverside," African American writer Richard Wright tells the story of a southern community besieged by a flood. Mann, Wright's main character, is trapped, and his wife is about to have a baby. But with the waters rising and widespread panic and greed drowning any feelings of sympathy his situation might otherwise evoke, Mann's only recourse is to use a stolen boat. As he rows against the current in a desperate attempt to get medical care for his wife, he again asks for help. But his cries are heard by "white folks." The white owner of the boat ignores Mann's pleas and shoots at him. He shoots back. Mann eventually reaches a hospital and finds his way to the "colored" section, only to discover that it is too late — his wife and unborn child are dead. But Mann has no time to grieve. He is immediately forced to help evacuate white patients from the hospital. Then, when he might have been able to save himself, he is asked to save more white people—this time, the wife and children of the white man he has killed in self-defense. After he helps them reach land, the family accuses him. "He shot daddy twice! . . . [H]e came back to the house. . . . He was going to kill us!" the son says. "White folks, have mercy!" Mann pleads. But they do not.[98]

Written in the 1930s, Wright's story about the limits of white sentimentality and mercy resonated with civil rights activists of the late 1960s. Ideas about childhood had helped defeat legal segregation. They had also, for a time, motivated many whites and blacks to support the black freedom movement. But like Mann, African American activists were exhausted with the work of saving or "redeeming" whites while black men, women, and children were still dying or living under the "veil," a fate some considered worse than death. Wright said that after he published "Down by the Riverside" in a collection of short stories purposefully titled *Uncle Tom's Children*, he realized he "had made a mistake": "I found I had written a book which even bankers' daughters could read and weep over and feel good about. I swore to myself that if I ever wrote another book, no one would weep over it; that it would be so hard and deep that they would have to face it without the consolation of tears." More than twenty years later, many civil rights activists made the same pledge.[99]

Four

· · · · · · ·

THE NAACP AND THE YOUTH

ORGANIZING TRADITION

In a 1956 evaluation of its youth programs, National Association for the Advancement of Colored People (NAACP) leaders recognized that young people had "played a significant and vital role" in advancing the cause of racial equality. The association noted that growing support for civil rights work among black adults and throughout the white community was "in large measure the result of intensive work by youth and college units." It also acknowledged that young people in the association had "contributed to increasing the Negro vote in the South," educating the public on racial issues, breaking discriminatory employment and school admission practices, and curbing police brutality. Moreover, in the past few years, the NAACP boasted, youth council members had conducted several successful protests against segregation. In Dallas, they had eliminated "Negro Day" at the state fair. In St. Louis, they had opened the White Castle restaurant chain to black patrons. In Louisville, they had broken Jim Crow practices in lunchrooms at Kress, Woolworth, and other department stores. In Philadelphia, youth council members had eliminated "Sepia Day" at skating rinks. And in Detroit, youth councils had integrated restaurants, bowling alleys, and other public facilities.[1]

Within a few years, reports of direct action by young people and observations of the "vital role" of youth in the civil rights movement would seem unremarkable. Indeed, in the early 1960s, perhaps most movement organizers, participants, and observers would have agreed with historian and activist Howard Zinn that "sharp action by the youngsters" had set the developmental pattern for the civil rights protest movement. Scholars of the movement subsequently have also acknowledged that the energy and boldness of young people during that time ignited the struggle for racial equality. Impatient and uncompromising, "youth led the way." But 1956 was before Freedom Summer, before Birmingham, before the Student Non-Violent Coordinating Committee (SNCC), before Greensboro, even before Little Rock. So how do we account for this earlier recognition of young people's role in shaping the movement or this evidence of direct action before 1960 among youth members of the supposedly legalistic and slow-moving NAACP?[2]

Scholars have determined that young people were often the first and most enthusiastic supporters of civil rights programs in local communities and that young people frequently pushed the movement toward direct-action strategies. Studies have shown that youth set examples of courage and determination that inspired both local and national support for civil rights. But in their overall analysis, scholars tend to trivialize the contributions of children and youth to the black freedom struggle. They measure the success of civil rights organizing on the recruitment and involvement of local adults or stress the influence of family stories and adult activism on young people who chose to participate in the movement, even when much of their evidence suggests that significant differences existed between the younger and older generations and that youth most often encouraged their reluctant elders to get involved, not the other way around. Scholars have also, if unintentionally, belittled young people and their contributions to the movement by referring to them, as Zinn did, as "youngsters," a term that adults used more frequently in the mid–twentieth century but one that does not invite serious consideration.[3] Moreover, scholars have yet to explore the militancy and influence of young people on the civil rights movement of the 1960s in the context of the history of youth involvement in the movement and historically grounded ideas about childhood and youth. Taking seriously the contributions of young people and putting their activism in the context of a youth organizing tradition as well as in the context of an African American organizing tradition can help us better understand the dynamics of the civil rights movement, the NAACP, and the actions of young people during one of the most militant and successful periods of the black freedom struggle.

While youth activism certainly exploded in the late 1950s and early 1960s, a tradition of youth involvement in the African American freedom struggle originated as early as the antebellum period. Nineteenth- and early-twentieth-century abolitionists and race leaders, however, envisioned a primarily passive role for young people in the nation's racial struggles. But in the 1930s, the NAACP expanded its youth program when it became clear that black youth wanted to actively participate in the civil rights movement. During the Great Depression, at the same time that public and private agencies began to pay greater attention to the problems of youth, young people began to play an increasingly vital and militant role in the association and the movement, a role that would become more apparent and even more significant after the Supreme Court outlawed segregated schools in 1954.

SHAPING YOUNG MINDS, SHAPING THE FUTURE

Although there is little more than anecdotal evidence remaining, mostly from antislavery and Civil War children's stories, adults seem to have imagined a place for children in racial struggles even before Lincoln abolished slavery in the South. Abolitionists worried that any "acts and treaties" they promoted would have little effect "if they, who are now children, should be unfriendly, or even indifferent to the cause." But antislavery advocates, who championed new middle-class ideas about the innate goodness of children rather than traditional notions of their natural depravity, believed that young whites could be easily "impressed and guided" toward sympathy and "practical kindness" for the victims of slavery. Transmitting antislavery principles through literature and wherever possible through personal contact became important antislavery strategies for abolitionists who hoped to instill in America's future citizens an abhorrence for human bondage. Albeit in some respects limited, the first role that adults envisioned for children in the civil rights movement was also significant. Indeed, many twentieth-century activists, from W. E. B. Du Bois to SNCC organizers, continued to regard teaching children to understand that whites and blacks have "common feelings and impulses" as an important strategy in the black freedom struggle.[4]

Abolitionist children's literature recognized young people's potential, both in the future and to a lesser extent in the present, for becoming important political actors in the antislavery cause. While more mainstream children's literature of the period tried to shape young minds through stories that stressed moral virtue and strict obedience, abolitionist primers and stories taught that slavery was a sin and that both enslaved and freed blacks deserved the sympathy and the help of young readers. *The Anti-*

Slavery Alphabet, for example, reminded its "little readers" of the horrors of slavery and encouraged them to take action against the cruel institution in their everyday lives at the same time it taught reading skills:

> Y is for youth—the time for all
> Bravely to war with sin;
> And think not it can ever be
> Too early to begin. . . .
> You are young 'tis true
> But there's much you can do.
> Even you can plead with men
> That they buy not slaves again.
> Sometimes when from school you walk
> You can with your playmates talk.
> Tell them of the slave child's fate
> Motherless and desolate
> And you can refuse to take
> Candy, sweetmeat, pie or cake
> Saying no—unless 'tis free
> The slave shall not work for me.[5]

Often criticized for their racist overtones by modern scholars, anti-slavery tracts and stories certainly reflected the paternalism of their writers. Yet abolitionist children's literature also demonstrated what literary theorists call "oppositional tendencies" for the period in which it was produced. Not until the middle decades of the twentieth century would mainstream children's literature commonly express multicultural themes and encourage young people to challenge, instead of simply accept, social and political institutions and hierarchies.[6] But in the early nineteenth century, abolitionist children's literature sought to weaken racial constructs while recognizing and promoting the agency of children. *The Anti-Slavery Alphabet* and *The Child's Anti-Slavery Book* encouraged white children to question the validity of laws that condoned the separation of families and the ill-treatment of people who were only superficially different. In addition, those books instructed children to do something, however small, to challenge slavery. One story in the latter collection even suggested that young readers follow the example of "good" Christians who helped slaves escape, although providing such aid might bring monetary fines and imprisonment.[7]

In the Union, popular Civil War children's literature addressed some of the racial themes of abolitionist children's literature. As historian James Marten shows, Civil War children's magazines and books made the evils of the slave system, its eradication, and the humane treatment of former slaves important issues. That literature also encouraged children directly to subvert the Confederacy's aims and the South's sociopolitical order by sending clothing and toys to "contraband" children or by teaching them to read. Scholars have noted that attacking the Confederacy through acts of benevolence in some ways encouraged feelings of white superiority and condescension toward blacks. But, as with abolitionists' writings for children, benevolent acts toward former slaves or even the idea of such acts could also help to undermine the nation's current racial politics. Moreover, both abolitionist and Civil War children's literature gave young people a central role in creating a new, less racially divisive political reality. If young whites read that blacks, like all children, depended on others for care and protection until they grew up, if white children saw blacks as similar, then the barriers between the races could be destroyed. Perhaps the idea of race might be eliminated as well.[8]

After the Civil War, whites and blacks alike recognized that the malleability of children's minds and their potential as political actors made children's literature an important medium in the struggle for equal rights. Most white southerners remained unwilling to allow their children to be socialized into a new sociopolitical order, however. Even during the Civil War, schoolbooks for children rolled off southern presses. In contrast to northern wartime writings for children, southern texts affirmed the beneficence of slavery—the absolute loyalty, dependence, simplicity, and inferiority of black slaves—and portrayed Yankees as would-be tyrants who wanted to turn all southerners into destitute children. The years following the war likewise saw the growth of a distinctly southern literature for children—a literature overwhelmingly political in its intent. Katharine Du Pre Lumpkin recalled that young southerners were taught "to love the Lost Cause." At home, school, and in Children of the Confederacy clubs, they learned "patriotic" songs such as "Dixie," memorized poetry that celebrated the Old South, and read biographies of Robert E. Lee and Stonewall Jackson and the "little volumes of Confederate memoirs then coming off many local presses." Literature produced for southern children gave history a peculiar slant and perpetuated negative images of blacks. Books such as *The Darkies ABCs*, *Kinky Kids*, and later Elvira Garner's popular

Ezekiel stories and Inez Hogan's books about Nicodemus depicted African Americans as barely intelligible, forgetful, easily fooled, and in need of guidance from whites.[9] Negative stereotypes of blacks encouraged children of both races to develop identities that justified the politics of Jim Crow. Providing representations of blacks in children's literature, then, became an especially significant political act and children's literature a somewhat obscure but nonetheless key site for maintaining an unequal sociopolitical order — or, conversely, for encouraging change.[10]

Negative images of African Americans dominated mainstream children's literature and helped justify segregation for the first half of the twentieth century. From the earliest days of Jim Crow, however, the black community sought to undermine America's racial order by providing an alternative black identity through literature. In 1887 Amelia E. Johnson, a Baltimore minister's wife, founded *The Joy*, an eight-page monthly periodical for black children that ran for two years. In 1890, Johnson published *Clarence and Corinne; or, God's Way*, considered by many to have been the first children's book written for black children by a black author, although it did not address racial themes. That same year, however, black teacher, politician, and businessman Edward A. Johnson wrote *A School History of the Negro Race in America*, which he hoped would help remedy the "sins of omission and commission on the part of white authors" who "left out the many credible deeds of the Negro" and either explicitly or implicitly taught "the inferiority of the Negro." A few years later, Paul Laurence Dunbar wrote *Little Brown Baby*. And in 1905, Silas Xavier Floyd published a collection of stories, *Floyd's Flowers; or, Duty and Beauty for Colored Children*, which was later revised and reprinted. Black churches addressed the lack of acceptable images in reading material for black children in 1896 with the founding of the National Baptist Publishing Board. In its first year alone, this organization oversaw the publication of seven hundred thousand pieces of Sunday school literature. In subsequent years, black churches continued to produce literature for children that defied the racial politics of the day. Especially common were stories about black heroes such as Frederick Douglass and Harriet Tubman. Black newspapers ran similarly positive and heroic stories about historic, contemporary, and fictional black characters in "children's pages" or designated children's issues. These newspapers also challenged the barefoot, watermelon-eating images of blacks that dominated mainstream children's literature by featuring photographs of real black children whose dress, robust health, and postures reflected white middle-class ideals.[11]

As chapter 1 also suggests, stories for and images of children in some ways perpetuated and even reinforced the racial and class hierarchies that lay at the heart of Jim Crow politics. Yet these stories and images also directly countered the stereotypes of blacks that whites used to preserve the nation's racialized political order. While most whites wanted white and black children to grow up thinking of themselves as fundamentally different from each other, the idealized photographs of black children that commonly appeared in black newspapers gave young blacks an image of themselves that correlated with the dominant cultural values of the day. Books and stories that African Americans (and some white advocates) created especially for children similarly defied the stereotypes and pseudoscientific propaganda that whites used to keep blacks of all ages in their place.

Civil rights activists throughout the twentieth century used widespread ideas about childhood and images of children to create public and political sympathy and support for the movement. But such images were also part of a consistent strategy to create positive race consciousness and support for civil rights among young people, especially young blacks. Favorable images of blacks, whether in the form of photographs of black children or books for children, promoted racial pride and the cause of racial equality among youth. They also proved to whites that blacks embraced middle-class values. In his study of the civil rights movement in Mississippi, Charles Payne explains that keeping the story before the children, or providing young people with clear examples of dignity and resistance to racism, played an important part in their activism. Early black freedom leaders seem to have reached the same conclusion.[12]

CREATING FUTURE RACE LEADERS: CHILDREN AND THE EARLY NAACP

Efforts by African Americans, as one literary theorist puts it, "to influence and perhaps control the future destiny of the culture" through young people's literature increased during the Harlem Renaissance. In 1920, W. E. B. Du Bois and the NAACP expanded the practice of designating children's pages in black newspapers and periodicals such as The Crisis by creating a separate magazine for black children. *The Brownies' Book*, Du Bois explained, was "designed . . . to be a thing of joy and beauty . . . and emulation . . . for all children, but especially for *ours*." Like Johnson's earlier magazine for black children, its pages countered the usual stereotypes of African Americans found in mainstream children's literature and featured stories that showed the moral, cultured, refined, and heroic sides of black life. This journal, however, was primarily political, not religious. It informed its young readers about notable historic and current events significant to African American life and domestic and international politics through features such as Du Bois's column, "As the Crow Flies." Such features connected young African Americans directly to politics and gave them a broader context for understanding and evaluating local and national affairs by recounting, for example, information about what was happening among India's "brown people," celebrations for returning black World War I regiments, antilynching conferences, the Irish independence movement, anti-Jewish pogroms in Russia and Eastern Europe, industrial strikes across the nation, and race riots in Washington, Omaha, Chicago, Texas, and Arkansas.[13]

More pointedly, *The Brownies' Book* tried to interest children in the NAACP's mission and work. Although financial difficulties led to its discontinuance after only two years, this attempt by what was quickly becoming the foremost civil rights organization suggests that race leaders attached considerable importance to the place of youth in the struggle for racial equality. They saw that one of the best ways to advance the race was to inform black children about racial issues, encourage them to emulate the examples of black leaders, both past and present, and to recruit them for civil rights work. After *The Brownies' Book* folded, *The Crisis* continued to publish material specifically for children through a monthly "Little Page" section and in 1929 began featuring a "Youthport" section (also fairly short-lived) that included information about NAACP junior council activities as well as literary pieces. The NAACP also campaigned to rid public libraries and schools of racist materials and to compile bibliographies of books deemed suitable reading for African American youth. During this period, notable black writers such as Arna Bontemps and Langston Hughes published children's books. Those involved in these projects clearly recognized what literary scholars and historians would later discover—that most children's literature mirrored the dominant culture of the period and that mainstream culture offered few positive words about African Americans.

Like southern whites determined to provide their children with images of blacks that perpetuated the status quo, African American activists and writers understood the impact and potential impact of reading materials on young minds, which controlled the future.[14]

As with antislavery advocates, adults in the early-twentieth-century movement for racial equality saw children and youth as important agents of change. But they, too, envisioned children and youth playing a primarily passive role. Literary scholar Katharine Capshaw Smith suggests that race leaders' attitudes toward young blacks shifted during the 1910s and 1920s. For her, the fact that texts increasingly addressed young people directly indicates a growing recognition "that children have power as active social participants." Some of the topics about which Du Bois wrote for youth further attest to a growing appreciation for young people's political consciousness. Notwithstanding this development, however, race leaders did not seem especially interested in the power of young people. Rather, they seemed to hope that if youth read positive stories about members of their race, learned about their history, and studied racial issues, they would become active civil rights workers when they got older. The NAACP encouraged black children to submit writings for association publications and rather vaguely to use their positive self- and race consciousness to do something for black Americans. As one typical poem, "To a Brown Boy," advised,

'Tis a noble gift to be brown, all brown,
Like the strongest things that make up the earth,
Like the mountains grave and grand,
Even like the very land,
Even like the trunks of trees —
Even oaks, to be like these!
God builds His strength in bronze . . .
Eagles are of this same hue . . .
I have mighty things to do.

Addressed specifically to a boy, even though it would have been read by both boys and girls, this poem suggests gendered notions of citizenship and race leadership. It also implies that children have "mighty things to do" in the future, not the present. Beliefs that children and youth were important mainly as future political actors dominated much of the reading material produced for black children in the first decades of the twentieth century. Those beliefs also dominated the NAACP's early organizational stance toward young people. Indeed, not until the 1930s did the organization recognize that youth could offer significantly more than future workers and leadership for the race.[15]

When it launched the "Youthport" section for young people in 1929, *The Crisis* explained that the association had "long had a Junior Division" with the object "to teach its members the history and achievements of the Negro race, to familiarize them with the lives of distinguished men and women that the race has produced, and to cultivate in them an appreciation of their worth; to develop inter-racial co-operation and understanding, and to train them in the work of the Association." As one young person speaking from the perspective of "Youthport" described its intentions and those of junior work in general, "I am going to try to instill in them, that because their face is black is not sufficient reason why they are not entitled to their rights." The junior division officially included young people between the ages of fourteen and twenty-one. However, much younger children joined as well. Junior members elected their own officers but worked under the guidance of the local adult branch and the adult director appointed for youth work. The NAACP primarily encouraged its young members to develop a positive sense of themselves and their race and to learn about the organization so that one day they would become full members and perhaps even leaders. That status would come only, as director of branches Robert Bagnall put it, "when this generation passes."[16]

Oratorical contests were one way the NAACP encouraged elementary through high school children to study "intensively and extensively . . . Negro History and Art." Those contests, however, often fulfilled a dual purpose for the association and indicated another important role that young people played in the early civil rights movement. The association could charge parents and community members money to observe how much their children had learned about their race and how articulate they had become on issues such as Negro patriotism and segregation. Many NAACP youth groups held speech contests and produced musical and dramatic programs, generally centered on racial themes. Such activities cultivated a positive sense of racial identification in youth; prepared them to challenge racial inequality by giving them experience in public speaking, discussion, and debate; and raised significant funds for other NAACP work. As these activities suggest, the NAACP also expected young people, in the words of one national leader, to "give entertainments for the Association." NAACP-

sponsored baby contests similarly entertained, promoted race pride, and
were one of the "easiest . . . quickest and cheapest way[s] to raise a large
amount of money." Junior members also raised money and showed their
commitment to civil rights by selling subscriptions to *The Crisis* and NAACP
Christmas seals.[17]

Junior members during this period also "helped" with adult work. What
exactly that meant other than distributing leaflets and ushering at meetings is unclear. The NAACP did use young people to raise money and clearly
considered "extending the influence of the Association . . . guiding the
child thought toward organization . . . getting them interested early in
life" so that "some of them may develop into excellent workers" as critical
to the cause of racial equality. The association, however, did not seem to
have a distinct sense of children and young people as important political
actors and civil rights workers while they remained young. There was no
official manual or yearly program outlining the work of junior divisions.
And considerable confusion arose about what young members should do,
who should be allowed to join junior divisions, how those divisions were
organized, and their relationship to senior branches. The NAACP's national
office was also confused about where junior divisions existed.[18]

That the NAACP lacked a clear program of action for young people and
instead talked about the importance of socializing children into the ideas
and work of the organization reflected prevailing attitudes toward children. Most child-centered institutions and organizations during the first
decades of the twentieth century considered socialization a one-way process. Schools and juvenile courts, youth recreation programs, and child-
centered urban reform efforts assumed that young people exercised little
agency and could simply be molded by proper environment, training, example, and adult organization and supervision into good Americans who
embodied dominant cultural values.[19] Experts increasingly regarded childhood and youth as important periods in an individual's growth and development, but child-rearing manuals stressed that parents, teachers, or other
adults involved with young people should strictly control that growth and
development.[20] *The Crisis* captured this way of thinking about childhood
with a 1919 article that reminded readers not to lose "precious time" in
"systematically" training "the little . . . unfolding mind."[21]

That article, however, also acknowledged that children and youth sometimes stepped out of the more passive role that most adults envisioned
for them. "Blockheads," and less dense parents, it humorously asserted,

should remember that children have a will of their own and that adults should take care to train but not to "kill the spirit of the little man." And indeed, even in the 1920s, black children and youth defied the expectations of the NAACP and most adults in the movement, who regarded junior councils only as a training ground for real civil rights work. In 1924, for example, more than 125 children and youth formed the Harriet Tubman Junior Division in Detroit. "The young people of Detroit are active and have hope to stir up things around here for the NAACP," their adult leader, Beulah Young, told the NAACP national office. How exactly they intended to "stir things up" is not altogether clear. Detroit youth members engaged in the usual kinds of NAACP junior branch activities: they discussed black history and current events and put on plays. Some youth members apparently were also involved with riots about housing segregation during the volatile summer of 1925. Whatever its activities, the group numbered more than two thousand members, and Young suggested that all 500 junior members age sixteen and older pay full membership fees and transfer to the senior branch. Partly because of internal dissent, the adult branch in Detroit had "been steadily going down," and she and others thought that the young members would provide "a strong working force" to renew the group's activities. Although some young people resisted the move, at least 350 pledged to transfer, while the remainder planned to continue their activities in the junior division. Youth, it seemed, wanted to be active in the cause of racial equality and could possibly serve as present — not just future — leaders in that cause as well.[22]

Despite the enthusiasm of young NAACP members, civil rights activism in Detroit seems to have fizzled rather than taken off. Records suggest problems among adult leaders in Detroit's senior division and tensions between adult and youth members over tactics and programs (or the lack thereof). Later conflicts between adult and youth branches throughout the nation, including Detroit, indicate that adults did not always appreciate the contributions of young people or take full advantage of their enthusiasm and activism. Moreover, adults sometimes saw youth members and branches as rivals instead of as partners in the cause of racial equality. Whether Detroit's adult members "killed their spirit" or something else happened, the potential for action and influence that Young saw in the youth with whom she worked apparently was not immediately realized. Yet despite this seeming failure, by late 1929 another "group of young people of talent and ability" "resurrected" the junior division, planned an "ambitious program," and made Detroit a center for youth work.[23]

THE ENTHUSIASM OF YOUNG PEOPLE: NAACP YOUTH COUNCILS IN THE 1930S

In the early 1930s, at least partly because of the grassroots efforts and enthusiasm of young people, the NAACP nationwide began to recognize young people's potential in the movement and to establish a more coherent program of action for them. In 1931, Bagnall wrote to the association's executive secretary, Walter White, to criticize the "middle-aged" character of most NAACP branches and outlined a tentative program to recruit "young people [and to] give full play to their activities." His proposal included activities traditionally associated with junior councils—debates, performances, entertainments, and fund-raising—and suggested that the association make a special effort to organize older "youth" as well as children. These older youth, NAACP leaders realized, might significantly aid the cause of racial equality by surveying the treatment of blacks in schools, recreational facilities, restaurants, and shops; assessing employment opportunities; working toward improving those opportunities; and organizing interracial events. Discussions about young people in the movement continued, and in early 1933, White approached the association's board of directors about the need for a "definite program for activity by Junior Branches." All too often, he remarked, "faithful, but elderly" NAACP members "discourage initiative on the part of young people." Meanwhile, he warned, "other activities and movements are occupying the attention of young people and gaining their support." The following year, White requested the cooperation of the Philadelphia branch (which had an active group of junior members) "in trying a laboratory experiment" with a youth program. "It seems to us at the National Office," he told branch president Charles Dorsey, "that one of the chief weaknesses of the NAACP is that we have never had the time, funds, or personnel to work out an adequate program for junior branches and for students in high schools and colleges." White and other leaders believed that the time had come to turn that weakness into a strength.[24]

Increased nationwide attention to the problems and issues of youth during the 1930s partly accounts for the NAACP's increased attention to its programs for young people. During the Great Depression, "youth" became a significant if somewhat ambiguous political category. In the early decades of the twentieth century, Progressive-era reformers turned their attention to the plight of America's young people, and psychologist G. Stanley Hall introduced the idea that adolescence was a significant category of human development. But not until the 1930s did public and private agencies really began to think of the problems and concerns of young people in their teens and twenties as unique and deserving of special and separate consideration from those of adults or young children. Not coincidently, many of the "problems of youth" that organizations such as the American Youth Commission addressed correlated with the NAACP youth programs' focus. For example, the commission and other groups made considerable efforts in the 1930s to assess and improve youth employment, recreation, and educational opportunities. At the same time, public and private agencies and reformers opened a national debate on educational inequalities, the outright absence of high school facilities for many of the nation's youth, and the question of federal aid for education. The availability of public and private grants to support programs for young people also suggests increased attention to youth issues and, since the NAACP worked to take advantage of these funding opportunities, an additional incentive or means for the association to develop a stronger youth organization.[25]

As White's memo suggests, the NAACP's increased interest in youth was also partly motivated by fear that other organizations, especially communist organizations, were winning young blacks' support and loyalty. NAACP leaders recognized that if they did not take advantage of the energy of black youth, someone else would. "There is the need for more activity and more aggressiveness on the part of our branches if we are to hold our own in competition with the Communists," one NAACP leader urged. In the mid-1930s, White worried that other organizations were "irretrievably [winning] the enthusiasm of . . . young people." "Young people today are thinking more deeply and intelligently about race and other problems than at any other time," he commented. And the "NAACP cannot hope to continue to function, or even to exist, nor has it any right to demand that it be permitted to continue in existence, unless there is constantly being added to it new blood, new ideas, new enthusiasm and new workers."[26]

The Scottsboro Boys case also confirmed the NAACP's "chief weakness" and helped convince the association to create a strong youth program. The NAACP had initially refused to represent the boys, whereas the Communist Party had defended them in court and encouraged the nation's youth to rally on their behalf. Young blacks realized that "any young negro [was] in danger of becoming another Scottsboro boy" and came out in unprecedented numbers to participate in mass meetings and demonstrations on behalf of the boys. Such actions demonstrated that youth could be significant political actors in their own right and that the more militant rhetoric and tactics of leftist groups appealed to them. The case may also have indicated to the NAACP that if it wanted mass support from the black community, it had to appeal to black youth, address their concerns, and adopt some of the more direct-action strategies that communist and labor groups already used. Scholars have emphasized the NAACP's initial inability to see the Scottsboro case outside of the organization's class biases and the time and effort wasted in the subsequent fight between the NAACP and the Communist Party for control of the boys' defense. These are certainly important aspects of the case. But Scottsboro points not just to the NAACP's failure to see across class lines but also to the association's failure to see the problems and potential activism of youth across class lines. As a 1924 article in *The Crisis* makes clear, the association only rarely even attempted to reach out to "other [lower] classes" of black youth. Widespread youth demonstrations in the wake of the Scottsboro Boys case plainly showed the NAACP that young blacks needed and wanted more than a positive sense of themselves and their race and that young people could do more—and wanted to do more—than give speeches and sell newspapers. On one level, the struggle for control of the Scottsboro case reflected a larger fight between the two organizations for control of black youth, a fight over which group best represented not only the interests of nine particular black boys but also all black youth in America.[27]

If the NAACP felt threatened by the Communist Party's eagerness to take up the cause of young African Americans and to use their energy to influence political and social change, young people themselves demonstrated (literally) that they were ready for change and wanted to take action. Historian Robert Cohen describes the growth of student movements, often leftist-oriented, in the early 1930s. He finds that in contrast to the apolitical spirit of university campuses during the 1920s, students across the nation were taking action on a variety of issues, including racial inequality, by the middle of the following decade. NAACP leaders witnessed the increasing political activism among college students and mass protests by black youth on behalf of the Scottsboro Boys. In addition, officials saw black and white youth coming together to address racial issues through a variety of forums, including the National Negro Congress, Southern Negro Youth Congress, National Student League, American Youth Congress, American Student Union, League of Young Southerners, Council of Young Southerners, YWCA and YMCA, and other religious organizations as well as smaller, local youth groups such as Baltimore's City-Wide Young People's Forum. These and other youth-centered organizations worked to expand citizenship rights and equal opportunities for African Americans through a wide range of often militant activities, among them boycotts, pickets, union organizing, voter registration campaigns, job training programs, the circulation of letters and petitions, and protests against police and mob violence, white primaries, and poll taxes and in favor of expanding cultural, recreational, and educational opportunities. The efforts of these organizations and similar work by youth around the globe (not coincidentally, in the summer of 1936, young people from thirty-six countries met in Geneva, Switzerland, for the first World Youth Congress) did not go unnoticed by the NAACP, the U.S. government, or young people. Articles in *The Crisis*, many written by youth, frequently reported on the work of student groups and conferences. They talked about student delegates going to India, interracial student meetings in Florida, YWCA forums in Mississippi, and National Student League Conferences. Articles also celebrated youth militancy. One, for example, described how black youth picketed the National Crime Conference because organizers refused to address the crime of lynching. Young people as well as adult NAACP leaders repeatedly noted that young people were eager for action and for cross-race alliances. "There is definitely a world youth movement," affirmed one young member in a speech at the NAACP's 1936 annual conference.[28]

The national NAACP office also received letters from extant junior councils pressuring them to develop a clear and dynamic program and "urgent requests" from college students for a youth organization designed to take advantage of a full range of "techniques of action." As Juanita Jackson, the NAACP's first youth director, explained, "Appeals have come from students all over the country. . . . [T]he Association has sensed the growing awareness of Negro youth to the problems which face them and their increasing desire to become a part of movements which are attempting to do something about them." In response, in March 1936 the NAACP introduced a new set of objectives and a national program for youth councils. Partly developed by young people and headed by Jackson, a recent college graduate,

NAACP Youth Secretary Juanita Jackson (fourth from left) and the Scottsboro Boys, 1937. Jackson's visit demonstrated the NAACP's commitment to the problems of the nine boys and all black youth. (Courtesy National Association for the Advancement of Colored People Records, Library of Congress, Prints and Photographs Division, LC-USZ62–116731)

former junior council member, and the leader of Baltimore's direct-action-oriented City-Wide Young People's Forum, the program greatly expanded the official role of young people in the black freedom movement and reflected an increased appreciation for their interests and activism.[29]

The NAACP directed its new program to young people between the ages of sixteen and twenty-five, a slightly older cohort than the junior councils. As before, however, both older and younger youth and even very young children joined. The association's age grouping reflected public and private officials' and researchers' tendency to define "youth" as young people in their teens and early twenties. The NAACP quickly began differentiating between "youth councils" and "college chapters," but in many ways those categories were more of an organizational than an ideological or experiential differentiation. In organizing youth, NAACP officials perceived that young people, whether they were fourteen or twenty-four, shared similar interests and ideas about civil rights issues and strategies and fewer constraints to keep them from acting on those ideas (as SNCC and Congress of Racial Equality (CORE) activists discovered when junior high and high school youth became the first to respond to the groups' organizing efforts in the early 1960s).

Like earlier NAACP programs, the association's new program sought to help young blacks develop a positive race consciousness and to guide them toward a lifelong commitment to NAACP work. But unlike previous programs, this one also asked youth to work toward specific civil rights goals. Not surprisingly, both because of the association's long-standing efforts to end lynching and young people's response to the Scottsboro Boys case, antilynching became an early nucleus for NAACP youth work. The NAACP also encouraged youth council members to campaign against other racialized political, economic, and social problems, such as racial injustices in the courts, Jim Crow practices, negative racial stereotypes in advertising, and debt peonage among sharecroppers and tenant farmers. The association suggested that youth work toward equal educational and employment opportunities and the right to vote. And, both recognizing and anticipating young people's opportunities and inclination for interracial work, NAACP youth leaders directed young members to pursue activities and forums for interracial cooperation in their communities. Moreover, unlike the earlier junior councils, which encouraged youth to learn about the association primarily so that they would later become adult members and race leaders, the new youth councils aimed, at least ostensibly, to develop "an intelligent, militant youth leadership."[30]

The NAACP instructed youth councils to achieve their objectives through a wide-ranging program of activities. Organizational materials counseled young people to "study and discuss" before taking action on racial issues but made clear that learning and talking about issues should be considered preparatory to further action and not become an end in itself. Correspondence outlining the national program charged, "Your youth council must be a center of *education, cooperation,* and *action.*" And Jackson told young members, "Remember, it is not enough to awaken; it is not enough to understand. We must act—and act now!" National youth program guidelines encouraged members to use their knowledge to conduct forums, hold mass meetings and rallies, organize Youth Consumers' Cooperatives and "buy where you can work campaigns," to create and distribute "dramatic" leaflets. An understanding of racial issues, the guidelines indicated, would help young members more effectively protest the absence of blacks on juries and police brutality, lobby and petition for antilynching legislation, direct voter registration drives, question political candidates on racial issues, circulate information on civil rights test cases, and publicize instances of racial injustice. National leaders recommended

THE YOUTH ORGANIZING TRADITION

we've been drafted for active duty by the

NAACP!

NAACP recruitment advertisement. The association used ideas about childhood to solicit support and to suggest that young people had an important role to play in the black freedom struggle. (Courtesy National Association for the Advancement of Colored People Records, Library of Congress, Prints and Photographs Division, LC-USZ62–118184) that young people study and address local issues and adapt the NAACP's national youth program to the local community context. Officials also instructed young members to take racial issues outside of their communities and into the national spotlight, a directive that members of Harlem's NAACP youth council exemplified in 1937 when they joined with white youth organizations to press for antilynching legislation by picketing in Times Square.[31]

The NAACP's more diverse and active youth program recognized that young people's enthusiasm, vigor, and fearlessness often stood in stark contrast to the "apathetic attitude of many adults." One program guide remarked that the new youth organization aimed to cultivate in "youth members a sense of their importance and worthwhileness" to the NAACP. "Developing constant activities" kept young people busy with civil rights work. Expanding the youth section of The Crisis made young people aware of what other youth groups were doing, spread ideas, and helped youth feel that they were a central part of an aggressive movement for change. Making concrete and attainable goals — for example, getting one hundred thousand youth to participate in a nationwide demonstration or organizing three hundred new youth councils during the next year — encouraged a "sense of destiny" among youth. A youth slogan, conferences, and "periodic nation-wide activities" stimulated a "sense of comradeship and national solidarity." And giving youth "a voice and representation in the creation and development of their national youth program" fostered a sense that their ideas mattered and that the youth council really was their organization. Although in the decades that followed young people would question whether the NAACP recognized fully their agency and potential, the association clearly made a considerable effort in the 1930s to expand its youth program and benefit from young people's desire to participate actively in the struggle for racial equality.[32]

NAACP youth programs after the mid-1930s also suggest that the association, often criticized for its primarily legalistic and conservative strategies, used a wide range of protest strategies, some substantially more confrontational than those traditionally associated with the organization. Even activities designed to support NAACP legal work often took on a militant quality in the hands of youth. While adults in the NAACP prepared legal briefs, raised money, and lobbied for new legislation, youth members held street demonstrations to publicize NAACP legal cases and protest unjust court decisions or questionable criminal charges against blacks. Historians have noted that in the 1930s, the NAACP used direct-action strategies to aid in its long-standing campaign for federal antilynching legislation.[33] Significantly, primarily youth councils and college chapters used direct-action techniques in those campaigns. Although reluctant to fully embrace direct action, the NAACP officially incorporated militant techniques into its program for young people. Perhaps not surprisingly, given what scholars have identified as the association's moderate tendencies, the inclusion of direct action and other more militant elements in the NAACP's national youth program often originated in suggestions from young people themselves. For example, a youth delegate to the advisory committee for the youth section proposed in 1936 that the NAACP sponsor an annual national youth demonstration against lynching. The advisory committee, partly composed of youth members, approved his idea as well as a resolution adopted by youth at that year's national conference calling for youth members to wear black armbands and arrange for local churches "to observe a moment of silent prayer . . . every time a lynching occurred." At that same meeting, likely because of widespread interest in direct action but also because she was a veteran youth activist who had engaged in picketing, boycotts, and mass meetings in the early 1930s, Jackson suggested that youth councils conduct rallies to support the NAACP education program, the association's current legal cases, and black youth who were victims of injustice. A youth delegate then proposed "that we have a Negro challenge segregation statutes and refuse to ride Jim Crow"; for practical reasons, however, such protests should occur only in areas with no danger of lynching. Both proposals passed.[34]

Most accounts of the civil rights movement associate the use of non-violent direct-action strategies with the late 1950s and 1960s when the Montgomery Bus Boycott, Freedom Rides, and sit-ins captured media and public attention. The youth protests of that period, however, did not reflect so much an entirely new energy and activism on the part of youth as they did a long tradition of youth activism that began during the 1930s when young people first engaged in direct action to challenge America's racial politics. Historians, however, have not fully explored the tradition of youth activism that began during that period.[35] That lack of attention can be attributed in part to the "failures" of those direct-action campaigns. Protests by young people during the 1930s and 1940s did not result in federal legislation for civil rights or the end of segregation in America. Yet their campaigns were significant. In some communities, black youth ended racial stereotyping in advertising and won new employment and recreational opportunities. Some communities even integrated theaters, restaurants, auditoriums, and unions. The Muskogee, Oklahoma, youth council stopped a radio commercial that played "Alabama Coon." The Gary, Indiana, youth council secured jobs for more than thirty-five young blacks with a "Buy Where You Can Work Campaign," ended "the practice of 'short weighting' in the stores," and opened school athletic competitions to Negro schools. Young members in Cincinnati won higher wages for black Works Progress Association workers and integrated New Deal recreational projects. And in New York, the Albany youth council put an end to derogatory pictures of blacks in local newspapers, while the Rochester council worked to break racist employment policies at Eastman Kodak. Young people's efforts to survey, publicize, and protest the grossly unequal conditions of black education helped make educational inequality an important and compelling public issue in the late 1930s and 1940s, a problem that the Supreme Court later became moved to remedy. Their efforts occasionally brought immediate improvements in black educational opportunities, such as transportation allowances and high schools for black students. And youth-led voter registration campaigns, such as the one conducted by the Greenville, South Carolina, youth council, were so challenging to the racial politics of the day that local police arrested and jailed the group's teenage president, William Anderson, on false charges. If historians have not taken seriously the activism of young people during the 1930s, white southerners did not make the same mistake.[36]

Youth activism also helped to reconstruct the social drama of lynching. As historian Grace Elizabeth Hale explains, early-twentieth-century southern whites used the "spectacle of lynching" to tell "a story of the entire white community in action . . . to protect southern 'civilization.'" But in the 1930s, the NAACP "shattered" this "narrative frame" by circulating detailed accounts that explained lynching as a story of white southern injustice instead of black bestiality.[37] Young people played a significant role in this transformation. Indeed, the NAACP's efforts to reframe lynching would likely have been less effective if not for the counterspectacles that young people staged. Mass demonstrations by well-dressed youth wearing black armbands turned lynching into a story of southern injustice and, perhaps more important, of respectable young black men and women acting to protect victims of white terrorism. That young women, including young white women, as well as young men demonstrated against lynching further challenged the white South's story that lynching protected pure white womanhood. In the same years that black youth began direct-action campaigns to end lynching, African American writer Richard Wright published a collection of short stories in which all of the characters represent a new type of Negro: they talk back and defy segregation, and "their spontaneous reaction is no longer to cringe, but to fight." Black youth in the NAACP seemed to be of the same type, and their demonstrations helped transform lynching incidents from a means of intimidation into a platform for militant protest.[38]

MILITANCY IN THE MOVEMENT

Direct action by youth in the 1930s also redrew the boundaries of acceptable civil rights activity. Scholars frequently note that the NAACP tended toward conservatism. For the leading civil rights organization, that conservatism had important consequences for the direction and pace of civil rights work. But, as historian Peter Lau has recently argued, "There was never a single NAACP." Lau's work on the movement in South Carolina clearly demonstrates that local branches, often through young members' actions and ideas, helped make the association a more responsive mass organization. The NAACP created a space for negotiation and militant civil rights protest in its youth program. By designing youth councils and college chapters that embraced direct action instead of redirecting the entire association toward more militant strategies, the NAACP legitimated those strategies without alienating its older, generally more moderate base of support. In 1937, White wrote an article on the role of the association's youth program in which he recognized the NAACP's moderate nature and expressed hope that young people would move the association in new directions: "The youth council will bring new life and new energy into the whole organization. The young people feel that the older people want to continue doing things the way they have always done them. The young people would like to try a different way." White explained that the constitution for the new youth program provided a way that young people could directly influence the whole branch by giving youth leaders and their adviser a place on the executive committee. He further clarified that youth participation on the committee should not be restricted to youth issues because it was "important for the young people . . . to bring the point of view of their age group to all the problems of the branch."[39]

THE YOUTH ORGANIZING TRADITION

Not all of the association's young people wanted to push the movement in new directions, and those who did were often disappointed that many adult members resisted new viewpoints, young people's energy, and different ways of doing things. The friction that arose between senior NAACP branches and youth councils certainly attests to the association's continuing conservatism. But conflicts between adult and youth members also suggest the relative militancy of young people within the association. Moreover, those conflicts indicate that although it was not an uncontested space, youth councils provided a space for young people, usually more open to new ideas than their elders, to come together and explore civil rights issues and strategies, to express their discontent with mainstream approaches, and sometimes to challenge more moderate elements within the organization. African American writer Louis Lomax has lamented that no one seriously or openly challenged the NAACP until 1958, believing that the lack of meaningful debate on civil rights work stymied the development of a more dynamic civil rights movement. Lomax's observations about the importance of debate and the NAACP's position as the uncontested leader of civil rights activities suggest that the internal debates between youth and senior branches may have been especially significant to the development of the black freedom struggle.[40]

After the mid-1930s, NAACP youth groups engaged in frequent and sometimes heated conflicts with adult leaders. Correspondence between branches and national leaders almost routinely mentioned "the friction that arises from time to time in the youth councils and the senior branches." In 1937, the youth council in Richmond, Virginia, commented in its first newsletter that "many youth councils have complained that there is a lack of cooperation from the senior branches." Although the youth editors said they were "glad to report this is not true with the Richmond Chapter," they also expressed hope that their newsletter and the "recent conference and the part Youth played in it" would "make a lasting impression not only on our own group but on the Adult Group. Too long," their article continued, "we have been criticized for inadequacy, incompetency and having an impulse to go headlong without thinking. . . . This has long been a false accusation which we truly hope to change."[41]

Young people's willingness to consider and act on ideas and strategies that senior members considered too radical resulted in similar and even more serious "false accusations" on a number of occasions. In 1941, national leaders received correspondence from James McClendon, president of the Detroit senior branch, that claimed that the city's youth councils had misused funds, had reported interorganizational conflict to the press, had tried to take control of the executive committee, and were "being influenced by outside left-winged organizations." In the investigation that followed, however, it became clear to national youth administrative assistant Edward Swan that McClendon's statement that youth members "resent our 'fogie' ideas . . . and 'general do nothing' program" was more accurate than any of his other charges. Swan noted in his report, "There is a very decided gap between youth council and senior branch thinking. . . . [T]he senior branch is ultra conservative while the youth council is ultra liberal. Lack of understanding has been somewhat accentuated because the senior branch continues to consider the Youth as immature, reckless, and unreliable; the youth council feels that the senior branch is conservative, slow and inactive on vital issues." Swan worried that under present circumstances, the relative inactivity and "autocratic control of the senior branch" would discourage youth members from transferring to that branch at the appropriate age, make association youth "good prey for extreme left-wing groups," and lead Detroit's entire NAACP organization to "die as a result of internal diseases." Swan suggested that the situation would improve if more democratic and responsive leadership developed in the senior branch and if it became "as active as the youth councils." Rather than siding with conservative elements in the branch, national leaders recognized that the city's youth council played a valuable role in opening discussion on civil rights issues and stimulating a more dynamic civil rights program.[42]

As in Detroit, conflict between NAACP youth councils and senior branches often arose because of "wide differences in . . . thinking" between the two groups. Senior members feared youth members' tendency toward radical ideas and strategies, and young people in the association resented the conservatism of their elders. Adults who felt threatened by the militant ideas and techniques of young people commonly dismissed their ideas by raising questions about youth members' lack of maturity and experience or by accusing them of being controlled by leftist groups. Some youth council members were indeed communists, and communists regarded NAACP youth councils, as they did other youth groups, as a good place to spread their influence. One 1940s directive pointedly declared, "The Party must recruit young people. . . . [T]he Communist Party needs the idealism, enthusiasm and energy that is characteristic of youth." The memo further identified Negro youth as the communists' "most important ally" and insisted that "every effort" should be made "to win them into activity." Finally, the document singled out NAACP youth councils as the "most important" Negro youth organization. Even so, adults in the association who wanted to discourage any militant civil rights activity often misrepresented communist numbers and influence in youth councils. For example, in 1947, one Flint, Michigan, adult leader accused the youth council of communist infiltration. After investigating the matter, national leaders concluded that no infiltration had occurred. Instead, it appeared that the youth council's "all out campaign against violations of the State's Civil Rights Law" simply challenged the status of adults in the organization and the senior branch's more conservative tactics.[43]

That campaign also exemplified how, long before Greensboro, young people in the NAACP fought Jim Crow with both direct action and other techniques. As part of its campaign, the Flint youth council initiated legal action against a skating rink owner who was violating Michigan's civil rights statutes. When the threat of legal action did not motivate the rink's owner to integrate, youth organizers sent interracial teams of young people to seek admittance. They also distributed leaflets, picketed the rink, and solicited the support of sympathetic groups, some of which were leftist, to help with direct-action activities. Perhaps just as significant as the protest activity of these youth was the national association's response to it. Instead of discouraging such militant activities, national NAACP leaders affirmed that "the Flint youth council does have a good program against racial discrimination" and that "the chief cause of the difficulty" was the "jealousy" of one adult leader and the general lack of cooperation and trust between the two groups. As in the Detroit case, the national office supported and even "congratulated" and expressed "abiding faith" in these militant efforts. Although such strategies generated fear among more conservative members and made them vulnerable to charges of communism, at least some youth councils did exactly as NAACP leaders had hoped, revitalizing the struggle for racial equality.[44]

Of course, not all national leaders supported all the militant activities of young people in the association. Youth director Ruby Hurley, for one, resisted members at the 1945 national youth conference at Wilberforce who attempted to pass controversial resolutions calling for youth action on the "opening of Palestine [to Jews fleeing Europe after World War II], the ousting of American troops from China, . . . withdrawal of English troops from Indonesia [and] Compulsory Military Training." According to the president of the New York City youth council, Clinton Henry Lewis, Hurley "voiced a 'dynamic' opposition" to their efforts at the conference and effectively blocked all mention of these politically charged resolutions in youth council materials and association press releases. In letters to both Hurley and White, Lewis expressed his belief in the NAACP's potential: "I see the organization as a dynamic institution taking the Negro towards political, economic, and social maturity. I see it as a bastion against reaction and a leader in the people's movements towards one world democracy." But Lewis warned that with Hurley more interested in "'Old Ladies Tea Conventions' and 'Debating Parties'" than anything constructive, and with the association generally "in the arms of abject complacency and degenerate indifference," those potentialities were not being met. As Lewis saw it, youth were committed to a more dynamic civil rights movement, and young people could lift the NAACP "from its present fascist-like and reactionary position" and create "a more progressive National Association."[45]

Despite his energy and convictions, Lewis apparently lost his battle with Hurley and resigned his position as youth council president. But his frustration with the association's unwillingness to take a militant stand on controversial (and perhaps peripheral) political issues and its suppression of young people's efforts to take action on those issues attests not only to the NAACP's conservatism but also to the relative militancy of young people within the organization and suggests that youth councils, college chapters, and national youth conferences provided young people with important forums for exploring issues and strategies, some of which conflicted with what many adults saw as the NAACP's proper direction. It also suggests that young people had a sense that they could shift the association's direction, that at least some young people regarded youth councils as a place from which to fight NAACP conservatism, and that the association had to consider and respond to young people's sometimes-radical ideas. Moreover, Lewis and the young people with whom he worked were likely more successful in their efforts to reshape the civil rights movement than they imagined. Not only did they help build traditions of youth activism and youth protest against conservatism within the NAACP, but they helped fashion new leadership. Gloster Current, a former youth council member, the coordinator for Detroit-area youth councils, and the adviser who helped Lewis and the other youth delegates at Wilberforce draft their resolutions, became director of branches shortly after this incident. From that position, Current remained a strong advocate of youth action, even youth militancy. Although elements within the association often resisted youth action, the NAACP perhaps unintentionally facilitated the influence of more militant ideas on its work in particular and on the movement in general by creating a strong program for young people and allowing a place for radicalism within the association's ranks.[46]

YOUTH AND THE GROWTH OF THE MOVEMENT

Young people's influence on the association grew during the 1940s as the NAACP expanded its program for young people. Although certainly part of a larger effort to broaden association membership, attention to recruiting youth members during World War II and the postwar period stands out. In 1941, the NAACP had 55 youth councils and 14 college chapters. By 1945, those figures had reached 200 and 33, respectively, and included numerous councils in the Deep South states of Louisiana, Florida, Georgia, South Carolina, and Alabama. Moreover, some councils had memberships in the hundreds and even thousands. The Knoxville, Tennessee, group, for example, had 1,184 members, while the Chattanooga branch had 853, Wilmington, Delaware, had 560, and Savannah, Georgia, had 514. Within another two years, forty-nine college chapters existed, including groups at such prominent Negro colleges as Fisk, Hampton, and Howard and at predominately white institutions including Bucknell, Bryn Mawr, Oberlin, Wayne State, Berkeley, Harvard, Stanford, and Princeton. Many of these councils, especially those in the North, West, and Midwest and on integrated college campuses, were interracial. A college chapter was also created at the University of Texas at Austin, the first all-white southern university to have an NAACP branch. Perhaps not coincidentally, each of these institutions became centers of youth civil rights activism in the late 1950s and 1960s. Other important centers of later youth civil rights activity such as Albany, Georgia, and Greensboro, North Carolina, also established youth councils in the 1940s. By 1951, the NAACP's youth program included 384 youth councils and 85 college chapters representing "nearly every principal city and . . . nearly every major college campus."[47]

As in the 1930s, attention to youth and their problems helped direct the NAACP's resources toward its youth programs. During the 1940s, international events, the seeming rise in juvenile delinquency rates, and evidence

Members of the Charlotte, North Carolina, NAACP youth council and their
adult advisers, 1942. (© Corbis)

of extreme poverty and prejudice among America's young people signaled
disturbing trends. In response, myriad experts and government agencies began to discuss publicly what they regarded as strong connections
among national security, the future of democracy, and the experiences of
America's youth. They warned that prejudice negatively affected personality development, democracy, and crime rates and that national security
demanded that all children in America realize their rights to good mental
and physical health and education.

Given the national attention to the problems of juvenile delinquency
and the NAACP's long-term efforts to encourage positive images of African
Americans and organize young people, it was not surprising that in August 1943, Hurley, newly appointed as the organization's youth director, expressed concern regarding that summer's urban riots. She cautioned youth
leaders and councils that "there were far too many young people between
the ages of 12 and 22 involved . . . not [as] bystanders or on-lookers, but
[as] actual participants." Young blacks, she affirmed, have "the right to object" to their second-class status, "but our protests and demonstrations are
effective only if conducted in an intelligent directed campaign of action."
Supporting the notion of militant youth action while condemning the violence of "frenzied mob[s]," Hurley indicated that the NAACP and its youth

councils needed to mobilize the energy and discontent of youth into more productive channels. Widespread fears about the frustration and rebellion of black youth as well as young people's obvious interest in racial protest led the association to intensify youth organizing efforts in the aftermath of the riots. At that summer's NAACP youth conference, participants discussed projects to "combat juvenile delinquency." Moreover, over the next year, the association organized an additional forty-eight youth councils and eight college chapters. Membership gains between the summer of 1943 and the summer of 1944 appear especially striking when compared to those made the previous year; from the summer of 1942 to summer of 1943, the association added only seven new youth councils and four college chapters.[48]

Many critics of the NAACP's youth program, including former youth members, complained that youth councils focused too much on social and recreational activities and not enough on civil rights action. The level of activism certainly varied by council. But even playing basketball and holding dances, especially since these were ostensibly interracial events, carried political meaning in mid-twentieth-century America. Those activities potentially broke the color line in what segregationists considered some of the most alarming settings. In addition, because juvenile delinquency was regarded as an important political issue, young blacks were seen as particularly prone to delinquent behavior, and appropriate youth recreation and social programs were perceived as vital deterrents, any activity that youth councils and college chapters planned along those lines took on a political cast. Michigan's Communist Party specifically emphasized "the youth-recreation side of the picture" when it evaluated Detroit's 1943 riots. According to those observers, the city's lack of recreational facilities for black youth was a central reason for the riots. And more important, African American leaders, at least confidentially, agreed with this assessment.[49]

The NAACP's social activities directed youthful energy away from riots, delinquency, and communism and toward constructive goals. Those activities challenged negative stereotypes of blacks and threatened Jim Crow. Moreover, the social and recreational focus of many NAACP youth councils sometimes encouraged young people to engage in more overt political action. National debate affirmed the importance of wholesome leisure-time opportunities for youth, Jim Crow practices generally restricted the social and recreational activities of young blacks, and African American youth were frustrated and angry about the racist restrictions that dictated their use of community facilities. In the late 1940s, one ten-year-old African American boy from New York expressed the feelings of many of his peers when he told an interviewer, "I don't like the way colored people look in the movies. They make 'em black, as black as a blackboard with big old thick lips. Sometimes they got on raggedly clothes. The white people look nice. It makes me mad." Other youth complained that they could not sit at lunch counters, were prevented from going on rides at Coney Island, were told they could not play by the river, encountered racism at museums, and got yelled at or attacked when they tried to play in parks, playgrounds, or on the streets. Recreational facilities were one of the most common ways that young people collectively experienced Jim Crow, and many young blacks deeply resented the racism they encountered in leisure-time spaces. Not coincidentally, most youth council direct-action campaigns in the 1940s targeted recreational facilities—theaters, auditoriums, restaurants, swimming pools, skating rinks, zoos, and playgrounds.[50]

If concerns about juvenile delinquency and recreational opportunities for young blacks informed the NAACP's youth program, so did other contemporary ideas about youth. During the 1940s, prominent social scientists, educators, and child welfare agencies engaged in public discussions about the rights of young people in a democratic society, their natural ability to transcend racial barriers, and their roles as leaders in forming a more just and peaceful world. Speakers at NAACP youth conferences affirmed these ideas, which NAACP lawyers later used in the *Brown* case. In 1945, one conference participant addressed the need to destroy damaging stereotypes of blacks and the feasibility of ending race prejudice and school segregation since "children know no prejudice except that handed down to them by parents [and] neighbors." At the same conference, noted black scholar and Wilberforce University president Dr. Charles H. Wesley reflected the thinking of many prominent educators when he told attendees that reorganizing school curricula to emphasize intercultural education and human relations and foster the dignity and worth of all students would help young people build a better world. Youth are "at the head," he asserted, "wherever we find things turning. . . . It is possible for youth to prove the falsehood of race." Other speakers at youth meetings, including notable figures such as First Lady Eleanor Roosevelt and New York black congressman Adam Clayton Powell Jr. similarly highlighted young people's ability to overcome the legacies of the past and play an active role in shaping a new world. Powell pointedly told NAACP youth that although they were not responsible for the current state of world and national affairs, it was their responsibility to "come face to face" with "right and wrong" and to challenge the "status quo." Young people at NAACP conferences readily accepted that responsibility. "We do hope in the future that Negro youth will not be denied a chance to take his rightful place in a democratic society," youth delegates at one conference asserted before pledging themselves "to a continuous fight against the evils of democracy until democracy becomes a reality for all." At another youth conference, delegates pledged "to condemn those who would keep silent in the face of the evils of segregation," declaring, "We will speak out against these undemocratic and un-American practices. We must be heard. We will be heard."[51]

THE WAR OF YOUTH

Scholars of the black freedom movement often describe World War II as a watershed event in the history of the movement, especially for the ways it heightened black Americans' expectations and made apparent the contradictions of American democracy.[52] The war was also a watershed in movement history for the attention it directed toward young people. Questions and fears about national security and the future of democracy led to questions about whether the nation was taking advantage of all its human resources and whether young Americans were growing up to understand and respect democracy or to be cynical and open to authoritarianism and crime. Perhaps more important, discussions of young people's lack of prejudice and their ability to create a more peaceful world dominated national debates about children and the nation's future. Those discussions helped shape a favorable ruling in the *Brown* case as well as the ways the media reported desegregation struggles. Discussions about young people's capacity to effect democratic change and youth's role in challenging the undemocratic elements of American society, however, also influenced the organizing and activism of young people in the 1940s, 1950s, and 1960s.

The militant rhetoric and democratic ideology of World War II and the subsequent cold war and the idea that young people were vital actors in the cause of American democracy shaped civil rights organizing efforts and the fight for racial equality. World War II made continued American racism difficult to excuse and gave rise to "scientific" and popular understandings of youth that justified young people's activism and heightened their ex-

pectations that they could change the world. Throughout the 1940s, young
people were commonly urged, in the words of one advocate, "to insure
the realization of their dreams and ambitions in a world of peace through
political action and political participation." That this particular statement
was made at a 1945 World Youth Week rally further attests to the perceived
importance of youth and their role in world affairs. First organized in the
spring of 1943, World Youth Week was specifically designed to encourage young people to "intensify their efforts . . . to ensure that our future
springs may be filled with happiness and security." In 1943, Congressman
Powell promoted a similar way of thinking when he told young people in
the NAACP that the "war we are fighting is the war of youth," counseling
them to continue their fight against America's fascists, otherwise known
as "crackers." The 1945 youth conference, organized around the theme of
"Youth and the Atomic Age," likewise highlighted the need for American
youth and "the youth of the world to work together . . . to cultivate the
science of human relationships and to make it possible for all people to enjoy the Four Freedoms in One World." A 1945 pamphlet about the NAACP
youth program and that year's youth conference similarly linked foreign
policy objectives and contemporary understandings of young people with
youth action against racism when it explained that the association's youth
program was about "building for total democracy." It also celebrated the
"intensity of youth's activity" and cited youth council antilynching demonstrations, attempts to eliminate segregation in public places, voter registration campaigns, and organizing efforts as especially indicative of young
people's success in building a democratic society. And a 1951 pamphlet
talked about the "Crusade for Freedom" being waged by NAACP youth.
Promoting the idea of militant youth activity against Jim Crow and reiterating the ideas that would soon help outlaw segregation, it asserted: "The
YOUTH OF AMERICA has the greatest stake in the country's future. . . . By
this same token, youth bear the greatest responsibility for the shaping of
America's future course of action. Their sense of fair play and good sports-
manship makes apparent to them the wrongs to which older generations
have grown blind. Through their vigilance, determination, and aggressive
leadership they can lead our country to an effective mending of the flaws
in her democracy."[53]

Ideas about the openness and power of youth and their responsibility
for creating a more democratic world influenced the way young people
thought about themselves. Clinton Henry Lewis certainly saw himself and

the other young people with whom he worked as the vanguard of change. At meetings and conferences, young NAACP members sang songs that affirmed "You've got to be taught to hate and fear" and "There is no task too great for [youth]: No job's too big to do. We shall change the city! Change the State!! And change the nation too!!!" Resolutions passed by youth members at national conferences often reflected both the democratic ideology of the era and young people's sense of mission. At the association's 1943 Emergency War Conference, youth participants militantly declared, "We Negro youth of America, living in a democracy would be traitors to our country and its principles if we ever ceased in our fight for absolute and complete freedom." At another conference, young people similarly resolved to "fight and work" like "our brothers in the armed forces . . . for a world in which all people, regardless of race, creed, or previous condition, shall determine their own destiny—a world in which Indians, Far Easterners, Africans, and Negro Americans, shall be free together with all mankind." And white students at the University of Tennessee called for blacks to be admitted to all university functions, for the school to invite black speakers to campus, and for interracial meetings. One student explained to the university's official student newspaper, "As long as segregation and discrimination exist within our country, we shall never be an effective leader in a world, three-fifths of whose people do not have white skins. We, the students on this campus, can, if we desire, do our share in bringing about a more just social system—a democracy with equal opportunity for all."[54]

Like their 1930s protests, the "fight and work" of young people during the 1940s has been forgotten.[55] During that decade, NAACP youth also desegregated theaters in Indiana, Illinois, and other midwestern states. They picketed Philadelphia Woolworth stores; demonstrated against segregated schools in New York and North Carolina; and integrated swimming pools and skating rinks in Cleveland as well as bowling alleys, unions, and automobile factories in Detroit and excursion steamers elsewhere in Michigan. Youth members broke discriminatory practices in dormitory housing and community services in university towns such as Bloomington, Indiana, and fought discrimination in restaurants, with some victories. Young people also blocked showings of racist films, won leading instead of servant roles for black youth in school productions, and conducted voter registration campaigns in Richmond, Virginia; Savannah, Georgia; Charleston, South

Young NAACP members protesting Texas segregation laws, 1947. (Courtesy National Association for the Advancement of Colored People Records, Library of Congress, Prints and Photographs Division, LC-USZ62-84483)

Carolina; and Birmingham, Alabama. Young people from around the country also passed resolutions on, lobbied for, and conducted letter writing and educational campaigns in support of the extension of social security, federal aid for education, a national health bill, antilynching legislation, fair housing and employment practices, and the elimination of poll taxes. They planned mass rallies, demonstrations, and educational campaigns during Negro History Week, Negro Youth Week, and Brotherhood Week. NAACP youth groups helped the U.S. Children's Bureau with its back-to-school campaign and protested unequal educational facilities and opportunities during National Education Week. Moreover, because experts during the 1940s hailed education, especially intercultural education, as an essential way to fight prejudice and achieve a democratic society, young people and the NAACP regarded many of these activities more as overtly political and potentially challenging to the nation's racial climate and less as simple educational programs. Young people's civil rights activities may not have led to the widespread use of direct action, brought federal civil rights legislation, or ignited the public imagination in the way that later youth protests did. Those activities did, however, break the color line in some areas and, more significantly, perpetuated and expanded a continuous tradition of youth organizing and direct action that had begun in the preceding decade.[56]

The variety and proliferation of youth protests during the 1940s attest to both the expansion of NAACP youth programs and young people's sense of their ability to challenge the undemocratic elements of American society. As the 1940s ended, NAACP officials likely sensed that young people would start to play an even more central role in the nation's struggle for racial equality. At the same time that Thurgood Marshall and other NAACP lawyers prepared their briefs for what would become the historic *Brown* ruling, a ruling that was partly based on ideas about young people and that gave schoolchildren important political roles, the association again reevaluated its youth program. The NAACP rejected a suggestion to simply boost membership numbers and revenues by organizing "Cub Councils" and "Cradle Rolls" (a term commonly used by African Methodist Episcopal Sunday schools) for very young children. Instead, the association moved to discourage adult branches from treating youth councils as subordinate, treatment that NAACP leaders recognized "stymied progressive activity" by youth. The association also planned to develop an even more overtly aggressive youth program. At the 1952 annual conference in Oklahoma City, which became a center of NAACP youth direct-action protest in the late 1950s, association head Roy Wilkins led a discussion on "Adapting NAACP Programs to the Needs of Today's Youth." He condemned young people who were preoccupied with social life and suggested that they do more, "especially on the community level . . . in breaking down discrimination and segregation, and in securing compliance" with laws in states that already had civil rights codes. Another particularly popular workshop taught young people specific "techniques for combating discrimination and segregation." The NAACP had previously taught youth members direct-action techniques. In 1944, for example, the association circulated "The ABC's of Mass Pressure" among its youth councils. This bulletin, based on a youth conference workshop by Current, told young members how to use the press and "dramatic demonstrations, parades, pickets lines, etc." to bring civil rights issues to the public. Drawing on the ideas of a professor at Michigan's Wayne University (now Wayne State University), Current instructed youth members on the differences between and effective uses of demonstrations and picket lines and about how to "use words, symbols, ideas, and the like" to attack Jim Crow. In the 1940s, making the public aware of civil rights issues and creating public sympathy were important objectives. But by 1952, the NAACP and its youth councils were decidedly more militant and focused on attacking segregation itself. During the 1952 workshop, leaders pointedly instructed youth attendees not to "compromise on the issue of discrimination" and told them that they should work with liberal elements in their communities against even "temporary segregation in any form . . . such as having certain times to go to a roller skating rink, or certain days to go to the zoo." Moreover, workshop participants staged "dramatization[s] of segregation as it actually takes place" in both ostensibly integrated and completely segregated communities. Teams of volunteers played the roles of ticket seller and minority patrons of a theater, and after each enactment, the audience evaluated and discussed the tactics and interactions.[57]

At the same time, the YWCA and YMCA voiced their "uncompromising" opposition to racial discrimination and pledged to "work though the means of peaceful non-violent efforts" for a more equitable social order. Student Ys had worked toward integration for several decades. As early as the 1920s, they had promoted interracial forums and instituted programs and study groups, and in the 1940s Y groups ended a variety of discriminatory campus policies across the country. In the 1950s, however, the organization increasingly encouraged its chapters to work with other youth organizations, such as the NAACP, "to set up desegregation committees on their campus to study and act on local problems."[58]

Although some NAACP youth groups in the 1950s continued to deserve the criticisms lodged by Wilkins and others, including youth members, for being more socially than politically oriented, young people in the NAACP increasingly applied militant strategies and direct-action techniques to real-life segregation dramas. By the late 1950s and early 1960s, examples of militant activity by young members—sit-ins by Wichita, Kansas, youth members or picketing conducted by Pittsburgh youth against workplace discrimination, for example—filled NAACP reports and press releases. Association leaders became even more explicit about their support of youth activism and about the militant role of youth in the organization. In 1955, Hurley, formerly the organization's youth director and now its field secretary, announced that "youth councils are much in demand" and urged branches to make a special effort to organize young members. "They want to take part and there is work they can do," she insisted. "We need YOUTH and YOUTH need the NAACP." Two years later, the association set goals to establish youth councils in every active branch and facilitate communication between youth councils and training efforts by holding additional statewide youth conferences. In 1957, the NAACP also held a mass youth rally in New York City to celebrate "Young Freedom Fighters." The rally featured youth speakers such as Jolee Frits, a white student who had lost her job because of her NAACP activities; Bobby Cain, the black student who had integrated Clinton High School in Tennessee; Fred Moore, who had had to resign his position as South Carolina State College student body president for leading resistance to a White Citizens' Council boycott; and Ernest McEwen, who had directed a student protest against anti-NAACP propaganda and was expelled from Mississippi's Alcorn College. This event both recognized the militant activities of young people and encouraged others to emulate these "YOUTHFUL HEROES OF THE SOUTH." The following year, the association similarly highlighted and encouraged young people's contributions to the movement by awarding its prestigious Spingarn Medal for civil rights work to the nine teenagers who had integrated Little Rock High and to Josephine Boyd, the first African American to graduate from an integrated school in North Carolina. In 1958 and 1960, the association appointed additional staff to help with youth organizing, especially in the South. In 1959, youth councils and college chapters, even in places such as Jackson, Mississippi, conducted a series of youth marches for freedom. And in the early 1960s, NAACP leaders routinely called for youth councils, "the fighting arm of the Association," to picket segregated stores and facilities. Officials even specified that senior branches provide financial and legal assistance, while "militant direct action projects should be assigned to youth."[59]

In some ways, this celebration of and focus on youth simply represented a response to the widespread activism of young people, and statements about the militant role of youth were simply descriptions of fact. But the NAACP had been responding to and encouraging youth activism since the 1930s, when it first organized youth councils and college chapters. Moreover, it had officially supported militant youth action on civil rights issues since that time. As direct-action protests by young people and media coverage of such protests escalated, many NAACP members and leaders expressed frustration that the association was not getting credit

for all the direct action in which NAACP youth engaged. Others, such as
the youth council members who started the Greensboro sit-ins or those
who "defected" to CORE, complained that even though they were or had
been NAACP members, they had decided to take militant action on their
own because the association was too conservative to do so.[60] Each side
was perhaps justified in its complaints. But both groups, like later scholars of the movement, missed the real significance of the NAACP's youth
programs and perhaps one of the most important contributions of the
NAACP to the black freedom struggle. To complain about failing to receive
credit for militant youth activity or to dismiss the association's role in that
activity was to miss the long-standing dialectical relationship between
young people, the NAACP, and its youth program. The NAACP helped create a youth organizing tradition on civil rights and to some degree even
encouraged young people to explore and engage in militant strategies.
Moreover, although the NAACP was certainly not the only organization
that helped build that tradition, the scope of its youth organizing efforts
and its position, as Lomax ruefully observes, as *the* civil rights organization of the first half of the twentieth century made the NAACP especially
significant to that tradition. Indeed, SNCC volunteers found an organizing
base among young people in Mississippi in 1964 at least partly because
Medgar Evers had helped form NAACP youth councils there in the 1950s.
And just a year earlier, in a fitting tribute to both their origins and their
focus, Tougaloo College demonstrators chose to call themselves the NAACP
(Nonviolent Agitation Association of College Pupils). But young people
had encouraged the (original) NAACP to organize youth, had challenged
the parameters of the organization's activity, and had pushed the association and thus the movement in more militant directions, exactly as those
Greensboro youth council members did when they sat down at the Woolworth counter in 1960.[61]

Five

. . . .

YOUTH UNLIMITED

YOUNG PEOPLE & THE SOUTHERN

CIVIL RIGHTS MOVEMENT, 1950–1965

At a memorial service for James Chaney, Andrew Goodman, and Michael Schwerner, James's eleven-year-old brother, Ben, made a speech: "I want us all to stand up here together and say just one thing. I want the sheriff to hear this good. WE AIN'T SCARED NO MORE OF SHERIFF RAINEY!" The young boy's attitude and words in the face of his brother's murder reflected what seemed in the 1960s to be a new energy and militancy among America's youth and especially among young southern blacks. A year earlier, after the death of Medgar Evers, members of the Evanston youth council of the National Association for the Advancement of Colored People (NAACP) expressed a similar sentiment: "We the Negro youth of today feel that our forefathers have exercised too much patience in the past—that the time has come for action—it is time NOW that freedom be achieved. . . . Please move over, because we are coming thru." And at a 1967 youth rally, seventeen-year-old Clarissa Williams insisted, "We intend to be the generation which will make black youth to be unlimited. We intend to be the generation that says, Friends we do not have a dream, we do *not* have a dream, we have a plan."[1]

Whether or not their militant attitudes were altogether different from those of black youth in the 1930s, 1940s, or early 1950s, Ben Chaney, the Evanston NAACP youth council, and Clarissa Williams all saw themselves as markedly different from previous generations of civil rights activists. In the eyes of the members of the new generation, whatever their elders had accomplished, they had been decidedly too fearful and patient, not direct and forceful enough about achieving racial equality. Most observers of and participants in the civil rights movement in the early 1960s agreed that there was something decidedly different about that generation's youth. In his 1960 essay for *The Nation*, "Finishing School for Pickets," historian and activist Howard Zinn noted that while alumni and friends of the college had once boasted that "you can always tell a Spelman girl" because she "walked gracefully, talked properly, went to church every Sunday, [and] poured tea elegantly," there was "something fundamental at work . . . setting free for the first time the anger pent up in generations of quiet, well-bred Negro . . . women." Zinn half joked that because of this "something fundamental," it was now perhaps more truthful to say, "You can always tell a Spelman girl—she's under arrest."[2]

Zinn's essay may have depicted one of the results of the change taking place among black youth, but it did not explain that change. Child psychiatrist Robert Coles, who was interested in understanding the motivations for and psychological effects of youth activism in the 1960s, said that the question most commonly asked him while he was working with children in the South was, "What kind of [young] person takes on this hard life of protest, of demonstration and frequent arrest?" Scholars of the movement have wondered the same thing, and their research into this question has greatly expanded our understanding of the civil rights movement. In *I've Got the Light of Freedom*, Charles Payne describes an African American organizing tradition and elucidates the influence of examples or "stories" of resistance on the young people who participated in the movement in the early 1960s. Others have similarly explored the continuity of generations and explained youth direct action as an extension or enactment of parental values. Scholars have also suggested that the greater racial liberalism and democratic ideology of the era, exposure to racialized political struggles in Africa, national media coverage of civil rights struggles, the Emmett Till case, and the *Brown* ruling all significantly influenced young Americans who decided to engage in nonviolent direct-action protests in the early 1960s.[3]

Coles recognized that scholars' and observers' attempts to explain why certain young people participated in protests reflected false upper- and middle-class assumptions that youth "will be hurt by the trials they assume." Such explanations also reflected the surprise that many people felt as they witnessed young people, who had grown up during a period widely regarded as one of cultural conformity and political conservatism, "breaking the 'docile generation' label with sit-ins, demonstrations and picketing." Coles tried to combat prevailing fears about youth activism. The articles he published in the 1960s on children and civil rights events indicated that young people who integrated schools or participated in protests proved remarkably resilient in the face of verbal and physical abuse inflicted by white segregationists and showed no signs of lasting psychological damage. In fact, he insisted, reiterating one of the themes that had made the NAACP's argument in the *Brown* case so compelling to the Supreme Court justices, the children who did *not* face the dangers or trauma of protest and simply accepted racial hierarchies suffered psychologically and spiritually.[4]

Scholars who have placed the youth activism of the 1960s within the context of an African American organizing tradition or who have stressed a tradition of liberalism in the families of young white volunteers have similarly tried to challenge false assumptions about that activism, particularly about its supposedly unprecedented and unexpected nature. The history of the NAACP's youth program presented in chapter 4 offers additional evidence that the youth protests of the 1960s represented not so much a break with the past as the continuation and escalation of a militant youth organizing tradition. But even in the context of a longer tradition of youth organizing and militancy (or an African American organizing tradition or a tradition of white liberalism), the aggressiveness, scope, and influence of youth activism in the 1950s and 1960s civil rights movement stands out. In fact, youth activism for civil rights became so widespread in this period that white segregationists felt the need to conduct an "all-out drive" to enlist students in their cause. "From coast to coast white youth are on the march for race and nation . . . to counter the wild hordes of Communist-inspired, Negro demonstrations," they insisted. Such rhetoric reflected negative racial stereotypes and was one of the usual cold-war-inspired excuses for dismissing African American demands. It also suggested a disingenuous assertion of white youth solidarity and, most important, a very real sense of fear about what segregationists knew to be autonomous black activism. White southerners' explanations of youth activism obviously are suspect, although they were right that, as one white southerner complained, the "young squirts [were] hell-bent on revolution."[5]

One way to begin to understand the qualitative and quantitative differences between earlier youth protests and youth activism of this period as well as its significance to the civil rights movement is to start with an understanding of childhood and youth as significant and separate developmental stages and of the relationship between those developmental stages and history. In *Daddy's Gone to War: The Second World War in the Lives of America's Children*, William Tuttle proposes that historians trying to understand social change can benefit from the work of developmental psychologists who have outlined different stages of human development, the most significant being those of childhood and youth. "Few people," Tuttle notes, would disagree that while "people continue to change throughout the life course . . . the earliest years are the most formative ones." He suggests that historians apply this understanding and "recognize that social change has differential effects based on whether children, adolescents, or adults are affected." Tuttle sees the intersection of "age, culture, and history" as determining individual development and shaping social change. And his research on children during the World War II era demonstrates that the age or developmental stage at which American children experienced the war affected their subsequent understanding of that event and their views of the world, the nation, and even themselves.[6]

Tuttle's theoretical framework is significant to an understanding of youth civil rights activists in the 1950s and 1960s. Some of those young activists were born during the war years that Tuttle examines, and all of them grew up in the highly charged ideological climate of World War II and the subsequent cold war. In the 1940s, the United States fought a war "for democracy and cooperation, and against racism and violence," and those ideas pervaded the media and were emphasized in the nation's schools. Tuttle notes that school-age children "were ideal [cognitive] receptors" for the democratic messages of the war and that they "developed moral stances tightly attuned to the United States' lofty war aims."[7] That such messages influenced young people is not to deny that they had agency or that socialization is a dialectic process. It is simply to suggest that adults were not affected by the democratic ideology and rhetoric of the era in the same way or to the same degree as young people, who were introduced to that ideology and rhetoric during their most formative years.

After years of working with black and white children in America's South as well as in racially divided South Africa, Coles realized that national ideologies greatly influence young people. He even suggested that "a nation's history becomes . . . a child's apparently idiosyncratic conscience." Coles was disturbed by the ways that children's conceptions of their nations led them to separate themselves from others, as when one young Afrikaner told him, "We won't be a country if apartheid ends; we won't be here; we'll disappear." But the connections that Coles observed between national identity and personal identity in children's minds could work to challenge the status quo as well, especially if, as was true in mid-twentieth-century America, national ideals, forged in the international arena, threatened the extant domestic order. At least partly because of those connections, Coles suggested, young people who did not challenge the rules of racism were more likely to suffer psychological distress than those who did. American children were especially sensitive to the democratic messages of the war and postwar period, and those messages became part of the way many young people understood their nation and themselves. Moreover, because of the intermingling of national and personal identity and the discrepancies between national ideals and sociopolitical realities, young people who grew up in the period were also potentially more sensitive to violations of American democracy than were their elders. In Howard University psychiatrist Fredric Solomon's terms, young people at the time had an especially great "yearning . . . to coincide their actions with their beliefs." Or, as the U.S. commissioner of education remarked in 1951, "Why, our children ask, don't adult community deeds measure up to adult living-room creeds?" Atlanta University students made precisely this point in 1960 when they took out a full-page advertisement in the *Atlanta Constitution* declaring, "We cannot tolerate in a nation professing democracy . . . the discriminatory conditions under which the Negro is living today. . . . The practice of racial segregation is not in keeping with the ideals of Democracy and Christianity."[8]

If young people were in some ways hypersensitive to the democratic ideology of the era and its infractions, they were also culturally conditioned to fight against violations of democratic principles, in part because of cultural and "scientific" understandings of children. During the 1940s and 1950s, social science researchers, educational experts, and child welfare advocates increasingly talked about childhood as a season of alternatives. Understandably, then, young people increasingly thought of themselves as "not as prejudiced as the older people," as one Louisiana student put it. Public discussions also focused on the central roles that young people would play in overcoming society's racial and religious prejudices, bringing about democratic change, and ensuring world peace. An early 1950s article in *National Parent-Teacher* captured both scientific and popular thinking about young people when it suggested that adults "stand aside and let young persons develop a social conscience not blacked by all our prejudices. . . . Give the kids an even chance and they will come up with something better than we can think of ourselves." Similar ideas even appeared in children's literature. Books for young people during this period increasingly featured young characters who met their needs by "self-direction" and "through social change" rather than by conformity to adult norms. Popular and award-winning children's book authors such as Lois Lenski, Joseph Krumgold, Elizabeth Yates, and Ann Nolan Clark created heroic characters, often racial or ethnic minorities, who challenged the social, political, and racial politics of the time. And the beloved Dr. Seuss consistently albeit humorously urged young readers to recognize societal constraints and to imagine new ways of ordering the world through his characters, whether it was young Gerald McGrew in *If I Ran the Zoo* or the boy narrator who eventually befriends a pair of unfamiliar pale-green pants in "What Was I Scared Of?" The young people who became involved in the direct-action protests of the 1950s and 1960s grew up during a time in which young people were told that America's youth were responsible for extending and enforcing the principles of American democracy.[9]

The actions of youth delegates at the 1950 White House Conference on Children and Youth suggest that ideas about young people's responsibility for changing the world and the democratic ideology of the era indeed influenced America's youth. Significantly, 1950 marked the first time organizers of the decennial conference invited youth to participate, indicating that national leaders in the fields of child health, education, and welfare acted on contemporary beliefs about the agency of young people and their role in strengthening American democracy. Conference sessions highlighted those beliefs and addressed national security issues, the problems of prejudice, and the state of American childhood. After attending one session that explored prejudice as "an obstacle to the working of democracy," youth delegates evidently felt "so deeply . . . about making practice conform to principle that they chose to protect their members from any racial prejudice by living all together in barracks furnished by the Army" instead of in segregated hotels in Washington, D.C. Moreover, youth participants passed a resolution calling "on all organizations connected with the conference to 'take positive action to eliminate the cause of discrimination and to foster an aggressive program of civil rights.'" In another resolution, they asserted that until "all races and conditions of men are commonly accepted, democracy itself cannot be on a firm foundation." Youth delegates to the NAACP's annual conferences and YWCA and YMCA members participated in workshops that stressed many of the same themes and supported similar resolutions. Discussions about youth and democracy clearly influenced the way young people saw themselves and encouraged them not only to consider but also to take action on civil rights issues.[10]

In the 1960s, Coles insisted that the black children with whom he worked, whether from the South or from northern ghettos, were as "politically conscious" as white middle-class college students; they had learned to tell the difference, as one rural ten-year-old figuratively put it, "between a piece of real meat and streak o'lean." According to Coles, their high level of political consciousness resulted from personal experiences with the politics of Jim Crow. "Unforgettable events" such as being told they could not drink from the same fountains as white children, Coles suggested, "very definitely help shape their attitude toward their nation and its political authority." Those experiences sometimes led children to refuse to recite the pledge of allegiance or to draw the flag. One of the Little Rock Nine, Melba Pattillo Beals, said that she was already so afraid of white people by the time she was three that she hid from her white-skinned cousin when she came to babysit and that early experiences with segregation stole "a teaspoonful of self-esteem each day." Many other African Americans throughout the twentieth century recorded having similar experiences. But if many young people in the 1920s, 1930s, and 1940s felt a certain helplessness in the face of Jim Crow—felt like they were "far too young to question the wisdom" of those who taught the rules of segregation and the meanings of race—a growing number of young people in the 1950s and 1960s did not. The shame Beals felt, especially as she watched the adults in her family "kowtow to white people," ultimately led her to take action against Jim Crow rather than surrender to it. And she was not the only one of her generation to respond aggressively.[11]

A striking expression of both the similarities and differences between young blacks and their elders was an exchange between Congress of Racial Equality (CORE) activist James Farmer and his father. Just before participating in the Freedom Rides, Farmer visited the aging man in the hospital: "I told him on the morrow I was going on a freedom ride. 'Well,' he asked, 'what's that?'" After James explained the plan, including where they were going, his father asked, "Alabama and Mississippi, too?" "Yes," James replied. The old man looked up and said, "Well son, I'm glad you're going on that, what do you call it, freedom ride, and I hope you survive it. I realize that to some of you this may be the last journey you'll ever take, but I'm glad you're going and I'll tell you why. When I was boy in South Carolina and Georgia . . . we didn't like segregation either. We hated it. It just burned us up inside. But we said, we thought that that was the way that things always had been and the way they had to be, and we thought there was nothing we could do about it, so we accepted it and put up with it even as we burned inside." Whereas the older Farmer had perceived segregation as "something that we were going to just have to endure," the younger man believed that he could do something about it.[12]

The young protesters of the 1950s and 1960s were not the first to recognize the discrepancies between the nation's democratic ideals and the realities of American democracy. They were not, as Coles put it, "the first Negro youths to dream of freedom." During the Great Depression, American Youth Commission researchers had noted "the submissive spirit of many elders and the restless rebellion of youth." In 1936, a Talladega student recognized his classmates' hopes as well as what he called their "lack of citizenship incentive" when he reported to the school newspaper that students sometimes tried to vote but gave up after being treated discourteously or did not bother to try at all because "it wouldn't do any good anyway." Anthropologist Hortense Powdermaker similarly observed "the intense and mounting bitterness of the younger Negroes" in the 1930s. Writing late in the decade, she noted, like the Talladega student, that bitterness "so far" was generally "helpless and undirected." By the early 1960s, however, that bitterness had a definite direction. Coles suggested a number of reasons why the "hopeful children" of that generation had become committed to action: those children had grown up in families that were generally less authoritarian, in a society with somewhat weaker social controls, and in a world in which local communities were less isolated "in time and space" than children of earlier generations. Most important, he suggested, only with the current generation had African Americans become "free enough or secure enough even to conceive of the true security of real freedom." Coles might have added that the democratic ideology of

World War II and the cold war and public discussions about the dangers of prejudice and about young people as important agents of democratic change influenced their perceptions of themselves and their possibilities. But in any case, he acknowledged, the combination of culture, history— "the historical moment," he called it—and young people's stage in human development led them to "strike out and claim, successfully, once forbidden territory." For Coles it was almost a given that young people became the main actors in America's racial battles. Their developmental stage left them more open to change and more willing to act than adults. But it took more to break down racial barriers than what he and other experts on childhood saw as young people's natural inclination to see past society's racial barriers. If young people were to challenge segregation, Coles explained, "this very time is their essential catalyst." [13]

YOUTH AND THE HISTORICAL MOMENT

Many scholars of the civil rights movement have suggested that changing expectations in the post–World War II era help explain the escalation of civil rights protests in the 1950s and 1960s. The war raised expectations among black Americans, especially returning soldiers, that the federal government would move to protect their rights as citizens and to destroy the nation's decidedly undemocratic laws and practices. [14] World War II also raised the expectations of young people and influenced their protests. Sometimes the children of former servicemen expected that their fathers' war service would end racial injustice: said one young black activist, "My father fought in France for this country, almost got killed. Why should he be afraid to vote? Why should he tell me that I'm not as good as some white kid, and why should he sit and 'yes' the white man all day and then come home and booze it up and tell us how rotten they are?" Another young black similarly explained what she expected from the war: "We have proved our worth to the nation and its cause. Would we have to beg . . . for a place in this commonwealth? No, the cause of national defense will have gained our tie to bind us to the side of our white brethren for a great and happier America." But even if their fathers had not served in the war, young people who grew up with the democratic ideology and rhetoric of World War II and the postwar period—who grew up, as sociologist Kenneth Keniston later noted, "more attuned to the historical currents in their lives than . . . most children"—developed a sense of their nation

Young African Americans
support the war effort
(and America's democratic
ideals) by purchasing
defense stamps, 1942.
(© Corbis)

and themselves as champions of tolerance, freedom, and peace. When the American Youth Commission contemplated its work on African American youth in late 1939, it recognized that with "world conditions . . . challenging the stability of our nation's democratic institutions . . . Negro youth [were] becoming increasingly conscious of political discriminations." As a result of that heightened consciousness, students across the nation, like Dillard University senior Marie Hawthorne, wondered if "this is a democracy with rights and privileges, why doesn't it exist?" And they increasingly demanded to be treated in accordance with America's democratic values, both for their own benefit and for "the progress of the nation." Young whites developed similar expectations about their country. Future Freedom Rider and Mississippi volunteer Peter Stoner, for example, recalled a visit to New Orleans where he was surprised to see segregated drinking fountains. "In my innocence," he recalled, "I believed what I had been taught that this was a democracy and a land of freedom." Many young people of this generation clearly developed heightened expectations about American society and their place in it. The ideology of the war shaped their assumptions about what life in America in general and their own lives in particular should look like. Like Clarissa Williams, other youth in this period grew up believing that they and all Americans should and could be "unlimited."[15]

Researchers in the 1950s found that young people all over the world expected "to see greater equality in their lifetimes." Nonwhite groups, they observed, tended to be somewhat more pessimistic about the possibilities. Yet with the exception of Afrikaners, who would not relinquish their racialized rule of South Africa until the 1990s, the youth these researchers interviewed wanted greater equality and believed it would happen. T. J. Woofter, who for decades had studied and helped expose the problems of black Americans, was among those who believed that some of this sense of racial progress was the result of new courses "dealing with the interracial situation in America" (some seventy-seven in southern colleges and universities by 1940), studies such as those published by the American Youth Commission, and the interracial work of YMCAS and YWCAS and other local and regional youth-centered organizations. "Literally hundreds of thousands of students in both northern and southern colleges have been exposed to the hard facts of race relations in the past thirty years. Their minds have been disabused in varying degrees of the folk myths about race," Woofter explained. As a result, he had great hopes for the time when "their generation" would control "southern policy." So did others who saw the results of interracial committees and programs or the human relations seminars and intergroup education curricula that many school districts across the nation implemented in the late 1940s. A public opinion survey found that most respondents believed that such interracial work positively affected racial attitudes and black-white relations. NAACP youth council members also sensed that intercultural education brought "noticeable improvement in race relations." And evidence certainly suggests that they were right. Some young people became involved in civil rights organizing after attending integrated schools. John Strand, for example, reported starting college as a Nixon supporter. But at Carleton, located in Minnesota, "my politics and I changed a lot [as a result of] meeting different kinds of people [and] having different kinds of experiences." Future activist Bob Zellner and four of his classmates at Alabama's all-white Huntington College did not have African American colleagues, but they certainly took their training in a sociology race relations course seriously. In fact, the administration requested that the students withdraw from school after discovering that they planned to visit the Montgomery Improvement Association to research the "racial problem" and its solutions for a class paper. (Administrators evidently told the students that the Ku Klux Klan would have been a more appropriate source of information for the assignment.) Officials at Millsaps also regarded interracial programs as potentially threatening. The private Jackson, Mississippi, college censored material from its sponsor, the National Methodist Church, because of the church's increasing racial liberalism, a practice that made at least some students, including future Tougaloo chaplain and civil rights activist Ed King, even more curious about African Americans and integration. A veritable crisis developed in 1958 when parents discovered that a group of students from Millsaps and nearby Tougaloo had for several years been participating in "race discussions." During the crisis, at least some white students, perhaps influenced by their interracial training, vehemently protested attempts to infringe on their "right to learn from whom I want to." More clearly, Carroll Murray, who interviewed African American students for a 1959 sociology class at Loyola University of the South was, like Zellner, directly affected by her social science studies. She wrote to her professor that "before speaking to these two girls I was not, in the least, concerned with the racial problem. To me, if [integration] came—it came; if it didn't—it didn't. I didn't feel anything about it, one way or the other. . . . But during the interview, I tried to put myself in these girls' place, and see how they really felt." Murray was not the only young white to be changed personally (and perhaps politically) by such experiences. One young "loyal [and perhaps typical] Southerner," initially harbored "a feeling of repugnance" at being required to interview a black person for her sociology class. In the end, she was surprised by the articulate student she questioned and by what she learned from him. Although her interracial encounter hardly inspired her to join the movement or to drop many of her original prejudices, even this young woman was at least "forced to look at one Negro's ideas," an experience that "broadened [her] considerably." And while African Americans may have had very different responses to such interactions, especially to interviews by patronizing if well-intentioned white students, they also tended to place "much value on such things as inter-racial meetings." In fact, in interviews from the late 1940s, black parents in New York City mentioned "early rich, integrated or intergroup, life experiences sponsored by YMCA and YWCA camps, social and civic groups" more than anything else as "things that are or might be done to improve relationships" between the races. Suggestive of the differences between the regions (the lack of integrated public education in the South) as well as their faith in education, upper-income parents in segregated St. Louis most often mentioned "mixed schools" as a way "for bettering relations."[16]

World War II and a greater focus on interracial issues and programs helped create a more favorable environment for civil rights activism. The war had also discredited racism and just as importantly had encouraged young Americans to see themselves as part of a larger world. Much as W. E. B. Du Bois discovered when he first traveled to Europe, many young blacks who grew up during and after World War II realized that they stood "not against the world, but simply against American narrowness and color prejudice." The war changed many young whites' perceptions as well. Bob Douglas, for example, remembered seeing an "entire battery of black naval men wiped out" while he was a nineteen-year-old serviceman. Because of such experiences and the "exhilaration of having won a war," he returned home to Arkansas with a sense that "everything"—including racial affairs—"was gonna be better." He and his friends considered themselves "all a little more liberal-minded than we had been, [and] a large number of us thought segregation was wrong." Perhaps also influential in shifting some young soldiers' perceptions of race were military training programs that encouraged servicemen to discuss significant questions, such as "What opportunities do Negros have to obtain education? What factors aside from the physical limitations of public schools systems affect Negros' educational opportunities? . . . When they have the opportunity, is the achievement of Negros comparable to whites?" Efforts by federal agencies and African American leaders to publicize the status of blacks during World War II also positively affected young people's attitudes. Researchers found that although white children's prejudice against blacks remained significant, it had nonetheless lessened considerably over the course of the war. Not all young people adopted more liberal attitudes toward race or more determined ideas about what their own future should hold, but by the 1950s, World War II and that era's ideas and ideals showed many young people and youth leaders that "the workings of the democratic process [had] become more meaningful [and that] Negro and white youth were living in a new world and a changed social milieu." As Carole Tuxeud, a student at Xavier University in New Orleans, plainly told a 1959 interviewer who asked her thoughts on Jim Crow and civil rights activity, "Times have changed."[17]

Two youth-centered events in the mid-1950s further shaped the "social milieu" of young Americans and strengthened both the expectations of young blacks and their sense of themselves as vital actors in the cause of racial equality: the Supreme Court ruling in the *Brown* case and the murder of fourteen-year-old Emmett Till. The 1954 *Brown* ruling specifically upheld not just the civil rights of black Americans but the rights of black children in America. Moreover, it put America's schoolchildren at the center of the nation's struggle for racial equality.[18] It seems hardly coincidental that young people became decidedly more militant in the years after the Supreme Court outlawed segregated schools, guaranteed young blacks the rights of childhood, and asked them to lead the nation in creating a new sociopolitical order. The *Brown* ruling no doubt heightened young blacks' expectations that their dreams of equality would be fulfilled. Indeed, historian R. Scott Baker has recently shown that "the Supreme Court's repudiation of state-sanctioned segregation inspired" the activism of South Carolina's black students, who believed the ruling signaled "new educational possibilities." Youth activists such as Lolis Elie, who got involved with the NAACP at New Orleans's Dillard University and later worked for CORE, attributed the rising consciousness among their generation to *Brown* as well. Elie recalled that "after the '54 decision, people started hearing about integrating the schools, and . . . there were places . . . where they had seen children being spat on, so . . . the oppression was somehow or another heightened." Harvey Gantt, a young South Carolina sit-in leader and the first African American admitted to Clemson, similarly recalled that "for a kid like me, [the day of the *Brown* decision] was a very significant day. I don't forget it." Young blacks from North Carolina and Louisiana interviewed in 1954 for Edward Murrow's *See It Now* program reported that they "liked" the ruling, felt that it would "affect them greatly," help them "get a better education," and "advance further." One interviewee called the decision "one of the most wonderful new things that happened in America and especially in the South in the last fifty years." According to poet Langston Hughes, the Supreme Court's decree gave "the Sit-In Kids and the Freedom Riders . . . a bit more to go on than" he had when he was growing up. Even if, as scholars have suggested, *Brown* "did not speak to the range of political, economic, and extralegal constraints" on the lives of black adults, it certainly did speak to the most obvious constraints on the lives of black children and youth.[19]

The ruling also raised the consciousness of some young whites. Zellner recalled that when he was in college, news about the *Brown* decision was everywhere, forcing people to think about it and ask questions about what was "the right thing to do." YWCA and Student Non-Violent Coordinating Committee (SNCC) activist Casey Hayden similarly regarded *Brown* as a turning point in her life. A senior in high school at the time of the ruling, she was "surprised that it was by law that schools were segregated. I always thought it was because people by choice lived in different neighborhoods," she recalled. "I was in journalism class and we would read the paper every day and discuss it. . . . I just thought that it was the most stupid thing I had ever heard of." Not all young whites responded to *Brown* with Hayden's perspective or commitment to racial justice. Murrow's *See It Now* special, for example, revealed that some young southern whites were "disappointed" in the ruling, believed blacks did not want integrated schools, or felt it would cause racial problems. Others on the program, however, admitted to being less against it than their parents, to being willing to "adapt," or to thinking that desegregated schools would "strengthen America in the end." The decision encouraged young people across America, including those not directly affected by the ruling and those who might never have previously thought about civil rights, to at least consider the plight of their black counterparts and the nation's system of segregation. For many youth (black and white), *Brown* brought, to use social theorist Pierre Bourdieu's framework, "the undiscussed into discussion, the unformulated into formulation." It shifted "the universe of possible discourse . . . the universe of the thinkable."[20]

The *Brown* ruling also reinforced and gave substance to the idea that young people were significant political actors. In effect, the Supreme Court's decision made America's schoolchildren responsible for changing the country's racist practices. In the aftermath of *Brown*, young blacks throughout the South, often despite the considerable misgivings of their parents and the intransigence of whites, readily accepted that responsibility and chose to push their local communities into compliance with the ruling. Although public school integration hardly proceeded with "deliberate speed," even limited progress in this area could affect young people considerably—whether physically or psychologically. Young blacks including Little Rock student Melba Pattillo Beals, who "understood education before [she] understood anything else" and whose parents had drilled into her that "education is your key to survival," would likely have been especially influenced by the ruling. Moreover, within two years of the ruling, at least 442 southern school districts had officially desegregated, and by the end of the 1956–57 school year, that figure reached 713. This was an indisputably significant if also disappointing result. For the first time, many young southern blacks, even those whose families did not share the education-centered culture of Beals's, could at least begin to imagine the end of Jim Crow schooling. And segregated schools were, by many accounts, young people's most familiar and often most humiliating experience with American racism. Perhaps also illustrative of shifting conditions and their influence on ways of thinking were the results of a Texas poll. In April 1954, just before the *Brown* ruling, only 19 percent of those questioned felt that "Negro children should have the right to go to the same school as whites." In August 1958, that number had almost doubled, and 67 percent of respondents believed that integration would be achieved across the state. At least some white youth, such as Ed King and his high school friends in Vicksburg, Mississippi, thought the *Brown* ruling "was a good thing" and immediately began "talking about how different it was going to be when black students came [to school] that September." The Southern Regional Council acknowledged the *Brown* ruling's impact on student activism when it identified the "resentment over the pace of school desegregation [as] one irritant which motivated students" to join demonstrations. This was a point with which young black militant Les Holingsworth would likely have agreed. Just about to graduate from high school in May 1954, he later recalled that his group of friends "thought that [because of *Brown*] we were gonna be able to go to whatever college we wanted to in the state, but we soon found out that that was really not the way it was going to be."[21]

IDENTIFYING WITH THE MOVEMENT

If the South in general was slow to implement the *Brown* ruling, the efforts of the Little Rock Nine, Dorothy Counts, Ruby Bridges, and other black schoolchildren to realize its promises were duly recorded by the national news media and witnessed by Americans throughout the country. Some black families even collected and circulated news clippings about these events. And, as chapter 3 explains, the stories the media told about school desegregation successes and failures further reinforced notions that young blacks deserved the rights of American childhood, that young people were important agents of democratic change, and that youth were considerably better than their elders at negotiating new sociopolitical relationships.

The media depicted the young people who integrated southern schools as heroes and leaders of democracy. But that was not always how readers, listeners, or viewers regarded those young people. The public's varied responses indicate that youth often reacted very differently than adults to the *Brown* ruling and subsequent efforts to enforce it. Many adults saw the children who desegregated schools as victims of racial violence and wanted to protect them. Others saw them as foolish and as asking for trouble. Young blacks, however, more commonly saw them as people to emulate. "John," a young black activist, captured a range of typical responses when he said that he "used to have dreams about" what he called "the Little Rock trouble." "We'd sit and watch that on that television set, and we'd get angry and my grandmother would say that those kids shouldn't try to go to that school and my mother wouldn't say anything and my father would curse those whites and say we should stay away from all of them . . . they can't be trusted, they're no good." After watching the reports, "John" would "go to bed and dream that I was one of those nine kids in Central High and that [Arkansas Governor Orval] Faubus came over to the school and I killed him with a machine gun." Unlike his grandmother, his father, and even his mother, who reacted to the prospect of school desegregation by separating themselves from the Little Rock Nine and expressing fears that reinforced racial hierarchies, "John" readily identified himself with the young people involved in desegregating America's schools and regarded both them and potentially himself as heroes.[22]

So, too, did SNCC activist Julian Bond, who, prior to Little Rock,

> had been a happy-go-lucky teenager. . . . My role models . . . were white teenagers, mostly Italian American youngsters who danced five afternoons a week on ABC's *American Bandstand*. . . . But suddenly the nine brave young people of Little Rock's Central High School—the Little Rock Nine—replaced my former idols. My new models didn't seem to wear the proper hip clothes, but they possessed something the *Bandstand* dancers did not—grace and courage under great pressure. . . . I learned all their names too. I knew of Ernie Green, at seventeen the most like me: a senior, who seemed to me to represent everything a college-bound young man should be.[23]

Ernest Green shows his textbooks to African American children after his first day of classes at Little Rock's Central High School, 1958. The Little Rock Nine and others like them became role models for other African American youth. (Courtesy *New York World-Telegram* and *Sun* Newspaper Photograph Collection, Library of Congress, Prints and Photographs Collection, LC-USZ62–126834)

Young people responded to later civil rights protesters in much the same way. As movement journalist David Halberstam explained, "If many of their parents were terrified of the words *Freedom Riders*, then the young felt differently." Youth wanted to be like the Freedom Riders, to join them. The movement often threatened older blacks such as one New Orleans resident who insisted "conditions [are] improving. . . . I'm satisfied—I don't give no trouble — don't get no trouble." Or those who told young New Yorker Julie Prettyman that segregation is "the way it is and nothing else can be done" and considered her "crazy" because she refused to go to the movies if it meant sitting in the balcony. Conversely, joining the struggle for racial equality offered young blacks a new source of status. Inside the civil rights movement, an observer explained, young southern blacks such as James Chaney escaped a "lifetime of being a 'boy.'" As one young participant recalled, "It was time for change." After all, "growing up to be a young Black man, [I] really had no opportunities." For young people, wearing CORE T-shirts, marching in protest demonstrations, and going to jail became a source of status and pride. Bond called being at the movement's forefront "ego-fulfilling." Many adult participants and later historians explained that young people joined protest demonstrations more readily than older people because they "did not have jobs and bills to pay [and] could afford to go to jail." As one contemporary sociology professor put it, young people were "energetic, mobile, and independent." But widespread youth activism cannot be wholly explained by young people's relative lack of responsibility.[24]

Children and youth perceived the movement in positive terms and individually as well as collectively identified with civil rights activists and activities. Bob Moses headed south and began his life as a civil rights organizer after seeing a *New York Times* photograph of young sit-in demonstrators. "I knew how they felt and I wanted to see, you know, what that was like," he later told fellow SNCC worker Joyce Ladner. Carolyn McKinstry, a participant in the Birmingham demonstrations, recalled that "it felt good, it felt right." Other youth similarly "loved the atmosphere" and saw themselves in the faces of the Freedom Riders. They admired and sometimes "fell absolutely in love with" young movement leaders. They "got caught up with the singing and talking" and "became totally engrossed" or "hooked," as Deborah Sanders Avery put it. Young people described protest demonstrations and mass meetings as "exciting," even "fun," despite the dangers. "It was fun to see Bull Conner riding down Second Avenue in that tank," remembered one youth. "It was fun seeing everybody around downtown and not spending any money, but yet they were happy." Activist and strategist James Bevel also suggested that young people had "courage and confidence" that their elders lacked. He noted that youth, especially girls, reacted to the violence of white police differently than adults did. Such gendered as well as age-influenced responses may well have resulted from the ways that boys and girls commonly experienced Jim Crow. A 1949 study concluded that southern black boys from both the upper and lower classes were more likely than their female counterparts to meet "aggression" and "discrimination" from whites. They were also more likely to feel "anger" rather than "inferiority" and to "fight" as a result of those encounters. This study also suggested, however, that girls more frequently argued with whites who harassed them and that upper-class southern girls were actually more likely than their male or northern counterparts to receive (or at least to report) "physical ill-treatment." Young people seem to have experienced and reacted to Jim Crow in complex, gendered ways. Some of this study's other findings are more straightforward, including the fact that "fear" and "indifference" were the least common responses of both boys and girls of all income and regional groups to their encounters with racism and Jim Crow.[25]

Whatever their experience with or understanding of America's racism, instead of responding to the "immediate fear" that paralyzed their parents, youth of both sexes increasingly saw and acted on the "logic" of nonviolence. As SNCC activist Courtland Cox explained, "There was nothing we could have done or . . . tried to do if we had met overwhelming force, but we didn't let that paralyze us in terms of . . . making our stance." Or as Birmingham youth protester Cleopatra Goree more blithely recalled, "You just didn't care. . . . You were just ready for whatever." Bevel also recognized that youth had "a kind of cohesion and camaraderie" that helped the movement spread. Organizing young people was relatively easy: when student leaders got involved, they quickly "got all the other students involved." As one high-school-age demonstrator later explained, after "somebody took the initiative . . . once one person went across, a bunch of us followed." For many young people, the struggle for racial equality became inextricably linked with local black youth cultures. A young Birmingham man described his connection to the movement: "It was interesting to me because everybody was doing it." And a Freedom Summer volunteer simi-

larly explained that he, too, became involved in the movement because "it was just the biggest thing around at the time."[26]

REJECTING JIM CROW ETIQUETTE

Many young blacks who became activists in the early 1960s had positive adult influences in their personal lives that helped counter the inescapable messages of Jim Crow. University of Maryland at Baltimore County president Freeman Hrabowski III, who participated in the 1963 Birmingham demonstrations as a youth, recalled that using textbooks discarded by white students, entering movie theaters through side entrances, and seeing only whites portrayed as successful on television and "Colored Only" signs everywhere "had an immeasurable impact on the psyches of young African-Americans" like him. Yet despite the negative influences of Jim Crow during what he described as a formative period of his life, Hrabowski also found that "constructive guidance in the home and neighborhood and moral lessons taught in the church, . . . inspirational stories in the Negro-owned newspapers and constant encouragement by teachers who told us we were very special" helped to balance those influences. Hrabowski's experiences as a child both sensitized him to the unfair obstacles that African Americans faced and gave him a sense that he could overcome those obstacles.[27]

R. Scott Baker, Aldon Morris, Diane Ravitch, and others have uncovered great examples of parents and teachers encouraging young people to challenge the constraints of Jim Crow. For many young blacks, however, there was often a catch to the sense of racial pride and self-esteem that parents and communities helped them to develop. As Andrew Young later explained, young blacks were frequently taught "to be strong to put up with all you're gonna have to put up with" rather than to try to change the situation. Moreover, if the activism and activist cultures of some young people in the late 1950s and early 1960s may be more easily explained, the young protester who dreamed of killing Faubus, like many others, both black and white, did not grow up in a home environment of racial liberalism with examples or stories of adults who defied Jim Crow or with the more balanced sense of himself that better-class blacks such as Hrabowski often possessed. "John" recalled that as a child, he had once sat down at the front of a bus. After the white woman next to him pushed him and told him "to get away and go to the back," which made him feel "bad and different," his grandmother "drove . . . home" that feeling with a lecture on Jim Crow etiquette. Then his father, "not happy with that . . . gave me the worst beating of my life. . . . I'll never forget him . . . telling me to keep my place." The story is striking for its resemblance to countless others told by African Americans who grew up in the first half of the twentieth century. Black militant James Forman called his similar racial awakening story "a cliché of the black experience." The story told by "John," however, is striking for another reason. Its young narrator linked, at least on some level, his early encounters with Jim Crow and especially his grandmother's and father's roles in enforcing segregation to his later experience watching the Little Rock Nine and his family's reactions to that event. Most significantly, his initiation into the politics of Jim Crow did not end with the "lessons" his elders taught him. The young people John watched on television taught him a different way to respond to Jim Crow—that is, by refusing to keep his place, by defying not only the rules of segregation but also his grandmother's and father's patterns for dealing with those rules. Watching events unfold in Little Rock made clear his elders' complicity in America's racial politics and gave him a sense that he, too, could challenge Jim Crow.[28]

Like "John," many young people resented the usual lessons their elders taught them about growing up in segregated America. They were grateful for those who rebelled "in their own way long before we were born." However, they were also angry, as one Tougaloo College protester explained, both about Jim Crow and about the fact that youth were being indoctrinated, purportedly for their own protection. Dillard and Xavier students suggested that one of the worst aspects of Jim Crow was the way parents on both sides of the color line programmed their children to obey racialized laws and customs, "with no sufficient explanation." First-year chemistry major Claude Smith even cited the "fear passed down from generation to generation" as "the main drawback" to achieving integration. Black children aged between ten and twelve from St. Louis and New York City, interviewed for a 1949 dissertation, also expressed dissatisfaction with their elders' collusion with Jim Crow politics. Most of the 150 young people questioned for this study, which attempted to gauge youth and adult responses to discrimination, regarded their parents' advice to "withdraw from" or "avoid" discriminatory situations and to "ignore" insults as inadequate or not particularly useful. In contrast, these children consistently valued their parents' much less frequent instructions to "fight back." One mother captured the different perspectives of young people and adults on Jim Crow etiquette when she admitted, "Of course, my children get mad, and they're always fussing when I tell them how to act. They say the white folks treat 'em bad, and they always razz 'em. Of course, I don't mind staying in my place." A young black girl articulated the difference between her reaction and her mother's reaction to being forced to change coaches on a train from New York to South Carolina: "I felt so bad, and I got real mad. I wanted to tell them a whole lot, to bawl them out. It sure did make me mad to have to move up there just because I was colored. I started talking about it. My mother wanted me to stop saying anything. She told me to shut up—that I was talking too loud. . . . It made me feel like we are so different. But I know that I'm just as good. No, what my mother says to me doesn't help." Particularly striking is this girl's frustration and anger with her mother, her sense that she was "so different" not only from whites but from her mother. Also striking is that whatever the advice or young people's assessments of it, the youth interviewed for this study, especially those identified as upper class, almost always followed their parents' instructions. The same did not seem to be true of young people a decade later.[29]

In a 1960 address, retired South Carolina attorney Marion A. Wright pointedly remarked that what struck him most about the current "student-led rebellion" was that the participants were protesting "not merely against custom, but also against the elders who manage our affairs." In 1940, black sociologist and American Youth Commission researcher E. Franklin Frazier noted that "even when [young people] take over the techniques of 'getting by' which the parents have worked out . . . these techniques have a different meaning for the children." In 1960, that meaning was expressed in a prizewinning essay by Nashville high school senior Nancy Glen, who obviously refused to adopt the technique of "getting by." In it she ordered those who accepted segregation simply to "shut your mouth and open your mind." Young people in this period were taking cues about how to act from each other rather than from what Wright called "the jaded and unimaginative" adults around them. And indeed, many young people who participated in civil rights protest demonstrations cited the influence of television and the examples of other black youth as key to the decision to join the movement.[30]

Faye Bellamy, for example, attributed her political consciousness and later activism partly to having "over the years on television watched people in the movement." Orthia Haley likewise explained that she and many others were prompted to act because "you see television and you read things and . . . certain things that sift down through to you." And future militant Cleveland Sellers recalled gathering with other students "around the TV in the student union over at the college to witness [the sit-ins]" and feeling proud of the participants' determination. "Eventually," he explained, "the enthusiasm spilled over and students at Voorhees became interested in taking part. . . . [T]hat's where the activism got drilled inside, and it kinda welled up and began to burn inside of me." News of protests by their counterparts in nearby Rock Hill similarly inspired Orangeburg, South Carolina, youth to take action.[31]

Other youth, too, "gleaned ideas" and courage from their peers around the nation. Carolyn McKinstry told interviewers that "there were a lot of things my parents didn't tell us." Only after watching the Freedom Riders on television did she even become "aware of the [Jim Crow] signs that were on the [bus] seats." McKinstry's parents had tried to protect their children from racism. They and many other better-class black parents developed tactics, such as driving their children rather than having them take the bus, to avoid potentially humiliating situations and to keep the children "safely naive." But McKinstry's mother and father could not hide the racism broadcast by televised news reports. And once their daughter realized what was going on and how other youth were dealing with it, she rejected her parents' strategies for coping with racism and made excuses to take the bus downtown. Like the youth she saw on television, McKinstry chose to challenge Birmingham's segregated system of public transportation by taking a seat at the front of the bus. She also began to attend mass meetings and participate in protest marches.[32]

Another young Birmingham activist similarly reported growing up with an inchoate awareness of inequalities that was brought to consciousness by media images of civil rights activists. She said that she "had always felt that there was something wrong between the races [and] didn't like the way Black people in [her] community would . . . become rather subservient in their demeanor when a White man came around." After "watching the Movement . . . on TV," her neighbors' behavior made more sense to her, and she began to investigate and become absorbed in civil rights work. Like many of his peers, Rallis Jones Jr. also grew up watching "demonstrations on TV and the marches." So, although in some ways his decision was

A police officer takes picket signs away from young Birmingham protesters, May 1963. Civil rights leaders may have debated whether or not they should "use" children in demonstrations, but young people in Birmingham had fewer qualms than their elders about participating in the movement. (Photograph by Ed Jones, *Birmingham News*; © Polaris Images Corporation)

tough, especially with his teachers and other adults warning him to stay away from the marches, when civil rights leaders came to his school, he and his friends were excited to join.[33]

THE EMMETT TILL GENERATION

Like the televised broadcasts and newspaper reports of young blacks attempting to desegregate schools, public facilities, and private businesses, the 1955 lynching of Emmett Till also inspired young people to reject the generally more cautious behavior of their elders and directly challenge America's racial barriers. Scholars have noted that the unpunished murder of this fourteen-year-old black boy "was branded indelibly into the memories of many young people across the south, both horrifying and galvanizing a generation." As one scholar explains, "Youngsters who saw Till's misshapen body in the photographs in *Jet* magazine later became the ardent staffers of SNCC and referred to the Till case as their political awakening." The Till case revealed the depths of southern racism, "stimulated," in the words of black congressman Charles Diggs, "a lot of interest and anger on the part of blacks all over the country," and demonstrated that something had to be done about Jim Crow. In the 1940s, the interracial secretary of the national YWCA suggested that for civil rights work to progress, "many young people in northern cities need to be shocked into an awareness of the bitter meaning of race prejudice." The murder of the Chicago youth produced just such awareness. But perhaps just as important, it gave young blacks an alternative way to respond to American racism and raised their expectations for how they should be treated. Although Till's lynching and the travesty of justice that followed certainly influenced them, Till's example of standing up to white men also made the incident a significant turning point in the lives of many young blacks, especially young southern blacks, and motivated them to take a stand against racism. Many future activists found in the stories that circulated about Till a new pattern for dealing with the politics of Jim Crow or found old patterns difficult to maintain after learning how Till defied racial customs and responded to the white men who tried to intimidate him.[34]

Mississippi native Anne Moody was the same age as Till. His lynching in some ways made her more afraid. But it also led her "to look upon Negro men [and women] as cowards." After the boy's murder, she could no longer "respect them for smiling in a white man's face, addressing him as Mr. So-and-So, saying yessuh and nossuh when after they were home behind closed doors that same white man was a son of a bitch, a bastard, or any other name more suitable than mister." Both her mother and her white employer told her to "just do your work like you don't know nothing" and to continue to respect the invisible color line that permeated southern race relations. But Till's murder changed her. From the moment she learned about his lynching, Moody refused, despite her fears, to allow her white employer to treat her with disrespect. She even quit her job when the woman accused her of stealing. "That's how you talk to white folks?" her mother said after witnessing one exchange between the girl and her employer. "How *am* I suppose to talk to her?" Moody asked, demonstrating that she now questioned her mother's way of responding to racism. Not unlike Till, Moody was no longer willing to stay in her place, to suffer "in silence and self-denial," like the adults around her. In an interview years later, she pointedly explained that Till's murder put a "distance" between her and her mother: "I just couldn't understand why they didn't get together, why they were whispering about it instead of . . . talking openly and trying to do something about it." Mississippi civil rights leader

Aaron Henry suggested that civil rights activism was not about "whether or not you're afraid but . . . what you do when you are afraid." And the Till incident influenced how many young people, especially young southern blacks, chose to answer that question.[35]

Sellers explained in his autobiography that as a child he had an "unquestioning acceptance" of segregation. That acceptance, he recognized, grew out of a "subtle, but enormously effective, conditioning process. The older people in the community," he said, "those who knew what segregation and Jim Crow were all about, taught us what we were supposed to think and how we were supposed to act." But community adults, Sellers suggested, understood that young people might not learn their lessons. They "were always afraid that we young people would take white racism too lightly. They were always urging us to 'be careful,'" he recalled. After writing about the way adults had conditioned him to respond to racism, Sellers immediately turned to the Till case. "The atrocity that affected me the most was Emmett Till's lynching. . . . Till was only three years older than me and I identified with him. I tried to put myself in his place and imagine what he was thinking. . . . I wondered how I would have handled the situation." He also likely imagined himself doing just what Till had allegedly done — talking back to white men, refusing to be a "boy." And with Till as a model, Sellers determined by the time he was sixteen that he "was ready for change."[36]

Not all young blacks responded to the Till case with the same courage and determination, but many, including activists such as Moody, Sellers, David Jordan, Joyce Ladner, and Julian Bond, became more critical of what they considered the phoniness and cowardice of adults and decided that they would rather have self-respect than jobs or college degrees or even physical safety. Literary scholar Christopher Metress has recently suggested that Till's lynching "represents well the power of unsettling experiences to produce disorder, [to] disrupt and disorient . . . to throw . . . ways of knowing into confusion." He argues that the way the Till story came to be remembered at times challenged "conceptions of redemption" and moved African Americans "toward a more violent form of engagement with hatred and oppression." And indeed, many young people became more committed to the black freedom struggle as a result of Till's death. "That whole ordeal and that terrible killing" were, as activist Howard Love explains, the "biggest thing" in his and his friends' minds "for a long number of years." Mississippi organizer and Freedom Rider Dave Dennis later identified "the roots of [his] protest" in his early involvement in the Shreveport NAACP youth council and in hearing about Till's murder when Dennis was just fourteen or fifteen. Bond similarly recalled that "like a whole generation of young blacks, I was given unforgettable insight into the cruelties of southern-style racism and moved along the path to later activism by the graphic pictures that appeared in *Jet* magazine of Emmett Till's swollen and misshapen body." It was also the one of the earliest and most prominent memories of activist Frank Smith, who "felt as if it literally happened right down the road because [he] knew so many black kids who could have . . . been caught up in absolutely ridiculous circumstances," just like Till. Even young southern whites, including future activists Bob Zellner and Ed King, were deeply affected by Till's murder. King, who was a freshman at Millsaps College in Jackson at the time, recalled his distress: "I didn't think things like that were possible — I mean, I thought lynching was something that hadn't gone on for twenty years, thirty years."[37]

And unlike adults, young people often responded to Till's murder by imitating the Chicago boy's behavior. Moody's mother and her white employer were right. Till, the product of a northern, urban black youth culture, did not have the same respect as most southern blacks did for the invisible color line that permeated the region's social, political, and economic landscape. And that, as whites such as Moody's employer and Roy Bryant and J. W. Milam as well as young blacks such as Moody knew, made Till threatening. He was not the first young person to take a stand against racism or the first youth to inspire others to take action against segregation. But his story was especially important because of the national and international media attention it received. Just as the NAACP and young black demonstrators rewrote the social drama of lynching in the 1930s, Till unwittingly helped to rewrite the script for southern race relations. Even Ben Chaney's remarks at his brother's 1964 funeral seem strikingly reminiscent of the comments that purportedly cost Till his life almost ten years earlier: "I'm not afraid of you. I'm as good as you are," Till allegedly told his white killers. Bryant and Milam likely exaggerated Till's defiance in their paid confession to *Look* magazine, but their account of Till's bold resistance perhaps made him an even more attractive role model for his generation. Till's refusal to accept second-class status, to be intimidated by white men, to trade his dignity even for his life, heightened young blacks' expectations and set the tone for youth activism of the late 1950s and 1960s. And that youth activism, in turn, set the tone for the civil rights movement.[38]

THE YOUNG PEOPLE'S MOVEMENT

In the award-winning documentary series, *Eyes on the Prize*, Diane Nash suggests that although "the media and history seem to record it as Martin Luther King's movement . . . young people should realize that it was people just like them, their age, that formulated goals and strategies and actually developed the movement." Scholars of the movement as well as other participants and observers at the time have also recognized that young people influenced the movement. Even so, much of youth's activism remains obscure and youth's influence un- or underappreciated. As former Selma student leader Charles Maudlin recently told interviewers, one "of the most unsung stories [of the civil rights movement] is about the significance of the student movement." The history of the NAACP's youth councils suggests that young people engaged in direct-action protests as early as the 1930s and that they pushed adults, the association in general, and the movement in more militant directions. This pattern of youth activism and influence characterized the most successful period of civil rights activity as well. Accounts of direct-action protests, adult responses to youth participation in the movement, and even the mentoring relationship between adult leaders and youth in the movement all suggest that young people participated and shaped the civil rights movement to an extent not yet fully recognized by historians or the public.[39]

When the Supreme Court ruled against segregated schools in 1954, few people knew that one of the cases included in that decision began with a student-led strike. Those who did, especially whites, often questioned whether the black students at Moton High School in Prince Edward County, Virginia, had independently orchestrated a schoolwide walkout, confronted white school officials, and enlisted the help of NAACP legal counsel. The white superintendent of schools certainly remained convinced that young strike leaders were simply "parroting the questions that someone else had given them," that they "were pawns in an adult conspiracy." The same was true in other cases of youth-initiated protest. For example, some people (black and white) believed the NAACP had paid the Tougaloo Nine to start sit-in demonstrations or that liberal faculty had unduly influenced them. One man, revealing his assumptions about adult control of the movement as well as about childhood and gender, even likened adult protest leaders to bad mothers who neglected their God-given responsibilities. Both, he argued, acted childishly and should be investigated by the Society for the Prevention of Cruelty to Children. Tougaloo chaplain Ed King and others associated with the demonstrations in Jackson, however, were quick to emphasize student autonomy. And today, sixteen-year-old Barbara Johns's impatience with the accommodationist stance of Prince Edward County's black adults and her boldness in organizing students and initiating the Moton strike are better known than during the 1950s. Yet the Prince Edward strike, like most other instances of student activism, especially those prior to the Greensboro sit-ins, still receives little attention. Moreover, scholars who relate the details of the protest implicitly question the agency of the young participants by either stressing adult influences on the young protesters or carefully reconstructing events to make clear that, as unexpected as it may be, Johns and the other student strike leaders acted without adult guidance. The details of the Prince Edward story, however, also highlight patterns of protest that show the differences between young people and adults and the not-so-surprising activism and influence of young people in civil rights protests.[40]

Adults certainly influenced Barbara Johns. The girl's grandmother, Mary Croner, had grown up hating the degradation blacks faced. She even rehearsed "passionate, unheard speeches" in the woods. "I would speak out and pretend the trees was listening," Croner recalled. Johns and other Moton High students also learned from and respected their principal, Boyd Jones, who secretly and in subtle ways supported their strike. And it was certainly "fitting," as Richard Kluger has suggested, that Johns would lead a challenge against segregation: in the 1930s, her uncle, Vernon Johns, the fiery pastor who occupied the pulpit of Montgomery's Dexter Avenue Baptist Church before Martin Luther King Jr., spearheaded black Prince Edward's fight for school buses. But Barbara Johns's determination and attitude differed in important ways from the approach taken by the older blacks who influenced her, which is not surprising given that she grew up in a time with very different opportunities and a very different sense of limits and possibilities. Rather than speaking to empty woods, Johns spoke to 450 of her peers in the school auditorium and to the entire black community at mass meetings, convincing them to strike until the white community met their demands. She also explicitly rejected her principal's patience and the idea, common among older generations of black community leaders, that persistently working with the white community was the best way to achieve greater equality. Like many youth members of the NAACP as far back as the 1930s, Johns saw action as a more effective approach than patience and, perhaps more significantly, believed that she could take action. And although many similarities exist between Barbara and Vernon Johns and although she undoubtedly learned much from her uncle, Vernon Johns was a man, a minister, and an accepted authority and leader. Barbara Johns's age, her gender, her status in the community, and some of her objectives and methods set her apart from her uncle. Young Johns recognized the many positive influences in her life, but she also recognized that most of the adults around her were incapable of the same boldness and were "unwilling to challenge . . . the system that degraded them."[41]

In addition, like Clarissa Williams seventeen years later, Barbara Johns had a plan, a plan that indicates that Johns regarded her generation as markedly different from that of her parents. From the moment they began to imagine their protest, Johns and the other student leaders involved knew that keeping their plan to strike a secret from adults was essential to its success. And after the strike started, the students "voted not to seek their parents' blessing" before proceeding. They even contacted NAACP lawyers and organized mass meetings without adult help or approval. "We knew we had to do it ourselves," Johns said, "and that if we had asked for adult help before taking the first step, we would have been turned down." After the protest began, the support of adults on the national, state, and local levels made possible an effective and sustainable challenge against Jim Crow education. But movement leaders knew that Johns's assessment was essentially right. At a mass meeting shortly after the Moton High protest began, one father stated that he wished that parents had known beforehand about their children's plans. The state NAACP secretary, Lester Banks, replied that as a parent himself, he agreed. "But," he continued, "I was glad they didn't because if they had told their parents there wouldn't have been a strike."[42]

THE DOUBLE CONSCIOUSNESS OF YOUTH

In the first years of the twentieth century, W. E. B. Du Bois talked about the double consciousness of African Americans—their sense of "twoness" as blacks and as Americans. The young people who participated in civil rights protests of the 1950s and 1960s demonstrated a different sense of twoness, a sense that had to do with their age, not their race. Despite the influence and even encouragement of adults, many young civil rights activists defined themselves in opposition to their elders and recognized that as youth they enjoyed a unique perspective and opportunity for change. As sixteen-year-old SNCC activist Lyn Wells explained, "The youth of this country is a vital part of any social movement because . . . they have not yet committed themselves to the rigid rules of conformity and complacency of the 'establishment' or society." Carolyn Smith, a Priest Creek Freedom Student, shared her sense of generational disparity when she complained that "the younger generation has more get up and go than the older generation had. If the previous generation had fought harder for freedom, we might have had a civil rights bill thirty years ago." Young people expressed similar sentiments when they wrote to movement leaders grumbling that parents considered civil rights work too dangerous. "I'm sure this is a frequent problem," one New York youth wrote, "and [I] would be greatly appreciative if you could in some way minimize my mother's fear." "My dam mom is just too conservative to let me participate. . . . We liberals have a tough time with 'right-wing' parents," another high school student explained. When interviewed by white sociology students in the late 1950s and early 1960s, black college students frequently voiced their support for the civil rights movement and criticized the older generation for considering them too radical. For young people, change was happening "*entirely* too slow[ly]." And "the elders," as Xavier student Floyd Banks put it, "do not know what it is about." Looking back on her participation in the movement, one former youth activist captured the gap between the generations when she remarked that in the 1960s, she and her friends "felt our own people were not really listening to something that was worthwhile." After she became an adult, however, she "understood how afraid they were of losing everything." A white volunteer in Mississippi expressed his sense of twoness when he explained that he was at "a crucial moment in life and that to return home," to choose the adult world "where everything is secure" over the new world he was helping to create, "would be to choose a kind of death." This young activist ultimately felt more "afraid of the kind of life [he] would fall into" at home than the dangers he faced doing civil rights work in Mississippi. And Franklin McCain, one of the four Greensboro youth who sat down at the Woolworth counter in 1960, later recalled being "real scared" while also being finally convinced that he and his friends needed to take action: "We'd been kicking the idea around, then we dared each other to do it, when somebody said we were just like our elders who talk and do nothing." The sit-in movement thus began with a conscious decision by young people to choose action and uncertainty over fear and some semblance of security and to create a self-identity that they saw as fundamentally different from that of their parents.[43]

Sympathetic southern attorney Marion A. Wright also had a sense of the differences between young people and adults and of what youth could accomplish on their own. He told students gathered in Durham, North Carolina, "If I were looking for advice I would turn to this group and others like it. . . . I would not be seeking primarily for information. That is not hard to come by. I would be seeking for a spirit, an attitude, a bent of mind, and sense of adventure. That is rare and priceless. . . . [Y]outh is the period of rebellion and rejection of the *status quo*." Wright went on to congratulate young civil rights activists for their lack of timidity and for their concern with the merit of ideas rather than with who got credit for them and to congratulate white students' willingness to "identify themselves with another's woes." Oberlin College president Robert K. Carr captured another characteristic of youth organizers as well as a central tenet of postwar educational theory when he said that "students recognize that formal learning in the classroom leaves something to be desired. They have a strong need for involvement in life itself." And Bob Moses made a similar point when he told interviewers that "the young black people were trying to say something about how they felt and they were expressing this not through talking but through doing."[44]

Civil rights leader Ella Baker came to many of the same conclusions. Perhaps best known for her influence on SNCC, Baker's involvement in civil rights activities and especially in youth organizing began decades before the famous Greensboro sit-ins. After graduating from Shaw University in the late 1920s, Baker moved to New York City, where she started a Negro history club at a Harlem Y, helped form youth consumer cooperatives and forums, and worked as a NAACP youth council adviser. In the 1940s, Baker promoted youth activism and helped to establish youth councils as an NAACP field secretary and then as a national officer. Just a few months after Greensboro, Baker used Southern Christian Leadership Conference (SCLC) funds to facilitate a student conference where young people could come together, talk about their experiences, coordinate their activities, and develop new strategies. She hoped the conference would help the students create an independent, youth-led grassroots organization that would attack racism on a variety of levels. Baker appreciated that young people had a different way of approaching civil rights than did most adults, a way that fit her more populist and direct approach to racial protest. And she feared that if adults and established civil rights groups took over the student movement and used it for their own purposes, much of what young people had to offer the movement would be lost.[45]

Young African American activist Kim Burwell later described some of what young people had to offer: "Young people don't think they know everything, they aren't as critical, they invest themselves whole-heartedly. . . . Adults are too skeptical—young people are more willing to plunge in and get things done. . . . Young people don't like a lot of talk, they like action—you have to give them something to do in order to draw them in." Indeed, SNCC, which grew out of the 1960 sit-ins and student conference, differed markedly from other civil rights organizations. The group's activists frequently expressed one of the main differences in its working philosophy in letters to high school students who wanted to know how to become members of the organization. One typical reply read, "SNCC does not have a membership in the ordinary sense. Working for SNCC is what makes you a member, not 'officially' but meaningfully."[46]

WE HAVE A PLAN

Young people's approach to civil rights organizing clearly differed from that of adults. But what also challenges common perceptions of youth activism is the fact that young people organized—that Barbara Johns and others like her had plans. Throughout the history of the NAACP's youth councils, adults in the association accused young members of acting rashly. Similar accusations surrounded youth attempts to challenge Jim Crow in the 1950s and 1960s. Some of these accusations were justified. One young Birmingham demonstrator recalled that his and his friends' participation in the movement was "more of an emotional thing," often "rather spontaneous." That youth got caught up in the movement and were willing to act on feelings other than fear, however, did not make their activism any less significant. Nor did it necessarily preclude rational thought and planning. Young protesters recognized that their emotions contributed to their activism; however, they also claimed to be practical. Youth often carefully considered both the constraints they would likely encounter and ways to challenge them. Young people in Marshall, Texas, for example, revealed judicious planning as well as their attitudes about gender when they excluded women from their first sit-ins. This group of students initially agreed that female participation would make passive resistance strategies too difficult for male activists to maintain. "I can't stand a man whippin' a woman—I can't stand that, that's too much pressure," one male participant explained. Young people also studied local racial problems and state and national laws, exploring different ways to approach the injustices of Jim Crow and calculating the risks and benefits of those approaches. In the 1960s, young people, as Robert Coles noted, left school and devoted months and even years of their lives to civil rights action.[47]

While commentators at the time, as well as later scholars of the movement, suggested that young people flocked to the movement because they had little to lose, one of the truly striking aspects of youth activism during this period is precisely how much young people were consciously willing to give up. Earlier strategies for achieving racial equality had required that black youth use their personal success to help uplift the race. Before the 1950s, African American leaders asked young people ambitiously to pursue higher education and good jobs and then to use their professional training, wealth, and socioeconomic standing to benefit the larger black community and the race. In contrast, the young people, black and white, who led the struggle for racial equality after *Brown* very often chose to sacrifice, at least for a time, educational aims, professional success, parental support, and material as well as physical well-being. Young activists frequently faced the wrath of school administrators and jeopardized their academic achievements and future economic status when they demonstrated. Throughout the South, high school principals and college presidents routinely expelled black students who engaged in protest activity. Countless young blacks postponed graduation or completely relinquished their dreams of a degree to spend more time on the movement. This was such a common phenomenon that Freedom School coordinator Liz Fusco tried to help students who dropped out of high school or were suspended or expelled find ways to graduate. White students also chose to prioritize the movement over scholastic endeavors. Youth from both races delayed schooling or elected not to attend prestigious northern schools to work in southern communities. Zellner, for example, was the only one of five white students involved in interracial activities at Alabama's Huntingdon

College to earn a degree (partly because of his status as an honors student) after school officials pressured them to withdraw. Julian Bond's father, the illustrious Dr. Horace Mann Bond, endorsed his son's civil rights activities until he quit school to devote himself full-time to organizing. Then the older man "was very much put out." Eleven years later, Julian Bond finally received his college degree. Others who joined the movement gave up foreign travel, jobs, and material possessions. Arkansas activist Howard Love described the concerns facing young people considering involvement in the movement: "We went through all the discussion about what the risks were and whether the administration would support us . . . which it didn't." Although others worried about their schooling, Love "didn't worry too much about compromising my education. I worried about losing my job, because I was working my way through school."[48]

Joining the movement might in some ways have been easier for young people than for adults. Frank James, a student, like Love, at Little Rock's Philander Smith College, suggested that he and other students "could do things that people who were heavy into their careers . . . would not do . . . and we were looking at the world we were about to enter . . . and the things we didn't like." But the fact that young people were at a stage in life where they could and would decide to join the movement more frequently than their elders does not in any way diminish the hard choices or the sacrifices they made. Similarly, Moody decided to forgo a medical career and work for the movement, and her explanation of her reasons for this decision is illustrative: "You've gotta survive as a human being with dignity and with grace, and we didn't have that, . . . so what's becoming a doctor? It's a prestigious thing to do, it would be fantastic if, here I am, the only black doctor in Centreville, or something, . . . and I just couldn't do it. . . . So I just took a B.S. in biology, and I became a full-time civil rights worker making $25.00 a week." For the Till generation, middle-class respectability and the traditional idea of "lifting as we climb" competed with visions of racial equality and self-respect. As a SNCC report explained, many students, once "merely concerned about 'getting a degree' as quickly as possible," were redefining their roles in the political process and their ideas about what qualified someone meaningfully to participate in society and lead a fulfilling life.[49]

Accounts from those who did not participate extensively in the movement reveal much about competing notions of success among young people and about what young people gave up. One of Ernest Green's friends admitted that she was not among those who integrated Little Rock's Central

High because she already had plans: "I was editor in chief of the paper [at the black high school], and you know, I had goals set for that year, and I was trying very hard to make certain my senior year would be a memorable one, in the sense of how I had projected it to be." SNCC activist Les Holingsworth first thought about getting involved in demonstrations in 1960 but had "other things on my mind." Moreover, he conceded, "I didn't have the guts." He bought a car instead, a decision that "kept me locked in debt, so it took away some of my freedom." Holingsworth also confessed that he did not become an organizer until later because he "wanted to be a playboy." Young people, like their elders, understandably found themselves torn between the movement and other opportunities for advancement, well-being, and satisfaction.[50]

Perhaps most remarkably, young civil rights workers were also well aware that their activism might bring physical harm and even death. Young people faced the same racist violence as adults. Their youth did not make them any less vulnerable to high-powered fire hoses, vicious dogs, or baton-wielding police or offer any greater protection against rocks, bombs, tear gas, or the fury of hate-filled mobs. It did not keep newspapers from printing their names and addresses. It did not keep them out of prisons or workhouses. An East St. Louis youth voiced the conscious commitment that many young people made to the movement when he said, "If death is what it takes, we have all oriented ourselves that if we have to die, we hope it will not be in vain. . . . We will continue this at any cost. . . . [W]e will go all the way, if it requires death, all the way." A young Montgomery demonstrator captured the sense of determination among young people and the very real risks they took: "Of course we were scared when the police on horses and motorcycles charged us. . . . Maybe the movement needs another martyr." Youth at the University of Texas at Austin recognized the high price that others were paying for racial equality and indicated their own determination to pay some of those costs—and to shame others into doing the same—in a newspaper article that recounted the beating of a black Houston man and the jailing of Nashville students. With such happenings, it asked, "Why are you buying in stores too cowardly to serve Negros? Why are you going to places your brothers cannot? Why are you saying, 'but, but, but'?"[51]

Young activists consciously made choices that involved significant, sometimes hidden, personal costs. Moreover, contrary to popular opinion, as Coles explains, even projects that appeared "spontaneous" often required planning, persistence, and negotiation. Johns and other student leaders at Moton met several times and attended Parent-Teacher Association and school board meetings for months before beginning the strike. Their actions involved detailed planning and coordination; they arranged to have the principal called away from the school, orchestrated a student assembly, made speeches, and handed out picket signs. Student organizers also considered some of the possible repercussions of their strike: they would likely not be able to attend school for an extended period, their parents might object to their actions, and they might be arrested. Johns and her friends, of course, had no way of knowing that Prince Edward County's whites would not surrender segregated schools until the mid-1960s, and their belief that collective action would prevent arrests was somewhat naive, but perhaps only in light of later civil-rights-related mass arrests. Their plans demonstrate, however, that these young activists thought ahead, took a practical approach to civil rights activity, and were not as constrained as adults were by their fears. Rather than not thinking about their actions, young protesters often just thought differently about civil rights activity than most adults and were more eager and willing to take action to change racial conditions. And in the end, at least in the Prince Edward example, whether local adults actively supported or opposed the strike, the majority of the students' parents expressed pride in what they recognized was "the responsible thoughtful way in which the students had staged the protest." Others who observed student protesters similarly recognized that "these are not young hotheads." Rather than being imprudent types, those who engaged in demonstrations often did so "as a witness to their faith." Or, as a Southern Conference Education Fund publication suggested, typical youth civil rights activists were like the Steele brothers of Tallahassee, Florida—excellent students, scholarship recipients, and accomplished musicians.[52]

White youth who voiced support for their black counterparts' protests likewise insisted that their decisions involved considerable deliberation as well as independence. As Birmingham-Southern College student Thomas Reeves explained in a particularly pointed letter to the editor of the *Birmingham Post-Herald*:

> Our action was not hasty or irrational even though it was entirely student created and inspired. Although we deliberately acted without involving our administration, we asked the opinions of

many local adult leaders before sending the petition. Perhaps we were brainwashed—that is, perhaps [our status as college students] has partially cleansed our minds of the prejudice, ignorance, and pettiness which has always been a part of our moral and educational environment. . . . I hope that a few people will realize that students are not impressionable children or brainwashed Communists, but that we are trying to be sincere and freedom-loving Christians. We are young, it is true, and we make mistakes like other people, but surely we are entitled to our own expressed opinion without threat of shame, ostracism and violence. We believe we have seen at least a glimpse of the truth . . . and, so far, we are not willing to turn our backs and blind ourselves.

Also telling was an exchange between Reeves and a white adult who wrote to the newspaper to praise the young man's "courage to speak out" and to express the belief that "you younger whites must be the ones to take action to arouse the rest of us" who cannot act because of "reprisals in jobs and otherwise." Reeves wrote back to explain that despite his youth, his civil rights work had carried serious consequences, costing him his church job and time in jail.[53]

OPPORTUNITY AND ACTIVISM

If their youth made them less constrained and more willing to act than adults, other generational differences also influenced students' actions. Johns explained that she and her friends were "really bothered . . . very angry" that they attended classes in tar shacks and rode discarded buses while white students in the district enjoyed nice facilities and equipment. Researchers exposed the discrepancies between white and black, rural and urban, northern and southern schools in the 1920s and 1930s. But not until later did many students witness the extent of those discrepancies firsthand. Whereas in 1930 less than 55 percent of American youth attended secondary schools, by 1950 more than 76 percent of fourteen- to seventeen-year-olds went to high school, and by 1960 that number had reached 89 percent. By the time the Supreme Court ruled against segregated public education, graduating from high school had become the norm for America's youth. Overall graduation rates for black youth remained lower than the overall national averages but had increased even more dramatically as many southern communities constructed their first high schools for black youth. Between the 1930s and 1940s, according to Ambrose Caliver, senior specialist on Negro education for the Office of Education, the number of black students attending high school more than doubled, and black high school graduation rates tripled. Maryland's Baltimore County, for example, opened three secondary schools for black students in the fall of 1938. Previously, the school district had provided high school training only to the few young blacks who passed special examinations and paid residentially based (which meant race-based) tuition fees. And significantly, as historian Peter Lau explains, the 1948–49 school year was the first during which Clarendon County, South Carolina, offered twelfth grade to its black students. The students' determination to improve their new but decidedly unequal educational circumstances (they had to pay fees and raise money for their own books and equipment, much of which the white principal never delivered) "helped propel the equalization campaign forward" and led to one of the cases decided with the *Brown* case. Attention to the recreational needs of youth in the 1930s also resulted in the expansion of extracurricular activities for high school students. American students, including black students, increasingly participated in school sports teams and diverse school clubs. And those activities or the lack of those activities or of facilities or equipment for them often contributed to black students' sense of racial injustice. Indeed, historians including William Chafe and Aldon Morris locate the origins of the later sit-in movement in black high schools, and R. Scott Baker finds that new school facilities and programs for South Carolina's black students positively affected their sense of racial pride and their political activism during the 1950s.[54]

The expansion of high school services for black youth and the proliferation of student clubs and sports in the 1940s and 1950s also gave Johns and many of her classmates opportunities to travel to other schools and towns for extracurricular activities. Those opportunities introduced them, at relatively young ages, to conditions outside their local communities. Earlier generations of young southern blacks, who often lacked any high school facilities or training, did not commonly enjoy such experiences. According to Johns, these experiences made her and her friends keenly aware of the differences between their own and other schools, especially schools for whites, as well as more angry and determined to do something about local racial conditions. The increasing availability of postsecondary and graduate schooling for blacks, including the desegregation of formerly all-white state universities, similarly raised young blacks' awareness, expectations, and determination. Before World War II, attending college was a rare privilege for most American youth, and especially blacks. In the 1940s, one U.S. congressman suggested that "education does not necessarily bring happiness; frequently it brings dissatisfaction because of an awareness of bad conditions. . . . [I]t first makes us aware of the improvements that should be made." A black New Orleans resident made a similar observation in 1959 to a Loyola University of the South sociology student: "The young people of this generation, especially, show a better understanding of the problem, and are more active in helping to improve it. . . . The schools are mainly responsible for this."[55]

African Americans commonly noted the increased opportunities available to black youth and recognized their effects on the younger generation. A southern black man who had earned a math degree told interviewers in the late 1940s that just a few years earlier, "Negro students could not get the education they can get to-day." Frank Walker, a New Orleans postal clerk, reflected that education was "going to change everything." In fact, he pointed out, the attitudes of local college students had already shifted, giving him "a feeling of genuine optimism." Hodding Carter, a white southern journalist who won a Pulitzer in 1946 for his editorials on racial tolerance, wrote an essay for the *New York Times Magazine* in anticipation of the Supreme Court's decision in the *Brown* case in which he told the story of a fictitious but true-to-life southern black family. Carter focused his story on the family's young nephew, a war veteran and University of Arkansas graduate student. The young man, a beneficiary of both the GI Bill— the 1944 legislation that gave returning servicemen college or vocational training benefits—and the recent integration of the state's preeminent postsecondary institution, questions the racial disparities that still exist and makes the older generation "uncomfortable" by continually arguing with his elders. From the author's perspective, the expanded opportunities available to younger blacks, especially those in urban areas, made them less satisfied than their parents with the pace of progress.[56]

Young people expressed dissatisfaction with better but nevertheless inadequate and inferior schools and educational programs. In interviews conducted in 1959 and 1960, southern black college students noted that educational facilities and opportunities had improved but complained about poorly equipped high schools with limited music, language, physical education, and advanced math and science classes. The schools were crowded and in disrepair. Reiterating the NAACP's arguments to the Supreme Court in *Brown*, students also suggested that discrepancies between white and black schools created an inferiority complex in young blacks. Many young people identified the negative mental and emotional effects of Jim Crow as its most disturbing aspect. Moreover, these students regarded education as "the equalizing factor." They clearly understood the connections between economic inequalities and educational inequalities. They knew that in America, "education provides the ladder of escape from low social and economic status." Taking a practical view of the matter, young blacks told their white interviewers that since segregated schools led to damaging psychological problems for both races and poor job prospects for African Americans, integrated schools were a fitting remedy. Respondents demonstrated an acute awareness of continuing educational inequalities and their consequences for personal well-being and future work opportunities. These comments also showed the influence of other popular arguments for integration: "Being segregated there's no chance to learn anything about each other, and . . . many great ideas . . . have been hampered," and the "worst part [of segregation] is the limitations of the education system. Russia is ahead and [if] we would realize the potentiality of the Negro as a scientist perhaps we would be more capable of competing with them." These youth had clearly internalized the cold war arguments for civil rights. In addition, they as well as Johns and her friends could more clearly see patterns of racism and compare their situation to that of others largely because of their expanded educational opportunities.[57]

Those experiences also helped young African Americans see themselves as part of a society that reached beyond the borders of their hometowns. The increasing mobility of young people during the post–World War II era and their growing connections to the outside world influenced civil rights protest. Increasing mobility—whether in the form of young urban blacks going south to visit relatives or attend college or young rural blacks going to urban centers for summer jobs, to visit family, or to participate in school programs—and an increasing awareness of the larger world through television and other media led to a determination to fight racism at home. Frank James, who became involved in demonstrations as a college student in the early 1960s, recalled that the crisis at Central High made him "aware of the situations in the states," and after he moved to Arkansas from Oklahoma, the more he traveled around the state, "the more rage grew in me." Bond similarly recognized "that the black world had this national character to it" after moving from Pennsylvania to Atlanta. That he and his friends read in the *Atlanta Daily World* about the Greensboro demonstrations and immediately started their own sit-in movement further testified to the national character of the black world and how it influenced young African Americans. Xavier student Sandra Baker reported that she "didn't really know integration until she was exposed to it in Nebraska [one summer] and then she *really* became dissatisfied with segregation." And the young men who started the Greensboro sit-in were inspired both by Little Rock students who visited their community and by news of the Montgomery Bus Boycott. Whatever the source of youth activists' information, young Claude Smith concluded that the "present generation [of black youth] are becoming aware of problems facing the world today and they realize that the only way of solving these problems is to" integrate. In other words, Smith, like many other youth, saw his personal and community struggles with segregation and discrimination in a national, even international context. Young activist Lolis Elie captured many of the reasons why the young people of the 1950s and 1960s (who he recognized were not the first "to say, well, Goddammit, I'm going to sit here [where blacks are not allowed]") had engaged in widespread protests:

> The fact that there was that decision [the *Brown* ruling] coinciding with the fact that [there were] probably more young black kids in college than any other time. . . . There was something bigger than your neighborhood. [You had] exposure to a larger world. . . . All the subtle things that don't come to your mind because you take it for granted make you a different kind of person, having a different kind of experience, unlike other generations that preceded you. . . . Going to college is more than just what you read in the books. . . . You're encountering a whole lot of other people, see, so that if somebody comes to New Orleans and tells me something different about their experience somewhere, it makes me a different person and it makes me . . . perceptive to different kinds of things. I would perceive certain experiences different than my parents did.

Coles was right. Young blacks in the 1950s and 1960s were growing up less isolated, and their experiences influenced the way they saw themselves and their situation, directly contributing to their activism. The same could likely be said about young whites. As the head of the NAACP, Roy Wilkins, suggested, "Any youngster who looks at the television or reads the sports page must suspect that there is something queer about the segregation arguments of adults."[58]

A POLITY OF THEIR OWN

As a high school student, Johns was also not isolated in the ways she experienced segregation and racism. That she shared this daily encounter with Jim Crow with hundreds of other young blacks influenced the action she took as well. Many of the examples or stories of black resistance to Jim Crow that young blacks witnessed or heard as they grew up included only examples and stories of individual blacks standing up to individual whites. Even new books on African American history, designed to inspire race pride in black youth and teach them about earlier instances of racial protest, highlighted the examples of individual blacks such as Frederick Douglass and Harriet Tubman or the accomplishments and successes of individual blacks such as Paul Robeson and Mary McLeod Bethune. Family stories of defiance and books about notable African Americans certainly challenged the doctrines of white supremacy and provided young blacks with positive role models. SNCC worker Charles Robertson, for one, noted that black history played a role in his activism: "We had the image and we knew who some of the great heroes were," he recalled. And the young people who started the Greensboro sit-ins acknowledged that books by and about blacks contributed to their decision to protest Jim Crow. Yet by focusing on individuals, those stories and books also implicitly suggested that challenging the color line was a solitary endeavor. Young people, especially as they entered the labor force as maids or stock boys, had isolated experiences with Jim Crow and sometimes defied the rules of racism as individuals. African American youth, however, more commonly experienced the strictures of Jim Crow collectively—at school or at recreational facilities, among other places. As adults, they might feel the constraints of Jim Crow more as individuals; as youth, however, their everyday shared experiences with segregation helped them see the collective nature of those constraints and encouraged them to confront Jim Crow collectively as well. Early militant civil rights protest activity most commonly involved those who experienced segregation collectively—that is, young people who experienced racism collectively in schools and identified themselves collectively as students, or working-class blacks who experienced racism

collectively in factories or other work environments and identified themselves collectively as workers. Barbara Johns certainly believed that students' shared oppression required collective action and solidarity, even
likening the Moton High strike to those conducted by unions.[59]

As he reminisced about growing up in the Jim Crow South, John Rice
noted that young people had their own "polity"—their own youth culture and organizational structure. This collective identity shaped and influenced civil rights protests. Johns called on student council and other
club leaders to help organize the Moton strike. In the 1960s, James Bevel
similarly approached student leaders and drew on the "cohesion and camaraderie" of young people to organize protest demonstrations. By engaging the help of student leaders in both Jackson, Mississippi, and Birmingham, Alabama, he helped mobilize hundreds of youth demonstrators
practically overnight, a feat he recognized to be impossible among adults
who lacked the close relationships and informal organizational structures
of youth. SNCC organizers likewise found organizing efforts among young
people much easier than among adults, in part because of existing youth
networks. SNCC organizers quickly discovered that freedom schools, for
example, were an effective way "to get into the schools" and coordinate
a statewide student movement. Around the country, youth synagogues,
Christian youth groups, and other organizations provided an organizing
base for youth civil rights protest activity and helped the movement spread
rapidly among young Americans. Even in the 1930s and 1940s, the NAACP
found that a few interested youth could result in councils that included entire school populations. Aware of young people's proclivity for networking,
the association also specifically encouraged young members to work with
established youth clubs and organizations to promote civil rights activities.
Local ministers, such as the Baltimore Bethel African Methodist Episcopal Church's Harrison J. Bryant, were often quite successful in recruiting
church youth for civil rights demonstrations as well. Moreover, as Bevel
noted, because "the students . . . had a community they'd been in since elementary school . . . if one of them would go to jail, that had a direct effect
upon another because they were classmates." In McComb, Mississippi,
after whites jailed fifteen-year-old Brenda Travis for protest activity and
the school principal expelled her, more than a hundred of her classmates
walked out of school and marched to city hall. Most of them subsequently
spent time in jail and engaged in other demonstrations. Students in Baton Rouge similarly refused to attend classes until the principal reinstated

seventeen schoolmates whom he had kicked out after they staged a sit-in at Kress. Jerome Smith explained that "the whole community thing" "set fire" to him about the Baton Rouge student movement. One of the Tougaloo students involved in library read-ins also talked about "the whole [student] community thing." She explained that "a lot of students were waiting for us when they brought us back in police cars," making her experience "a joyful time" instead of a time of fear. And Ernest Green, the first black student to graduate from Little Rock's Central High, similarly alluded to the importance of youth communities in civil rights protest when he acknowledged his friends who remained at the all-black Horace Mann School and decidedly in the background of civil rights struggles, for being "super supportive" as he "cracked this white institution."[60]

Because of "group pressure," even youth who "held back at first [sometimes] wound up leading" protest activities, as in the case of one Texas girl who got involved after being "badgered for her reluctance. . . . You gotta go along with the program. You can't say 'I'm not going,'" classmates told her and other wary bystanders. Youth in Montgomery similarly pressured their peers to boycott classes rather than ride city buses during the 1955 demonstrations. "Students would affect other students," one former NAACP youth council member recalled. Another youth activist explained that the movement "became sort of hot, white hot," so young people only had to decide how to become involved, not whether to join. An Arkansas protester similarly described the way the movement worked: "If something was happening in Mississippi or happening in Alabama, in particular if young people are doing it, you felt we ought to be doing it here, and that's how most things happened." And Julia Washington Bond captured the way that her son, Julian, and many other youth thought about the demonstrations when she told an interviewer that despite the dangers associated with joining the sit-in movement, "there was hardly any way to escape it. [And] pretty soon there were no onlookers left, because it was very hard for students to see everybody else doing something that they weren't doing."[61]

Johns's reliance on established student leaders and networks and her success in mobilizing widespread support for the protest first among young people and then among adults in the black community characterized much of the later civil rights movement. In 1957, a national education journal suggested that "if you get a child interested in doing something, his parents will soon be drawn into it too." The article described how young Americans in Europe fostered better international relations with their foreign peers. But young blacks similarly worked as "ambassadors in blue jeans" in their communities. Throughout the South, young African Americans functioned as liaisons between civil rights groups or ideas and local blacks. The work of scholars such as Charles Payne and John Dittmer confirms that throughout Mississippi, young people were often the first and most enthusiastic supporters of civil rights activity and that their participation and influence made a "sustained statewide movement possible." In Delta towns and urban centers alike, "hard-headed" young people such as June Johnson and the McGhee brothers pulled "their reluctant elders into the movement after them."[62] Peter Lau's study of South Carolina and Christina Greene's work on North Carolina have similarly shown that young people were a vital part of the "driving force for change" in local communities within those states. Participants in and observers of the movement in the 1960s talked about the influence of young people on the movement as if it were a new phenomenon. Many people saw sixteen-year-old SNCC activist Lyn Wells as stating the obvious when she asserted that "the role of high school students across the nation in the civil rights movement has changed a great deal in the last few years. In many southern towns high school students took the initial step to become active in the 'movement' and were *later* followed by their parents." The role of young people had changed, or perhaps more accurately, perceptions of young people's role in the movement changed with the "intense generational self-consciousness" of the baby boom. As the movement became larger and more visible, more and more young people became determined to move with or without their elders. America's domestic-centered political culture also helped to direct attention to the activism of young people and to shift perceptions of their activism. Moreover, perceptions of change and national media coverage of youth protests further encouraged young people to become active in the struggle for racial equality. Yet as the Prince Edward example illustrates, young people influenced the movement and inspired adult activism throughout the postwar period.[63]

A CHILD SHALL LEAD THEM

If Johns feared that adults would not initially support her plan, she also believed that after she and her peers took action, their example would motivate adults to join the fight. One of the first student leaders whom

Johns approached about the strike recalled talking with her about the inferiority of their school and their parents' lack of progress with the white school board. After their discussion, Johns insisted, "Our parents ask us to follow them, but in some instances . . . a little child shall lead them." Johns's statement reflected in religious terms the political and cultural ideas about childhood and youth then so prominent in public discussions about education, national security, and the future of American democracy. Whether or not she recognized the connections between her biblical reference and contemporary debates about young people as important agents of sociopolitical change, Johns certainly recognized the possible political dimensions of the comment. Not unlike Martin Luther King Jr., she drew on the black community's religious culture and America's child-centered political culture to promote action against white supremacy.[64]

The children of Prince Edward did indeed lead their elders. The Reverend L. Francis Griffin, who usually spearheaded community efforts against racial inequality in the county, regarded the student strike as an important "means of rallying the black community." He was inspired by the students and told Farmville's black adults that "anybody who would not back these children after they stepped out on a limb is not a man. . . . Anybody who won't fight against racial prejudice is not a man." Griffin's challenge to the black community recognized the bold action of the Moton High students as an essential stimulant to further community activism. But by conflating a willingness to fight prejudice with manhood, it also contradicted Johns's vision of children as vital actors in the cause of racial equality and diminished their part in the protest. Johns had hoped to stir widespread support for the student strike by telling community adults, "Don't let Mr. Charlie, Mr. Tommy, or Mr. Pervall stop you from backing us. We are depending on you." She stressed the young strikers' relative courage and determination in the face of white retaliation and their hope that adults would support their actions instead of surrendering to whites as usual. Griffin, however, stressed the students' helplessness and youth and the need for adults to take the lead in the protest. A sermon Griffin gave a few months later, enthusiastically received by his congregation, similarly highlighted ideas about children and corresponding notions of adulthood instead of acknowledging the autonomy and actions of the young protesters. Griffin's speech also employed the same social science arguments about racism's effects on young people that would help sway the Supreme Court to rule against segregated schools a few years later:

"When I look and see healthy colored babies, I think how God has brought them into the world properly and how the rotten system of the Southland will twist them into warped personalities, cringing cowards, unable to cope with the society into which they were unwillingly thrown and which they have a God-given right to enjoy. . . . I'm willing to die rather than let these children down."[65]

Speeches and newspaper stories with similar ideas became even more common after the *Brown* ruling asked schoolchildren to take the front lines in the battle against segregation, especially in the 1960s, when student demonstrations spread across the South and captured widespread media attention. In the early part of the decade, for example, high school and college students in Baltimore circulated a brochure that attributed students' heightened concern for civil rights to their relative temporal proximity to the first moment they "realized that all people are not treated equally." In addition to contrasting the innocence of childhood with the social construction of race, it more poignantly asked readers,

> How many times a day do you see children? Most of us see them quite often, playing in parks with laughter and joy, on their way to school with serious faces, when we tuck them in at night and hear their last little confidential whispers of the excitement and thrills which have befallen them. Much of our community life is taken up with children, educating them, protecting them, loving them. But do we really think of them? Do we stop to think how many times a Negro child is told that he cannot go into this or that store and have an ice cream soda? Do we wonder whether a white child is troubled over the contradiction of ideals, when he is told, on the one hand, that God loves all men, and, on the other hand, that Negros are dirty and inferior and unworthy of his friendship?

The publication went on to ask for community support "so that we will never have to teach our children to fear and discriminate."[66]

Remarks such as Griffin's and young people's strategies for promoting civil rights suggest the significance of ideas about childhood and young people's activism. They also suggest one reason why young people's contributions to the civil rights movement have remained obscure for so long. Widespread beliefs about childhood cast youth, despite evidence to the contrary, as dependent and innocent victims. Johns and her classmates hardly seemed "cowards, unable to cope with . . . society." And the young

Baltimore students had obviously overcome their warped childhoods. As
historian Genna Rae McNeil argues, "Committed black struggle grew out
of health, not pathology." Nevertheless, Griffin and later Martin Luther
King Jr. and other adult leaders of the civil rights movement as well as
journalists and sometimes youth used young people's activism and widespread notions of childhood and the psychological dangers of segregation
to shame black adults and white America into supporting the movement.
Implicitly or explicitly juxtaposing the activism of young people and ideas
about childhood with the inactivity of adults and ideas about adulthood,
and in particular manhood, encouraged black adult action and white sympathy — whether in Prince Edward, Birmingham, McComb, Baltimore, or
Jackson. But speeches such as Griffin's also implied that civil rights activism was rightly the province of adults, especially adult men, and that adult
activism was inherently more valuable than youth activism.[67]

Bevel, known for his work organizing young people, convinced Martin
Luther King Jr. to let young people join the 1963 Birmingham demonstrations by bringing up the idea of children's agency. Because children could
not be sheltered from the effects of racial prejudice, Bevel reminded King,
children had the right to protest segregation. Moreover, Bevel suggested,
if children as young as five could choose Christ, then they could hardly
be considered too young to choose to act on their faith.[68] But if Bevel recognized the agency of youth, many other adult organizers failed to fully
appreciate young people's potential contributions or their autonomy. Instead of seeing young people as independent political actors, they more
commonly talked about "using" children. They saw letting schoolchildren
march as simply a tactic, a means to an end.[69] Revealing a bias for adult
participation and diminishing the idea of young people as independent
agents of change, the SCLC's Wyatt Tee Walker commented about Birmingham, "We knew we were right to use the children." "We had run out of
troops. We had scraped the bottom of the barrel of adults who could go.
. . . [W]e knew we needed to involve the students." After the Birmingham
campaign, U.S. attorney general Robert Kennedy similarly indicated that
he saw civil rights protest as an inherently adult activity when he pressured King not to "use" children in future protests. King agreed with Kennedy's premise and decided that the next major civil rights campaign, the
March on Washington, would at least officially be restricted to older youth
and adults.[70]

Because of widespread beliefs about childhood, "using" young people in the Birmingham campaign was an effective tactic. Whites and blacks around the country responded when they saw dogs, fire hoses, and police batons subduing schoolchildren. King, who had only hesitantly approved the participation of child protesters, was "jubilant" to see the overwhelming support for the movement among adults that the children's participation generated. But King, who at times recognized "the immensely responsible [and creative] role of students," regarded youth participation primarily as a strategy for dramatizing civil rights issues rather than as an expression of young people's determination to fight for racial equality. For King and for many adult leaders, the participation of thousands of young people in Birmingham and other civil rights campaigns and their willingness to confront the dangers of white supremacy, stand up for their rights, and go to jail seemed less significant than the national attention and adult support for the movement their participation brought.[71]

Organizer Frank Smith showed his bias for adult participation when he expressed excitement that in the fall of 1963 (after the spring Birmingham demonstrations and the 15 September church bombing), local adults in Mississippi, "as opposed to youth," began "to play a larger role." Aaron Henry told the NAACP national office that "the best asset we have" was not that young people were determined to make the Clarksdale, Mississippi, boycott work but that the schoolchildren who initiated the boycott "have won the support of their parents in not going downtown." In 1964, many Freedom Summer volunteers in Mississippi, despite their youth, similarly demonstrated that they valued adult participation and issues over youth participation and projects. CORE initiated freedom schools in part to organize "a student force" for civil rights work. Ultimately, however, volunteers considered freedom schools politically valuable primarily "when canvassing was impractical." Moreover, voter registration work carried much more status than freedom school work. As one volunteer put it, "Running a freedom school is an absurd waste of time." Not surprisingly, given the low status of freedom schools, women more commonly worked there as teachers while most of what volunteers considered the "really important political work" went to men. A few freedom school teachers revealed a similar focus on adult participation and a belief that civil rights activities were more appropriate for adults when they complained that "the older people, who should be most willing to cooperate in any way possible, are often the most uncooperative in the community. . . . If only the adults of the community would wake up and see what they are really doing to their children by keeping them at home, the Summer Project in McComb would probably be the most successful in the state." Many years later, one organizer insisted that despite public opinion and much evidence, "it was primarily the older people who were instrumental to SNCC."[72]

Scholars of the civil rights movement, even those who have greatly expanded our understanding of civil rights organizing, especially organizing on the local level, and challenged many traditional assumptions about the movement, have similarly focused on adult activism. Implicit and at times explicit in their accounts of the civil rights movement is the idea that youth activism was an important means of inspiring adult activism but that "youngsters" had themselves been inspired by adults and an adult African American organizing tradition and that adult participation was preferable to and innately more significant than youth participation. These studies have encouraged scholars to question how the media and historians have framed the civil rights movement. Focusing on violence, big events, and national leaders has discouraged "more complex understandings of the movement and its evolution" and obscured much of the organizing process.[73] Understandings of the movement have also been obscured, however, by assumptions about the role of youth and the relative value or lack of value of youth organizing.

THE REAL TRANSFORMATION

SNCC organizer Michael Thelweel observed that the "gap between generations lies like a blight on every Negro community. . . . [A]ny gathering of Negroes in Mississippi consists of teenagers and older people." His comment reflects the unspoken presumption, common in many historical studies of the movement, that what really mattered in Mississippi and elsewhere was the presence of local adult leadership and an adult tradition of protest or that youth sometimes inspired adults to join or sympathize with the movement. The emphasis is always on adult participation—the lack of it causes a "blight," its presence marks a significant turning point. Parents, teachers, and other adults certainly inspired some young people to take action against Jim Crow. And instances of adults supporting civil rights protests after young people engaged in direct action and especially after whites hurt young protesters filled civil rights organizations' reports and press releases. Young people undoubtedly inspired adults to join the movement. But without diminishing the importance of adult influence on

youth, adult activism, or young people's influence on adult activism and
leadership, especially at the local level, we need to take more seriously the
activism of young people and see it not merely as an important precursor
to adult civil rights involvement but also as a measure of the movement.
We need to recognize the importance of young people's willingness in the
1950s and 1960s to challenge the status quo despite adult hesitance and
the continued threat of racial violence.[74]

One of the most remarkable stories about the movement in the late
1950s and 1960s is that regardless of adult activity and in spite of adult
inactivity, young people identified with and participated in the movement
throughout the South. The gap between the generations was less a blight
than a positive indicator of significant differences between the members
of the younger generation and their parents. Students and local youth may
only have been used as "auxiliary help when adults were willing to lead"
community organizing efforts, but young people could always be counted
on to help with organizing, whatever the role. Organizers and scholars
often suggest that the most striking aspect of Freedom Summer was that
whites paid closer attention to Mississippi's racial violence and that in
some communities, black adults worked to secure voting rights. But young
blacks also flocked to freedom schools, with or without their parents' permission and despite white terrorist attacks on those schools, in numbers
that defied organizers' most optimistic expectations. Young people eagerly
canvassed neighborhoods, encouraging adults to get involved and to register to vote. Indeed, because of youth autonomy and enthusiasm for the
movement, Bob Moses considered laughable a Mississippi judge's propo-
sition that SNCC organizers were "the leaders who are causing young children to be led like sheep to the pen to be slaughtered." In Jackson, black
community leaders similarly realized that they had no control over young
protesters. As Tougaloo president A. D. Beittel explained, "The students
have already made up their minds." It was less important, in the words
of one teenage activist, that "parents have cowered down and refused to
take a stand" than that Mississippi youth were determined to integrate
libraries and lunch counters and to register voters or that even twelve-
year-olds were eagerly playing the part of Rosa Parks on Jackson's city
buses. As freedom school teachers in McComb observed, "Negro youths
have proved that they are willing to help their race in any way that they
can." White volunteer Sandra Adickes certainly had a sense of the value of
youth activism when she wrote in her diary that one of the local girls "is a

Civil rights workers at a Freedom Press office in Hattiesburg, Mississippi, 1964.
(© Bettman/Corbis)

fantastic worker—I love the way the adults begin by being amused by her
and then go on the defensive. The introduction is usually, 'Have you went
to register?' and no excuse will serve." And perhaps the most remarkable
story about Birmingham was not that young people helped to "awaken the
conscience of the white man" or spur black adults to action but that young
blacks, including Freeman Hrabowski, readily joined the demonstrations
and that they came to see, in his words, that "the voices of the young were
significant, and that young people could think and act responsibly, and
that our actions could change the course of history and the world . . . that
not only did we have the right to sit at lunch counters or enter buildings
through the front door, but that we had the responsibility to claim those
rights."[75]

Martin Luther King Jr. and others may have thought the SCLC was
"using" young people in Birmingham, but young people had a different
perspective. As Bevel had insisted, this was their fight, too. One teenage
SNCC activist explained that although students had "long been talked
about as young and impressionable," "these very students" were "forming
definite convictions about the world around them" and taking "the lead
in our society in putting their convictions to test." Student demonstrators
complained that "people always give us this line about being the leaders

of tomorrow; that's bunk, we're the leaders of today." Johns and the other Moton High students saw themselves as capable, independent actors. Moreover, she explained exactly who, if anyone, was "using" whom when she wrote about "the pride I had in the parents (and others) who supported us. They were at first bewildered by it all — but they attended the meetings in full strength. . . . They stood behind us — timidly at first but firmly." Young people in Jackson, Mississippi, expressed a similar sentiment when they congratulated Tougaloo faculty who had followed their example and "had taken to agitatin' Jackson restaurants." High school "friends of SNCC" in the Washington, D.C., area likewise demonstrated their sense of autonomy and worth when they wrote a letter to the White House requesting that the president meet with them. "President [Lyndon] Johnson will undoubtedly be very pleased and interested in seeing this delegation of students," it read. "We are the most vital part of the Great Society that the president *and we* are trying to build." Civil rights organizers throughout the country repeatedly discovered that young people considered themselves significant political actors in their own right and were determined to move with or without anyone else's support. "The kids were going to do it anyway. . . . [T]hey were holding their own mass meetings and making plans. . . . [W]e didn't want them to have to do it alone," one so-called leader of the Albany movement explained. And one young activist, when asked if he considered King the leader of the movement, replied, "Hell no! I'm my own leader!"[76]

False assumptions about youth organizing or the subordinate position of young people in the movement often led to accusations that black adults were "using" children, as in Prince Edward and Birmingham, or that organizers such as those in Mobile, Alabama, lacked any real support for their programs because most participants were young. Such assumptions also resulted in newspaper stories about adults leading youth demonstrations, most notably when the *New York Times* labeled white organizer Bob Zellner, who had just arrived in town and only reluctantly participated, the leader of a McComb student strike. Adickes told a similar and fairly typical story about spontaneously going to the Hattiesburg Public Library with a group of local black youth who requested library cards, were refused, and sat down to read. The police chief soon arrived and identified Adickes as the leader. Her response: "I'm not the leader, I'm a friend of these girls." The group then moved on to the local Kress lunch counter. Assumptions about youth clearly obscured the role of twenty-five black high school students in Galveston, Texas, who sat down at local lunch counters with copies of the U.S. Constitution and chanted, "We'll take a seat and sit for a week." Confronted with this display of student activism, a white manager requested that the students "secure the help of a responsible Negro adult who might talk the situation over with the managers of the stores." The youth, less concerned with recognition than success (another characteristic of youth organizing), enlisted the help of (or perhaps "used") a "responsible Negro adult committee" that negotiated with the white manager to work out an acceptable time frame for integration. A few weeks later, *Life* magazine featured a picture of an interracial group of four local adult religious leaders holding a sign that read, "Welcome to Galveston." The "quiet negotiations" of these "catalysts," the magazine reported, had resulted in integrated lunch counters. There was no mention of the real catalysts — the youth whose not-so-quiet protest had initiated those negotiations.[77]

It is not surprising, then, that our historical memory is similarly clouded by assumptions about youth and adults. We commemorate Martin Luther King Jr.'s birthday instead of the anniversary of the Greensboro sit-ins. When we think of the Montgomery Bus Boycott, we think of King and Rosa Parks, not Claudette Colvin. Months before Parks (the girl's NAACP youth council adviser) refused to give up her seat, the fifteen-year-old Colvin "electrified Montgomery's black community" when she was beaten and jailed for refusing to move to the back of a city bus. Nor do we remember the key role that other Montgomery young people played by boycotting buses en masse (students represented a large percentage of usual riders), shuttling people around town, and passing out leaflets. When we see images of crowds marching across the Edmund Pettus Bridge or on the road to Alabama's capitol, we also rarely consider young people's part in the Selma campaign. But as local youth activist Charles Robertson told interviewers, one of the "important" aspects of the Selma movement was "that while . . . there were many adults involved . . . kids were the ones who were the first leaders, the advance leaders, and the parents came [later] to make sure that they were okay. . . . It was high school students who really played a very dynamic role. The kids were educating the parents." The Virginia historical marker erected to commemorate the Moton High protest credits Griffin as the leader of the strike. There is a plaque with his likeness, the dates of his birth and death, and a short tribute. Moreover, when we do remember young people, we usually talk about them as victims, not as significant political actors, or about how extraordinary they were. Young

Marchers on Selma's Edmund Pettus Bridge, 1965. Young people were central to the success of the Selma voting rights campaign. (© Flip Schulke/Corbis)

activists such as Johns may have been extraordinary, but the nation proved full of such extraordinary youth.[78]

Liz Fusco, CORE's freedom school coordinator, understood that the "real transformation of Mississippi" and of the movement could be measured by the increased questioning and activism of young people. Bevel recognized the movement's source of strength when he organized youth in the early 1960s and later when he urged Martin Luther King Jr. to take up the issue of peace in Vietnam, insisting, "We must have an issue that speaks to young people." Given Ella Baker's long-standing support of youth activism and organizing, it seems fitting that *Fundi*, a film documentary of her life, features a song written by one of the student leaders of the Albany movement and a founding member of the SNCC Freedom Singers, Bernice Reagon, to capture her point of view and celebrate the role of young people in the movement:

> To me young people come first, they have the courage where we fail
> And if I can but shed some light as they carry us through the gale
> The older I get the better I know that the secret of my going on
> Is when the reins are in the hands of the young who dare to run
>   against the storm.

Bob Moses expressed both his feelings about youth activists and the larger significance of young people in the civil rights movement when he said,

Young activist, ca. 1950s. Not only were ideas about childhood used to encourage black adults to join the movement, but young people were on the front lines pushing for black voting and other civil rights. (Courtesy National Association for the Advancement of Colored People Records, Library of Congress, Prints and Photographs Division, LC-USZ62–126802)

"We can't count on adults. Very few who 'have the time' . . . are not afraid of the tremendous pressure they will face. This leaves the young people to be the organizers, the agents of social and political change. . . . They operate at extreme disadvantage; they suffer from the most backward educational system in the U.S. . . . It is a sign of hope that we have been able to find young people to shoulder the responsibility for carrying out the voting drive. They are the seeds of change." Gerald Hoag, a black New Orleanian, similarly identified "the attitude of the younger people [as] his greatest source of optimism." The mother of student leader Charles Maudlin, reportedly the first person in Selma to register to vote under the 1965 Voting Rights Act, acknowledged the role that her son and other local young people played in the movement when she told *Jet* magazine, "If it were not for the children we would not have gotten out to vote." And Maudlin himself insisted that "the movement was spearheaded [by young people] between the ages of 9 and 21," who "were the ones who changed the nation primarily . . . broke down the walls of segregation in this era and . . . were responsible for helping to liberate . . . everybody." Fifteen-year-old Mississippian Joyce Brown penned words that many observers saw as symbolizing her generation's attitude: "Here I have come and here I shall stay / And no amount of fear, my determination can sway." And young movement participant Teresa Clark wrote in the *Palmer's Crossing Freedom News* words that resonated with her peers and that we can hope will resonate with young people today: "Deep down I know that we shall overcome someday. . . . I will continue to fight for peace for all Americans."[79]

AFTERWORD

THE POLITICS OF CHILDHOOD,

THE POLITICS OF CHILDREN

Not long before I began research for this project, the Smithsonian Institution published a collection of photographs taken in the Mississippi Delta during the 1980s and 1990s. The book is filled with images of children. The images bear a striking similarity to those captured by New Deal photographers in the 1930s and Student Non-Violent Coordinating Committee photographers in the 1960s. A young girl squints as she chops cotton. Children play barefoot in the dirt. Others look hopelessly out the window of a shack. And four children huddle together in their (one) bed, their clothes dirty and torn. At the end of the book, the photographer remembers his own childhood. He grew up watching televised images of civil rights protests and the violent intransigence of segregationists. As a thirteen-year-old during the summer of 1964, he had been sure that America would not "turn its eyes from places such as the Mississippi Delta." But it had. And more than thirty years later, he, like earlier civil rights activists, was using images of children to highlight the gap between American ideals and realities, to encourage the nation to reconsider the plight of its underprivileged youth, and to recognize "their desire for freedom . . . and their voices."[1]

Others, including scholars, journalists, and political activists, have continued to demonstrate the elusiveness of racial equality by showing that the lives of many black children, whether in the rural South or urban America, still bear no resemblance to the childhood we idealize.[2] Recently, images of the many young and mostly black victims of Hurricane Katrina have reminded us that our nation is failing African American children and their families in fundamental ways. Moreover, ideas about childhood and images of children have been used throughout America's history and continue to be used to elicit support for a wide variety of social and political causes. Public and political groups commonly draw on the nation's beliefs about childhood as they debate everything from abortion, education initiatives, and health care to labor issues, environmental policies, First Amendment rights, and war. Indeed, when I began this project, the saga of young Elián González was used to raise questions about restrictive U.S. immigration policies, and the murdered teenagers at Colorado's Columbine High School were made the face of arguments against lax gun-control laws. Those two examples demonstrate the ways that ideas about childhood influence American politics and political discussions today. But they are also good examples of the limits of basing pleas for social and political change on ideas about childhood. In neither case did images of children or appeals to ideas about childhood effect significant reform on those issues.

Still, while there are limits to the politics of childhood, I must admit that I have some hope that placing ideas about childhood and young people themselves at the center of the history of the black freedom movement will help bring renewed interest in African American civil rights and perhaps even greater attention to the structural nature of American racism and racial inequality. Maybe looking at young people and ideas about them in history will encourage us to take action so that our nation's institutions and services, legal frameworks, and communities reflect what has been largely a rhetorical and theoretical commitment to children, to equality, and to justice. I have more hope, however, in the politics of children — that young people, especially if they are encouraged, will continue, as one observer of youth protests in the 1960s put it, "to shatter our histories" and "create explosions that sweep away . . . our [nation's] secrets" and injustices.[3]

THE CHILDREN'S CHARTER (1930)

PRESIDENT HOOVER'S WHITE HOUSE CONFERENCE ON CHILD HEALTH AND PROTECTION, RECOGNIZING THE RIGHTS OF THE CHILD AS THE FIRST RIGHTS OF CITIZENSHIP, PLEDGES ITSELF TO THESE AIMS FOR THE CHILDREN OF AMERICA

I. For every child spiritual and moral training to help him to stand firm under the pressure of life.

II. For every child understanding and the guarding of his personality as his most precious right.

III. For every child a home and that love and security which a home provides; and for that child who must receive foster care, the nearest substitute for his own home.

IV. For every child full preparation for his birth, his mother receiving prenatal and postnatal care; and the establishment of such protective measures as will make child-bearing safer.

V. For every child health protection from birth through adolescence, including: periodical health examinations and, where needed, care of specialists and hospital treatment; regular dental examinations and care of the teeth; protective and preventive measures against communicable diseases; the insuring of pure food, pure milk, and pure water.

VI. For every child from birth through adolescence, promotion of health, including health instruction and a health program, wholesome physical and mental recreation, with teachers and leaders adequately trained.

VII. For every child a dwelling-place safe, sanitary, and wholesome, with reasonable provisions for privacy; free from conditions which tend to thwart his development; and a home environment harmonious and enriching.

VIII. For every child a school which is safe from hazards, sanitary, properly equipped, lighted, and ventilated. For younger children nursery schools and kindergartens to supplement home care.

IX. For every child a community which recognizes and plans for his needs, protects him against physical dangers, moral hazards, and disease; provides him with safe and wholesome places for play and recreation; and makes provision for his cultural and social needs.

X. For every child an education which, through the discovery and development of his individual abilities, prepares him for life; and through training and vocational guidance prepares him for a living which will yield him the maximum of satisfaction.

XI. For every child such teaching and training as will prepare him for successful parenthood, home-making, and the rights of citizenship; and, for parents, supplementary training to fit them to deal wisely with the problems of parenthood.

XII. For every child education for safety and protection against accidents to which modern conditions subject him—those to which he is directly exposed and those which, through loss or maiming of his parents, affect him indirectly.

XIII. For every child who is blind, deaf, crippled, or otherwise physically handicapped, and for the child who is mentally handicapped, such measures as will early discover and diagnose his handicap, provide care and treatment, and so train him that he may become an asset to society rather than a liability. Expenses of these services should be borne publicly where they cannot be privately met.

XIV. For every child who is in conflict with society the right to be dealt with intelligently as society's charge, not society's outcast; with the home, the school, the church, the court and the institution when needed, shaped to return him whenever possible to the normal stream of life.

XV. For every child the right to grow up in a family with an adequate standard of living and the security of a stable income as the surest safeguard against social handicaps.

XVI. For every child protection against labor that stunts growth, either physical or mental, that limits education, that deprives children of the right to comradeship, of play, and of joy.

XVII. For every rural child as satisfactory schooling and health services as for the city child, and an extension to rural families of social, recreational, and cultural facilities.

XVIII. To supplement the home and the school in the training of youth, and to return to them those interests of which modern life tends to cheat children, every stimulation and encouragement should be given to the extension and development of the voluntary youth organizations.

XIX. To make everywhere available these minimum protections of the health and welfare of children, there should be a district, county, or community organization for health, education, and welfare, with full-time officials, coordinating with a state-wide program which will be responsive to a nationwide service of general information, statistics, and scientific research. This should include:

a) trained full-time public health officials, with public health nurses, sanitary inspection, and laboratory workers;
b) available hospital beds;
c) full-time public welfare service for the relief, aid, and guidance of children in special need due to poverty, misfortune, or behavior difficulties, and for the protection of children from abuse, neglect, exploitation, or moral hazard.

FOR EVERY CHILD THESE RIGHTS, REGARDLESS OF RACE, OR COLOR, OR SITUATION, WHEREVER HE MAY LIVE UNDER THE PROTECTION OF THE AMERICAN FLAG.

GENEVA DECLARATION OF THE RIGHTS OF THE CHILD (1924)

Adopted 26 September, 1924, League of Nations

By the present Declaration of the Rights of the Child, commonly known as the "Declaration of Geneva," men and women of all nations, recognizing that mankind owes to the Child the best that it has to give, declare and accept it as their duty that, beyond and above all considerations of race, nationality or creed:

1. The child must be given the means of requisite for its normal development, both materially and spiritually;
2. The child that is hungry must be fed; the child that is sick must be nursed; the child that is backward must be helped; the delinquent child must be reclaimed; and the orphan and the waif must be sheltered and succored;
3. The child must be the first to receive relief in times of distress;
4. The child must be in a position to earn a livelihood, and must be protected against every form of exploitation;
5. The child must be brought up in the consciousness that its talents must be devoted to the service of fellow men.

UNITED NATIONS DECLARATION OF THE RIGHTS OF THE CHILD (1959)

G.A. res. 1386 (XIV), 14 U.N. GAOR Supp. (No. 16) at 19, U.N. Doc. A/4354 (1959)

PREAMBLE

Whereas the peoples of the United Nations have, in the Charter, reaffirmed their faith in fundamental human right and in the dignity and worth of the human person, and have determined to promote social progress and better standards of life in larger freedom,

Whereas the United Nation has, in the Universal Declaration of Human Rights, proclaimed that everyone is entitled to all the rights and freedoms set forth therein, without distinction of any kind, such as race, colour, sex, language, religion, political or other opinion, national or social origin, property, birth or other status,

Whereas the child, by reason of his physical and mental immaturity, needs special safeguards and care, including appropriate legal protection, before as well as after birth,

Whereas the need for such special safeguards has been stated in the Geneva Declaration of the Rights of the Child of 1924, and recognized in the Universal Declaration of Human Rights and in the statutes of specialized agencies and international organizations concerned with the welfare of children,

Whereas mankind owes to the child the best it has to give,

Now therefore,

The General Assembly

Proclaims this Declaration of the Rights of the Child to the end that he may have a happy childhood and enjoy for his own good and for the good of society the rights and freedoms herein set forth, and calls upon parents, upon men and women as individuals, and upon voluntary organizations, local authorities and national Governments to recognize these rights and strive for their observance by legislative and other measures progressively taken in accordance with the following principles:

Principle 1

The child shall enjoy all the rights set forth in this Declaration. Every child, without any exception whatsoever, shall be entitled to these rights, without distinction or discrimination on account of race, colour, sex, language, religion, political or other opinion, national or social origin, property, birth or other status, whether of himself or of his family.

Principle 2

The child shall enjoy special protection, and shall be given opportunities and facilities, by law and by other means, to enable him to develop physically, mentally, morally, spiritually, and socially in a healthy and normal manner and in conditions of freedom and dignity. In the enactment of laws for this purpose, the best interests of the child shall be the paramount consideration.

Principle 3

The child shall be entitled from his birth to a name and a nationality.

Principle 4

The child shall enjoy the benefits of social security. He shall be entitled to grow and develop in health; to this end, special care and protection shall be provided both to him and to his mother, including adequate pre-natal and post-natal care. The child shall have the right to adequate nutrition, housing, recreation and medical services.

Principle 5

The child who is physically, mentally, or socially handicapped shall be given the special treatment, education and care required by his particular condition.

Principle 6

The child, for the full and harmonious development of his personality, needs love and understanding. He shall, wherever possible, grow up in the care and under the responsibility of his parents, and, in any case, in an atmosphere of affection and of moral and material security; a child of tender years shall not, save in exceptional circumstances, be separated from his mother. Society and the public authorities shall have the duty to extend particular care to children without a family and to those without adequate means of support. Payment of State and other assistance towards the maintenance of children in large families is desirable.

Principle 7

The child is entitled to receive education, which shall be free and compulsory, at least in the elementary stages. He shall be given an education which will promote his general culture and enable him, on the basis of equal opportunity, to develop his abilities, his individual judgment, and his sense of moral and social responsibility and to become a useful member of society.

The best interests of the child shall be the guiding principle of those responsible for his education and guidance; that responsibility lies in the first place with his parents.

The child shall have full opportunity for play and recreation, which should be directed to the same purposes as education; society and the public authorities shall endeavor to promote the enjoyment of this right.

Principle 8

The child shall in all circumstances be among the first to receive protection and relief.

Principle 9

The child shall be protected against all forms of neglect, cruelty and exploitation. He shall not be the subject of traffic, in any form.

The child shall not be admitted to employment before an appropriate minimum age; he shall in no case be caused or permitted to engage in any occupation or employment which would prejudice his health or education, or interfere with his physical, mental or moral development.

Principle 10

The child shall be protected from practices which may foster racial, religious and any other form of discrimination. He shall be brought up in a spirit of understanding, tolerance, friendship among peoples, peace and universal brotherhood, and in full consciousness that his energy and talents should be devoted to the service of his fellow men.

NOTES

ABBREVIATIONS

AYC Papers   American Youth Commission Papers, American Council on Education Records, Hoover Institution Library and Archives, Stanford University, Palo Alto, Calif.

CBP   Children's Bureau Papers, National Archives II, College Park, Md.

CCCP   Children's Crusade for Children Papers, Manuscripts Division, Library of Congress, Washington, D.C.

CCP   Constance W. Curry Papers, Special Collections Department, Robert W. Woodruff Library, Emory University, Atlanta, Ga.

CORE Papers   Congress of Racial Equality Papers, Collections on Microfilm, Library of Congress, Washington, D.C.

EKC   Ed King Collection, Mississippi Department of Archives and History, Jackson, Miss.

GEB Papers   General Education Board Papers, Rockefeller Archive Center, Sleepy Hollow, N.Y.

HLP   Hylan Lewis Papers, Amistad Research Center, Tulane University, New Orleans, La.

IAP   Inez Adams Papers, Amistad Research Center, Tulane University, New Orleans, La.

JHFP   Joseph H. Fichter Papers, Special Collections and Archives, J. Edgar and Louise S. Monroe Library, Loyola University–New Orleans, New Orleans, La.

JLC   Joyce Ladner Collection, Mississippi Department of Archives and History, Jackson, Miss.

LC   Library of Congress, Washington, D.C.

MEC   Medgar Evers Collection, Mississippi Department of Archives and History, Jackson, Miss.

NAACP Papers   National Association for the Advancement of Colored People Papers, Collections on Microfilm, Library of Congress, Washington, D.C.

NABR	*Newsweek* Atlanta Bureau Records, Special Collections Department, Robert W. Woodruff Library, Emory University, Atlanta, Ga.
OHP	Oral History Project, Birmingham Civil Rights Institute, Birmingham, Ala.
RG	Record Group
RLSP	Richard L. Stevens Papers, Manuscript, Archives, and Rare Book Library, Robert W. Woodruff Library, Emory University, Atlanta, Ga.
RWL	Manuscript, Archives, and Rare Book Library, Robert W. Woodruff Library, Emory University, Atlanta, Ga.
SCLC Papers	Southern Christian Leadership Conference Papers, Collections on Microfilm, Library of Congress, Washington, D.C.
SEPC	Social Ethics Pamphlet Collection, Yale Divinity Library, Yale University, New Haven, Conn.
SHC	Southern Historical Collection, University of North Carolina, Chapel Hill, N.C.
SNCC Papers	Student Non-Violent Coordinating Committee Papers (microfilm), Martin Luther King Jr. Center, Library and Archives, Atlanta, Ga.
SOSC	Save Our Schools Collection, Amistad Research Center, Tulane University, New Orleans, La.
SRCP	Southern Regional Council Papers, Manuscript, Archives, and Rare Book Library, Robert W. Woodruff Library, Emory University, Atlanta, Ga.
USM	Historical Manuscripts, McCain Library and Archives, University of Southern Mississippi, Hattiesburg, Miss.

INTRODUCTION

1 Eugene Green, "Political Socialization," 189.
2 While scholars have done much to help us understand childhood as a social construct and to explore young people's agency and experiences, few works have addressed issues of race or looked at African American youth in the twentieth century. Important works that look at race and black youth include Wilma King, *African American Childhoods*; Ritterhouse, *Growing Up Jim Crow*; Sallee, *Whiteness*; Illick, *American Childhoods*; Mintz, *Huck's Raft*; Lindenmeyer, *Greatest Generation*; Tuttle, *Daddy's Gone*.
3 The seminal work on sentimental versus economic conceptions of childhood in America is Zelizer, *Pricing*.
4 A growing literature addresses these points and stresses the importance of the 1930s to the black freedom struggle. See, for example, Patricia Sullivan, *Days of Hope*; Lau, *Democracy Rising*; Kelley, *Hammer and Hoe*; Tuck, *Beyond Atlanta*;

Greene, *Our Separate Ways*; McNeil, *Groundwork*; Honey, *Southern Labor*; Korstad, *Civil Rights Unionism*; Goluboff, *Lost Promise*; Aldon D. Morris, *Origins*. See also Jacquelyn Dowd Hall, "Long Civil Rights Movement."

5 See, for example, Goluboff, *Lost Promise*; McNeil, *Groundwork*; John P. Jackson, *Social Scientists*; Dudziak, *Cold War Civil Rights*; Kluger, *Simple Justice*; Lau, *Democracy Rising*.

6 Implicit and sometimes explicit in my study is the idea that *Brown*, despite its limitations and failings, was indeed a watershed in movement history. My argument about the reasons for and the larger significance of *Brown* supports Dudziak's contention that *Brown* and the civil rights movement cannot be separated from their cold war context ("*Brown*"; *Cold War Civil Rights*). It also supports Derrik A. Bell Jr.'s idea that *Brown* represented a "convergence of interests," although the convergence I see differs from the one on which he focuses ("*Brown*").

7 See May, *Homeward Bound*. On the "response of the masses" to the case and its impression on NAACP legal counsel Charles Houston, see McNeil, *Groundwork*, esp. 109, chap. 9.

8 Ideas about childhood limited civil rights efforts in much the same way that beliefs about women's special qualities limited the scope and success of the women's movement. See Joan W. Scott, "Gender."

CHAPTER ONE

1 *Chattanooga News* quoted in *New Republic*, 26 August 1931, Part 6, Reel 8, Frame 346, NAACP Papers.

2 *Real Story of Scottsboro*; William Pickens, editorial, *New York Herald Tribune*, 15 April 1931, Part 6, Reel 8, Frame 108, NAACP Papers.

3 Goodman's essential *Stories* notes that northern supporters highlighted the youth of the defendants, while white southerners focused on ideas about white womanhood, but his book does not examine the case in terms of historically grounded ideas about childhood and youth. *Norris v. Alabama* (294 U.S. 587 [1935]) made it all the way to the Supreme Court, which ruled against the South's systematic purging of blacks from jury rolls. On childhood in the 1930s and federal efforts to protect childhood, see Lindenmeyer, *Greatest Generation*; Mintz, *Huck's Raft*, 233–53.

4 *Scottsboro*; *The Nation*, 3 June 1931, Part 6, Reel 8, Frames 163–64, NAACP Papers.

5 *Real Story of Scottsboro*. Documents such as the "Children's Charter," which expanded the notion of the state as parent, may have represented northern normative views of childhood. The North moved much more quickly to abolish child industrial labor and to adopt programs and policies such as mothers' pensions and compulsory schooling requirements that were designed to protect children.

6 *Omaha Guide*, 3 April 1932, Part 6, Reel 8, Frame 623, NAACP Papers; "Letter from Birmingham, Alabama," 4 May 1931, Part 6, Reel 2, Frame 835, NAACP Papers.

7 "Appealing to the Nation's Conscience," *Chicago Sunday Bee*, 24 May 1931, Part 6, Reel 8, Frames 140–41, NAACP Papers; black activist and labor organizer Robert Weaver quoted in Patricia Sullivan, *Days of Hope*, 87–88.

8 W. E. B. Du Bois, *Black Reconstruction*, 726. Du Bois specifically referred to historians of the Reconstruction, but his comment applies more broadly.

9 In its coverage of the case, *The Crisis* stressed that the NAACP was "eager to save the boys" and did not want organizational conflict to jeopardize "the lives of eight boys" ("Statement by the NAACP," 82–83).

10 W. E. B. Du Bois, *Darkwater*, 193, 4. Swedish feminist and reformer Ellen Key proposed that the twentieth century should be "the century of the child" and was widely quoted by Progressive-era reformers.

11 W. E. B. Du Bois, *Souls*, 209, 2, 208, 212, 213.

12 Weld, *American Slavery*, 7–9; "Declaration of the American Anti-Slavery Society," 265; Pennington, "Life of a Slave Child," 221; Stowe, *Uncle Tom's Cabin*, 409; Jacobs, *Incidents*, 62; Louisa J. Hall, "Birth," 42–44.

13 Washington, *Up from Slavery*, 5, 4, 36.

14 W. E. B. Du Bois, *Souls*, 56. On Du Bois and especially his shift toward greater militancy, see David Levering Lewis, *W. E. B. Du Bois*.

15 W. E. B. Du Bois, *Darkwater*, 81, 18–19, 11–12.

16 Gaines, *Uplifting the Race*, 45, 78, 107.

17 On early-twentieth-century racial progress strategies, including their gendered nature, see Gaines, *Uplifting the Race*. See also Shawn Michelle Smith, *Photography*; Darlene Clark Hine, "Rape."

18 W. E. B. Du Bois, *Darkwater*, 16–17, 11.

19 James Bond, "Education," 41, 60.

20 W. E. B. Du Bois, "Our Baby Pictures," 298–99. On race leaders' strategies, see Stephanie J. Shaw, *What a Woman Ought to Be*; Shawn Michelle Smith, *Photography*; Bragg, "Marketing," chap. 5. On eugenicists' use of children's photographs and the ways that Du Bois challenged prejudicial racial hierarchies through the use of visual imagery, see also Shawn Michelle Smith, *American Archives*; Shawn Michelle Smith, *Photography*. Portraits of better-class black families similarly enshrined sentimental conceptions of childhood. See, for example, the two by James Van Der Zee that Gaines includes in *Uplifting the Race*, 69, 108. In the first sit two well-dressed little girls, leaning on their mother, with one holding a stuffed animal; in the second, a little boy in a sailor suit stands next to his mother, a little dog at his heels. This second picture portrays an image of childhood health and innocence while suggesting future patriotic, perhaps even militant, manhood (particularly since the boy's father, dressed in a military uniform, also appears in the photograph). In the 1910s and 1920s, all issues of *The Crisis* included photographs of black children, especially the "children's number" (the October issue). On middle-class ideals, racial uplift, and photographs of black children, see also Mary Niall Mitchell, "'Rosebloom and Pure White.'"

21 On typical images of black children, see Wilma King, *African American Childhoods*,

119–36. On the NAACP's efforts to combat stereotypical images, see also Katharine Capshaw Smith, "Childhood." With thirty thousand subscribers by 1913, *The Crisis* had become "required reading in many black homes" (Darlene Clark Hine, Hine, and Harrold, *African-American Odyssey*, 403).

22 Faith Adams, "Question to Democracy."

23 In "Our Baby Pictures," W. E. B. Du Bois admitted that it was "true, these . . . selected children [come] mostly from the well-to-do" (298). See also Katharine Capshaw Smith, "Childhood."

24 Murphy, *Problems*, 166–67. Murphy was involved in industrial child-labor reform in the South.

25 Katharine Capshaw Smith, "Childhood," 804–7; W. E. B. Du Bois, *Darkwater*, 202–203; Du Bois in *The Crisis*, October 1926, 6, 283.

26 *The Crisis*, September 1919, 250; Lindenmeyer, *Right*.

27 See Sallee, *Whiteness*, 118; Lindenmeyer, *Right*. Beginning in 1915, the Children's Bureau collected some statistics on maternal and infant health for blacks.

28 On black parents' struggle to maintain control of their children after the Civil War, see Fields, *Slavery and Freedom*; Zipf, "Reconstructing 'Free Woman'"; Farmer, "'Because They Are Women'"; Rebecca Scott, "Battle"; Fluke, "Planters"; Schmidt, *Free to Work*, chap. 5.

29 Horace Mann Bond, *Education*, 284. Spargo, *Bitter Cry*, first published in 1905, examined "the problem of poverty as it affects childhood." It went through seven printings before 1916 and, as scholars have noted, "played an important part in the growing agitation for child labor legislation" (xiii). Kelley and Wald had come up with the idea for and lobbied for the creation of a federal agency devoted to the needs of children. On the Children's Bureau and early-twentieth-century child welfare reform, see Lindenmeyer, *Right*; Ladd-Taylor, *Mother-Work*.

30 See Horace Mann Bond, *Education*, chap. 14, titled "The Forgotten Child." Other significant studies on black youth include three sponsored and published by the AYC: Allison Davis and Dollard, *Children of Bondage*; Charles S. Johnson, *Growing Up in the Black Belt*; and Frazier, *Negro Youth*. The youth commission also prepared a summary volume of "general information now available about Negro youth," Reid's *In a Minor Key*. Powdermaker, *After Freedom*, includes an analysis of black youth. For an analysis of these AYC publications, see Daryl Michael Scott, *Contempt and Pity*, 19–69.

31 As chapter 3 suggests, black leaders never fully moved away from the need to prove the respectability of African American children.

32 Horace Mann Bond, *Education*, chap. 14; Sallee, *Whiteness*, 105–6.

33 Significant studies that address this topic include Lindenmeyer, *Right*; Sallee, *Whiteness*; Zelizer, *Pricing*; Linda Gordon, "Putting Children First"; Linda Gordon, *Heroes*; Ladd-Taylor, *Mother-Work*; Nasaw, *Children*; Lasch, *Haven*; Platt, *Child Savers*; Cravens, "Child-Saving"; Ronald D. Cohen, "Child-Saving."

34 Zelizer, *Pricing*, 66, 209; Sallee, *Whiteness*, 150. Sentimental ideas about childhood helped to undermine slavery, some early twentieth-century reformers were indeed

concerned about minority children, and a few Progressive-era philanthropists were moved to help black children when confronted with the discrepancies between idealized childhood and black childhood. Letters between Edgar Murphy and Jane Addams, for example, suggest their concern. See Sallee, *Whiteness*, 154. Washington's participation in the 1909 White House Conference on Dependent Children similarly suggests that national child-welfare reformers were concerned about the plight of America's black children. The Anna T. Jeanes Fund and Julius Rosenwald Fund were especially notable private efforts that improved the education of rural black youth. But even child-welfare reformers sympathetic to black children had not been above using white fears about "negro domination" to further their efforts to "save" white children from "the new slavery in the New South," child labor. See Sallee, *Whiteness*, 52, 92–93. Sallee explains that Murphy and other Alabama reformers who supported Negro industrial education and otherwise criticized the use of racial scare tactics used those tactics when arguing against child labor by calling up fears of white racial degeneracy. In chapter 5, Sallee discusses "rehabilitating" the image of poor white children.

35 Schuyler, *Weight*, 180, 210–12, 156–58, 184–87.

36 Lindenmeyer suggests that the Children's Charter, filled as it was with "romantic clichés about the rights of childhood," "did little to solve the crisis facing increasing numbers of children and their families as the economic depression worsened" (*Right*, 170). Lindenmeyer may be right, especially in the short run, and Children's Bureau officials were certainly disappointed by President Hoover's lack of concrete action on children's issues. The charter may have been significant after all, as was Hoover's long-standing involvement in the rights of childhood and child welfare. The Children's Bureau had already promoted the idea of the "rights of childhood" (as had Hoover in his efforts related to World War I relief efforts), but the Children's Charter clearly outlined those rights. On Hoover and children's rights, see Marshall, "Herbert Hoover," 1–2, 11–12; Marshall, "Humanitarian Sympathy." The charter further popularized ideas about children's rights, since, as Lindenmeyer notes, the charter "was reproduced as posters and fliers and distributed throughout the United States" (*Right*, 170). *The Crisis* ran an article on the conference at which the charter was created and suggested that it represented a step forward for black Americans (Butler, "Forward," 374–75).

37 See, for example, *The Child*, November 1936, December 1939; Abbott, "Message." Photographs of idealized black children, however, surrounded Abbott's article, indicating the NAACP's reluctance fully to abandon its earlier strategy. The Children's Bureau's increased attention to black children resulted partly from its increased attention to the issue of agricultural child labor and to the problems of rural children.

38 See "Beautiful Child Contest"; "Winners in *The Crisis* Beautiful Child Contest"; Jenkins, "Gifted Negro Children"; "Give These Youngsters a Chance"; W. E. B. Du Bois, Postscript, January 1933, 20–22.

39 W. E. B. Du Bois, "Is the NAACP Lying Down?," 354; Alexander, "Wandering Negro

Boys," 107, 118. As other scholars explain, the NAACP's involvement in the Scottsboro case also reflected a shift in how the association looked at grassroots organizing and at class in general. See, for example, Kelley, *Hammer and Hoe*; Goodman, *Stories*; Fairclough, *Better Day*; Patricia Sullivan, *Days of Hope.*

40 See, for example, G. Stanley Hall, *Adolescence*; Demos and Demos, "Adolescence"; Kett, *Rites*; Fass, *Damned*; Austin and Willard, *Generations*; Macleod, *Building Character.*

41 The shift to sentimental over economic valuations of childhood was accompanied by the ascendance of a transitional stage of development between sentimental childhood and economic adulthood. Youth was also a period in which young people would transition from a stage of sexual innocence to a stage of sexuality. On fears about youth, see, for example, Mintz, *Huck's Raft*, 249–53.

42 Rainey, *How Fare American Youth?*, 34. See also Howard M. Bell, *Youth Tell Their Story*; Chamberlain, "Our Jobless Youth"; Mintz, *Huck's Raft*, 243–44; Lindenmeyer, *Greatest Generation*, 218, 230.

43 Lindenmeyer, *Greatest Generation*, 218, 230. The National Youth Administration and Civilian Conservation Corps also provided recreational opportunities, literacy instruction, cooperative schools, scholarships, and vocational training for youth. AYC Executive Committee meeting minutes indicate widespread support for the idea that "harm is being done by the employment of young people under the age of 20." See, for example, minutes from 4–5 May 1936, 9, Box 1, Folder 20, AYC Papers.

44 See Lindenmeyer, *Greatest Generation*; Mintz, *Huck's Raft*, 213–53; Hawes, *Children*; Lynd and Lynd, *Middletown*; Fass, *Damned*; Kett, *Rites*; Modell, *Into One's Own*; Mintz and Kellogg, *Domestic Revolutions*; Schrum, *Some Wore Bobby Sox*. Between 1900 and 1930, high school enrollment rose 650 percent. In 1935, the Lynds suggested that "no two generations of Americans have ever faced each other across as wide a gap in their customary behavior" (quoted in Mintz and Kellogg, *Domestic Revolutions*, chap. 7 n. 26). Powdermaker's study, *After Freedom*, noted that young people responded much differently to Jim Crow than their elders, and the AYC-sponsored studies referenced in this chapter explored the generation gap. The commission's studies sometimes use the term "teenage" but use quotation marks, indicating that it was not yet widely used.

45 Douglass, *Secondary Education*, 40–41; Chamberlain, "Our Jobless Youth"; Chambers, *Youth-Serving Organizations*, ix; Minutes, 4–5 May 1936, 18, Box 1, Folder 20, AYC Papers; Rainey, *How Fare American Youth?* On the commission's continuing concern about youth problems and the competition between democracies and other political groups for youth, see "Proposal for Continued Support of a Youth Commission," 18 June 1941, 4, Box 556, Folder 5945, GEB Papers.

46 The best example was perhaps Boys State, formed in 1935 by the Illinois American Legion as a counter to fascist countries' "Pioneer Camps." On Boys State, see Urbiel, "Making of Citizens." The NAACP reorganized its youth program in 1936 at least partly because young blacks seemed to be drawn to leftist organizations. The

new NAACP youth program was decidedly more militant and gave young people a more active role in the movement.

47 See Chambers, *Youth-Serving Organizations*. The commission imagined a hugely comprehensive and influential role for itself. See, for example, "A Proposal for the Development of a Comprehensive Program for the Care and Education of American Youth," Entry 11, Box 1, Folder 9; "Memo to Directors of the Study from Robert Sutherland," 1 October 1938, Box 11, Folder 2; "Plan for Publicizing and Implementing the Findings and Recommendations of the American Youth Commission," 15 July 1938, Box 11, Folder 5; "Letter to Dr. Floyd W. Reeves from Robert Sutherland," 12 May 1941, Box 18, Folder 10, all in AYC Papers. That John W. Studebaker, the U.S. commissioner of education from 1934 to 1948, was a member of this commission suggests its influence and its relationship to federal agencies. Moreover, its parent organization, the American Council on Education, had been formed during World War I partly to serve as a liaison between the federal government and educational institutions. Other executive committee members of the commission included Will W. Alexander, Clarence A. Dykstra, Dorothy Canfield Fisher, Willard E. Givens, Henry I. Harriman, George Johnson, Mordecai W. Johnson, Chester H. Rowell, William F. Russell, Henry C. Taylor, Miriam Van Waters, Matthew Woll, Owen D. Young, and George F. Zook. The AYC Papers include biographies of these committee members (see Entry 11, Box 17, Folder 2). Commission studies (as planned) were also widely quoted by public figures and the national media. *Life* magazine dedicated its entire 6 June 1938 issue to the commission's findings. See also Chamberlain, "Our Jobless Youth"; Eleanor Roosevelt, "Why I Still Believe." My evidence challenges Walter A. Jackson's contention in *Gunnar Myrdal* that social scientists who studied race relations in the 1930s "were rarely heard by top policymakers in Washington or by the general white reading public" (105). The AYC did not pay significant attention to Native American youth, but during this period, the Bureau of Indian Affairs began to reevaluate its programs for young Native Americans. See Bloom, "Rolling." On youth movements, see also Robert Cohen, *When the Old Left Was Young*. On the influence of the AYC, see also "Report of the Director to the Commission," 15 April 1940, 1, Box 9, Folder 10, Howard Y. McClusky Collection, Bentley Historical Library, University of Michigan, Ann Arbor, Mich.; George Zook to Dr. E. E. Day, "A Proposal for the Development of a Comprehensive Program for the Care and Education of Youth," Box 555, Folder 5940, GEB Papers; "Accomplishments of the American Youth Commission, 1935–1940," 11 November 1940, 7–9, Box 555, Folder 5944, GEB Papers; Donald J. Shank to Flora M. Rhind, "RE: Continued Implementation of the Work of the American Youth Commission," 29 November 1942, Box 556, Folder 5945, GEB Papers; Paul T. David to Robert J. Havighurst, 2 December 1939, Box 555, Folder 5943, GEB Papers.

48 Howard M. Bell, *Youth Tell Their Story*, 2; Rainey, *How Fare American Youth?*, 21, 19. In the commission-sponsored *Secondary Education*, Douglass suggested that depending on a young person's desires, part-time employment after the age of sixteen

and full-time work after the age of twenty were acceptable (127). Executive committee meeting minutes sometimes suggest that it is "wiser to postpone employment" until age 20. See, for example, those from 4–5 May 1936, 9, Box 1, Folder 20, AYC Papers. Young people were more ambivalent about child labor. Howard M. Bell's study, *Youth Tell Their Story*, indicates that young people interviewed "were almost equally divided as to how far government regulation [of child labor for fourteen- and fifteen-year-olds] should go" and a few (3.5 percent, a number Bell calls "negligible") thought that child labor, at least for those ages, was not a governmental concern at all (224–28). In some ways, the AYC sought to promote social cohesion without calling into question the extant politico-economic order. On the birth of sociology as an antidote to the widespread social unrest that resulted from industrialization, see Wolf, *Europe*.

49 Rainey, *How Fare American Youth?*, 63; Douglass, *Secondary Education*, 14, 32–33, 72–74. The commission's executive committee meeting minutes frequently mention discussions on these points. A sense of these conditions and fear of youth maladjustment prompted the previously cited studies on Negro youth and personality sponsored and published by the AYC in the early 1940s. On child-rearing in the era, see Hulbert, *Raising America*; Mintz, *Huck's Raft*, 213–32.

50 Douglass, *Secondary Education*, 36. For a summary of scholarship on the effects of the Great Depression on America's families, see Mintz and Kellogg, *Domestic Revolutions*, chap. 7.

51 U.S. Committee on Economic Security, *Social Security*, 229; Mintz, *Huck's Raft*, 235; Lindenmeyer, *Greatest Generation*, 206. Carey McWilliams, John Steinbeck, Paul S. Taylor, Dorothea Lange, and other liberals generally defined the problems of agricultural migrants in terms of families rather than in terms of labor. Their focus reflected widespread concerns about American families and ensured attention to the problems of agricultural migrants, although it also shaped and limited reform efforts.

52 Minehan, *Boy and Girl Tramps*, xiii–xvi; Rainey, *How Fare American Youth?*, 35.

53 Howard M. Bell, *Youth Tell Their Story*, 17, 48. Bell called transient youth "the Wild Boys of the road" (they were commonly called "wild children"). Minehan's study notes that the public generally did not acknowledge the presence of girls among transients. The commission itself did not direct much attention to the specific problems of transient youth. (Migrant youth were an altogether different group that traveled with their families and received significant attention.) And "the boy and girl tramp problem" was generally seen as a pre-1934 problem — before New Deal programs took effect. See Chamberlain, "Our Jobless Youth." But the presence and problems of young transients seemed to influence the commission, which was clearly concerned with establishing conditions that would dissuade youth from leaving home and having to support themselves financially.

54 Howard M. Bell, *Youth Tell Their Story*, 40, 140–43, 135; Douglass, *Secondary Education*, 35–40.

55 Howard M. Bell, *Youth Tell Their Story*, 40, 140–43, 135. See also Douglass, *Sec-*

ondary Education, 35–36, 39–40; May, *Homeward Bound*. Minehan's *Boy and Girl Tramps* has a chapter on "Sex Life" that discusses the casual attitude of young transients toward sex and the permeability of racial boundaries in the sexual relationships of transient youth. Wolf has suggested that sociology as a discipline (which he shows is intimately tied to government interests) locates "the causes of disorder in family and community" in isolation from more basic economic and political forces (*Europe*, 7–13).

56 Rainey, *How Fare American Youth?*, 77, 80; Howard M. Bell, *Youth Tell Their Story*, 160.

57 Howard M. Bell, *Youth Tell Their Story*, 162–68, 97. Bell specifically argued that "the weight of the national burden of unemployment could be substantially decreased by the elimination of large numbers of school-age youth from the labor market" (98). AYC statistics showed that crime peaked between the ages of twenty and twenty-four. Scholars such as Gilbert have explained that data indicating high rates of crime among youth are distorted since some behaviors deemed criminal in youth are not criminal in adulthood (*Cycle of Outrage*, 66–79). In any case, perceptions of youth criminality were perhaps as significant as actual criminal behavior; commission studies showed that 8.4 percent of white youth surveyed spent most of their free time "loafing," compared to 14.3 percent of Negro youth. Loafing was sixth on the list of principal leisure-time activities for white youth and second for black youth. The primary leisure-time activities of white male youth who lived on farms were loafing, reading, or some type of individual sport. Higher rates of loafing among black and rural youth were attributed not to race or natural inclinations but to the absence of constructive alternatives and lower educational levels. Judges agreed. A judge in Delaware, for example, attributed "the number of colored children coming before the court" to the lack of recreational facilities and worked with local charities to open a playground and community center ("Child-Welfare Services," 156). Organized social activities (with adult supervision) were deemed preferable to individual activities (team sports were better than individual sports, and so forth). My discussion of New Deal recreational programs is based on Lindenmeyer, *Greatest Generation*, 230–32.

58 Presenters, some of them AYC researchers, at a 1940 conference on "The Needs of Negro Youth at Howard" mentioned commission findings and declared their intentions to make "its work known" (George Johnson, "An Analysis of the Youth Problem," in "Report of the Proceedings of the Conference on the Needs of Negro Youth," Howard University, 15–17 July 1940, Box 100, Folder 10, HLP). The commission had at least three executive board members who could be singled out as racial liberals: Will Alexander (former executive director of the Commission on Interracial Cooperation and 1928 winner of the Harmon award, given for services to American race relations), writer Dorothy Canfield Fisher (see chap. 2), and Edith Stern (daughter of Julius Rosenwald, who helped black communities build hundreds of schools between 1912 and 1932). On the Rosenwald schools, see Hoffschwelle, *Rosenwald Schools*. Some progressive educators, such as those associated

with the *Social Frontier*, questioned the AYC's liberalism, mostly because it did not call into question laissez-faire capitalism. See "A Commission for the Study of Youth," *Social Frontier*, November 1935, 38–39, Box 556, Folder 5947, RG 23, Series 1, Subseries 3, GEB Papers.

59 "American Youth Commission Executive Committee Meeting Proceedings," 16 September 1935, Washington, D.C., 79, Box 2, Folder 1, AYC Papers; Woofter, "Status," 592. Du Bois was not altogether convinced that the way Woofter framed his research furthered the NAACP's aims. See W. E. B. Du Bois, "Woofterism," 81–83; W. E. B. Du Bois, *Philadelphia Negro*. Youth-centered agencies such as the AYC and the National Youth Administration were among the most progressive on issues of race and the most forthright in addressing racial inequalities during the 1930s. On the racial liberalism of the National Youth Administration, see Patricia Sullivan, *Days of Hope*; Badger, *New Deal*, 207–8; Kirby, *Black Americans*, 110–21; Natanson, *Black Image*, 38–39. Family studies scholars have noted that during the 1930s, the nation began to pay more attention to African American family systems, define them as problematic (or pathological), and suggest ways that the social sciences could help. See, for example, Nobles and Goddard, *Understanding the Black Family*, chap. 1. Those scholars point to AYC studies as important research that came out of this period. In the 1920s, Du Bois had published statistics detailing educational inequalities in *The Crisis*. See Patricia Sullivan, "Prelude to *Brown*," 164; "A Proposal for a Study of Negro Youth," 1937, Box 558, Folder 5966, RG 23, Series 1, Subseries 3, GEB Papers.

60 On the wide-ranging and lasting influence of these commission studies see, for example, Nobles and Goddard, *Understanding the Black Family*. Scholars often emphasize that these studies began with the idea of the Negro as a problem. And indeed, studies sponsored by the AYC certainly assumed that something was "wrong" with African American families and youth. They actually began, however, with the idea that there was something wrong with America's youth and the way the nation was dealing with them as well as with the assumption that black youth suffered most from the problems of American youth, a minor but perhaps significant difference.

61 Reid, *In a Minor Key*, foreword, 3–4. Reid's book addressed these and other related points; see also point 14 of the "Children's Charter."

62 Robert L. Sutherland, *Color, Class, and Personality*, 19, 29, 40, 10–12.

63 Ibid., 3; Allison Davis and Dollard, *Children of Bondage*, 171.

64 Rainey, *How Fare American Youth?*, 95. Rainey, a longtime educator, was president of Bucknell University just prior to serving as the AYC's director and was named president of the University of Texas Board of Regents in 1939. There he waged an ultimately unsuccessful stand for academic freedom and was fired in 1944. He ran unsuccessfully for governor of Texas in 1946 with the support of labor, minorities, and independent progressives. On Rainey, see Cox, "Rainey Affair"; "Homer P. Rainey." Rainey's papers are at the Western Historical Manuscript Collection, University of Missouri, Columbia, Mo. Patricia Sullivan (*Days of Hope*) and others

have talked about the "discovery" of rural poverty in the 1930s. On the relation-
ship between blacks, the New Deal, and 1930s politics, see also Sitkoff, *New Deal*.
Contemporary accounts that exposed rural poverty include Agee and Evans, *Let
Us Now Praise*; Raper, *Preface*; Raper and Reid, *Sharecroppers All*. See also Horace
Mann Bond, *Education*.

65 Edwards, *Equal Educational Opportunity*; Rainey, *How Fare American Youth?*, 107.
The argument that many or even most young people were not capable of being
educated had long hindered the expansion of public education in America. Although such arguments had lost considerable weight by the 1930s, even when they
concerned racial and ethnic minorities, the AYC still saw it necessary to include
some defense of the idea that all youth could benefit from formal education. See
also Douglass, *Secondary Education*, 73–74; Howard M. Bell, *Youth Tell Their Story*,
66.

66 Rainey, *How Fare American Youth?*, 131, 127; Douglass, *Secondary Education*, 75;
Howard M. Bell, *Youth Tell Their Story*, 63, 57. See also Horace Mann Bond, *Education*.

67 See, for example, Lumpkin and Douglas, *Child Workers*, 77. Lumpkin and Douglas
extensively used the Children's Bureau's research and other studies. Work by Ben
Shahn and Arthur Rothstein was especially critical of the state of rural life, black
as well as white. And Jack Delano took photos of dilapidated Negro schools. See
Natanson, *Black Image*. Natanson notes that most of Delano's shots featured new
black schools and presented images of black students that fit idealized notions of
childhood and obscured the difficulties and inequalities that black young people
in the rural South faced. In part this was to show the positive effects of the New
Deal. See also various images reprinted in Thompson and Austin, *Children*.

68 See Lindenmeyer, *Greatest Generation*, 228–29. Grants from these agencies were
used to pay the salaries of rural teachers. See, for example, Work Projects Administration, *Final Statistical Report*, 111, 113. See also Wilkerson, *Special Problems*, 135–
37, 139–43. Comparisons of educational emergency relief to black schools and to
white schools indicated that black schools needed more aid (given relative population statistics) than did white schools.

69 Douglass, *Secondary Education*, 88, 77; Edwards, *Equal Educational Opportunity*,
77, 72–76; Howard M. Bell, *Youth Tell Their Story*, 130; "American Youth Commission: Present and Anticipated Major Recommendations," 30 October 1939, Box
555, Folder 5943, 3, GEB Papers; Douglass, *Secondary Education*, 119–21, 133. The
AYC did not advocate the federalization of public schools but rather called for the
"freedom and flexibility of local [school] authorities" along with federal funding
(Douglass, *Secondary Education*, 122–30). See also U.S. Advisory Committee on
Education, *Report*, 19–46; Dawson, "Federal Government." Douglass's study made
clear that the "angle of the rights of children" was secondary to considerations of
national security. This fits with my argument in chapter 2 that ideas about children's rights and particularly about black children's rights became increasingly
influential and politically significant in the 1940s and 1950s. During this period,

fears about national security grew, and children's rights became increasingly connected to national security considerations. During the 1920s, states assumed increasing financial responsibility for local schools (and assumed greater control of local schools). See Kolb and Brunner, "Rural Life." AYC researchers at times directly suggested that the state of southern schools merited the end of dual school systems. In general, however, the commission used much more diplomatic tactics than did early-twentieth-century reformers, who basically defined the problem of industrial child labor as a southern problem and tried to shame southern states into passing child-labor legislation. On public schools during the 1930s and the work of black social scientists during that decade, see also Tyack, Lowe, and Hansot, *Public Schools*, esp. 179–83.

70 Douglass, *Secondary Education*, 71, 121. On the work of the Federal (later National) Council of Churches in the 1920s and 1930s, see Ellsworth, "Women." Ellsworth notes that the women involved in council programs became experts on the issue in the 1930s and 1940s and were asked to provide information about migrant children to various public and private agencies and to speak at conferences. The council also employed black women to work with black migrant children, and although the council respected Jim Crow, the fact that it recognized and addressed the needs of black migrant children in the 1920s remains significant. It would perhaps be useful to explore connections between the National Council of Churches' work among migrants in the 1920s and 1930s and the council's work among southern blacks in the 1950s and 1960s that Findlay describes in *Church People*. Examples of articles published in the 1920s include Gleason, "Raising Children"; McGill, "Children"; Agnes E. Benedict, "Young Nomads"; Fuller, "Child Labor." For other references to agricultural child labor, see the bibliography of McWilliams, *Ill Fares the Land*. Although this earlier research on agricultural child labor did not receive widespread public attention or support at the time it was published, it was widely cited in the 1930s, when the nation became more willing to address the problem because of the Great Depression. On the factory-like conditions of agricultural labor, see McWilliams, *Factories*.

71 Gertrude Binder, "The Child Laborer is Still With Us," clipping, Box 55, National Child Labor Committee Papers, Manuscripts Division, LC; Lumpkin and Douglas, *Child Workers*, 60–61; *Child Welfare League of America Bulletin*, February 1937, 4, *Christian Century*, 21 March 1934, clipping, *Garment Worker*, 26 February 1937, clipping, all in Box 55, National Child Labor Committee Papers, Manuscripts Division, LC. Advocates commonly pointed out that as disturbing as census data on the rates of child labor were, that data did not even include a significant number of child laborers because the census did not ask any questions about the labor of children under the age of ten. A 1938 study estimated that 11 percent of spinach workers in South Texas were under fourteen years of age. A Works Progress Administration study found that among Hidalgo County migrant workers in Texas, 27 percent of the children were under ten, and 80 percent of all children between the ages of ten and fourteen worked (Menefee, *Mexican Migratory Workers*, 19). Many issues

of *The Child* in the 1930s and 1940s included articles on agricultural child labor. See also McWilliams, *Factories*, 321.

72 Lumpkin and Douglas, *Child Workers*, 4–5; McWilliams, *Factories*, 316–17; McWilliams, *Ill Fares the Land*, 118. See also Hahamovitch, *Fruits*. In 1932, after the depression drastically increased the numbers of unemployed and of transients, the federal government created the Committee on Care of Transient and Homeless (known after 1939 as the Council on Interstate Migration). This committee, like the Farm Security Administration, helped bring emergency relief to migrants.

73 Woofter, "Possibilities," 125; Henry Hill Collins Jr., *America's Own Refugees*, 260. On Mexican American education and segregation, see Gonzalez, *Chicano Education*, esp. chap. 5.

74 In the 1940s, the nature of the migrant problem again shifted and gave advocates even more reasons to insist on equal educational opportunities for America's youth. What was referred to as "destitute migration" diminished, at least in terms of public significance, as migration for defense jobs took center stage. After just one year, the Tolan Committee (House Select Committee to Investigate the Migration of Destitute Citizens), formed in 1940, was renamed the Select Committee Investigation of National Defense Migration. With World War II, migration became a way of life for thousands of American families of all economic standings. Indeed, the U.S. Census Bureau classified almost one out of every five children born between 1941 and 1947 as "migrant." Families migrated to bomber factories, shipping yards, army bases, and navy posts across the country. Rachel Love, whose father, an Army Air Corps instructor, was reassigned every two months, attended five different schools in one year. Tuttle, *Daddy's Gone*, 51; Henry Hill Collins, *America's Own Refugees*; Lamb, "Migration," 335–37. See also "Child Labor"; Gonzalez, *Chicano Education*, 76. That World War II made migration a way of life in America made educational disparities even more alarming. More than ever, advocates had compelling reasons to insist on equal educational opportunities for the nation's youth. The reasons for educational equality would only multiply during the cold war.

75 Numerous child welfare advocates, researchers, and agencies described the deficiencies of migrant children in these terms and recommended public schools and strict compulsory education as the best remedy for the children's problems. See, for example, Anderson, "Highlights," 112; Maddox, "Farm Security Administration," 111; Henry Hill Collins, *America's Own Refugees*, 262; Newlon, *Education*, 203. Even agencies not necessarily focused on youth echoed the AYC's recommendations. At the 1940 Interstate Conference on Migrant Labor, for example, officials from a variety of agencies and states agreed that one of the main areas for action on the migrant problem lay in providing services such as schools, public health, and housing to migrant children and their families (McCall, "Migration," 132).

76 "American Council on Education—American Youth Council: Studies of Negro Youth," n.d., 1, Box 555, Folder 5944, GEB Papers. This document also outlines publication and sales figures for the volumes on black youth. In *Survey Graphic*, for example, Chamberlain argued that despite the commission's and others' apparent faith in education, "Education is a weak bulwark for democracy if democracy can't

deliver the goods in the form of jobs, a future, or just plain hope" ("Our Jobless Youth," 580). Commission members would have agreed with Chamberlain but would also have suggested that education would help youth get better jobs, secure them more stable futures, and give them hope. Lumpkin and Douglas also felt that compulsory and universal education would not fully eliminate child labor—that federal legislation was needed (*Child Workers*, 85). On the commission's hopes to influence racial politics, see, for example, "Proceedings," Washington, D.C., 17–18 October 1937, 170–99, Box 8, Folder 1, AYC Papers; Woofter, *Southern Race Progress*, 120.

77 "Saturday Morning Session," American Youth Commission Executive Committee Meeting, 24 May 1941, 168–89, Box 20, Folder 2, AYC Papers.

78 W. E. B. Du Bois, *Darkwater*, 193; Charles S. Johnson, "Negro Rural Youth," in "Report of the Proceedings of the Conference on the Needs of Negro Youth," Howard University, 15–17 July 1940, Box 100, Folder 10, HLP; Powdermaker, *After Freedom*, 302, 299, chap. 15. Researchers thought it significant that blacks' enthusiasm for education directly following the Civil War had not been dampened by the meager state of black education (Allison Davis, Gardner, and Gardner, *Deep South*, 420).

79 See Howard M. Bell, *Youth Tell Their Story*, 98. Goluboff, *Lost Promise*, describes the Justice Department's shift from defining civil rights in terms of both race and labor to a definition that included only race and the NAACP's shift from fighting for both economic and educational equality to focusing on just educational equality.

80 W. E. B. Du Bois, *Philadelphia Negro*, 351. Du Bois's question was specifically about the city of Philadelphia but was implicitly directed at all American cities.

CHAPTER TWO

1 Swedish feminist and reformer Ellen Key quoted in Frank, "Childhood and Youth," 753; W. E. B. Du Bois, *Souls*, vii. See also Ellen Key, *Century*.

2 "Press Release," Box 11, CCCP; "Report of Children's Librarians, New York Public Library, March 26, 1940," Box 6, CCCP. On Fisher, see Madigan, *Keeping Fires*. On the A.D. 1212 Children's Crusade, see Runciman, *History*, 139–44; "Chronica," 213.

3 Faith Baldwin, "Portrait of a Child," 1–2, 4, Box 10, CCCP; "There Is a Lamp," Box 23, CCCP; "No 'Isms' but Americanism," Box 23, CCCP; Sarah Cleghorn, "A Prayer for the Children's Crusade," Box 11, CCCP.

4 The Mein Kampf Fund (proceeds from the sale of Hitler's book in America) covered the campaign's administrative expenses. See Box 25, CCCP; Syndicated Cartoons, Box 22, CCCP; "Children's Crusade," *Newsweek*, 13 May 1940, Box 10, CCCP. On other humanitarian campaigns, see Marshall, "Herbert Hoover," 3. Frankfurter was an associate justice of the Supreme Court when it made its ruling in the *Brown* case.

5 "Radio Address," Box 11, CCCP; "The 'Ayes' Have It," in Box 22, CCCP; Johanna M. Lindlof, "Children without a Country," Box 23, CCCP.

6 Amelia Josephine Burr, "Our Father," Box 6, CCCP.

7 Mildred Douglas, "What Democracy Means," Box 11, CCCP; Beth Adicaff, "The Children's Crusade," Box 6, CCCP; Ruth Keough, "My Opinion of the Children's Crusade," Box 6, CCCP; "The Brotherhood of Youth" (Syndicated Cartoon), Box 22, CCCP; Caliver and Douglass, "Education," 134; "Library Committee," Box 6, CCCP. See also other miscellaneous materials, Boxes 6, 11, CCCP.

8 "Untitled," Box 23, CCCP; Raymond Gram Swing, "Crusade for Children," *Esquire*, May 1940 (nationally syndicated), Box 10, CCCP; "Untitled," Box 10, CCCP; Hand County Newsletter, April–May 1940, Box 11, CCCP; Irving Fineman, "A Letter to My Sons," Box 10, CCCP.

9 Gladys English, "Untitled," Box 6, CCCP; Franklin D. Roosevelt, "Radio Script," Box 11, CCCP; "Untitled," Box 23, CCCP; "Children's Crusade," *Newsweek*, 13 May 1940, Box 23, CCCP; Irving Fineman, "A Letter to My Sons," 2, Box 10, CCCP; Robert Nathan, "To the Children," Box 23, CCCP. On World War I propaganda and childhood, see Marshall, "Herbert Hoover," 4–6.

10 May, *Homeward Bound*.

11 Aristotle quoted in Greenstein, *Children and Politics*, 3. On the development of American public education, see Cremin, *American Education*; Kaestle, *Pillars*; Kaestle and Vinovskis, *Education*; Rudolph, *Essays*; Block, "Politics."

12 Such an understanding of the connections between children and politics helps explain why education for girls and women generally came much later in America than it did for boys. It also helps explain why separate schools for blacks were so blatantly unequal—black children were not future citizens, at least not future full citizens.

13 See "Proceedings," Washington, D.C., 16 September 1935, 148–49, Box 2, Folder 1, AYC Papers.

14 Runciman, *History*, 139–44; Josephine Baker, "To the Editor" (nationally syndicated), Box 10, CCCP; "Children's Crusade," *Newsweek*, 13 May 1940, Box 10, CCCP. Fisher told other committee members, "I think the study of Negro youth should be adopted if we don't do anything else" ("Minutes," 5 May 1936, 44, Box 1, Folder 20, AYC Papers). The crusade in some ways presaged a late 1940s "Zeal for Democracy" program in the nation's schools that, as Hartman notes, "encouraged students to think of American democracy in normative fashion, and to define it solely in opposition to totalitarianism" (*Education*, 70–71).

15 Faith Baldwin, "Portrait of a Child," 2, Box 10, CCCP. On minstrelsy, see Hale, *Making Whiteness*, 151–54; Lott, *Love and Theft*.

16 In *Making Whiteness*, Hale argues that whiteness became the "unspoken but deepest sense of what it means to be an American" (xi).

17 Zeligs, "Children's Intergroup Concepts," 115, 121–25; Zeligs, "Racial Attitudes."

18 Zeligs, "Children's Intergroup Concepts," 116; *Life*, 6 June 1938, 364. Only one photograph in the issue included any African Americans—a black child who appeared incidentally as part of a zoo scene.

19 Gordon Gillette, "Radio Address," 26 April 1940, Box 11, CCCP; "Speech to Federation of Women's Clubs" (later rebroadcast via radio), 2 February 1940, Box 11,

CCCP; "Untitled," Box 22, CCCP; "Untitled," Box 10, CCCP; "No 'Isms' but Americanism," Box 23, CCCP.

20 Vera Flory, "Strange Things," *Morning Tennessean*, 5 May 1940, Box 10, CCCP; Cheney Junior High School Students, "Letters," Box 6, CCCP.

21 Katharine Lenroot, "Radio Address," WMAL, 16 March 1940, 10:45–11:00 A.M., Washington, D.C. (rebroadcast via other stations), 5–7, Box 22, CCCP.

22 On the legislative priorities and successes of women voters in the 1920s and 1930s, see Schuyler, *Weight*, 180, 210–12; Franklin D. Roosevelt, "White House Conference," 263; Marshall Field, "A Guide for Wartime Planning for Children," 1942, Reel 50, Frames 145–52, National Consumer's League Papers, Manuscripts Division, LC. Lindenmeyer's important work, *Right*, does not note this new emphasis at the 1940 conference. Instead, she is more concerned with what she sees as the decline and weakening of the Children's Bureau after it was transferred to the Social Security Administration in 1946. Rather than just stripping it of the power and prestige it carried as a separate, independent agency, this move may have expanded the bureau's vision and influence in significant ways. The creation of the Department of Health, Education, and Welfare in 1953 perhaps resulted partly from the Children's Bureau's ability to spread its ideas about the "whole child" and government's responsibility toward children.

23 Franklin D. Roosevelt, "White House Conference," 263; "Conference on Children," 171.

24 Katharine F. Lenroot, "The Objectives of Democracy for Its Children," speech to California Congress of Parents and Teachers, 22 July 1940, 4, 102 IF 14-68, Box 10, 1-0-4, CBP; Perkins, "General Child Welfare," 239 (a reprint of a nationally syndicated radio broadcast); *Children Bear the Promise of a Better World . . . Their Education Is Democracy's Strength*, Defense of Children Series 7 (Washington, D.C.: U.S. Department of Labor, 1942), 1; *Children Bear the Promise of a Better World . . . Through Play They Learn What Freedom Means*, Defense of Children Series 8 (Washington, D.C.: U.S. Department of Labor, 1942), 1.

25 In *Social Scientists for Social Justice*, John P. Jackson notes that during the late 1930s and 1940s, social scientists increasingly researched race prejudice, the genesis of race prejudice in children, and the construction of racial identity. He attributes this new interest in the subject partly to the increasing numbers of graduate students pursuing studies in psychology and sociology. Such research also seems to have been encouraged by increasing interest in the rights of childhood and the government's responsibilities for securing those rights and by the success of the Children's Bureau, the AYC, education experts, and child welfare advocates in making the experiences of children and youth and childhood itself significant public and political topics.

26 Franklin D. Roosevelt, "Speech to Congress," 16 May 1940, quoted in Katharine Lenroot, "The Objectives of Democracy for Its Children," 2, IF 14-68, Box 10, 1-0-4, CBP; Oettinger, "Current Concern," 128. Oettinger was chief of the Children's Bureau.

27 "Proceedings," Washington, D.C., 17–18 October 1937, 190, Box 8, Folder 1, AYC Papers. In *Right*, Lindenmeyer notes that while the bureau had long been interested in protecting the "emotional security" of children, the 1940 conference reflected "the new trend in child welfare policy of placing greater importance on children's emotional health" (206). Hulbert notes that during the 1920s, child experts began talking about the "personality" and "maladjustment" of children and identified childhood as "the golden period for mental hygiene." She also comments on the national security anxieties of the 1940 White House Conference (*Raising America*, 106–10, 172). For other factors that shaped the movement's direction, see Goluboff, *Lost Promise*; McNeil, *Groundwork*; and Jacqueline Dowd Hall's thoughtful synthetic article, "Long Civil Rights Movement."

28 Katharine Lenroot, "The Objectives of Democracy for Its Children," 4, 13, IF 14-68, Box 10, 1-0-4, CBP; Katharine Lenroot, "Radio Address," 5, Box 22, CCCP. The first significant study on racial difference in minority children was Klineberg, "Experimental Study." A number of scholars began looking at race prejudice and identity during the 1930s, and the first studies on prejudice and personality were published during that decade as well. Early studies on prejudice and personality development often focused on whites. One especially significant study on the effects of racial prejudice and personality development came out shortly before the 1940 White House conference. See Hartley, *Problems*; John P. Jackson, *Social Scientists*, 20–42. The AYC's studies on black youth were published in 1940 and 1941, and they, too, looked at the influence of race and racism on personality development. Commission papers also indicate that the group tried to popularize its findings among professionals, policymakers, and the general public before these studies were published.

29 Ewin, "Opportunity," 83. Similar themes began to dominate more localized public discussions. See, for example, Markowitz and Rosner, *Children*; Children's Bureau Commission, "Children's Charter," 248; "Eighth Graders Examine Their Attitudes," 360; Zeligs, "Children's Intergroup Concepts," 115–19; Edward L. Adams et al., "Attitudes," 337; Chein and Laks, "Attitudes," 367, 366. Chein and Laks were research associates of New York City's Committee on Unity. On "the damaging psychology of race," see also Herman, *Romance*, 174–99. On child expert thinking and research at the time, see also Hulbert, *Raising America*, chaps. 6, 7.

30 Bettelheim and Janowitz, *Social Change*; Lane, "Education-Centered Community," 274. Lane was a professor of education at New York University. See Sherman, "Is Education Inciting Race Hate?," 6; Alpenfels, "Price," 5; W. H. Kilpatrick, Stone, and Cole, "Frame," 564; Adamic, "Will Racism Lead," 12. Contrary to what Guinier argues in "From Racial Liberalism," the "new integrationist orthodoxy" did not fail "to connect its version of the [negative impact of racism on] the psychology of blacks with an equally probing analysis of the psychology of whites." Instead, partly because racism was deemed bad for whites and for national security, advocates began arguing for greater contact between the races (101). Guinier is right, however, to note that the ideology of racial liberalism did not fully take into account

the psychological benefits of segregation to whites (102). See Arter, "Effects." Arter's article references a number of studies conducted during the 1940s and 1950s.

31 Lillian E. Smith, *Strange Fruit*, 57, 60, 97, 198, 206.

32 Allen, "Strange Fruit." See W. E. B. Du Bois, *Souls*, 3; Lillian E. Smith, *Strange Fruit*, 344, 366.

33 Rachel Davis Du Bois, "Sharing Cultural Values," 485; Bishop, "Character," 28; Alpenfels, "Price," 6; Lane, "Education-Centered Community," 274; Adamic, "Will Racism Lead," 13.

34 Lillian E. Smith, *Strange Fruit*, 169, 88; Kenneth B. Clark and Clark, "Racial Identification"; Radke, Trager, and Davis, "Social Perceptions," 442. On the Clarks' research and clinical work, see Markowitz and Rosner, *Children*; Herman, *Romance*, 192–99. Kenneth Clark was also involved with AYC research in the 1930s. Radke, Trager, and Davis's study, sponsored by New York's Bureau for Intercultural Education, was widely quoted — for example, in "Missouri's Children at the Mid-Century," White House Conference on Children and Youth: Jefferson City, Missouri, March 1951, 42, 102 IF, 14-68, Box 14, 0-1-0-48, CBP.

35 Lane, "Education-Centered Community," 273; Caliver, "Negro Child," 236; *Fair Chance*; Overstreet, "High Art," 23–24; Kenneth B. Clark and Clark, "Race Prejudice"; Lillian E. Smith, *Strange Fruit*, 340–41. Caliver was senior specialist in the education of Negroes under the Federal Security Department of the U.S. Office of Education.

36 See Gilbert, *Cycle*, 79, 133–34. On the New York committee and the attitudes of prominent individuals in the city, such as Judge Justine Polier, see Markowitz and Rosner, *Children*. Psychologist Erik Erickson's emphasis on the importance of ego and personality formation similarly supported the work of child advocates and other scholars trying to direct attention to the problems of prejudice in children. Scholars have noted that Myrdal's book promoted "new" theories of juvenile delinquency and relied heavily on the work of other scholars. See, for example, Gilbert, *Cycle*, 130–31. Myrdal's work especially reflected the AYC's work, and many of the scholars who contributed to *An American Dilemma* also contributed to commission publications. On Myrdal and the influence of *An American Dilemma*, see esp. Walter A. Jackson, *Gunnar Myrdal*; Southern, *Gunnar Myrdal*. On juvenile delinquency, see also Mintz, *Huck's Raft*, 291–302.

37 Melvin A. Glasser, "Citizen Responsibility for Child Welfare," address presented at the Church Conference of Social Work, Atlantic City, N.J., 25 April 1950, 14, 102 IF, 14-68, Box 10, 0-1-1-14, CBP; Blanshard, "Negro Delinquency," 117, 118, 121, 122. Blanshard was executive director of both the Society for the Prevention of Crime and the Foreign Division, Recruitment and Manning Organization, of the War Shipping Administration.

38 Caliver and Douglass, "Education," 134; W. H. Kilpatrick, Stone, and Cole, "Frame," 561; Olive Applegate, "Pied Pipers of Crime," 2, 102 CF, 49-52, 7-2-2-2, Box 438, CBP; W. Howard Jackson, "The Rising Tide of Color," *Voice of Tomorrow*, April 1933,

14, Schomburg Center for Research in Black Culture, New York Public Library, New York, N.Y.; "Hyde Park Youth Project of the Welfare Council of Metropolitan Chicago," 1958, Box 107, Folder 8, HLP. In *Cycle of Outrage*, Gilbert notes that the Children's Bureau and its experts generally sought to describe young offenders as victims instead of as criminals (149). On Wright, see Rampersad, *Richard Wright*, 898.

39 Wright, *Native Son*, 463, 453, 542, 551, 670. Wright's novel emphasizes many of the same themes stressed in Allison Davis and Dollard, *Children of Bondage*; Frazier, *Negro Youth*; and Charles S. Johnson, *Growing Up in the Black Belt*, which were published at the same time as *Native Son*.

40 Buck, "Save the Children," 197–98; Fisher, introduction, ix–xi; Wright, *Native Son*, 671; Wright, "How 'Bigger' Was Born," 866; "Report of the Director to the Commission," 15 April 1940, 6, Box 9, Folder 8, Howard Y. McClusky Collection, Bentley Historical Library, University of Michigan, Ann Arbor, Mich. Buck, who grew up in China, championed the rights of all children, especially Amerasians (a term she coined). She established the first interracial, international adoption agency in the United States and supported civil rights and women's rights, and her books often addressed racial themes. She also adopted seven children, including two African Americans. Fisher's introduction was quoted, not insignificantly, in Robert L. Sutherland's *Color, Class, and Personality*, 14–15. The director of the AYC suggested that the commission's studies were startling in much the same way as Wright's book and considered their publication in the wake of *Native Son* "probably fortunate," since they would garner more public attention.

41 Alpenfels, "Price," 4; Lawson, *To Secure These Rights*; *Civil Liberties and Human Rights Public Affairs Newsletter*, 10 October 1949, 7, RG 73, Series 3, Box 37, Folder 4, SEPC; Ferguson, "Public-Spirited Youth," 4; W. H. Kilpatrick, Stone, and Cole, "Frame," 565; Fitch, "Thumbs Down," 21, 22; Annie Lee Davis, "Attitudes," 83; Mackenzie, "How to Keep Your Child," 79–80 (condensed from an article in the *New York Times*). See also Moon, *High Cost*. On the rise of cultural pluralism and its relationship to *Brown*, see also Daryl Michael Scott, "Postwar Pluralism."

42 Vernon J. Williams Jr., *Rethinking Race*, 29–20, 34–35, chap. 3; Stocking, *Delimiting Anthropology*, 34, 41, 46; Liss, "Diasporic Identities," esp. 131–32, 137; Bateson and Mead, *Balinese Character*, xvi; Ruth Benedict, *Patterns*, 10, 254, 271. On "the collapse of the doctrine of instinctive prejudice," see Vernon J. Williams Jr., *From a Caste to a Minority*, 137–41. Williams also notes that "one of the toughest obstacles to overcome for those who studied race relations before the mid-1920s was the idea that prejudice was difficult, if not impossible, to remove from whites" (25).

43 Steven Lawson, *To Secure*, 156; Lenzy Patton, "Letter," 18 August 1953, CF 53-7, 0-2-9-1, Box 561, CBP; Rice, *I Came Out*, 26, 28–29.

44 Woodward, *Strange Career*; Bettelheim and Janowitz, *Social Change*, 290. Ritterhouse has also used the Woodward thesis to talk about the racial socialization of black and white children (*Growing Up Jim Crow*, 7–8).

45 Petry, "My Most Humiliating Jim Crow Experience," 63–64.

46 Coggins, "I Hate Negroes," 71. Such racial awakening stories were also a way for adults to shape or reinforce beliefs about childhood. Such stories reinforced both the idea that childhood was a period of innocence and the idea that racism was unnatural—a learned system of belief.

47 Lillian E. Smith, "Why I Wrote *Strange Fruit*," 47–49. Lillian Smith's *Killers of the Dream* commented even more explicitly on the relationships among childhood, racism, and white supremacy.

48 Lillian E. Smith, *Strange Fruit*, 108–9.

49 See Lillian E. Smith, "'Georgia Primer,'" 7–11; Lillian E. Smith, *Strange Fruit*, 109–14.

50 Lillian E. Smith, "Why I Wrote *Strange Fruit*," 49, 47; Keesecker, "Supreme Court Decisions," 4; Ford, "Teacher Looks," 264; Lillian E. Smith, *Killers of the Dream*, esp. 64, 25–27, 77, 38–39; Ethel Popel Shaw, *Personal Adventures*, 22; Annie Lee Davis, "Attitudes," 85. Brownie Ledbetter, a white southerner who promoted integration in the early 1960s, remembered that her family had "lots of discussions" about contemporary theories of racial prejudice and children and that she personally had bought "eleven of Lillian Smith's *Killers of the Dream*. . . . [W]e read that and we just craved it" (Brownie Ledbetter, interview by George King, n.d., 13, 27, Box 10, Folder 20, SRCP).

51 Haynes, "Clinical Methods," 317; W. H. Kilpatrick, Stone, and Cole, "Frame," 572, 556; "Children and Your Democracy's Future," Governor's Committee for Illinois on the Mid-Century White House Conference for Children and Youth, 20, 102 IF 14-68, Box 1, CBP; Felix, "Teacher's Role," 1–2; Studebaker, "Education of Free Men," 5; Scheele, "School," 31, 35; Lenroot, "American Childhood," 5; Pete McKnight valedictory address quoted in Gaillard, *Dream*, 23. See also Goodykoontz, "Life," 104. Haynes was executive secretary of the Department of Race Relations of the Federal Council of the Churches of Christ in America. Felix, a medical doctor, was chief of the Mental Hygiene Division of the Public Health Service. Anthropologists such as Ruth Benedict similarly saw schools as key sites for developing tolerance and correcting the mental illness associated with prejudice. As she put it (albeit not talking specifically about race), "One of the most effective ways in which to deal with the staggering burden of psychopathic tragedies in America . . . is by means of an educational program which fosters tolerance in society" (*Patterns*, 273–74).

52 Box 1, CBP; Dodson, "Social Action," 345; Davie, "Minorities," 454–55; Rainey, *How Fare American Youth?*, 133; Burrell, "American Education," 450; Chambers, "Culture Conflicts," 467; Myrdal quoted in Kirp, *Just Schools*, 32. Dodson edited the *Journal of Educational Sociology*, directed curriculum research at the Center for Human Relation Studies at New York University, and served as the executive director for Mayor LaGuardia's Committee on Unity from 1944 to 1947. Chambers was associated with the American Youth Commission of the American Council on Education. On Myrdal's emphasis on education as a solution for racial problems or at least the public's selective reading of Myrdal's recommendations, see Walter A.

Jackson, *Gunner Myrdal*. In her essential book on twentieth-century school reform, Ravitch notes a 1930s consensus among American educators that teachers should be social engineers. She suggests that the political potential of this sentiment was lost, however, and that postwar schools aimed to "adjust young people to" the social order rather than to challenge it (*Left Back*, 327). Although this statement is true in many respects, some educators, child welfare advocates, civil rights activists, and even laypeople continued to link public schools with sociopolitical change. On public schools in the period, see also Hartman, *Education*, esp. chap. 3.

53 See Lindenmeyer, *Right*, 205–6. The 1950 Mid-Century White House Conference on Children and Youth focused even more on the importance of personality development and education.

54 Caliver, "Negro Child," 236; Caliver, "Secondary Schools," 320. See also Caliver, "Project," 5; Rayburn, "That Civilization May Survive," 9; Meyer, "New Values," 14. On schools and foreign policy needs, see also Hartman, *Education*, esp. 70–71, chap. 3.

55 Patricia Sullivan, "Prelude to *Brown*," 164; Myrdal, *American Dilemma*, 902–3. On Myrdal and his study, see Walter A. Jackson, *Gunnar Myrdal*; Brameld, "Educational Costs," 41, 44; Studebaker, "Communism's Challenge," 1, 3.

56 Roucek, "Future Steps," 499–500; Lundberg, "Security," 9; U.S. Children's Bureau, *Controlling*, 7; Meyer, "New Values," 14; Caliver, "Secondary Schools," 320; Isadore Wexler, "An Adventure in Neighborhood Councils," June 1948, CF 102, 49-52, 8-6-0, Box 434, CBP; Brameld, "Educational Costs," 44; "Organized Labor Speaks," 100. Lundberg had been associated with child welfare reform since the Progressive era, and when the Children's Bureau expanded in 1915, she headed its Social Service Division.

57 Frost, "Protocol," 343; Lenroot, "American Childhood," 4; Buck, "Save the Children," 196; Schwellenbach, "Put Children First," 136; Eliot, "Furthering Individual Well-Being," 21; "University of Chicago Round Table Equality of Educational Opportunity—A Radio Discussion by Robert Redfield, George Stoddard and Louis Wirth," 13 July 1947, 12, RG 73, Series 3, Box 121, Folder 1, SEPC. Frost was an assistant professor of education at Brooklyn College. Schwellenbach was secretary of labor. Eliot was chief of the Children's Bureau.

58 On the relationship between *Brown* and the cold war, see especially Dudziak, *Cold War Civil Rights*; Dudziak, "*Brown*"; Rosenberg, *How Far the Promised Land?*; Klarman, *From Jim Crow to Civil Rights*.

59 Acheson quoted in Dudziak, *Cold War Civil Rights*, 101; YWCA, *We Need Atomic Understanding!*" (rare pamphlet), 2nd ed., 1946, RG 73, Series 3, Box 38, Folder 3, SEPC; Katharine F. Lenroot, "A Democracy's Responsibility to Its Children," February 1941, 5, CBP. Acheson's comment was made in a letter dated 2 December 1952 and was included on page 8 of the U.S. amicus curiae brief in support of the petitioners/appellants in *Brown v. Board of Education*, 347 U.S. 483 (1954).

60 "Universal Declaration," 140–41; Katharine F. Lenroot, "A Democracy's Responsibility to Its Children," February 1941, 3–4, CBP; Lundberg, "Security," 9; see Dud-

ziak, *Cold War Civil Rights*. In *From Jim Crow to Civil Rights*, Klarman misses some
of "the larger culture and . . . historical moments" that the justices shared with
the American public and that made "judicial invalidation of segregation conceivable" and made it especially conceivable that the Supreme Court would choose an
education case involving schoolchildren to invalidate segregation, even if, as he
suggests, blacks themselves were more interested in securing voting rights, ending
police brutality, and finding fair employment (310, 391). See also John P. Jackson,
Social Scientists, which explores important connections between the work of social
science researchers, especially sociologists, and the *Brown* case. Borgwardt argues
that the United Nations Declaration of Human Rights and America's rhetorical
support of its principles created a "cognitive dissonance . . . that itself constituted
a kind of engine of historical change . . . as political leaders struggled to narrow"
the gap between their actions and their words (*New Deal*, 56). This gap would
be especially apparent when ideals about childhood were compared to the actual
treatment of children in America. There is, of course, much more to the context of
Brown than ideas about childhood. This framework is meant to help us understand
Brown but certainly does not replace the thoughtful work on *Brown* and the black
freedom struggle done by other historians.

61 Studebaker, "Education of Free Men," 6; Patricia Sullivan, "Prelude to *Brown*," 165;
Phillipson, "Follow-Up," 132; U.S. Children's Bureau, "Conclusions," 2; Studebaker,
"Education Moves," 35; W. H. Kilpatrick, Stone, and Cole, "Frame," 557; Douglass,
Secondary Education, 18; Spock, "Development," 85; *Curriculum in Intergroup Relations*, 4; Buck quoted in Isadore Wexler, "An Adventure in Neighborhood Councils," CF 102, 49-52, 8-6-0, Box 434, CBP. Phillipson was the executive secretary of
the Midcentury Committee for Children and Youth. In the 1930s and early 1940s,
the AYC promoted the idea that children needed to "experience democracy." See,
for example, "Executive Committee Meeting," 2–4 May 1936, 21–23, Box 1, Folder
20, AYC Papers. These kinds of ideas appeared in *The Crisis* in the early 1930s. See,
for example, Rachel Davis Du Bois, "Building Tolerant Attitudes," 336; Gardner,
"Changing Racial Attitudes," 336. During and after World War II, anthropologists
such as Margaret Mead and Gregory Bateson focused on the need to "plan an
integrated world" through "a disciplined science of human relations" (Bateson and
Mead, *Balinese Character*, xvi).

62 Benjamin and Brooker, "UNESCO," 9; U.S. Office of Education, *How Democratic Is
Your School?*, 2; Blanshard, "Negro Delinquency," 122.

63 W. H. Kilpatrick, Stone, and Cole, "Frame," 568; Brameld, "Educational Costs,"
45; Fitch, "Thumbs Down," 22; Chein and Laks, "Attitudes," 374; George Edmund
Haynes, "Road toward Interracial Peace," *Interracial Education*, n.d., 3, RG 58,
Series 3, Box 54, Folder 770, YMCA Student Division Papers, Yale Divinity Library,
Yale University, New Haven, Conn.; Alpern, "Role," 363; Burgum, "Promise," 344.
On the intercultural education movement, see also Selig, "Cultural Gifts."

64 Mary Linda Helfant, "Springfield Schools Have Become Laboratory in Education
for Democracy," *Springfield (Mass.) Sunday Union and Republican*, 5 September

1943, RG 73, Series 3, Box 12, Folder 1, SEPC; Halligan, "Community's Total War," 375; "Three Boards," 5; Tipton, "'Mass Truancy,'" 6.

65 Lenroot, "Children," 2–3; Rice, *I Came Out*, 184; Lillian E. Smith, *Strange Fruit*, 354, 356; W. E. B. Du Bois, *Darkwater*, 217.

66 Mnookin, *In The Interest*, 8.

67 *Brown v. Board of Education*, 347 U.S. 483, 494–95 n. 11 (1954); Arter, "Effects," 186; "Morally Right Decision," 29–31. On other ways the NAACP and the Department of Justice might have promoted racial equality and the NAACP's growing awareness that attacking *Plessy* was the best way to advance its cause, see Goluboff, *Lost Promise*. John P. Jackson, *Social Scientists*, offers a compelling account of the relationship between social science researchers and the *Brown* decision. Patterson, *Brown*, explores criticisms of the *Brown* decision's reliance on social science research, noting that southerners on the Court warned Chief Justice Earl Warren not to use social science in the ruling. But Patterson suggests that Warren's inclusion of social science research was not unmindful and that of the five cases covered in the *Brown* ruling, the Topeka case took "top billing" precisely because the psychological arguments on which the Legal Defense Fund attorneys relied in that particular case "resonated" with the presiding judge in Kansas and with the Supreme Court (chaps. 2, 3, esp. pp. 35, 69). These arguments suggest that the justices' rulings were indeed motivated by ideas that linked racial prejudice to the rights of childhood and that Warren considered those ideas essential to the explanation of the Court's decision to the American public. I believe that Warren made this decision partly because those ideas were already well known and widely accepted by the general public. Including social science research made the ruling more tolerable and even compelling to whites not otherwise convinced by notions of black equality. The AYC had begun as early as the late 1930s to "make thousands of common people 'psychologically ready' for the implementation of its recommendations, including its recommendations on black youth." See "Plan for Publicizing and Implementing the Findings and Recommendations of the American Youth Commission," 15 July 1938, 3, Box 11, Folder 5, AYC Papers. For contemporary criticisms of the use of social science research in *Brown*, see Cahn, "Jurisprudence." See also Daryl Michael Scott, "Postwar Pluralism," which looks at the *Brown* decision, public debates about social science research on racial prejudice, and the role of the nation's schools in terms of postwar cultural and therapeutic pluralism. Ideas about childhood made the "new psychologicalized and medicalized . . . knowledge about [race,] society and the psyche" compelling to the Supreme Court. As Scott says, the Court was not "steeped in psychology" (79). The justices (and the American public) were, however, steeped in American (and international) ideals about childhood and the rights of childhood. See also Daryl Michael Scott, *Contempt and Pity*, which looks at the history of social science research on black personality and how it has been used to support both conservative and liberal racial ideologies and politics. Walter A. Jackson, *Gunnar Myrdal*, examines research on intercultural education, prejudice, and psychological damage. On *Brown* and personality

damage, see also Herman, *Romance*, 195–98. On *Brown* in general, see also Armor, *Forced Justice*; Greenberg, *Crusaders*; Howard, *Shifting Wind*; Klarman, *From Jim Crow to Civil Rights*; John P. Jackson, *Social Scientists*; Kluger, *Simple Justice*; Patterson, *Brown*; Ravitch, *Troubled Crusade*; Tushnet, *Making Civil Rights Law*; Wilkinson, *From Brown to Bakke*.

68 In *Cold War Civil Rights*, Dudziak makes a compelling case for the impact of national security issues in the *Brown* decision. Her analysis, however, does not explain why the Court did not choose another case for declaring the unconstitutionality of segregation. Moreover, she notes that in arguing the case, the NAACP referred only briefly to the "Cold War argument" and instead emphasized the findings of social science experts. In its opinion, the Court likewise stressed the "importance of education to our democratic society" (*Brown*, 1954). Dudziak is right to suggest that the absence of national security rhetoric in *Brown* does not mean that the Court was not influenced by such considerations, but to ignore what the Court chose to discuss in its opinion may be distorting as well (102–4). In *How Far the Promised Land?*, Rosenberg also explores the international context of the ruling and the civil rights movement. He focuses on the "color-conscious internationalism" and rhetoric of movement leaders (1).

69 "Universal Declaration," 141; "University of Chicago Round Table Equality of Educational Opportunity—A Radio Discussion by Robert Redfield, George Stoddard and Louis Wirth," 15–16, RG 73, Series 3, Box 121, Folder 1, SEPC.

70 McNeil, *Groundwork*, 137; Robert L. Carter, *Matter of Law*, 93–96, 99, 115, 119–26; *Answers for Action*, 3; "Selected Highlights," 59; *Brown*, 1954; Sherrill T. Wills to the Editor (Ralph McGill), 30 September 1957, Box 24, Folder 1, MSS 252, Ralph McGill Papers, RWL. On early NAACP legal strategies, see McNeil, *Groundwork*, chap. 10.

71 Goluboff, drawing in part on my research, has also talked about the importance of the "education context" of the *Brown* ruling (*Lost Promise*, 243–50). Because Dudziak believes that civil rights reforms were about improving America's image abroad, she focuses on the "symbolic value" of the Supreme Court decision (*Cold War Civil Rights*, 90).

72 *Intercultural Education News*, November 1944, 2. McNeil notes that NAACP legal counsel Robert L. Carter recognized that "racial segregation was merely a symptom, not the disease" ("Before *Brown*," 1433). My work suggests that myriad social scientists and education experts as well as civil rights activists recognized that racial prejudice and not just segregation was the problem—which was why they pointed to schools and young people as the remedy.

73 Caliver and Wilkins, "Education," 111. In "'Whole United States,'" Payne asks, "What does it mean that supporters and opponents of segregation alike overestimated the impact of *Brown*? What does that imply about the level of understanding of the racial system?" (84). We might, however, instead ask what it implies about beliefs about childhood that both sides expected schoolchildren to effect a social and political revolution in race relations. On "massive resistance" and other south-

ern strategies for combating desegregation, see, for example, Townsend Davis, *Weary Feet*, 55–57; Lassiter and Lewis, *Moderates' Dilemma*; Benjamin Muse, *Virginia's Massive Resistance*; Robert Collins Smith, *They Closed Their Schools*; James J. Kilpatrick, *Southern Case*; Robbins L. Gates, *Making*; Klarman, *From Jim Crow to Civil Rights*. For a nuanced look at white resistance (and accommodation) in Mississippi, see Crespino, *In Search*.

CHAPTER THREE

1 Hansberry, *Movement*, 2, 122–23.
2 See, for example, Payne, *I've Got the Light*, 413–41. On the media, journalists, and the movement, see also Roberts and Klibanoff, *Race Beat*.
3 Klarman, *From Jim Crow to Civil Rights*, argues that "*Brown* increased the salience of the segregation issue, and in 1954 many Americans, if forced to take a position, could only be integrationists" (366). Klarman's comment suggests that a Supreme Court ruling necessarily raises public awareness of an issue and encourages people to take sides. I would suggest that "many Americans . . . could only be integrationists" because the court chose to rule against segregation in a children's case and because of widespread beliefs about childhood. In *The High Cost of Prejudice*, noted writer and literary critic Bucklin Moon had pointed out that because the "most important . . . symbols which control the community . . . are firmly opposed to any change in the status quo," the nation seemed headed in a direction "not too different from Nazi Germany" (xv). See also Ariès, *Centuries*; Pollock, *Forgotten Children*, chaps. 1, 2.
4 "Morally Right Decision"; Sitkoff, *Struggle*, 28.
5 See Metress, *Lynching*; Till-Mobley and Benson, *Death*; Huie, *Wolf Whistle*; Huie, "Shocking Story"; Whitfield, *Death*; Feldstein, "'I Wanted'"; Whitaker, "Case Study." See also Houck, "Killing Emmett"; Hendrickson, "Mississippi Haunting"; Pollack and Metress, "Emmett Till Case"; Harold and DeLuca, "Behold the Corpse." On *Life's* coverage of the Till case, see Wendy Kozol, *Life's America*, 153–56.
6 Scholarly works that examine lynching in the Jim Crow South generally note that lynching began to decline as an acceptable form of public entertainment by the 1940s, with the Till case revealing both significant change and disturbing continuities in the murder of blacks in the South. See, for example, Brundage, *Lynching*; Hale, *Making Whiteness*; Jacquelyn Dowd Hall, *Revolt*; Wiegman, "Anatomy"; Whitfield, *Death*; Zangrando, *NAACP Crusade*. On the Till case in particular, see also Payne, *I've Got the Light*, 54.
7 See, for example, Hampton and Fayer with Flynn, *Voices*; Martin Luther King Jr., *Stride*; Moody, *Coming of Age*; Aldon D. Morris, *Origins*; Payne, *I've Got the Light*; Sellers with Terrell, *River*; Sitkoff, *Struggle*; Whitfield, *Death*; Juan Williams, *Eyes*; Metress, "On That Third Day."
8 Hampton and Fayer with Flynn, *Voices*, 5–6. See also Feldstein, "'I Wanted,'" 295.
9 Whitfield, *Death*, 104, 145–47; Payne, *I've Got the Light*, 39–40; Joyce Ladner quoted

in Whitfield, *Death*, 90; Ladner, "South," 23; Myrlie Evers quoted in Hampton and Fayer with Flynn, *Voices*, 6; "State Papers," 1; *Commonweal* quoted in Whitfield, *Death*, 46. Many of the articles cited here appeared in papers all over the country courtesy of the Associated Press. Just two weeks before Till's murder, a sixty-year-old Mississippi farmhand was killed for voting in a primary. In May, two weeks passed before the *New York Times* mentioned the killing of a respected black Mississippi leader, Rev. George Lee.

10 Wilkins quoted in "Muddy River," 18; Feldstein, "'I Wanted.'"

11 "Mississippi," 29; Everett, "Till Nearly Missed," 12; "Negro Describes," 1; "The Law: Trial by Jury," 18. See also Brownmiller (a Freedom Summer volunteer in Mississippi), *Against Our Will*, 245–48; "Death in Mississippi," 603; Chisholm, "Letter." On southern press descriptions of Carolyn Bryant, see Houck, "Killing Emmett," 242–43, 246.

12 "Mississippi," 29.

13 Kempton, "He Went," 112; Clyde Gordon, "Letter"; Everett, "Till Nearly Missed," 1; "The Law: Trial by Jury," 18; "Mississippi," 29; Colin and Elliot, "Mother Waits," 30; Feldstein, "'I Wanted,'" 272, 296 n. 48. Nearly fifty years after her son's murder, Mamie Till-Mobley stressed similar ideas in *Death*.

14 "Negro Describes"; Everett, "Till Nearly Missed"; "Jury Deliberations"; "The Law: Trial by Jury," 18.

15 "Mississippi," 29; "Designed to Inflame," 20; "Jury Deliberations." On Carolyn Bryant's testimony (including that fact that she never named Till) and southern newspapers' descriptions of Till and events at the store, see Houck, "Killing Emmett," 245–51.

16 Huie, "Shocking Story," 46–47; *Chattanooga News* quoted in *New Republic*, 26 August 1931, Part 6, Reel 8, Frame 346, NAACP Papers. Some scholars have noted that Huie's description of Till emphasized his size (Till was big for his age). But Huie's physical description of Till should be considered in contrast to his description of Milam's physical appearance (Milam was considerably bigger than the boy) and in the context of the jury's ruling on the case.

17 Hirsch, "50,000 Mourn"; "State Papers," 1; *Winston-Salem Journal* quoted in "Press and Emmett Till," 11; Clyde Gordon, "Letter"; *Jackson Mississippi State Times* quoted in "Aspects of the Till Case," 12; *Chattanooga Times* quoted in "Press and Emmett Till," 11.

18 Wakefield, "Justice," 284; *Atlanta Constitution* quoted in "Press and Emmett Till," 10; "Charge Two Men"; "Boy Goes Home," 32.

19 Huie, "Shocking Story," 50, 48. See also W. E. B. Du Bois, *Souls*, 209–13; Lillian E. Smith, *Strange Fruit*, 112–13.

20 Clyde Gordon, "Letter"; Wakefield, "Justice," 284.

21 See Feldstein, "'I Wanted'"; Wendy Kozol, *Life's America*, 154.

22 Gunter, "Wives Serious"; "'Were Never into Meanness,'" 34; Kempton, "Baby Sitter"; "Mississippi," 29.

23 "Murder Trial," 16; Huie, "Shocking Story," 46; Feldstein, "'I Wanted,'" 281.

24 See Whitfield, *Death*, 45, 100, 105, 66. See also C. Eric Lincoln, 5 October 1962, quoted in Whitaker, "Case Study," 182.

25 *Shane*; Huie, "Shocking Story," 46.

26 Roy Wilkins quoted in Juan Williams, *Eyes*, 52; Evers quoted in Hampton and Fayer with Flynn, *Voices*, 6; Diggs quoted in Juan Williams, *Eyes*, 49, 44; Whitfield, *Death*, 82, 90. On Till's murder as a stimulus for future activists, see Payne, *I've Got the Light*, 54–56; Moody, *Coming of Age*, chap. 10; Townsend Davis, *Weary Feet*, 267; Fredrick Harris, "It Takes a Tragedy." Pollack has explored the ways that the deaths of children in fiction (including fictional accounts of the Till murder) exposed adult behavior and the violent nature of white southern male culture ("Grotesque Laughter"). On reactions to the Till case, see also Box 2, Folder 19, MEC.

27 Bradley quoted in Juan Williams, *Eyes*, 57; Lenroot, "Children," 3.

28 Lentz, *Symbols*, 41, 45; Garrow, *Protest*; Landphair, "'For the Good,'" 248; Steinbeck, *Travels*, 220. To be sure, some white southern newspapers and periodicals continued to reflect the views of die-hard white supremacists. What seems striking in looking at the southern press, however, is how sympathetically many "white" southern papers treated civil rights struggles after 1954, especially when those struggles involved children. This phenomenon resulted partly from the availability and use of Associated Press and United Press wire services. On press coverage of the civil rights movement and its shifting nature, see also Roberts and Klibanoff, *Race Beat*.

29 Steinbeck, *Travels*, 227–28. In their recent study of the press and the civil rights movement, Roberts and Klibanoff note the ways that images of and stories about children "get to the conscience of the white man," to use Martin Luther King Jr.'s words (*Race Beat*, 307; see also 164, 316–24).

30 "Morally Right Decision," 30–31. For a critical look at some of *Life*'s coverage of the movement and the magazine's use of family ideals, see Wendy Kozol, *Life's America*.

31 "Time of Testing"; Roberts and Klibanoff, *Race Beat*, 164.

32 Henry Louis Gates Jr., *Colored People*, 25–26; *New York Times* reporter Benjamin Fine quoted in Juan Williams, *Eyes*, 102; Moseley, "Negro Parents"; see also Bates, *Long Shadow*, 69–71, 116–20.

33 "Battle of Nashville," 14–15, 16; Morin, "Deceptive Calm"; Ford, "Teacher Looks," 264; Steinbeck, *Travels*, 228. Payne, among others, decries simplistic portrayals of racists. I agree that such portrayals allowed others at the time and continue to allow those writing and reading about civil rights today to distance themselves from racism. Such one-sided portrayals of racists (at least during the civil rights movement) often appeared in the press juxtaposed to images of children. What made racists appear "stupid, vulgar, and one-dimensional" was not just that they were racist but that they did not show respect for cultural ideas about the sanctity of childhood. See Payne, *I've Got the Light*, 418.

34 Former U.S. senator and University of North Carolina president Frank Porter Graham talking about Counts quoted in Gaillard, *Dream*, 10; Counts's father

quoted in Gaillard, *Dream*, 3; Ford, "Teacher Looks," 264; *A First Step toward School Integration* (CORE pamphlet), June 1958, RG 73, Series 3, Box 31, Folder 16, SEPC.

35 Gaillard, *Dream*, 7–8.

36 Beals, *Warriors*, xx–xxi; "South's Closed Schools," 21; "School's Out," 38.

37 *New York Amsterdam News* quoted in Hughes, *Fight*, 158; "School's Out," 38; "Crisis in Education," 25; Roy Wilkins, "Integration Crisis in the South," in *In Search*, ed. Wilson, 372; Cummings, Query Editor, Newsweek WUX, 1960, Box 14, Folder: "Segregation New Orleans," NABR; "Southern Schools in the Sputnik Age," *Southern Newsletter*, December 1957, 12, RG 73, Series 1, Box 31, Folder 3, SEPC.

38 "Russians Push"; Hughes, *Fight*, 157; "What Orval Hath Wrought," 13; *Times of Indonesia, Mexico City El Nacional*, and *Tokyo News* quoted in "As Others See Us"; *Atlanta Constitution* quoted in "Southern News Briefs," *Southern Newsletter*, October 1957, 9, RG 73, Series 1, Box 31, Folder 3, SEPC; Ethel Williams, "Testimony before the Subcommittee on Integration," 15 June 1962, Reel 14, Frames 420-22, CORE Papers, addendum.

39 Moseley, "Negro Parents"; "South's Closed Schools," 24; Dhonau and Roberts, "Negro Says"; Knebel, "Dixie's New Rebels," 20; "Students and Parents."

40 Lillian E. Smith, *Strange Fruit*, 356; "School's Out," 38–39; Jane Reif, "Crisis in Norfolk," 14–15, Box 1, Folder 23, SOSC; Knebel, "Dixie's New Rebels"; "And the Students? They Didn't Vote," *Nashville Tennessean*, 20 November 1958, clipping in "Save Our Schools: A Roundup of Southern Press Opinion," 28, Box 1, Folder 19, SOSC. On the Mothers' League, see Cope, "Thorn"; Carbine, "Arkansas Junior"; Knebel, "Dixie's New Rebels"; "South's Closed Schools," 24; Emery, "Can You Meet"; Elizabeth Huckaby, interview by George King, January 1992, 7–8, Box 10, Folder 15, SRCP; Roy Reed, interview by George King, December 1991, 9, Box 11, Folder 8, SRCP; "Integration," 34; Kempton, "Upon Such a Day," 114; Reeves, "'So What?'" Huckaby, a vice principal for girls at Central, also insisted that the few white students who heckled their black peers were "egged on by . . . organized groups that their parents were in" (13).

41 Wilkins, "At Youth," 388; Father Mario W. Shaw, "Student Leadership in Race Relations: Workable Programs," outline of address given at the third annual Kentucky College Conference on Intergroup Relations, n.d., 2, Box 5, MSS 520, RLSP; *Civil Liberties and Human Rights Public Affairs Newsletter*, 10 October 1949, 6, RG 73, Series 3, Box 37, Folder 4, SEPC; "Students and Parents"; Query Editor, from Emerson, Newsweek WUX, For Nation: New Orleans, 1, 3, Box 13, Folder: Segregation: New Orleans, NABR; "Negro Girl Is Jeered at Harding," *Charlotte Observer*, 5 September 1957, 1, 6, Box 6, Folder: "Integration—School Opening Sept. 1957," NABR; Cope, "Thorn," 184; "What Orval Hath Wrought," 12; Ralph McGill, "Experimenting with Ignorance," *Atlanta Constitution*, July 1961, clipping, Box 2, Folder 1, SOSC.

42 Query Editor, from Emerson, Newsweek WUX, For Nation: New Orleans, 1, Box 13, Folder: Segregation: New Orleans, NABR; Kempton, "Upon Such a Day," 114–

15; Raab and Lipset, *Prejudice*, 36; Marvin Wall, "Women, Children to the Front as Klan Storms Stone Mountain," n.d., clipping, Marvin Wall, "Save Some Klansmen while We Can," n.d., clipping, both in Box 10, Folder 6, CCP; "South's Closed Schools," 24. Central High principal Jess Matthews made similar comments about "hoodlumism" and "organized adult backing" to a group of educators in 1958 (quoted in Cope, "Thorn," 183).

43 Wilkins, "At Youth," 389; Roy Wilkins, "Address at the Meeting of NAACP Branches in Mississippi," Jackson, Miss., 3 June 1956, 6, Box 2, Folder 38, MEC; "South's Closed Schools," 21; Cothran, "Integration," 12; "Minutes, Academic Freedom and Due Process Equality Committees of the ACLU," Part 19, Series B, Group II, Box E-6, National Association for the Advancement of Colored People Papers, Manuscripts Division, LC. The way the national press framed stories about school integration in the 1950s also mirrored the way the NAACP had framed discussions of school integration in the Midwest in the mid-1940s. For example, when Gary, Indiana, integrated its schools, *The Crisis* ran stories reminding readers that "an untold number of experiments have proven that children do not have prejudices but acquire them from adults." School strikes in Gary, the magazine explained, were being led by subversive organizations. Not only were student strike leaders being coached by adults, but six of those student leaders "were 'D' average students and considered 'bad actors' by the teaching personnel," and one of them was a "zoot-suiter" who had only lived in the area for three weeks (Jensen, "Intolerance"; Hamilton quoted in Roberts and Klibanoff, *Race Beat*, 210).

44 Clippings and reports in "Delaware Case," *Philadelphia Evening Bulletin*, 22 September 1954, Part 3, Series C, Reel 1, Frame 159, NAACP Papers; "Graduation: Big Day—Somewhere for All Our Graduates," *Arkansas Gazette*, 24 May 1959, Box 8, Folder: "Little Rock—Stop Cross, etc.," NABR. The *Gazette* was also concerned that Arkansas had lost talented youth to other states.

45 *Answers for Action*, 15; "10 Students from 'Protest' High Schools Observe Integrated Classes in New York," 19 October 1954, clipping, Box 8, Folder 8, IAP.

46 Payne, *I've Got the Light*, 418; Crespino, *In Search*, 4; Juanita Signal, interview by Ernest Doclar, April 1949, 2, Box 40, Folder 9, JHFP. On education-centered activism in South Carolina, for example, see Lau, "From the Periphery." On the Mississippi petitions, see "Handwritten Note," August 1955, Box 2, Folder 7, MEC; see also Kluger, *Simple Justice*; Landphair, "'For the Good'"; "Five Point Action Program," 12. On the long struggle for educational equity in South Carolina both before and after *Brown*, see R. Scott Baker, *Paradoxes*. On Houston's views and parental activism for equal education in Washington, D.C., see McNeil, *Groundwork*, 134, 190–91, 198, 209.

47 James Baldwin, *Notes of a Native Son*, 95; Beals, *Warriors*, 6–7.

48 James Farmer, "Emancipation Proclamation—(Unfinished Business)," 100th Anniversary Celebration of the Emancipation Proclamation, International Convention of Christian Churches, Miami Beach, Fla., 14 October 1963, Reel 3, Frames 576–80, CORE Papers, addendum; Baldwin, *Notes*, 94; Gaillard, *Dream*, 3; Fos-

ter and Foster, *Silent Trumpets*, 54; Forman, *Making*, 113; Montgomery boycott participant quoted in Rowan, "Cradle," 138; Birmingham demonstrator Robbie Smith, interview by Horace Huntley, 1 November 1995, 191, Volume 11, Section 3, OHP; W. E. B. Du Bois, *Souls*, 217–18, 263; "The Law: The Tension of Change," 26; Robert L. Carter, *Matter of Law*, 64; McNeil, *Groundwork*, 191, 212.

49 Wallace, "Restraints," 100, 106–7.

50 Bradley, "Afraid"; Dillard, "Children"; "Memorandum to Members," 1 December 1954, American States' Rights Association Papers, Archives Department, Birmingham Public Library, Birmingham, Ala.; "Editor Sez," 19; New Orleans segregationists quoted in Landphair, "'For the Good,'" 246; Armand J. Duvio, paid advertisement, 9 September 1961, unidentified clipping, Box 2, Folder 12, SOSC; Eastland quoted in "South Will Fight," 6; Kamp, *Lawless Tyranny*; Jim Johnson, "Let's Build a Private School," 12; Mrs. W. C. Todd to Editor (Ralph Emerson McGill), 30 September 1957, Box 24, Folder 1, Ralph McGill Papers, RWL. Segregationists used similar strategies to encourage parents to ban or protest interracial-themed books. See, for example, Erwin Knoll, "Is This What You Want Your Child to Read?," *Fiery Cross* (Tuscaloosa, Alabama), n.d., Box 6, MSS 629, NABR.

51 Flyer, National Socialist White People's Party, n.d., Box 12, Folder 21, MSS 921, Black Print Culture Collection, Special Collections Department, RWL; Landphair, "'For the Good,'" 142; "Reports from White Citizen's Councils," July 1956, Box 31, Simon E. Sobeloff Papers, LC; "Summary of the Milford School Incident," Part 3, Series C, Reel 1, Frame 159, NAACP Papers; Stanley M. Andrews, undated letter, "Save Our Schools," a special project of Liberty Lobby, Folder 3, Ku Klux Klan Papers, SHC; *Don't Be Brainwashed!* (pamphlet), n.d., Box 14, Folder: Segregation New Orleans, NABR. On these types of tactics, see also Roberts and Klibanoff, *Race Beat*, 201.

52 See, for example, Dabney, "Virginia's 'Peaceable, Honorable Stand,'" 52; "Louisiana Argues Issue"; Putnam, "This Is the Problem!"; George J. deBourbon, "The Black Menace," Box 31, Simon E. Sobeloff Papers, LC.

53 Edward Benjamin, "Note to *What It's All About*," 1958, RG 73, Series 2, Box 121, Folder 8, SEPC; *Fact Finder*, 30 April 1966, RG 73, Series 2, Box 121, Folder 8, SEPC.

54 Frank L. Britton, *American Nationalist*, n.d., RG 73, Series 2, Box 121, Folder 8, SEPC.

55 "Boy Goes Home," 32; "St. Augustine Ku Klux Klan Meeting" (SNCC report), n.d., 2, RG 73, Box 31, Folder 16a, SEPC; Dhonau, "Negro Girl." White southerners' arguments reveal their discomfort with growing youth agency. White adults may have found integration particularly disturbing because of other contemporary challenges to their authority and ways.

56 George W. Cheek, "The Pending Tragedy in the South," 14, File 41.2.15, SRCP; Medford Evans, "As New as Childhood," 6–7, 15; Mrs. I. M. Brown, "Call to Negroes"; Sitkoff, *Struggle*, 27; Stanley M. Andrews, undated letter, "Save Our Schools," a special project of Liberty Lobby, Folder 3, Ku Klux Klan Papers, SHC; *Arkansas*

Faith, December 1955, 10; J. H. White to Dr. E. J. Stringer, 25 August 1954, Part 3, Series C, Reel 1, Frame 716, NAACP Papers; Posey, "Negroes Enter." Here again, white southerners used the ideas and the kinds of arguments about childhood that had convinced the Supreme Court to rule in favor of integration to argue against it. Another example is the way that some southern school boards used "the psychological qualification of the pupil" and "the psychological effect [of attending certain schools] upon the pupil" to segregate students under "freedom of choice" plans (see Sitkoff, *Struggle*, 27).

57 *Brown v. Board of Education*, 347 U.S. 483, n. 11; "A Negro Father," "Letter to the Editor," *Atlanta Morning Star*, 8 June 1954, Part 3, Series C, Reel 1, Frame 444, NAACP Papers; Tobias, "Implications," 613; Mississippians for Public Education, "Urges Parents to Keep Sending Children to Public Schools" (press release), 24 August 1964, Box 1, Folder 6, CCP; Brownie Ledbetter, interview by George King, n.d., 12, Box 10, Folder 20, SRCP; "Fact Sheet for SOS Discussion Leaders," Box 1, Folder 13, SOSC; "Press Release," Box 1, Folder 11, SOSC; M. M. Smith "Spring Street School" (PTA address), 18 November 1958, Box 1, Folder 18, SOSC. White Atlantan Ralph McGill made arguments similar to these in a particularly pointed editorial, "What Price Political Glory: Sacrificing the Children," *Nashville Tennessean*, May 1963, clipping, Box 8, Folder 10, IAP. On southern white women's efforts to keep schools open, see Lorraine Gates, "Power"; Miller, "Challenging"; Frystak, "Elite White Female Activism."

58 Roy Wilkins, "Address at the Meeting of NAACP Branches in Mississippi," Jackson, Miss., 3 June 1956, 6, Box 2, Folder 38, MEC; George W. Cheek, "The Pending Tragedy in the South," 9, File 41.2.15, SRCP; *Fact Finder*, 30 April 1966, RG 73, Series 2, Box 121, Folder 8, SEPC; Herbert Ravenel Sass, "Mixed Schools and Mixed Blood," n.d., 6, Box 24, Folder 1, Ralph McGill Papers, RWL; "South Will Fight," 9–10. Roberts and Klibanoff note that southern white editors such as James J. Kilpatrick "used social science when it fit the racial and cultural stereotypes [they] wanted to believe and discounted social science as irrelevant when it didn't." Kilpatrick (and others) "grabbed everything [they] could" in their defense of segregation (*Race Beat*, 115).

59 Garrow, *Protest*, 149–53. Garrow's discussion of political culture draws on Pye, "Political Culture"; Verba, "Comparative Political Culture," 513, 516; V. O. Key, *Public Opinion*, 275.

60 May, *Homeward Bound*. On the postwar American family ideal, see also Wendy Kozol, *Life's America*; Spigel, *Make Room*.

61 "Freedom Fighting Family," *Jet*, 20 June 1963, cover; Reston, "I Have a Dream . . . ," 285; Russell Baker, "Capital Is Occupied," 291; Martin Luther King Jr., "I Have a Dream." There were, of course, speakers other than King at the March on Washington, and King had more to say about the movement than that he had a dream for children. It seems striking, however, that almost immediately (at least in the national media and in popular memory) the march became connected with sentimental ideas about childhood.

62 Kirp, *Just Schools*, 25.

63 Martin Luther King Jr., "Letter." Fairclough and other scholars have noted that the
Southern Christian Leadership Conference "skillfully attuned its methods and its
message to the idealism of the black church. . . . SCLC worked with the grain of
Southern black history and culture" (Fairclough, *To Redeem the Soul*, 403–4). Perhaps just as important, King also "worked with the grain" of American culture.

64 Halberstam, *Children*, 443.

65 See, for example, Branch, *Parting*, 750–53; James Bevel, interview by Spike Lee,
in *Four Little Girls*; Fairclough, *To Redeem the Soul*, 126, 137; Kennedy, "Negro";
Roberts and Klibanoff, *Race Beat*, 319; Bevel quoted in Hampton and Fayer with
Flynn, *Voices*, 134. See also Branch, *Parting*, chaps. 20–21; McWhorter, *Carry Me
Home*, chaps. 15–16. Garrow, *Protest*, explores how images of violence in the Birmingham and Selma campaigns captured support for the movement. It was, however, not just images of violence that moved the public and their political representatives; rather, images of violence against children were chosen time and again
to convey the meaning of civil rights events and issues. Waskow, *From Race Riot*,
argues that the photograph of a Birmingham police dog leaping at the throat of a
black schoolboy turned "the 1960s generation of 'new Negroes' . . . into a major
social force. . . . Intense pressure upon President John F. Kennedy to initiate federal action began to be applied the moment that photo appeared. . . . [F]inancial
and political support for all organizations in the civil rights movement multiplied
at once." After the Birmingham campaign, the movement "meant not only an abstract demand for social change but the concrete and immediate protection of
their children" (234).

66 King and Kennedy quoted in Fairclough, *To Redeem the Soul*, 229, 126; Halberstam,
Children, 438–39. Halberstam also looks at the debate among civil rights leaders on
using children in the Birmingham campaign (438–40); Adam Clayton Powell Jr.,
"Keynote Address," Virginia Union University, Richmond, Va., 17–19 November
1944, Part 19, Series B, Reel 5, Frame 273, NAACP Papers; Ellison, *Invisible Man*.

67 "'My God,'" 20; "For 14 Hours"; "Hands at the Fuse"; "Terror Reigns."

68 "Hands at the Fuse." In Spike Lee's interview with the Reverend John Cross Jr. and
his wife, Julia, in *Four Little Girls*, Julia Cross indicated that her first reaction to the
Sunday school bombing was to assume that it was the work of the Soviets. See also
Branch, *Parting*, chap. 23; McWhorter, *Carry Me Home*, chaps. 27–28.

69 "Day a Church Became a Tomb"; Southern Conference Education Fund, Press Release, 17 December 1962, Part 3, Series 11, Box 126, Reel 6, Frames 597–99, SCLC
Papers; "Minister Had Sought"; "'This Is Freedom's Price.'"

70 "Day a Church Became a Tomb"; National Association for the Advancement of
White People leader Bryant Bowles quoted in William G. Weart, "Ten Negroes
Back in Milford School," *New York Times*, 28 September 1954, clipping, Part 3,
Series C, Reel 1, Frame 207, NAACP Papers; "City Leaders Express Grief"; "City's
People All Victims." To be sure, not all white southerners regretted the bombing.
Indeed, despite numerous leads and widespread interest in the case, not one of the

murderers was brought to justice until 2001. One speaker at a Klan rally suggested that medals should be pinned on the killers: The murder of the girls "wasn't no shame," he said. He then went on to voice the white South's most extreme views on race and childhood: "In the first place, they ain't little. They're 14 or 15 years old — old enough to have venereal diseases, and I'll be surprised if all of 'em didn't have one or more. In the second place, they weren't children. Children are little people, little human beings, and that means white people. . . . They're just little Niggers" ("St. Augustine Ku Klux Klan Meeting" [SNCC report], n.d., 2, RG 73, Box 31, Folder 16a, SEPC).

71 "Auspice," "To the Editor"; "City's People All Victims," 21; "Alabaman's Great Speech," 44B; "Who's Responsible," 3; Gene Patterson editorial in *Atlanta Constitution* quoted in Roberts and Klibanoff, *Race Beat*, 351–52.

72 Willie Morris, *North*, 32, 33, 40.

73 Martin Luther King Jr., "Eulogy."

74 James Weldon Johnson quoted in Gaines, *Uplifting*, 248; "Berkeley," Telegram to Martin Luther King Jr. and the SCLC, 16 September 1963, Part 1, Series 1, Subseries 3, Reel 7, Frame 269, SCLC Papers; Woods, "Letter"; "Senators Call."

75 Payne, *I've Got the Light*, cites Norrell, "One Thing," as one example of "normative history" — history that attributes change and movement success to the ascendance of shared democratic values (421–22). Much of the recent scholarship on the civil rights movement has done much to show the many (often local grassroots) forces and factors that helped push the black freedom struggle. Still, this type of progressive narrative seems to have considerable staying power, especially in popular memory.

76 Diane Nash, in an interview for Spike Lee's film, *Four Little Girls*, indicated that the voting rights campaign in Selma was "born" in the aftermath of the Sunday school tragedy. She and Bevel, like many others, personally "felt that in order to respect ourselves as an adult man and woman, we could not let little girls be killed." Moreover, she and other activists saw voting rights as a way to give blacks a greater capacity to "protect children." Roberts and Klibanoff relate that those sympathetic to the black freedom struggle in Kennedy's administration believed that "exposure of the segregationists' point of view, the public disclosure of their private convictions . . . was essential to break through to a public that might prefer complacence" (*Race Beat*, 330). In many cases, the segregationist point of view was most clear and most disturbing to the American public when racism was directed against children.

77 James Farmer, "Emancipation Proclamation — (Unfinished Business)," 100th Anniversary Celebration of the Emancipation Proclamation, International Convention of Christian Churches, Miami Beach, Fla., 14 October 1963, 9, Reel 3, Frame 580, CORE Papers, addendum.

78 Ibid., 3–9; Jerry Levin, producer, *Under Discussion: Civil Rights and the Law*, 9 August 1964, 10:00–11:30 P.M., 10, transcript of WNEW TV program, Box 3, Folder 4, IAP.

79 Gloster B. Current, "ABC's of Mass Pressure," in "Report of 1944 Youth Conference," Part 19, Series B, Reel 5, Frames 236–53, NAACP Papers.

80 Press Releases (1962–64), Subgroup A, Series 7, Reel 13, Frames 829, 850, 871, SNCC Papers; "Running Incident Summary for the Month of July, 1965," Reel 55, Frame 1002, SNCC Papers.

81 See, for example, Webb and West, *Selma, Lord, Selma*; Payne, *I've Got the Light*, esp. chap. 7; Dittmer, *Local People*; Sitkoff, *Struggle*.

82 Forman, *Making*, 518. In his autobiographical *If White Kids Die*, Reavis tells of an incident where at a mass meeting, a SCOPE worker said that a fourteen-year-old girl had recently died chopping cotton. Reavis questioned the veracity of the story (55). Whether or not it was true, its telling suggests that the speaker recognized that it was the type of story that would motivate the crowd.

83 "Will She Live," 119; Miles College Student Body Demonstration flyer, Small Collections 97-SC-0046, Birmingham Civil Rights Institute, Birmingham, Ala.; Advertisements, Pamphlets, and Order Forms for *The Streets of Greenwood* and *A Dream Deferred*, Reel 36, Frames 9–11, 204–5, 213, 215, 225–27, 232–34, 244, 249, 253, 256–60, SNCC Papers.

84 Hansberry, *Movement*, 18, 14, 16, 19, 50, 100, 45, 17, 106; Fitch, "Thumbs Down," 21. The SNCC photos were intended to be used as a documentary record and as visuals in publications and mass media. The photos were also supposed to "service the field" and "service friends of SNCC" as well as "act as a source of income" ("Aim of SNCC photos," Reel 36, Frame 668, SNCC Papers).

85 See Payne, *I've Got the Light*, 374; "Aim of SNCC Photos," Reel 36, Frame 668, SNCC Papers; *Where Would We Be . . . without a Handful of Rocks?* (pamphlet), n.d., Box 16, Folder: SNCC #2, NABR.

86 *Cracking the Color Line* (pamphlet), n.d., Reel 13, Frames 1–18, CORE Papers, addendum.

87 Anna Holden, *A First Step toward School Integration* (pamphlet), CORE, June 1958, Box 9, Folder 11, IAP.

88 Lomax et al., *Mississippi Eyewitness*, 53, 56, 58.

89 Thomas Merton, *The Black Revolution* (pamphlet), Part 3, Series 9, Subseries 3, Reel 4, Frames 559–67, SCLC Papers.

90 McNeil, "Before *Brown*," 1458; Robert L. Carter, *Matter of Law*, 173; Paul Stern, "What Price Integration?" Reel 3, Frames 524–28, CORE Papers, addendum.

91 R. Scott Baker, *Paradoxes*, 150. In "The Media and the Movement," Julian Bond quotes journalist Nicholas Von Hoffman, who noted in 1964 that "the political position of the freedom movement is such that Negroes only win public sympathy when they are the beaten, not the beating, party." Bond further comments that in the late 1960s, "in the eyes of many whites former victims had become oppressors" (34–35).

92 See Joan W. Scott, "Gender."

93 Maurice O. Williams, *Constructing*, 83, 135. Wendy Kozol similarly argues that by placing social protest into a conventional, family-centered, idealized narrative,

Life "limited and even distorted knowledge about different social groups" (*Life's America*, 143).

94 Garrow, *Protest*, 164–65.

95 James Baldwin, "Fifth Avenue, Uptown," 650. Sperber has suggested a compelling framework for thinking about why some representations are more successful or "more contagious," to use his metaphor, than others ("Anthropology").

96 Rita Schwerner quoted in Payne, *I've Got the Light*, 395; Martinez, *Letters*, 22. SNCC organizer Charles Sherrod, an African American, commented, "White people don't care anything about us, but they care about their children. . . . If their children came South—the children of these white people, the good guys, the good thinkers—then money [and attention] would come with them" (quoted in Olson, *Freedom's Daughters*, 240).

97 Lomax et al., *Mississippi Eyewitness*, 23, 50–52, 12.

98 Wright, "Down by the Riverside," 324–25.

99 See W. E. B. Du Bois, "Of the Passing of the First-Born," in *Souls*, 349–54; Chris McNair (father of Denise McNair, one of the four girls killed in the Sunday school bombing), interview by Spike Lee, in *Four Little Girls*; Wright quoted in Embree, "Native Son," 53.

CHAPTER FOUR

1 "Study and Evaluation of NAACP Youth Program," 1956, Part 19, Series D, Group 3, Reel 16, Frames 418–25, NAACP Papers.

2 Howard Zinn, "Albany," 8 January 1962, Series 5, Folder 6, Aubrey Neblett Brown Jr. Papers, Virginia Historical Society, Richmond, Va.; Dittmer, *Local People*, 122. On the importance of young people to the movement, see also Payne, *I've Got the Light*; Olson, *Freedom's Daughters*; Carson, *In Struggle*; Belfrage, *Freedom Summer*; Reavis, *If White Kids Die*; Inge Powell Bell, *CORE*; Halberstam, *Children*; Blumberg, *Civil Rights*. Kelley, "Riddle," suggests the significance of unorganized youth subcultures to civil rights politics.

3 See esp. Payne's otherwise brilliant and essential *I've Got the Light*. Hughes, like Zinn and other contemporaries of the movement, similarly used the term "youngsters." Hughes also referred to student protesters as the "Sit-In Kids," another, probably unintentional yet rather patronizing way to refer to courageous albeit young activists (*Fight*, 155, 185). Mintz explains that before World War II, adults commonly referred to teenagers as "youngsters" and that the term implied a lack of independence (*Huck's Raft*, 267). On the history of youth organizing and for a criticism of the neglect of youth in history, see Robert Cohen, *When the Old Left Was Young*, esp. xix.

4 "London Convention," 88, 93, 96, 98. Marten, *Children's Civil War*, explores children's participation in the Civil War and Civil War children's literature. See also Marten's documentary reader, *Lessons of War*.

5 *Anti-Slavery Alphabet*, 16, 1.

6 See Taxel, "Reclaiming"; Lystad, *From Dr. Mather*; Zipes, "Second Thoughts," 27. Indeed, as Karcher, *First Woman*, notes, Lydia Maria Child lost her editorship of the first popular children's periodical, *Juvenile Miscellany*, when she began publishing what to most Americans at the time were radical anti-slavery stories (169).

7 See *Child's Anti-Slavery Book*. On race and children's literature of this period, see also Murray, *American Children's Literature*, 117–28.

8 On Civil War children's literature, see Marten, *Children's Civil War*, esp. 38–45.

9 On post–Civil War trends in children's literature, see Marten, *Children's Civil War*, 54; Lumpkin, *Making*, book 3; *Darkies ABCs*; *Kinky Kids*; Garner, *Way Down*; Garner, *Ezekiel*; Garner, *Ezekiel Travels*; Hogan, *Nicodemus*. This was one of the first of at least twelve books about Nicodemus and one of at least seventeen by Hogan about black children.

10 Joan W. Scott has suggested that identity production is always a contested and therefore highly political endeavor ("Evidence of Experience"). Scholars have argued along the same lines that German children's literature "played a complicitous role in the development of authoritarian personalities" and the formation of a highly prejudicial national state. See Zipes, "Second Thoughts." In *Making Whiteness*, Hale explores the ways that whiteness has been constructed and reconstructed through a variety of cultural and social forms and events, such as fiction, advertising, and lynchings. Children's literature is another form in which racial identity has been created and justified. On racial stereotyping in early-twentieth-century children's literature, see Murray, *American Children's Literature*, 134–36.

11 A. E. Johnson, *Clarence and Corinne*; Edward A. Johnson, *School History* (the University of North Carolina library has electronically published the full text and additional information about this volume; see ⟨http://docsouth.unc.edu/church/johnson/menu.html⟩ [22 November 2008]); Floyd, *Floyd's Flowers*; Ritterhouse, *Growing Up Jim Crow*, 224–31; Fraser, "Black Publishing," 24, 21; Daphne Muse, "Black Children's Literature," 11–12. Spillers's introduction to the reprint edition of *Clarence and Corinne* makes a number of important criticisms of this text, including that luck plays the central role in determining the characters' fate. Yet the book's significance as an "oppositional" text can be seen when viewed in the context of the period in which it was produced (a period in which similar criticisms would hold true for the majority of fiction produced for children and youth). On *Floyd's Flowers* and other early twentieth-century etiquette books for black children, see Katharine Capshaw Smith, "Childhood." For more on racial uplift literature and photographic images of black children, see Bragg, "Marketing," introduction, chap. 5. Mary Niall Mitchell has also written about photographic images of black children ("'Rosebloom and Pure White'").

12 See esp. Gaines, *Uplifting the Race*, 45. See also Katharine Capshaw Smith, "Childhood"; Ritterhouse, *Growing Up Jim Crow*; Fraser, "Black Publishing"; Daphne Muse, "Black Children's Literature"; Bragg, "Marketing"; Stephanie J. Shaw, *What a Woman Ought to Be*; Payne, *I've Got the Light*, 218.

13 W. E. B. Du Bois, "As the Crow Flies," 23–24. Du Bois originally published a series

of articles under the title "As the Crow Flies" in *The Brownies' Book*, which eventually folded. In the late 1920s, Du Bois revived the series and began including news briefs and short opinion pieces in *The Crisis* under the same title. On the *Brownies' Book* and other NAACP publications for young people, see also Bragg, "Marketing," chap. 5.

14 Advertisement for the *Brownies' Book* in *The Crisis*, September 1919. In addition to issues of the *Brownies' Book*, see Violet Joyce Harris, "*Brownies' Book*." Hughes's and Bontemps's work for children included *Popo and Fifina*, *You Can't Pet a Possum*, and *Sad-Faced Boy*. On black children's literature, see also Norton, *Through the Eyes*, 62; MacLeod, *American Childhood*; Banfield and Wilson, "Black Experience," 4; Mac-Cann and Woodard, *Black American*; Katharine Capshaw Smith, *Children's Literature*. On race leaders' efforts to counter racist stereotypes in children's literature, see also Murray, *American Children's Literature*, 136–40, 165–67. Leftists had a similar sense about the potential of children's literature, and their work also sought to break down American racism. See Mickenberg, *Learning*.

15 Katharine Capshaw Smith, "Childhood," 799; Newsome, "Bronze Legacy." Newsome was a frequent contributor of children's items. She contributed the monthly "Little Page" for *The Crisis* beginning with the October 1925 issue and became the critic for "Youthport" when *The Crisis* initiated this section for young people in October 1929. Membership rolls indicate that throughout the history of the NAACP, black female youth joined the association as frequently as black male youth. Male youth seemed to more often hold positions of leadership within the organization, and NAACP rhetoric often reflected a gender bias. Yet female youth held positions of leadership and were much more likely to hold positions of leadership in youth councils than were women in adult branches. In addition, women often served as adult advisers for youth councils. On Newsome and children's literature in *The Crisis*, see Katharine Capshaw Smith, *Children's Literature*; Bragg, "Marketing," chap. 5.

16 "Junior Crisis," 348, quoting the Junior Division Constitution; Laws, "How Youthport Shall Be Conducted," 26. On the ages of junior members, see, for example, Mellie M. Brinkley (chair, Junior Work Committee, Philadelphia, Pa.) to Robert Bagnall, 26 June 1926, Part 12, Series B, Reel 7, Frame 134, NAACP Papers (which indicates that the Philadelphia junior group included children from ages seven to eighteen); Robert Bagnall, "Letter to the Executive Committee, Subject: Junior Division," 24 February 1925, Part 19, Series A, Reel 1, Frame 42, NAACP Papers.

17 See, for example, Robert Bagnall (director of branches) to Wilfred Newman, 11 December 1929, Part 12, Series C, Reel 11, Frame 546, NAACP Papers; Inez Williams, "Letter," 62. Bagnall suggested that junior divisions should encourage youth to study the lives of Negro leaders, history, literature, and art and to engage in public speaking, discussion, and debate ("Letter to the Executive Committee, Subject: Junior Division," 24 February 1925, Part 19, Group A, Reel 1, Frame 42, NAACP Papers).

18 Annie Jones to NAACP National Office, Part 12, Series B, Reel 7, Frame 122,

NAACP Papers; Special Assistant to the Secretary, "Report of Youth Work" (to National Board of Directors), stamped 25 June 1938, Part 19, Series A, Reel 3, Frames 72–78, NAACP Papers.

19 See, for example, Tiffin, *In Whose Best Interest?*; Nasaw, *Children*; Clapp, *Mothers*; Lindenmeyer, *Right*; Cavallo, *Muscles*.

20 See, for example, Ladd-Taylor, *Raising a Baby*; Macleod, *Age*; Hulbert, *Raising America*; Stearns, *Anxious Parents*; Julia Grant, *Raising Baby*; Weiss, "Mother-Child Dyad."

21 See "Infancy" and "Childhood," *The Crisis*, October 1919, 287.

22 Ibid.; Beulah Young to Robert Bagnall, 17 March 1924, Part 12, Series C, Reel 11, Frame 981, NAACP Papers; "Officers of Junior NAACP"; Robert Bagnall to Fred Williams (president, senior NAACP branch, Detroit), 31 October 1924, Part 12, Series C, Reel 11, Frames 1024–25, NAACP Papers; "Largest Branch"; "Boys and Girls." Until the 1970s child-rearing advice almost always used male nouns and pronouns in gender-neutral situations. See Weiss, "Mother-Child Dyad"; Ladd-Taylor, *Raising a Baby*; Macleod, *Age*; Hulbert, *Raising America*; Stearns, *Anxious Parents*; Julia Grant, *Raising Baby*. Especially when referring to issues of agency and future action, there seems to have been a greater concern that male children be encouraged to develop a sense of independence and competence. On youth activism in 1920s Detroit, see also Bragg, "Marketing," 182–85. On conflicts over segregated housing in Detroit during this period and on the city's NAACP branch in the 1920s, see Boyle, *Arc*.

23 Robert Bagnall to James Weldon Johnson, 22 December 1924, Part 12, Series C, Reel 11, Frame 1022, NAACP Papers; Robert Bagnall to Fred Williams (president, senior NAACP branch, Detroit), 31 October 1924, Part 12, Series C, Reel 11, Frames 1024–25, NAACP Papers; Wilfred Newman to Robert Bagnall, 7 December 1929, Part 12, Series C, Reel 12, Frame 547, NAACP Papers; Robert Bagnall to Wilfred Newman, 11 December 1929, Part 12, Series C, Reel 11, Frame 546, NAACP Papers. On later youth council activism in Detroit, see Meier and Rudwick, *Black Detroit*, 80–82, 91–92.

24 Robert Bagnall to Walter White, "What Can Youth Movement Do," 29 September 1931, Part 19, Series A, Reel 1, Frame 13, NAACP Papers; Walter White to Board of Directors, 2 February 1933, Part 19, Series A, Reel 1, Frame 50, NAACP Papers; Walter White to Charles W. Dorsey, 21 December 1934, Part 12, Series B, Reel 8, Frame 263, NAACP Papers. Perhaps not coincidentally, the first youth director, Juanita Jackson, had been a member of the Philadelphia junior council as a graduate student.

25 For example, National Youth Administration Bulletin 4 outlined four projects to help with youth employment, community development, and recreational leadership, especially in rural areas. On funding as a possible incentive, see, for example, "Letter to Foundation for a Grant to Youth work," 1939, Part 19, Series A, Reel 3, Frames 376–87, NAACP Papers.

26 Daisey E. Lampkin to Walter White, 12 March 1938, Part 12, Series C, Reel 17,

Frame 851, NAACP Papers. Such sentiments were expressed throughout the 1930s, especially in connection with youth organizing (Walter White to Philadelphia Branch, 5 March 1936, Part 12, Series B, Reel 8, Frames 548–49, NAACP Papers).

27 Winston, *Life*, 27; "Boys and Girls," 272. On Scottsboro, see also Kelley, *Hammer and Hoe*, chap. 4; Goodman, *Stories*; Fairclough, *Better Day*; Patricia Sullivan, *Days of Hope*. Sullivan suggests that "the Scottsboro case challenged the NAACP to broaden the focus of its campaign against lynching" (88). Specifically, it challenged the group to expand its program for young people and to include direct action as part of its newly enlarged program for youth.

28 J. Franklin Bourne, "Youth Hurls a Challenge," Youth Night address at the NAACP 27th Annual Conference, Baltimore, 1 July 1936, Part 19, Series A, Reel 2, Frames 9–13, NAACP Papers. Robert Cohen, *When the Old Left Was Young*, esp. 43, 133; Balien, "I Attended," 67–68; Harlow, "Youth," 251; Streator, "Negro College Radicals," 47; Maurice Gates, "Negro Students," 232–33, 251; Ovington, "Students," 181. Bourne went on to say that "such movements are exemplified by the recently formed American Students Union, which includes in its platform a clause denouncing discrimination and promoting racial understanding and cooperation." On 1930s student action against racial inequality, see Robert Cohen, *When the Old Left Was Young*, 204–24. For information about many of these youth groups, see also Kelley, *Hammer and Hoe*, chap. 11; Richards, "Southern Negro Youth Congress"; *Official Proceedings*; Lau, *Democracy Rising*, 156–73; Egerton, *Speak*, 458–59. See also Florant, "Youth." Fairclough, *Better Day*, notes that the Southern Negro Youth Congress formed in 1937 after a student protest at Virginia State College in Petersburg (177). Some of these youth organizations were influenced or supported, at least periodically, by the Communist Party. On 1930s youth activism, see also Mintz, *Huck's Raft*, 245–48; Pahl, *Youth Ministry*; Lindenmeyer, *Greatest Generation*, 106–8. For young people's awareness of world youth movements, see "Youth around the World," *March of Youth*, May 1941, 4, Schomburg Center for Research in Black Culture, New York Public Library, New York, N.Y. On the Baltimore forum, see McNeil, "Youth Initiative." McNeil describes a close relationship between the NAACP and the forum and argues that it gave the association an opportunity to "observe the efficacy of the leadership of youth and young adults [and] draw from the forum's elected leadership . . . to launch a nationwide NAACP youth movement" (75). Not everyone agreed that black youth had become more activist-oriented. See, for example, Hughes, "Cowards," 226–28.

29 Juanita E. Jackson, "Letter to College Presidents," 21 October 1936, and "Letter," 4 March 1936, Part 19, Series A, Reel 1, Frames 85, 60, NAACP Papers. In 1933, the NAACP invited a few "interested and intelligent young people" to attend a conference to help map out a new youth organization. See Walter White to Board of Directors, 2 February 1933, Part 19, Series A, Reel 1, Frame 50, NAACP Papers. In addition, from 29 June to 5 July 1936, 210 youth delegates met to establish a national program and decide on methods and techniques, a meeting that would be repeated annually. See Lawrence, "National Youth Program." On the Baltimore

Young People's Forum, see "Baltimore Youth," 89; Pahl, *Youth Ministry*, 75; Mc-
Neil, "Youth Initiative." Bragg, "Marketing," explores the "formalization and re-
energization of [the NAACP's] youth branch system" 422.

30 The Scottsboro case was considered a "legal" lynching. In a letter to White, Philadelphia branch president Charles W. Dorsey suggested that antilynching "form
the very nucleus for the Junior work" (25 January 1935, Part 12, Series B, Reel 8,
Frame 264, NAACP Papers). His suggestion reflected his observations of young
people's interests. Moreover, much of the NAACP's national youth program from
1936 through the 1940s focused on antilynching activities. See Ovington, "Students." See also "Objectives of Youth Council," 5, Part 19, Series A, Reel 1, Frames
70–76, NAACP Papers.

31 Juanita Jackson to the Youth Members of the NAACP, 5 August 1936, Part 19,
Series A, Reel 1, Frame 81, NAACP Papers; "Appendix VII: Suggestions for Program Activities to Achieve the Objectives," 8–11, Part 19, Series A, Reel 1, Frames
73–76, NAACP Papers; "N.A.A.C.P. Youth Council News." The Harlem youth
council was not only singled out by *The Crisis* for its activities but was criticized by
many from the black better classes for demonstrating outside of Harlem, suggesting that this protest perhaps represented a somewhat new and more visible kind
of demonstration. This demonstration also provided a good example of the interracial work in which youth members engaged: the youth council organized and
sponsored the larger United Youth Committee against Lynching that conducted
this demonstration. The group participated in a number of other demonstrations,
mass meetings, fund-raising activities, and pressure campaigns. In the 1930s, the
YMCA and YWCA advocated similar objectives for their youth groups. Y members were encouraged to "study the problems of minority races" but to "avoid the
peril of merely academic study" and take steps in their local communities to end
racist practices. Not incidentally, like the American Youth Commission, many Y
leaders considered their interracial activities "the most fruitful work done by the
YMCA in any of its departments of activity in the last decade." See, for example,
"Toward Interracial Education: A Program Paper," Group 58, Series 3, Box 770,
YMCA Student Division Papers, Yale Divinity Library, Yale University, New Haven,
Conn.; "Minutes of Interracial Education Committee," 20 January 1936, Group 58,
Series 3, Box 54, YMCA Student Division Papers, Yale Divinity Library, Yale Uni-
versity, New Haven, Conn.

32 L. Pearl Mitchell, "Importance," 282; "Essential Elements in Building a National
Youth Movement," 1936, 2–3, Part 19, Series A, Reel 1, Frames 104–5, NAACP
Papers.

33 See Meier and Rudwick, "Origins," 343.

34 "Minutes of the Advisory Committee of the Youth Section of the 27th Annual Con-
ference," New York, 15 July 1936, Part 19, Series A, Reel 1, Frames 98–101, NAACP
Papers. On Jackson's earlier activism, see Pahl, *Youth Ministry*, 75; McNeil, "Youth
Initiatives." In another article, McNeil notes that NAACP legal counsel Charles
Houston considered legal challenges to racial inequality just one part of the as-

sociation's work. He also saw the importance of building a mass organization and engaging in other forms of protest ("Before *Brown*," 1447).

35 One especially notable exception to the lack of attention to youth activism is Mc-Neil, "Youth Initiative." See also Meier and Rudwick, "Origins," 244, 322, 331–44; Meier and Rudwick, *Black Detroit*, 80–82, 91–92. Recent scholarship, such as Lau's *Democracy Rising*, depicts the NAACP as a more responsive and complex organization.

36 See correspondence between the Muskogee council, the Pet Milk Company, and Roy Wilkins, January 1939, Part 19, Series A, Reel 5, Frames 354–55, NAACP Papers; Juanita Jackson to Youth Presidents, 18 January 1937, Part 19, Series A, Reel 1, Frames 111–12, NAACP Papers; "Annual Report Youth Work," 31 December 1938, Part 19, Series A, Group 1, Reel 3, Frames 4–8, NAACP Papers. In the late 1930s but especially in the early 1940s, a few youth councils and college chapters attacked racial segregation in public and private facilities, with some success. See, for example, "Youth Activities Report from the 6th Annual Youth Conference," 1944, Part 19, Series B, Reel 5, Frames 220–29, NAACP Papers. See also various issues of the *NAACP Youth News Letter*, Part 19, Series C, Reel 27, NAACP Papers. For the efforts of youth councils from Baltimore, South Carolina, Virginia, Arkansas, Oklahoma, Michigan, and Mississippi, see "Campaign against Inequalities in Education," 15 October 1937, Part 19, Series A, Reel 1, Frames 135–39, NAACP Papers. The NAACP Papers contain numerous references to the Anderson case, which also became a rallying point for youth demonstrations throughout the country. See, for example, William F. Richardson, "Notes of the President," *Voice of Youth* (Richmond, Va., Youth Council), September 1939, Part 19, Series A, Reel 5, Frame 1007, NAACP Papers; James H. Robinson (acting youth secretary) to Officers of Youth Councils, 10 August 1939, Part 19, Series A, Reel 3, Frames 230–31, NAACP Papers; "Draft of the Youth Pamphlet," Part 19, Series A, Reel 3, Frames 444–47, NAACP Papers. On Anderson, see also Lau, *Democracy Rising*, 101–5.

37 Hale, *Making Whiteness*, 222–27.

38 Burgum, "Promise."

39 Lau, *Democracy Rising*, esp. 10; Walter White, "Youth Council," 215.

40 Lomax, "Negro Revolt." Lau, *Democracy Rising*, similarly urges a more complex understanding of the NAACP and demonstrates a comparable dialectical relationship between local branches and the national association. Although he does not focus on youth, Lau also shows that young people were often on the forefront of civil rights activity in South Carolina. Greene, *Our Separate Ways*, reveals that young people were pushing the movement in Durham, North Carolina, although her (important) focus on gender perhaps keeps her from recognizing important age-related aspects of civil rights activism.

41 See, for example, Muskogee, Oklahoma, Branch to Frederic Morrow (branch coordinator), 23 February 1939, Part 19, Series A, Reel 5, Frame 361, NAACP Papers; "The Aftermath," *Voice of Youth* (Richmond, Va., Youth Council), July 1939, Part 19, Series A, Reel 5, Frame 1001, NAACP Papers.

42 James J. McClendon to Madison S. Jones Jr., 17 April 1941, Part 19, Series B, Reel 11,
Frame 105, NAACP Papers; James J. McClendon to Walter White, 18 March 1941,
Part 19, Series B, Reel 11, Frames 91–92, NAACP Papers; Edward M. Swan to Madison S. Jones Jr., 16 April 1941, Part 19, Series B, Reel 11, Frames 99–100, NAACP
Papers. Shortly thereafter, Gloster B. Current, a former youth council member and
a future director of branches, became the Detroit branch's executive secretary. In
Black Detroit, Meier and Rudwick describe the central role that Detroit's youth
councils played in 1940s union organizing and strike activities as well as the conflict between adult and youth members (80–93).

43 "National Youth Commission Report," RG 73, Box 28, Folder 1, SEPC; Edward M.
Swan to Madison S. Jones Jr., 16 April 1941, Part 19, Series B, Reel 11, Frames
99–100, NAACP Papers. Studies of the civil rights movement often point out that
charges of communist activity, especially in the late 1940s and 1950s, commonly
followed civil rights groups and organizers. Such accusations were made both by
those who wanted no changes to America's racial politics and by those who were
engaged in civil rights work but feared the ideas and techniques of more liberal
civil rights activists.

44 Robert Bone to Gloster B. Current, 15 December 1947, Part 19, Series B, Reel 14,
Frames 28–30, NAACP Papers; "Program Outline, Submitted by the Youth Council to the Flint Branch Executive Board with Copies to the National Office and
State Executive Board," 13 December 1947, Part 19, Series B, Reel 14, Frames 33–
34, NAACP Papers; "Testimony of Mrs. Vasolonyer Baxter, Youth Council Advi-
sor," 22 December 1947, Part 19, Series B, Reel 14, Frames 41–42, NAACP Papers;
"Meeting with Youth Officers," stamped 10 January 1948, Part 19, Series B, Reel
14, Frames 44–45, NAACP Papers; Dr. J. L. Leach, "State Conference of Branches
to Officers and Members of the Youth Council NAACP," 16 February 1948, Part
19, Series B, Reel 14, Frame 55, NAACP Papers. One youth council member was a
communist (but he refused to hold office in the council because of the possibility
of charges of infiltration), and the campaign attracted the support of young people
outside of the youth council, including socialist youth, which further opened the
council to charges of infiltration.

45 See Clinton Henry Lewis to Roy Wilkins, 6 February 1946, Part 19, Series B, Reel
23, Frames 667–68, NAACP Papers; Clinton Henry Lewis to Endor Harriss [sic],
6 February 1946, Part 19, Series B, Reel 23, Frame 665, NAACP Papers; Clinton
Henry Lewis to Ruby Hurley, 6 February 1946, Part 19, Series B, Reel 23, Frame
669, NAACP Papers.

46 Lewis's resignation was only indirectly related to his dispute with Hurley. After
his confrontation with Hurley, senior branch leaders questioned the legality of his
election to office, so he resigned and ran again. See Clinton Henry Lewis to Ruby
Hurley, 12 February 1946, Part 19, Series B, Reel 23, Frame 672, NAACP Papers.
On Current and youth work in Detroit, see Meier and Rudwick, *Black Detroit*,
80–82.

47 "Report of the Youth Secretary for 1944," Part 19, Series B, Reel 5, Frames 217–

24, NAACP Papers; *NAACP Youth News Letter*, November 1942, Part 19, Series C, Reel 27, Frames 22–23, NAACP Papers; "Directory of Youth Councils and College Chapters," 1945, Part 19, Series B, Reel 9, NAACP Papers; Youth Work Committee Meeting, 4 October 1944, Part 19, Series C, Reel 27, Frames 413–14, NAACP Papers; "NAACP College Chapters," 12 May 1947, Part 19, Series C, Reel 27, Frame 464, NAACP Papers; *NAACP Youth Councils*; *Crusade for Freedom* (pamphlet), 1951, Part 19, Series B, Reel 10, Frame 867, NAACP Papers. Perhaps not coincidently, many of SNCC's Freedom Summer volunteers came from these colleges. White civil rights leader Casey Hayden, among others, went to the University of Texas at Austin. On the activism of students there, see Rossinow, *Politics*. On the racial makeup of NAACP chapters, see, for example, "NAACP College Chapters," 12 May 1947, Part 19, Series C, Reel 27, Frame 464, NAACP Papers. This document listed thirty-six all-Negro chapters, ten interracial groups, and three all-white chapters. The association as a whole expanded its membership and its membership base (beyond the middle class) during this period as well. See Goluboff, *Lost Promise*, 190. Still, the growth of youth and college branches stands out.

48 Ruby Hurley to NAACP Youth Councils, August 1943, Part 19, Series C, Reel 27, Frame 34, NAACP Papers. Hurley's comments were specifically about Harlem's 1 August riots, which she witnessed. In July 1943, Hurley received correspondence from Mary Louise Rogers, president of Swarthmore College and affiliated with the U.S. Student Assembly, pointing out that "ninety percent of the Detroit rioters were between the ages of 15 and 25" (Mary Louise Rogers to Ruby Hurley, 7 July 1943, Part 19, Series C, Reel 22, Frame 788, NAACP Papers). News media also stressed the youthfulness of that summer's rioters, and the riots figured prominently in public discussions of juvenile delinquency and the frustration of young blacks. In the early 1940s, the NAACP also initiated what it called a "new project" to organize young people between the ages of twelve and sixteen into junior youth councils (*NAACP Youth News Letter*, October 1942, Part 19, Series C, Reel 27, Frames 20–21, NAACP Papers). See also *NAACP Youth Councils*; Youth Work Committee Minutes, 4 October 1944, Part 19, Series C, Reel 27, Frames 413–14, NAACP Papers. Ella Baker, hired by the NAACP in 1941, was especially active in setting up southern youth councils in the 1940s. See Olson, *Freedom's Daughters*, 140; Ransby, *Ella Baker*. In 1943, Ralph Ellison suggested that "the zoot suit conceals profound political meaning; perhaps the symmetrical frenzy of the Lindy Hop conceals clues to great potential power—if only Negro leaders would solve this riddle" (Kelley, "Riddle"). NAACP youth councils perhaps represented Negro leaders' attempt to "solve the riddle" and harness the potential political power of youth that Ellison saw reflected in black youth culture.

49 "The Detroit Race Riot" (confidential report), 6 July 1943, 7, Box 107, Folder 8, HLP.

50 Goff, *Problems*, 82, 13–18, 24, 28, 38, 81. On youth council and college chapter direct-action campaigns of this sort, see, for example, "Report of the Youth Secretary for 1944," Part 19, Series B, Reel 5, Frames 698–708, NAACP Papers; "Items

from Youth Councils," March 1949, Part 19, Series C, Reel 27, Frame 160, NAACP Papers.

51 "Conference Report," 1945 Youth Conference, Wilberforce, Ohio, Part 19, Series B, Reel 5, Frames 698–708, NAACP Papers; Charles H. Wesley, "Excerpts from Keynote Address," 1945 Youth Conference, Wilberforce, Ohio, Part 19, Series B, Reel 5, Frame 707, NAACP Papers; Adam Clayton Powell Jr., "Keynote Address," Annual Youth Conference, Richmond, Va., 1944, Part 19, Series B, Reel 5, Frames 268–77, NAACP Papers; Statement by youth adopted at the Regional Leadership Training Conference, Chattanooga, Tenn., March 1950, Part 19, Series C, Reel 27, Frame 196, NAACP Papers. Eleanor Roosevelt was the keynote speaker at the 1943 youth conference (*NAACP Youth Councils*; "Statement of NAACP Youth Councils," Adopted by Youth Councils at the Emergency War Conference, Detroit, Mich., 5 June 1943, Part 19, Series C, Reel 27, Frames 31–32, NAACP Papers). Youth delegates at this conference were both male and female. It seems likely that the use of the male pronoun "his" in this example belies a gendered perception of citizenship rights. The aims of the civil rights movement were often discussed in male-centered terms, although women sometimes challenged this male-centeredness, most famously at SNCC's Waveland conference. See Carson, *In Struggle*; Sarah Evans, *Personal Politics*. Gaines, *Uplifting the Race*, explores earlier challenges to the male and middle-class biases of the African American civil rights movement.

52 See, for example, Dittmer, *Local People*; Patricia Sullivan, "Southern Reformers"; Norrell, "One Thing"; Sitkoff, *Struggle*; Aldon D. Morris, *Origins*; Chafe, *Civilities*; Norrell, *Reaping*.

53 Helen Gahagan Douglas Speech at World Youth Week Rally at Carnegie Hall, 21 March 1945, quoted in *NAACP Youth News Letter*, March 1945, Part 19, Series C, Reel 27, Frame 86, NAACP Papers; Frances M. Damon to Ruby Hurley, 27 January 1944, Part 19, Series C, Reel 23, Frame 12, NAACP Papers; Adam Clayton Powell Jr., "Keynote Address," Annual Youth Conference, Richmond, Va., 1944, Part 19, Series B, Reel 5, Frames 268–77, NAACP Papers; "Call to Wilberforce Youth Conference, Youth and the Atomic Age," 27–30 December 1945, Part 19, Series B, Reel 5, Frames 649–652, NAACP Papers; *NAACP Youth Councils*. The 1940s saw the proliferation of youth events. Negro Youth Week, for example, began in 1941.

54 Rodgers and Hammerstein, "You've Got to Be Taught"; "Youth Goes Marching On" (to the tune of "The Battle Hymn of the Republic," 1861, by Julia Ward Howe), in *NAACP Songbook*, ca. 1950, Part 19, Series C, Reel 13, Frame 630, NAACP Papers; "Statement of NAACP Youth Councils," adopted by Youth Councils at the Emergency War Conference, Detroit, Mich., 5 June 1943, Part 19, Series C, Reel 27, Frames 31–32, NAACP Papers; "Report of Resolution Committee," 1942 Youth Conference, Part 19, Series C, Reel 27, Frame 22, NAACP Papers; Bob Ewing, "What Can We Do about Segregation?," reprint from *Orange and White*, 27 February 1953, Box 8, Folder 6, IAP. Singing Freedom Songs seems to have been a standard part of NAACP youth council activities at least as early as the mid-1940s.

55 Fairclough, *Better Day*, talks about the 1946 school boycott in Lumberton, North Carolina, instigated by NAACP youth council members (203).

56 See, for example, *NAACP Youth News Letter*, April 1943, Part 19, Series C, Reel 27, Frames 29–30, NAACP Papers; *NAACP Youth News Letters* and correspondence from Ruby Hurley about Youth Council activities, 1942–47, Part 19, Series C, Reel 27, NAACP Papers; *NAACP Youth Councils*. On NAACP youth council work in Charleston, see R. Scott Baker, *Paradoxes*, 106. On Detroit youth council activism, see Meier and Rudwick, *Black Detroit*, 80–93. Meier and Rudwick argue, however, that direct action did not form "a continuous tradition in black protest" ("Origins," 387).

57 Gloster B. Current to Walter White, 25 April 1951, Part 19, Series B, Reel 20, Frames 624–27, NAACP Papers; Ruby Hurley to Gloster Current, 18 January 1951, Part 19, Series B, Reel 10, Frame 862, NAACP Papers; "Report of the National Youth Work Committee to the 43rd Annual Convention of the NAACP," Oklahoma City, Okla., 27 June 1952, Part 1 supplement, Reel 6, Frame 945, NAACP Papers; Gloster B. Current, "ABC's of Mass Pressure," in "Report of 1944 Youth Conference," Part 19, Series B, Reel 5, Frames 236–53, NAACP Papers; Jimmie Lewis Franklin, *Journey*; Sitkoff, *Struggle*, 59; *Cosmopolitan* (AME Sunday school), 9 January 1938, Box 7, Folder 17, MSS 921, Black Print Culture Collection, Special Collections Department, RWL. On the direct-action protests by Oklahoma City's youth councils during the 1950s, see Luper, *Behold*. On the Oklahoma City (and 1958 Wichita, Kansas) youth council demonstrations, see also V. P. Franklin, "Patterns"; Collier-Thomas and Franklin, *My Soul*, 89–90, 105; Southern Regional Council, "The Student Protest Movement" (special report), 1 April 1960, Box 25, Folder: Student Civil Rights, RLSP.

58 "Seminar Task Group on Christian Social Responsibility in the Field of Integration," RG 73, Box 37, Folder 3, SEPC; Elizabeth Harrington, "Report on the Work of the Joint Interracial Education Commission," March 1936, 3–17, RG 58, Series 3, Box 54, Folder 769, YMCA Student Division Papers, Yale Divinity Library, Yale University, New Haven, Conn. See also, for example, Margaret L. Reid, "A Study of the Programs of American Student YMCA's in the Fields of Social Responsibility and World Relatedness," 1950, RG 73, Series 3, Box 86, Folder 15, SEPC. The World Student Christian Federation and YMCA Papers, both at the Yale Divinity Library, are other good sources for information on the relationship between the Christian youth movement and twentieth-century race relations. See also Egerton, *Speak*, 426.

59 See V. P. Franklin, "Patterns," 205; Ruby Hurley, "News and Action," September 1955, 3, Box 2, Folder 3, MEC; Internal Affairs Document, 1957, 2, Box 2, Folder 14, MEC. On the Pittsburgh NAACP youth activism, see James Collins, "Taking the Lead." On "early sit-ins," see also Aldon D. Morris, *Origins*, 188–94. On NAACP youth activism in the early 1960s, see Meier and Rudwick, *CORE*, 101–34. On youth council direct-action campaigns, see, for example, press releases and reports in Part 19, Series D, Reel 16, NAACP Papers. On the Salute to Youth Rally,

see "Youth Tell of Fight for Freedom in South" (press release), 29 May 1957, Part 19, Series D, Reel 17, Frames 504–5, NAACP Papers; Herbert Wright to Cleveland Robinson, re: Civil Rights Fighter's Rally, 22 April 1957, Part 19, Series D, Reel 17, Frame 419, NAACP Papers; Mammoth Youth Rally (flier), n.d., Part 19, Series D, Reel 17, Frame 483, NAACP Papers; "NAACP Intensifies Its Youth Program in the South" (press release), 30 January 1958, Part 19, Series D, Reel 16, Frames 214–15, NAACP Papers; Gloster Current, "Better Understanding between NAACP Branches and Youth Councils," ca. 1963, Part 19, Series D, Reel 16, Frames 298–305, NAACP Papers; "Minutes of the Executive Board of the NAACP Jackson, Mississippi," 4 March 1959, Box 1, Folder 2, MEC. See also, for example, Gloster Current to Branches, Youth Councils, and College Chapters, 31 March 1960, Box 1, Folder 76, EKC.

60 On the NAACP's failure to receive credit for the direct action of its youth members, see, for example, A. Thoressa Whittaker (president of Nashville Youth Council) to Julie Wright, 20 September 1961, Part 19, Series D, Reel 20, Frames 148–49, NAACP Papers. Carson notes that of the student protesters who belonged to political or civil rights organizations, "the largest number were members of youth groups affiliated with the NAACP" (*In Struggle*, 14). On the views of youth council members, see Inge Powell Bell, *CORE*, 97–98; Blumberg, *Civil Rights*, 226. Waskow contends that the "invention" of the sit-in occurred on 1 February 1960. This assertion is especially problematic as is the general consensus among historians that young activists in the 1960s were unaware of a tradition of black protest. Even if earlier sit-ins did not catch on nationally and youth in the 1960s considered their actions a break with the past, it seems unlikely that NAACP youth council members would be completely unaware that the tactic had been used by other and earlier youth councils, especially since the association's youth newsletters and correspondence talked about direct-action campaigns and youth workshops taught direct-action techniques. What was different and challenging about the Greensboro sit-ins, in addition to the fact that they received substantial media attention and led to other student direct-action campaigns, was that they occurred in the South, which was also perhaps why they received such attention and generated such a response among southern students (although they were not the first youth direct-action protests to take place in the South). Still, most of the earlier direct-action campaigns by young people in the NAACP took place in the Midwest or in southern border states such as Kentucky and Missouri. On the consensus among historians on this point, see Meier, "Toward," 214–15. Olson, *Freedom's Daughters*, mentions that Pauli Murray and some of her classmates at Harvard, "among others," conducted sit-in demonstrations as early as the 1940s (147). Sitkoff mentions youth protests (including the Oklahoma City NAACP youth council protest) of the late 1950s (*Struggle*, 59). In *I've Got the Light*, Payne suggests that "SNCC put the NAACP in a position where it was forced to support some direct-action project," an argument that again does not take into account the association's long-standing support of direct action by its own youth councils (100). Joanne Grant

has emphasized the "mass character of the NAACP" and how civil rights leader Ella Baker, who was so influential in the development of SNCC, had earlier in her career encouraged the development and activism of NAACP youth councils (*Ella Baker*, 50–51). On the Greensboro students' connection to the NAACP, see Aldon D. Morris, *Origins*, 197–99.

61 Lomax, "Negro Revolt"; Julie Zaugg, "Tougaloo Movement Minutes," 17 October 1963, 3, Box 2, Folder 69, EKC. Evers was especially excited by the number of youth joining the NAACP in 1956 and 1957 (Medgar Evers, "Annual Report Mississippi State Office," 1956, 7, 1957, 4, Box 2, Folder 39, MEC). Lau has found that support for CORE in South Carolina came primarily from NAACP chapters (*Democracy Rising*, 219). Joyce Ladner listed SNCC as the only civil rights organization with which she was associated prior to 1968, a telling illustration of the tendency to disassociate the NAACP from youth activism. Ladner had been an active NAACP youth council member since the late 1950s, and in the early 1960s, her council supported student protests in the Jackson area. See Wilma A. Dunaway, "Directory of Southern Sociologists Who Were Civil Rights Activists prior to 1968," Box 3, Folder 12, JLC; Miscellaneous Documents, Box 3, Folders 1, 2, JLC. See also Payne, *I've Got the Light*; Dittmer, *Local People*; Jonas, *Freedom's Sword*. On the Greensboro sit-ins, see Chafe, *Civilities*, chap. 3.

CHAPTER FIVE

1 Ben Chaney quoted in Huie, *Three Lives*, 231; "Wait a While — Tomorrow Is Another Day," *Teen Impact* (Evanston branch NAACP youth council), June 1963, Part 19, Series D, Reel 2, Frames 376–78, NAACP Papers; Williams quoted in Weinraub, "Brilliancy," 670. On Ben Chaney, see Blake, *Children*, 206–16.

2 Zinn, "Finishing School," 71, 73. Perhaps indicative of other black colleges and decades, Howard University students in the second decade of the twentieth century described and sometimes complained about the pressures of and focus on campus sorority and fraternity life. See the life histories written by Howard students, Box 100, Folder 3, HLP. Jacquelyn Dowd Hall also notes that "many young activists of the 1960s saw their efforts as a new departure and themselves as a unique generation" ("Long Civil Rights Movement," 1253).

3 Coles, "Children," 90; Payne, *I've Got the Light*, 417. See also Inge Powell Bell, *CORE*; Blumberg, *Civil Rights*; McAdam, *Freedom Summer*; Olson, *Freedom's Daughters*; Dittmer, *Local People*; Gaillard, *Dream*; Dudziak, *Cold War Civil Rights*; Sitkoff, *Struggle*; Whitfield, *Death*; Carson, *In Struggle*; Armstead L. Robinson and Sullivan, *New Directions*.

4 Coles, "Children," 90, 86; Albert Manley (president of Spelman) quoted in Zinn, "Finishing School," 73. Coles was not the only researcher to make such arguments.

5 "American States Rights Party Emphasis on Youth," *White American*, October 1964, Box 19, Folder: *The White American*, NABR; "32 Athens Students Joined, Klan

Says," *Atlanta Constitution*, 3 October 1963, clipping, Box 10, Folder 6, CCP; "Hear-Ye White Youth," n.d., Box 8, Folder: "Klan-Hate Groups," NABR; Edwin Lofton, "Letter to the Editor," *Jackson Daily News*, 4 April 1958, Box 2, Folder 107, EKC. Meier urges scholars of the civil rights movement to recognize discontinuities as well as continuities in movement history, specifically suggesting that it may be fruitful for historians to explore generational change or rebellion and its significance to the movement ("Toward").

6 See Tuttle, *Daddy's Gone*, 236–41. The most significant developmentalists Tuttle discusses are Erik Erikson and Jean Piaget. Erikson makes a similar argument. In "Youth," he suggests that "in youth . . . the life history intersects with history. . . . Historians on the whole make little of this; they describe the visible emergence and the contest of autonomous historical ideas, unconcerned with the fact that these ideas reach down into the lives of generations and reemerge through the daily awakening and training of historical consciousness in young individuals" (20).

7 Tuttle, *Daddy's Gone*, 118.

8 Coles, *Political Life*, 62–71, 201; "Motivation of Students' Role in Protest Is Studied," *Voice of the Movement*, (reprinted from the *Washington Post*), 2, Box 2 Folder 80, EKC; McGrath, "Citizenship," 84; *Atlanta Constitution*, 9 March 1960, clipping, Box 1, Folder 4, CCP. McGrath's statement directly followed comments criticizing adults who preached against discrimination but demonstrated racial or religious prejudice in their actions and attitudes. The ad also stressed black military service and the international relations/national security problems caused by America's racial prejudice; see Tuttle, *Daddy's Gone*, 239. Tuttle suggests that Japanese American children in relocation camps became especially "sensitized . . . to violations of democracy" (118). I think his point can be applied more broadly.

9 Mary Ann Perich, interview by Carole Tuxeud, 1959, Box 42, Folder 15, JHFP; Ferguson, "Public-Spirited Youth," 5; Seuss, *If I Ran the Zoo*; Seuss, "What Was I Scared Of?" On trends in children's literature, see Lystad, *From Dr. Mather*, 164, 194. Coles noted that many young activists cited J. D. Salinger's *The Catcher in the Rye* as having had a significant influence on them, and young white activist Mary King recalled that Eva Knox Evans's *All about Us* was her favorite book growing up—it also helped shape her perceptions of race as a child (Coles, "Reconsideration"; Mary King, *Freedom Song*, 51–52). That the Alabama state legislature voted to ban Garth Williams's *The Rabbits' Wedding*, a picture book in which black and white rabbits married, suggests that white southerners saw children's literature during this period as potentially subversive. On that controversy, see "Shades of Hitler!" The 1940s and 1950s also saw an increase in the publication of more marginal children's books that questioned America's racial politics, such as Beim and Beim, *Two Is a Team*, and Eva Knox Evans, *All about Us*. Mickenberg explores these and other less well-known leftist or leftist-influenced children's literature of the period that sometimes dealt with racial themes. She also notes that children's literature influenced student activism for civil rights. One Greensboro protester, for

example, cited Hughes and Meltzer, *Pictorial History*, as a source of inspiration for the sit-ins (Mickenberg, *Learning*, 276). On children's literature of the period, see also Murray, *American Children's Literature*.

10 Mary Taylor, "To You, Our Children: A Citizen's Conference Charts a Course toward the Future Well-Being of Children and Youth," *The Child*, February 1951, 108–9. The 1950 conference included four hundred delegates under age twenty-one. Some adults apparently "rejected youth participation" at this conference, while others saw youth participation as important "for what it does for them." All future conferences, however, included youth delegates and increasingly recognized youth as full contributing participants (106). See Phillipson, "Follow-Up."

11 Coles, *Political Life*, 29, 35; Beals, *Warriors*, 6; Coggins, "I Hate Negroes," 71. In 1956, E. B. White suggested that "the sense that is common to one generation is uncommon to the next." He noted that southern congressmen defended segregation by saying that "'separate but equal' . . . had been founded on 'common sense.'" But White pointed out that that was not the common sense of the present generation ("Letter," 166). Payne notes "evidence of growing race consciousness" and entitlement among the younger generation of African Americans growing up in the post–World War II period (*I've Got the Light*, 21–23). On young people's experiences with Jim Crow and their significance to the social, political, and economic order, see Ritterhouse, *Growing Up Jim Crow*.

12 James Farmer, "Emancipation Proclamation—(Unfinished Business)," 100th Anniversary Celebration of the Emancipation Proclamation, International Convention of Christian Churches, Miami Beach, Fla., 14 October 1963, Reel 3, Frames 576–80, CORE Papers, addendum; Richmond Smiley, interview by Marcel Reedus, 13 March 1996, Box 14, Folder 1, SRCP. Although not technically a youth himself at the time, James L. Farmer Jr. was certainly inspired by younger people (whom he also inspired by taking the kind of action that they admired) and had been at the forefront of civil rights activism since his student days. On young people pushing Farmer's activism, see, for example, John Lewis with D'Orso, *Walking*, 143–45, 164–66. Ritterhouse has found that children and youth in the pre-*Brown* era were often angry about segregation and the racism that created it, but they usually accommodated themselves to its realities by their late adolescent years (*Growing Up Jim Crow*, 180–223). My exploration of the history of the NAACP youth councils in chapter 4 suggests that access to civil rights youth organizations and forums in which they could discuss and explore racial issues with their peers encouraged young people to continue to resist racism rather than to adapt to it.

13 Coles, "Children," 90–92. See also Coles, "On Courage"; Robert Coles, "Comments on *Youth in Social Action*" (from *Science and Psychoanalysis* 1966), Box 14, Robert Coles Papers, SHC; American Youth Commission, press release, 22 September 1940, 2, Box 556, Folder 5950, RG 23, Series 1, Subseries 3, GEB Papers; "The Negro College and Citizenship," *Talladega Student*, February 1936, 10, Box 47, Folder 1, Lillian Voorhees Papers, Amistad Research Center, Tulane University, New Orleans, La.; Powdermaker, *After Freedom*, 333. Powdermaker noted that age

rather than socioeconomic status determined "what the Negro thinks and feels about white people" (325). Historians in some ways have taken for granted the participation of young people in the civil rights movement of the 1960s. Payne, for example, says, "That many young people eagerly joined the movement is not surprising" (*I've Got the Light*, 177). We need to consider more carefully, however, why young people in the post–World War II era felt they could express the anger that, as Payne notes, older generations of blacks also felt (and began to express once they saw young people taking action against racism). Karl Marx famously suggested that the material conditions of one's existence establish not only one's expectations but even one's most basic desires and aspirations (*Economic and Philosophic Manuscripts*). Social theorist Pierre Bourdieu similarly argued that "conditions of existence . . . impos[e] different definitions of the impossible, the possible, and the probable." Significantly, Bourdieu suggested that early (childhood) experiences form "the basis of perception and appreciation of all subsequent experience" and account for generational conflict (*Outline*, 78, chap. 2).

14 See, for example, Dittmer, *Local People*; Dalfiume, "'Forgotten' Years"; Thornton, "Municipal Politics"; Norrell, "One Thing"; Patricia Sullivan, "Southern Reformers"; Gavins, "NAACP." In their study of the origins of direct action, Meier and Rudwick find that African Americans "continuously reinvented" direct-action strategies "in response to shifting patterns of race relations and the changing status of blacks in American society." According to their research, "waves of direct action" occurred when blacks experienced "critical changes in their status," such as those experienced during World War II ("Origins," 387).

15 Quoted in Coles, "Serpents," 199; Deloney, "What Negro Youth Expects," 254; Keniston, *Young Radicals*, 75; Robert L. Sutherland, "A Recommendation for a Demonstration Project in the Personality Adjustment of Negro Youth," 1939, 2, Box 558, Folder 5966, RG 23, Series 1, Subseries 3, GEB Papers; Marie Hawthorne, interview by Bonnie Smith, 29 January 1959, Box 42, Folder 16, JHFP; Claude Smith, interview by Mickey Korndorffer, 7 April 1960, Box 41, Folder 21, JHFP; Peter Stoner, "A Glimpse into the Past: A Few Words about My Civil Rights Days," 1998, Peter Stoner Papers, USM.

16 Gillespie and Allport, *Youth's Outlook*, 10–11; *College Courses*, 3; Woofter, *Southern Race Progress*, 168. See also, for example, "The Nation's Press Comments on ADL's New Freedom Pamphlet, Miracle of Social Adjustment," reprint of Richard L. Lyons and Eve Edstrom, "Integration Called Miracle of Social Adjustment Here," *Washington Post and Times Herald*, 11 February 1957, Box 229, Folder 3, HLP; "A Study in Public Opinion: Racial Attitudes of the Negro Survey Forms" (Ohio), n.d., Box 15, Folder 41, Black Print Culture Collection, Special Collections Department, RWL (which also found that most respondents thought black and white children should be educated together); "First Partial Report of the Resolutions Committee," 1944, Part 19, Series B, Reel 5, Frame 729, NAACP Papers. At least eight Freedom Summer volunteers came from Carleton, a Minnesota liberal arts school. The school's first black collegiate student graduated in 1949 (*Carleton Voice*,

Summer 1999, Box 3, Folder 3, Kathleen Dahl Freedom Summer Collection, USM; Eric Hilleman (Carleton College archivist), correspondence with author, 24 July 2007; Bob Zellner, interview by Worth Long, 15 April 1996, 2, Box 5, Folder 17, SRCP). On the Millsaps crisis, see "White Citizen's Council Challenges Millsaps' Head," *Concern*, 28 March 1958, 3; Jim Waits, "Race Discussion Causes Crisis," "Integrated Meetings Held at Millsaps," *Jackson Daily News*, 6 March 1958; *Purple and White Surplus* (Millsaps's alternative student paper), all in Box 2, Folder 107, EKC; Ed King, interview by Joyce Ladner, n.d., 2–3, Box 3, Folder 42, JLC; Barbara Bell, interview by Carroll Murray, 6 February 1959, Box 41, Folder 16, JHFP; Leon Septh, interview by Ann Bee, 29 January 1959, Box 41, Folder 17, JHFP; Gerald Hoag, interview by I. Joseph Jeffrion Jr. (interviews with black New Orleanians), 1949, 2, Box 40, Folder 8, JHFP. Ninety-three percent of upper-income parents in New York considered intergroup meetings effective (Goff, *Problems*, 73–74). Perhaps also significant was the fact that universities such as Fisk, the University of Chicago, and New York University were offering baccalaureate degrees in race relations (Box 8, Folder 7, IAP). In the 1930s, at least one black student suggested that the lack of courses on racial issues bore partial responsibility for the current lack of unified social consciousness and group action on civil rights ("The Negro College and Citizenship," 10, Lillian Voorhees Papers, Amistad Research Center, Tulane University, New Orleans, La.). The Eleanor Roosevelt Memorial Foundation singled out "inter-group relations specialists . . . as one of the keys to a peaceful and constructive resolution of the nation's racial crisis." President Kennedy endorsed the idea of and plans for human rights leadership training ("President Kennedy Hails Human Rights Leadership Training Program Launched by Eleanor Roosevelt Memorial Foundation" [news release], October 1963, National Association of Human Rights Workers Archives, Amistad Research Center, Tulane University, New Orleans, La.).

17 Du Bois, *Darkwater*, 9; Bob Douglas, interview by George King, December 1991, January 1992, Box 10, Folder 1, MSS 934, SRCP; Instructional Aids for Use in Connection with ASF Manual, M 5, "Leadership and the Negro Soldier," n.d., 3, Box 107, Folder 13, HLP; Zeligs, "Races," 6; "Revolution in Main Street: Youth and Law Transform a Society," *World Communique* (YMCA), May–June 1961, 11, RG 73, Box 37, Folder 5, SEPC; Carole Tuxeud, interview by Mary Ann Perich, Box 41, Folder 15, JHFP. Aldon D. Morris also suggests the "huge gap between America's democratic rhetoric and its racial practices" motivated youth activism (*Origins*, 222).

18 In the 1970s, Orum suggested that the *Brown* ruling helped inspire black youth activism (Orum, "Patterns," 275; Orum, *Black Students*). Orum's argument in general does not take into account the long history of youth activism and gives perhaps too much credit to adult black leaders.

19 Rudy Lombard and Lolis Elie, interview by Joyce Ladner, n.d., 31, Box 3, Folder 38, JLC; Murrow, *See It Now*; Hughes, *Fight*, 204; Payne, "'Whole United States,'" 91. Martin, "'Stretching Out,'" also examines the influence of *Brown* as well as the Till case on African American activism. On South Carolina youth activism after *Brown*

and for the Gantt quotation (and for information about Gantt), see R. Scott Baker, *Paradoxes*, 108, 115, 146, chaps. 6–8. See also John Lewis, *Walking.*

20 Bob Zellner, interview by author, 2 May 2008; Casey Hayden, interview by Joyce Ladner, 2 July 1978, 2, Box 3, Folder 40, JLC; Murrow, *See It Now*; Bourdieu, *Outline*, 168–70. We might also say, to again use Bourdieu's framework, that *Brown* provided young African Americans with "the material and symbolic means of rejecting the definition of the real that [had been] imposed on them" (*Outline*, 169). Evidence shows that the *Brown* ruling also affected the race socialization messages that black parents gave their children. A recent study suggests that after *Brown*, black parents were less likely to teach "deference to and fear of whites" and more likely to convey a sense of individual pride to their children (Tony N. Brown and Lesane-Brown, "Race Socialization Messages," 201, 206–7).

21 Melba Pattillo Beals, interview, n.d., 5, Box 11, Folder 4, MSS 934, SRCP; Don Shoemaker, Southern Education Reporting Service Press Release, 7 September 1957, Box 6, Folder: "Integration — School Opening Sept. 1957," MSS 629, NABR; To Query Editor, *Newsweek*, n.d., 7, Box 13, Folder: Segregation and Mood South, NABR; Ed King, interview by Joyce Ladner, n.d., 3–4, Box 3, Folder 42, JLC; Southern Regional Council, "The Student Protest Movement" (special report), 1 April 1960, Box 25, Folder: Student Civil Rights, RLSP; Les Holingsworth, interview by George King, January 1992, 7, Box 10, Folder 16, SRCP. Kentucky officials anticipated that by the end of the 1957–58 school year, 80 percent of the state's black population would be attending integrated schools, all of Missouri's large cities would be integrated, half of Oklahoma's school population would be integrated, and Alabama, Arkansas, Maryland, North Carolina, Tennessee, Texas, and West Virginia all had achieved or planned to achieve some (albeit an often token) measure of integration. On the Southern Education Reporting Service, see Egerton, *Speak*, 616–17.

22 Quoted in Coles, "Serpents," 198.

23 Julian Bond, "Media and the Movement," 27–28.

24 Halberstam, *Children*, 391; Louis Dabney, interview by Paul Steen, 5 April 1949, Box 40, Folder 9, JHFP; Julie Prettyman, interview by Joyce Ladner, 27 April 1978, 10–11, Box 3, Folder 48, JLC; Huie, *Three Lives*, 95; Jones, "He Who Perpetrates"; Willie Osborne, interview by Binnie Myles, 17 November 1995, Volume 11, Section 7, OHP; Julian Bond, interview by Bob Hall and Sue Thrasher, December 1975, 15, Box 1, Folder 15, SRCP; Bagdikian, "Negro Youth's New March"; Blumberg, *Civil Rights*, 118; Hampton and Fayer with Flynn, *Voices*, 131; Morris F. Berkowitz quoted in Peter Kahn, "The Activist Students: They Take Part Increasingly in Social, Political Protests," *Wall Street Journal*, reprinted in *Selma Times-Journal*, 13 September 1965, Box 5, Folder: Civil Rights — Students, RLSP. Some older blacks commonly argued that greater equality would "happen in the Lord's good time." See, for example, Mr. Long, interview by Homer Maines Jr., April 1949, 5, Box 40, Folder 9, JHFP. In 1955, while searchers were looking for Emmett Till's body, "the body of a 14-year-old boy who liked to wear a CORE-lettered tee shirt was fished from the Big Black River near Canton, Miss." (Welsh, "Valley," 52).

25 Bob Moses, interview by Joyce Ladner, n.d., 4, Box 3, Folder 44, JLC; Carolyn Mc-Kinstry, interview by Horace Huntley, 23 April 1998, 9–10, Volume 35, Section 1, OHP; Miriam McClendon, interview by Horace Huntley, 8 November 1995, 6–9, Volume 11, Section 4, OHP; Deborah Sanders Avery, interview by Horace Huntley, 6 May 1998, 7, Volume 35, Section 4, OHP; Goff, *Problems*, 25, 36–38, 48–50. This study found that lower-income boys in St. Louis were the most likely to act on their aggressive impulses. It also suggested that the fact that girls more often reported feelings of inferiority might "indicate that in the process of development girls tend toward a heightened awareness of self." A number of scholars and participants have noted that girls often participated in movement activities more than boys because they faced less danger if they transgressed the color line and consequently grew up with less fear of white retaliation than boys. See, for example, Olson, *Freedom's Daughters*, 202. Girls did face the danger of rape, but it was unlikely to happen in a public setting. On the role of youth in the Birmingham demonstrations, see also *Mighty Times*.

26 Courtland Cox, interview by Joyce Ladner, 17 April 1978, 15, Box 3, Folder 34, JLC; Cleopatra Goree, interview by Horace Huntley, 29 April 1998, Volume 35, Section 2, OHP; Rallis Jones Jr., interview by Horace Huntley, 15 November 1995, 7–9, Volume 11, Section 6, OHP; Robert C. Smith, interview by Horace Huntley, 8 November 1995, 5, Volume 11, Section 3, OHP; Carl Imiola Young, *Carleton Voice*, Summer 1999, 21, Box 3, Folder 3, Kathleen Dahl Freedom Summer Collection, USM.

27 Hrabowski, "Role." Stephanie J. Shaw, *What a Woman Ought to Be*, similarly describes the ways that the black better classes tried to counter the negative influences of Jim Crow and give young black girls a positive sense of themselves, their race, and their future possibilities. Payne, *I've Got the Light*; Inge Powell Bell, *CORE*; Blumberg, *Civil Rights*; R. Scott Baker, *Paradoxes*; and others make similar points.

28 Andrew Young, interview by Eliot Wigginton, 8 July 1981, 6, Box 5, Folder 16, SRCP; "John" quoted in Coles, "Serpents," 197–98; Forman, *Making*, 20. On the socialization of black children in the Jim Crow South, see Ritterhouse, *Growing Up Jim Crow*. I do not mean to discount the importance of positive racial socialization efforts. R. Scott Baker, for one, makes a compelling case for the considerable influence of well-educated, progressive teachers on the rising generation of black activists. Building on the work of Ravitch, Tyack, and others, Baker suggests that "a new generation of teachers" promoted an activist stance toward racial inequalities. As he argues, the student activists of the 1950s and 1960s "were products of a generation of institutional development in African American schools and colleges" (*Paradoxes*, 38–43, 105–7, 118–20). See also Ravitch, *Left Back*, 377; Tyack, Lowe, and Hansot, *Public Schools*, 183–84. Other scholars similarly argue that student activism spread during this period at least partly because of the availability of a "visible protest model." See Aldon D. Morris, *Origins*, 222; Chafe, *Civilities*, esp. chap. 3.

29 James Cleo "Sam" Bradford quoted in Marian A. Allen, "Tougaloo College Involvement during the Civil Rights Movement; Emphasis: The Tougaloo Nine," 1 May   313
   1989, 4, Box 1, Folder 9, Tougaloo Nine Collection, Mississippi Department of Archives and History, Jackson, Miss.; Marie Hawthorne, interview by Bonnie Smith,
   29 January 1951, Box 41, Folder 16, JHFP; Claude Smith, interview by Mickey
   Korndorffer, 7 April 1960, Box 41, Folder 21, JHFP. In 84–94 percent of the cases
   that children reported to them, parents advised their children to withdraw from or
   avoid difficulties with whites, but children did not always choose to report interracial incidents to their parents (Goff, *Problems*, 62, 48–51, 57–59, 68, 81, 84). On
   young people and racial etiquette, see also Ritterhouse, *Growing Up Jim Crow*.
30 Marion A. Wright, "The Student's New Role," address before the Southern Student Human Relations Seminar of the U.S. National Student Association, Min-
   neapolis, Minn., 19 August 1960, Box 5, Folder: Civil Rights—Students, RLSP;
   E. Franklin Frazier, "Negro Urban Youth," address, Conference on the Needs of
   Negro Youth, Howard University, 15 July 1940, Box 100, Folder 10, HLP; Nancy L.
   Glenn, "Shut Your Mouth and Open Your Mind," *Nashville Tennessean*, reprinted
   in the *Tennessee Council on Human Relations Newsletter*, July–September 1963, 5,
   Box 8, Folder 3, IAP. Medgar Evers noted the importance of television and an
   expanded vision of the world to the movement when he said, "Tonight the Negro
   knows from his radio and television what happened today all over the world. He
   knows what black people are doing and he knows what white people are doing.
   . . . He knows about the new free nations in Africa. . . . Then he looks at his home
   community" (quoted in Roberts and Klibanoff, *Race Beat*, 337). *Brown* and young
   people's expanded sense of the world seem to have significantly affected young
   blacks' "sense of limits." What had once been seen as "the natural world" no longer
   seemed "self-evident and undisputed," to use Bourdieu's terms (*Outline*, 164).
31 Faye Bellamy, interview by Joyce Ladner, n.d., Box 3, Folder 28, JLC; Orthia Haley,
   interview by Joyce Ladner, 2 August 1978, 1, Box 3, Folder 41, JLC; Cleveland
   Sellers, interview by George King, June 1992, 2, Box 6, Folder 15, SRCP; Gaither,
   "Orangeburg," 9; Margaret L. Reid, "A Study of the Programs of American Student
   YMCA's in the Fields of Social Responsibility and World Relatedness," 1950, RG
   73, Series 3, Box 86, Folder 15, SEPC. On the Orangeburg student protests, see
   William Hine, "Civil Rights and Campus Wrongs," 315–33; Meier and Rudwick,
   CORE, 116–19; Lau, *Democracy Rising*, 218.
32 Carolyn McKinstry, interview by Horace Huntley, 23 April 1998, 6–7, Volume 35,
   Section 1, OHP; Amende, "Silence," 134.
33 Miriam McClendon, interview by Horace Huntley, 8 November 1995, 5–6, Volume
   11, Section 4, OHP; Rallis Jones Jr., interview by Horace Huntley, 15 November
   1995, 6–7, Volume 11, Section 6, OHP. Julian Bond has noted that "mainstream
   media coverage helped to spread news of southern civil rights activities to an audience far beyond the immediate locales where protests were taking place. This in
   turn helped to stimulate further activism, encouraging the growth of a genuine
   southern-wide mass movement" ("Media and the Movement," 26).

34 Townsend Davis, *Weary Feet*, 267. See also Whitfield, *Death*, 80; Payne, *I've Got the Light*, 54–56; Moody, *Coming of Age*, chap. 10; Metress, "On That Third Day"; Diggs quoted in Juan Williams, *Eyes*, 49; YWCA Secretary Yolanda Barnett paraphrased in Robert O. Blood, "Race Relations and New Haven Church Youth," 17, RG 73, Series 3, Box 66, Folder 9, SEPC.

35 Moody, *Coming of Age*, 110, 105–7, 128; Anne Moody, interview by Debra Spencer, 19 February 1985, 4–5, Box 2, Folder 39, MEC; Aaron Henry, interview by Jack Bass and Walter DeVries, 2 April 1974, Interview A-0107, Southern Oral History Project, SHC; Amende, "Silence," 135.

36 Sellers with Terrell, *River*, 10–16. In a 1992 interview, Sellers talked about the trauma of Till's murder, about his desire to avenge Till's death, and about Till as "a hero in my mind" (Cleveland Sellers, interview by George King, June 1992, 3, Box 6, Folder 15, SRCP).

37 Metress, "On That Third Day," 18, 21–22; Julian Bond, "Media and the Movement," 26–27); Ladner's notes and transcripts of various interviews with former civil rights activists, Box 3, Folder 69, JLC, esp. Cindy Breuning, "Jail Cells, Gender and Culture: A Perspective on the Civil Rights Movement in Mississippi, Interview by Dr. Joyce Ladner," n.d., 4; Howard Love, interview by George King, 14 January 1992, 12, Box 10, Folder 21, SRCP; Frank Smith, interview by Joyce Ladner, n.d., 13–14, Box 3, Folder 51, JLC; Bob Zellner, interview by Worth Long, 15 April 1996, 1, Box 5, Folder 17, SRCP; Ed King, interview by Joyce Ladner, n.d., 10, Box 3, Folder 42, JLC; Coles, "Serpents," 199. Bourdieu similarly suggests that "crisis is a necessary condition for a questioning of doxa," which he defines as our unconscious, seemingly natural "knowledge of the social world" (*Outline*, 169, 164).

38 Moody, *Coming of Age*, 107; Huie, "Shocking Story," 50. On the Till case's influence on youth activism, see also Fredrick Harris, "It Takes a Tragedy," 35–38.

39 Nash quoted in Juan Williams, *Eyes*, 131; John Jackson, Maudlin, and Murphy, interview, 6.

40 Superintendent T. J. McIlwaine quoted in Kluger, *Simple Justice*, 471; "Board Meeting Minutes, RE: Tougaloo College Students 'Read-In,' First Christian Church of Jackson," 17 April 1961, Box 1, Folder 2, Tougaloo Nine Collection, Mississippi Department of Archives and History, Jackson, Miss.; R. D. Robinson to Ed King, 4 June 1963, Box 2, Folder 51, EKC. Part of the unwillingness or reluctance of whites to consider the agency of black protesters was possibly because they made tremendous efforts to orchestrate white student protests and indoctrinate white children with white supremacist values. This was not the first or last example where whites and some blacks refused to acknowledge the agency of young people in the movement. See, for example, Payne's discussion of student protests in McComb, Mississippi, in *I've Got the Light*, 120. Lyles, "To Upset the City Fathers," examines civil rights protests in Mobile, Alabama. His research similarly indicates that whites commonly accused black adult organizers of using children as pawns and that organizers did not have any real support for their projects because much of their support came from young people. See also Olson, *Freedom's Daughters*, 79–

82; Kluger, *Simple Justice*, 467–80. On the Prince Edward protest, see also Robert Collins Smith, *They Closed Their Schools*; Robert Collins Smith, "Prince Edward County"; Foster and Foster, *Silent Trumpets*; Peeples, "Perspective"; Peeples, *Prince Edward County*; Neil Vincent Sullivan, *Bound*; Turner, "'Liberating Lifescripts.'"

41 Quoted in Olson, *Freedom's Daughters*, 82; Kluger, *Simple Justice*, 467, 470, 480, 467. On the importance of the "habitus" to one's "construction of reality" and to the questioning of reality, see Bourdieu, *Outline*, chaps. 2, 4.

42 See Kluger, *Simple Justice*, 469–71; Banks quoted in Robert Collins Smith, *They Closed Their Schools*, 55. On the important relationship between youth activism and community activism, see McNeil, "Youth Initiative," 70–75; R. Scott Baker, *Paradoxes*; Aldon D. Morris, *Origins*; Chafe, *Civilities*.

43 W. E. B. Du Bois, *Souls*, 3; Lyn Wells, "Purpose and Objectives of a Nation-Wide High School Conference," 1965, 3, Reel 55, Frame 955, SNCC Papers; Carolyn Smith, manuscript, n.d., Box 2, Folder 2, Joseph and Nancy Ellin Freedom Summer Collection, USM; Peter Gruenstein to SNCC, 1 April 1965, Reel 46, SNCC Papers; Matt Kessler to SNCC, 21 March 1965, Reel 46, SNCC Papers; Branda Hopkins, interview by Vivian Tumann, 7 April 1960, Box 42, Folder 1, JHFP; Floyd Banks, interview by Mary Lynn Dawon, 8 April 1960, Box 41, Folder 20, JHFP. See also other interviews in JHFP, Boxes 41–42; Jacqueline Byrd, who was fourteen when Bob Moses came to McComb and she started participating in civil rights work, quoted in Olson, *Freedom's Daughters*, 20; Elizabeth Sutherland, *Letters*, 23; un-identified clipping, n.d., Box 1, Folder 2, CCP. In the 1960s, perhaps influenced by the actions of young civil rights protesters, Keniston suggested that young people "have a kind of double consciousness, one part oriented to the adult world which they will soon enter, the other part geared to their version of the youth culture." Youth often "feel estranged and distant from what their elders represent" and can "see that older people are often genuinely confused themselves" ("Social Change," 213). McCain and other demonstrators also acknowledged their parents' support for and apprehension regarding their children's actions. Ritterhouse's research on young people in the Jim Crow era also suggests that the differences that the Prince Edward youth and other young activists sensed between themselves and the adults in their communities reflected a larger pattern of youth versus adult responses to segregation. Young people, she finds, even in the first decades of the twentieth century, were often angry and, in the words of one southern black woman, "ready for the fist." But because of their sexual maturation and increasing participation in the workforce, by the time they reached adulthood, African Americans usually reached some sort of accommodation with Jim Crow to survive (Ritterhouse, *Growing Up Jim Crow*, 182). Also pertinent is Ritterhouse's analysis of Charles S. Johnson's data from *Growing Up in the Black Belt*. Age, she notes, figured signifi-cantly in Johnson's findings. According to Johnson, the very different judgments about and levels of hostility toward the white race made by older and younger blacks indicates that black youth increasingly rejected stereotypes. Ritterhouse suggests that these data may instead indicate black young people's increasing ac-

commodation to whites (53–54, 209). My research on the history of the NAACP's youth councils correlates with Ritterhouse's findings that black youth were much less willing to accommodate to whites than were adults and much more inclined to engage in militant civil rights strategies. Powdermaker also observed differences between young people and their elders in the 1930s: most black adults in "Cotton-ville . . . go about their business taking the treatment they have become used to and shaking their head over the young folks who are laying themselves open to so much trouble" (*After Freedom*, 353). On the Greensboro sit-ins, see also Chafe, *Civilities*, 109–20.

44 Marion A. Wright, "The Student and a Changing Society," address before the student body of North Carolina College, Durham, N.C., 20 March 1961, 1–2, 9–10, Box 5, Folder: Civil Rights—Students, RLSP; Carr quoted in Peter Kahn, "The Activist Students: They Take Part Increasingly in Social, Political Protests," *Wall Street Journal*, reprinted in *Selma Times-Journal*, 13 September 1965, Box 5, Folder: Civil Rights—Students, RLSP; Bob Moses, interview by Joyce Ladner, n.d., 10, JLC.

45 See Payne, *I've Got the Light*, 82–89, 302; Grant, *Ella Baker*; Ransby, *Ella Baker*. Other important works that address Baker's role include Carson, *In Struggle*; Olson, *Freedom's Daughters*. Scholars such as Payne stress the mentoring relationships that notable civil rights leaders such as Baker, Medgar Evers, Aaron Henry, Rosa Parks, and Amzie Moore had with young people (all of whom were involved in NAACP youth councils and often in other youth organizations). But perhaps those leaders worked so closely with young people because of what young people offered them—perhaps young people influenced them as much as they influenced young people. Indeed, Baker and others—for example, Lillian Smith—often talked about getting their strength and vision from young people.

46 Kim and Dollie Burwell (daughter and mother), interview by Melynn Glusman, 19 April 1995, Interview G-0193, Southern Oral History Project, SHC; "Letter to Mr. Tiger (Brooklyn)," Reel 46, Frame 1083, SNCC Papers. SNCC commonly received letters from young people who wanted to "join" SNCC, and SNCC organizers commonly responded by questioning the idea or value of formal membership and organization.

47 See Willie Osborne, interview by Binnie Myles, 17 November 1995, Volume 11, Section 7, OHP; Rallis Jones Jr., interview by Horace Huntley, 15 November 1995, Volume 11, Section 6, OHP; Miriam McClendon, interview by Horace Huntley, 8 November 1995, Volume 11, Section 4, OHP; "Intensive Report on Marshall Sit-Ins," *Texas Observer*, 8 April 1960, 5, Box 1, Folder 4, CCP; Coles, "Serpents," 193. On the rational planning involved in youth civil rights activism, see also Aldon D. Morris, *Origins*, chap. 9. Morris also shows the importance of "preexisting [and ongoing community] resources"—adult organizational and institutional support for student-initiated demonstrations (206). See also Chafe, *Civilities*.

48 Peter Stoner, "A Glimpse into the Past: A Few Words about My Civil Rights Days," Peter Stoner Papers, USM; Bob Zellner, interview by Worth Long, 15 April 1996, 2,

Box 5, Folder 17, SRCP; Bob Zellner, interview by author, 2 May 2008; Julian Bond, interview by Bob Hall and Sue Thrasher, December 1975, 16, 21, Folder 15, SRCP; Howard Love, interview by George King, January 1992, 10, Box 10, Folder 21, SRCP. Political scientists have recently suggested that scholars need to combine organizational explanations and psychology-centered theories of social movements. See Goodwin, Jasper, and Polletta, *Passionate Politics*. See also Fredrick Harris, "It Takes a Tragedy." On racial uplift strategies, see, for example, Stephanie J. Shaw, *What a Woman Ought to Be*; Louis Hunton Berry, "Youth Faces Tomorrow," *Voice of Tomorrow*, March 1933, 5, Schomburg Center for Research in Black Culture, New York Public Library, New York, N.Y.; "What of the Young Negro Graduates," *Children's Call*, June 1932, 2, Schomburg Center for Research in Black Culture, New York Public Library, New York, N.Y.; "Success through Service," *Voice of Tomorrow*, March 1933, 3, Schomburg Center for Research in Black Culture, New York Public Library, New York, N.Y.

49 Frank James, interview by George King, January 1992, 3, Box 10, Folder 17, SRCP; Anne Moody, interview by Debra Spencer, 19 February 1985, 10, Box 2, File 39, MEC; "Yours for Freedom" (SNCC), 29 March 1965, Box 2, Folder 20, Joseph and Nancy Ellin Freedom Summer Collection, USM. Also reflective of this sentiment is a statement by Carl Holman, editor of the *Atlanta Inquirer*, the Atlanta student movement newsletter: "Cadillacs, split-level houses or freedom? To the students, freedom is the highest goal" (quoted in Tuck, *Beyond Atlanta*, 121). "Lifting as we climb" was the motto of the National Association of Colored Women.

50 Elizabeth Eckford et al., interview, n.d., 93, Box 10, Folder 1, SRCP; Les Holingsworth, interview by George King, January 1992, 12–14, Box 10, Folder 16, SRCP; Lottie Shackleford, interview by George King, February 1992, 4, Box 11, Folder 11, SRCP. Also telling about what young people gave up for the movement is the sense of loss that some activists later expressed about the choices they made to support desegregation efforts. Beals, *Warriors*, is one such account. R. Scott Baker, *Paradoxes*, includes other examples (163–65).

51 Roosevelt Peabody quoted in "Intensive Report on Marshall Sit-Ins," *Texas Observer*, 8 April 1960, 2, Box 1, Folder 4, CCP; Peter Kahn, "The Activist Students: They Take Part Increasingly in Social, Political Protests," *Wall Street Journal*, reprinted in *Selma Times-Journal*, 13 September 1965, Box 5, Folder: Civil Rights— Students, RLSP; R.D., "The Chilled Sunlight," *Texas Observer*, 11 March 1960, 4, clipping, Box 1, Folder 4, CCP.

52 In 1959, whites in many Virginia communities elected to close public schools rather than comply with integration orders. Prince Edward remained without public schools until 1964. On Virginia's "massive resistance," see Lassiter and Lewis, *Moderates' Dilemma*; Benjamin Muse, *Virginia's Massive Resistance*; Robert Collins Smith, *They Closed Their Schools*; James J. Kilpatrick, *Southern Case*; Robbins L. Gates, *Making*. On the details of the Moton High strike, see Kluger, *Simple Justice*, 467–72, 476–80. Kluger specifically notes that NAACP legal counselors were struck by how well-organized and determined the youth were (477). Many

civil rights organizers noted that young people "wanted something to do" (SNCC organizer Jesse Harrison quoted in Belfrage, *Freedom Summer*, 177; see also Robert Collins Smith, *They Closed Their Schools*, 53). J. Robert Keever comments on Virginia Union University protests in *Presbyterian Outlook*, 21 March 1960, 4, Box 1, Folder 12, CCP. "Who Leads the Sit-Down?: This Family is Typical," *Southern Patriot*, April 1960, Box 1, Folder 12, CCP. John Lewis's *Walking* also details the kind of planning that went into youth civil rights activity.

53 Thomas Reeves, "Letter to the Editor," *Birmingham Post-Herald*, March 1960, W. P. Ingram to Thomas Reeves, 20 March 1960, Thomas Reeves to W. P. Ingram, 28 March 1960, all in Box 1, Folder 4, CCP.

54 Johns quoted in Kluger, *Simple Justice*, 467; Caliver, "Certain Significant Developments," 114–17; Lindenmeyer, *Greatest Generation*, 224, 112, 138–39, 117, 146–47; Lau, "From the Periphery," 115; Chafe, *Civilities*, 23–24, chap. 3; Aldon D. Morris, *Origins*, 190, 196–97; R. Scott Baker, *Paradoxes*, 105–6, 118–24, 140–46, chaps. 6–8. See also Robert Collins Smith, *They Closed Their Schools*, 31. Like many rural southern communities, Farmville, in Prince Edward County, Virginia, did not have an African American high school until 1939 (Kluger, *Simple Justice*, 460). Baker's book also details the improvements white school boards made to South Carolina's black schools (greater expenditures for facilities, programs, and teachers' salaries) in the 1940s and early 1950s. Opportunities for black high school students in Birmingham also expanded considerably in the late 1930s and 1940s.

55 Rayburn, "That Civilization May Survive," 9; Raymond Tillman, interview by I. Joseph Jeffrion Jr., 1949, 6, Box 40, Folder 8, JHFP.

56 Mr. Johnson, interview by Betty Earle, April 1949, Box 40, Folder 8, JHFP; Frank Walker, interview by Joan Forshay, April 1949, Box 40, Folder 9, JHFP; Hodding Carter, "Segregation's Way," 34.

57 Sandra Baker, interview by Diane Gruber, 6 February 1959, Box 41, Folder 16, JHFP; "Report to the Board of Education, City of Chicago, by the Advisory Panel on Integration of the Public Schools," 31 March 1964, 10, Box 229, Folder 1, HLP; Eddie Trigs, interview by Kay Foster, January 1959, Box 41, Folder 16, JHFP; Ray Black, interview by Betty McGarry, 7 April 1960, Box 41, Folder 19, JHFP; Other Interviews, Boxes 41–42, JHFP. Although both girls and boys in these interviews talked about the psychological aspects of Jim Crow and to a lesser extent (or in conjunction with the psychological aspects) the educational and economic repercussions of segregation, in the 1959 interviews only girls identified the "social" aspects of segregation as especially disturbing (interview summary, January 1959, Box 41, Folder 18, JHFP). This finding fits with Delvin's important new research on gender and youth civil rights activism (*Linda Brown v. Board*).

58 Frank James, interview by George King, January 1992, 1–2, Box 10, Folder 17, SRCP; Julian Bond, interview by Bob Hall and Sue Thrasher, December 1975, 6–7, 13–14, Box 1, Folder 15, SRCP; Sandra Baker, interview by Diane Gruber, 6 February 1959, Box 42, Folder 16, JHFP; Claude Smith, interview by Mickey Korndorffer, 7 April 1960, Box 41, Folder 21, JHFP; Rudy Lombard and Lolis Elie, interview by Joyce

Ladner, n.d., 33–34, Box 3, Folder 38, JLC; Roy Wilkins, "Address at the Meeting of NAACP Branches in Mississippi," Jackson, Miss., 3 June 1956, 7, Box 2, Folder 38, MEC. Bond was not the only Atlanta student leader to have lived in another state (Tuck, *Beyond Atlanta*, 111). Wilkins's statement, which included a direct reference to Willie Mays, also suggests the importance of integrated professional sports to the civil rights movement. Laurie Beth Green, "Rejecting Mammy," explores the importance of mobility and the rural/urban exchange from the post–World War II era to civil rights protest. On Greensboro, see Chafe, *Civilities*, 113. Historians have shown that young black soldiers' experiences outside their own communities and the United States similarly influenced their responses to segregation once they returned home. Many scholars have talked about the media's role in civil rights protests of the 1950s and 1960s. Their accounts often give too much agency to the media and not enough to civil rights protesters. We need to consider television as one way — but certainly not the only way — that blacks and especially young blacks in the 1950s began to cross local community boundaries and in so doing began to imagine crossing local racial boundaries. Also contributing to (as well as symptomatic of) the explosion of youth activism in the early 1960s was the growth of correspondence among student organizations. Such correspondence spread news of student protests and support nationwide. See, for example, *U.S. National Student Association Civil Rights Newsletters*, weekly reports that began February 1961, Series 6, Folder 544, North Carolina Council on Human Relations, SHC.

59 See, for example, the stories related by Payne in *I've Got the Light*, 216, 218–19; Curtis, *Fighters*; Becker, *Negro*; McKean, *Up Hill*; Charles Robertson, interview by Joyce Ladner, n.d., 16, Box 3, Folder 49, JLC; Kluger, *Simple Justice*, 468–69. On the Greensboro youth, see Chafe, *Civilities*, 112–13. I do not mean to deny the collective/shared nature of all racial oppression in the United States but only to suggest that it was not always perceived in collective terms. As many scholars have shown, better-class blacks often differentiated their oppression from that of the lower classes, and blacks often accommodated themselves to many aspects of American racism even though they might challenge whites who tried to demand deference from them individually. See, for example, Greenwood, *Bittersweet Legacy*; Gaines, *Uplifting the Race*. Conversely, whites might see themselves as racial liberals based on their individual interactions with blacks but still countenance the collective oppression of African Americans under segregation or other racist policies. On working class black militancy, see Hunter, *To 'Joy My Freedom*; Kelley, *Race Rebels*; Honey, *Southern Labor*. Perhaps one reason why NAACP youth councils were usually more militant than adult branches had to do with their collective identity and shared experiences as youth. Adult members, who tended to be from the better classes and work in professional capacities, often in isolation either from lower-class blacks or from whites, came to the association as individuals, many of them already adept at negotiating or avoiding racial boundaries in their personal lives.

60 Rice, *I Came Out*, 26; Pahl, *Youth Ministry*, 76; Bevel's observations quoted in Blum-

berg, *Civil Rights*, 118, and Hampton and Fayer with Flynn, *Voices*, 131; Payne, *I've Got the Light*, 120, 185–86; Olson, *Freedom's Daughters*, 206–8; "Prospectus for a Summer Freedom School Program," Reel 38, Frames 326–28, 957–59, SNCC Papers; Johns, "Baton Rouge"; Jerome Smith, interview by Joyce Ladner, August 1978, 28–29, Box 3, Folder 52, JLC; "Ethel Sawyer Adolphe Recalls Library Sit-In," n.d., Box 1, Folder 8, Tougaloo Nine Collection, Mississippi Department of Archives and History, Jackson, Miss.; Ernest Green quoted in Hampton and Fayer with Flynn, *Voices*, 51. See also Ernest Green interview, n.d., Box 10, Folder 6, SRCP. On the spread of youth activism and its relationship to local movement centers, see Aldon D. Morris, *Origins*, chap. 9.

61 "Intensive Report on Marshall Sit-Ins," *Texas Observer*, 8 April 1960, 2, Box 1, Folder 4, CCP; Mary F. Witt, interview by Mausiki Scales, 17 April 1996, 8, Box 14, Folder 5, SRCP; Frank James, interview by George King, January 1992, 4, Box 10, Folder 17, SRCP; Howard Love, interview by George King, January 1992, 12, Box 10, Folder 21, SRCP; Julia Washington Bond, interview by Kathryn Finkelstein, 9 March 1976, 3, 13–14, Box 1, Folder 14, SRCP. White organizers such as Mary King and Casey Hayden became involved in the movement through the National Student YWCA. See Mary King, *Freedom Song*. My mother-in-law, Miriam Allen de Schweinitz, attended civil rights rallies as a member of Whitman College's YWCA. She also went with a YWCA delegation to a civil rights conference in Chicago. Letters from youth to SNCC organizers indicate that young people used a variety of religious and secular youth organizations to build a base for civil rights protest activity (Reel 46, SNCC Papers). Through its youth program, the NAACP was affiliated with a number of larger youth organizations or federations of youth organizations. The influence and significance of these youth federations on the civil rights movement deserves further scholarly consideration. On the significance of youth communities, see also Austin and Willard, *Generations*.

62 Mason, "Ambassadors," 8; Payne, *I've Got the Light*, 118, 225.

63 Lau, *Democracy Rising*, 85; Greene, *Our Separate Ways*; Lyn Wells, "To All SNCC Projects and Offices," 1965, Reel 55, Frame 902, SNCC Papers; Mintz, *Huck's Raft*, 314. On student activism in Baton Rouge, see also Sinclair, "Equal," 359–66.

64 John Stokes, student body vice president and state president of the New Farmers of America (the African American version of 4-H) quoted in Kluger, *Simple Justice*, 468. This quotation also appears in Robert Collins Smith, *They Closed Their Schools*, 34. On King's use of Isaiah 11:6, see Wilma King, *African American Childhoods*, 155.

65 Griffin and Johns quoted in Kluger, *Simple Justice*, 478–79; Sermon, 28 July 1951, quoted in Kluger, *Simple Justice*, 480. Griffin's use of social science arguments about the effects of racial prejudice and segregation on children and the black community's overwhelming response to his speech offer additional evidence that those arguments were less obscure and more important to the *Brown* ruling and civil rights developments than scholars have previously recognized.

66 Civic Interest Group Brochure (Baltimore, Md.), ca. 1960, Box 2, Folder 10, CCP.

67 Johns quoted in Kluger, *Simple Justice*, 478–79; McNeil, *Groundwork*, 11. Scholars have critiqued the emphasis on men's contributions to and participation in the civil rights movement and the lack of attention to women's often more obscure yet just as vital contributions. See, for example, Crawford, Rouse, and Woods, *Women*; Giddings, *When and Where*; Grant, *Ella Baker*; Greene, *Our Separate Ways*; Darlene Clark Hine, King, and Reed, *We Specialize*; Olson, *Freedom's Daughters*; Parks with Haskins, *Rosa Parks*; Jo Ann Gibson Robinson, *Montgomery Bus Boycott*; Robnett, *How Long?*; Deborah Gray White, *Too Heavy*.

68 See Halberstam, *Children*, 440–43. On the children's march in Birmingham, see also Branch, *Parting*, 752–802.

69 See, for example, Fairclough, *To Redeem the Soul*, 124.

70 Walker quoted in Hampton and Fayer with Flynn, *Voices*, 132, and in Fairclough, *To Redeem the Soul*, 124. King's decision to restrict participation in the march directly countered Bevel's original idea that it would specifically be a children's march. Bevel's concept of a children's march was based on the beliefs that America would pay attention if young people were involved and that children were eager to participate. See Halberstam, *Children*, 442–43.

71 Martin Luther King Jr., "A Creative Protest: American Students in the Struggle for Freedom," Durham, N.C., 16 February 1960, Box 1, Folder 12, CCP.

72 On Smith's attitude, see Payne, *I've Got the Light*, 393; Aaron Henry quoted in Dittmer, *Local People*, 122; "Prospectus for a Summer Freedom School Program," Reel 38, Frames 326–28, 957–59, SNCC Papers; Staughton Lynd, "Mississippi Freedom Schools: Retrospect and Prospect," Reel 38, Frame 335, SNCC Papers; Volunteer quoted in Payne, *I've Got the Light*, 305; McAdam, *Freedom Summer*, 107; "A Word from the Editors," *Freedom's Journal*, August 1964, Reel 38, Frame 265, SNCC Papers; Charles Cobb quoted in Payne, *I've Got the Light*, 178. Cobb was trying to correct the idea that outside youth activists were more central than local adults in the Mississippi movement, but like Payne, Cobb at times further obscures the important role that local youth played.

73 Payne, *I've Got the Light*, esp. 395; Dittmer, *Local People*. This focus on local adults in the movement nonetheless has filled in an important gap in movement history.

74 Thelweel quoted in Dittmer, *Local People*, 125. In just one example of youth influence on adult activism, the SCLC reported that after witnessing police brutality against student demonstrators, "the entire membership of the Martin (NC) County Teachers Association signed their names to a petition" (Press Release, 9 September 1963, Part 3, Reel 3, Frame 546, SCLC Papers). R. Scott Baker's *Paradoxes* is another important recent work that tells us something about youth activism but stresses adult influences on the younger generation.

75 Payne, *I've Got the Light*, 129; Bob Moses, "Letter from Magnolia Jail," 1 November 1961, *The Liberator*, 12 November 1961, 5, Box 2, Folder 5, CCP; A. D. Beittel to Bayard T. Van Hecke, 19 April 1961, Box 1, Folder 2, Tougaloo Nine Collection, Mississippi Department of Archives and History, Jackson, Miss.; "Twelve

Year Old Girl May Be Another Rosa Parks," *The Liberator*, 12 November 1961, 5, Box 2, Folder 5, CCP; Sandra Adickes, Freedom Summer Journal, 14 July 1964, 16, Sandra E. Adickes Papers, USM; "A Word from the Editors," *Freedom's Journal*, August 1964, Reel 38, Frame 265, SNCC Papers; Joyce Brown, "The House of Liberty" (a poem by a fifteen-year-old McComb freedom school student that was widely circulated in SNCC correspondence and promotional materials), Reel 55, Frame 186, SNCC Papers; Thomas Merton, "The Black Revolution," Part 3, Series 9, Subseries 3, Reel 4, Frames 559–67, SCLC Papers; Hrabowski, "Role," 3. Both Payne and Dittmer demonstrate that young people were among the first and sometimes only supporters of civil rights in local communities. Payne specifically notes that McComb, which is usually described as a "failure," was only a failure in the narrowest sense because young people there began to identify with and participate in the movement. But both scholars also tend to value adult over youth participation and even minimize the contributions of "youngsters." The use of the demeaning term "youngsters," especially in an era in which scholars are well aware of the importance of language, makes it even more difficult for readers to value young people as significant and independent political actors. Branch, *Parting*, also teaches us much about youth activism of the period, but he, too, emphasizes adults—especially Martin Luther King Jr. Many volunteers commented on young people's unexpected and overwhelming response to the freedom schools. See, for example, Staughton Lynd, "Mississippi Freedom Schools: Retrospect and Prospect," 26 July 1964, 1, Reel 38, Frame 333, SNCC Papers. Freedom schools had been at least partly developed to "raise the expectations" of black youth, but their participation suggests that their expectations had already been raised.

76 Bevel quoted in Hampton and Fayer with Flynn, *Voices*, 131–32; Peter Kahn, "The Activist Students: They Take Part Increasingly in Social, Political Protests," *Wall Street Journal*, reprinted in *Selma Times-Journal*, 13 September 1965, Box 5, Folder: Civil Rights—Students, RLSP; Lyn Wells, "To All SNCC Projects and Offices," 1965, Reel 55, Frame 902, SNCC Papers; Johns quoted in Robert Collins Smith, *They Closed Their Schools*, 53; *Voice of the Movement*, 23 April 1964, Box 2, Folder 79, EKC; Lyn Wells to W. Marvin Watson, 6 May 1965, Reel 55, Frame 900, SNCC Papers; Albany leader quoted in Carson, *In Struggle*, 58; "Dinez" quoted in "Residential Freedom School Report," August 1965, Reel 35, Frame 81, SNCC Papers. Similar comments about youth taking action or being ready to take action regardless of adult or organizational support surrounded movement activities. See Dittmer, *Local People*, Payne, *I've Got the Light*; Reavis, *If White Kids Die*. Scholars have pointed out that Zellner's race shaped perceptions of him as the "leader" of the march. One reason why King and others saw using children merely as a strategy was that they saw themselves as engaged in an effort to "redeem and enlighten" whites. Young people, conversely, were often less interested in redeeming whites than in doing something to change America's racist sociopolitical order, which helps explain SNCC's transformation from nonviolence to militancy. On the SCLC's philosophy, see Thomas Merton, "The Black Revolution," Part 3, Series 9, Subseries 3, Reel 4, Frames 559–67, SCLC Papers.

77 On youth participation in Mobile, see Lyles, "To Upset the City Fathers"; on Zellner, see Payne, *I've Got the Light*, 403; Dittmer, *Local People*, 110–11; Sandra Adickes, Freedom Summer Journal, 14 August 1964, 11, Sandra E. Adickes Papers, USM; on the Galveston case, see Kenneth Morland, "Lunch-Counter Desegregation in Corpus Christi, Galveston, and San Antonio, Texas," Special Report, Southern Regional Council, 10 May 1960, Series 1, Box 2, Reed Sarratt Pappers, SHC. See also "Look at the World's Week," 28. As Dittmer notes, SNCC organizers worried that locals might think that SNCC was using their children. The Galveston students were led by sixteen-year-old Kelton Sams, who reported that they had "no outside help from the NAACP or from any other city, but wanted to do something and were affected by 'but were not trying to imitate' the South-wide sit-ins" ("Galveston: A Contrast," *Texas Observer*, 8 April 1960, 5, Box 1, Folder 4, CCP).

78 Olson, *Freedom's Daughters*, 92–93; Mary F. Witt, interview by Mausiki Scales, 17 April 1996, 5–9, Box 14, Folder 5, SRCP; Robertson, interview; Robert Collins Smith, "Prince Edward County," 2. Perhaps the best expression of young people's lack of concern for recognition was Joyce Brown's poem, "The House of Liberty," which starts, "I came not for fortune, nor for fame, / I seek not to add glory to an unknown name" (Reel 55, Frame 186, SNCC Papers).

79 Liz Fusco, "Freedom Schools in Mississippi 1964," Reel 68, Frames 224–26, SNCC Papers; Bevel quoted in Fairclough, *To Redeem the Soul*, 362; Reagon, "Ella's Song"; Moses quoted in Payne, *I've Got the Light*, 250; Gerald Hoag, interview by I. Joseph Jeffrion Jr. (interviews with black New Orleanians), 1949, 2, Box 40, Folder 8, JHFP; John Jackson, Maudlin, and Murphy, interview, 6, 15; Joyce Brown, "The House of Liberty," Reel 55, Frame 186, SNCC Papers; Teresa Clark, "Palmer's Crossing Freedom School," *Freedom News*, 23 July 1964, 5, Box 1, Folder 2, Sandra E. Adickes Papers, USM. "Ella's Song," written and performed by Bernice Johnson Reagon, is sung as if Baker is speaking and even uses some of Baker's words. Moses's current "Algebra Project" suggests that he continues to see young people as the "seeds of change." See Moses and Cobb, *Radical Equations*.

AFTERWORD

1 See Light, *Delta Time*, 33, 49, 85, 15, 112, 125.

2 Marian Wright Edelman's work with the Children's Defense Fund is a prime example. As historian Ethan Sribnick explains, Edelman developed an "ideology of children's rights" as a strategy for addressing the problems of poverty and race in the politically conservative climate of the 1970s (and today) ("Marian Wright Edelman"). Other examples include Jonathan Kozol, *Amazing Grace*; Kotlowitz, *There Are No Children*. Kozol taught in Boston's public schools in the late 1960s but lost his job as a result of pressure from white parents who were upset in general about efforts to end de facto segregation through busing and specifically about his efforts to teach black poetry and literature.

3 Cottle, *Time's Children*, 323–24.

BIBLIOGRAPHY

ARCHIVAL SOURCES

Ann Arbor, Mich.
  University of Michigan, Bentley Historical Library
    Howard Y. McClusky Collection
Atlanta, Ga.
  Emory University, Robert W. Woodruff Library, Manuscript,
        Archives, and Rare Book Library
    Black Print Culture Collection
    Constance W. Curry Papers
    Ralph McGill Papers
    Newsweek Atlanta Bureau Records
    Southern Regional Council Papers
    Richard L. Stevens Papers
  Martin Luther King Jr. Center, Library and Archives
    Southern Christian Leadership Papers (microfilm)
    Student Non-Violent Coordinating Committee Papers (microfilm)
Birmingham, Ala.
  Birmingham Civil Rights Institute
    Oral History Project
  Birmingham Public Library, Archives Department
    American States' Rights Association Papers
    Southern Regional Council Papers (copies; originals in Atlanta, Ga.)
Chapel Hill, N.C.
  University of North Carolina, Southern Historical Collection
    Robert Coles Papers
    Ku Klux Klan Papers
    North Carolina Council on Human Relations Papers
    Reed Sarratt Papers
    Southern Education Board Papers
    Southern Oral History Project

College Park, Md.
    National Archives II
        Children's Bureau Papers
Hattiesburg, Miss.
    University of Southern Mississippi, McCain Library
            and Archives, Historical Manuscripts
        Sandra E. Adickes Papers
        Kathleen Dahl Freedom Summer Collection
        Joseph and Nancy Ellin Freedom Summer Collection
        Peter Stoner Papers
Jackson, Miss.
    Mississippi Department of Archives and History
        Medgar Evers Collection
        Ed King Collection
        Joyce Ladner Collection
        Tougaloo Nine Collection
New Haven, Conn.
    Yale University, Yale Divinity Library
        Social Ethics Pamphlet Collection
        YMCA Student Division Papers
New Orleans, La.
    Loyola University–New Orleans, J. Edgar and Louise S. Monroe
            Library, Special Collections and Archives
        Joseph H. Fichter Papers
    Tulane University, Amistad Research Center
        Inez Adams Papers
        Hylan Lewis Papers
        National Association of Human Rights Workers Archives
        Save Our Schools Collection
        Lillian Voorhees Papers
New York, N.Y.
    Schomburg Center for Research in Black Culture, New York Public Library
        General Research and Reference Division
        Photographs and Prints Division
            William Pickins Photograph Collection
Palo Alto, Calif.
    Stanford University, Hoover Institution Library and Archives
        American Council on Education Records
Richmond, Va.
    Virginia Historical Society
        Aubrey Neblett Brown Jr. Papers
Sleepy Hollow, N.Y.
    Rockefeller Archive Center
        General Education Board Papers

Washington, D.C.

Library of Congress

Collections on Microfilm

Congress of Racial Equality Papers

National Association for the Advancement of Colored People Papers

Southern Christian Leadership Conference Papers

Manuscripts Division

Children's Crusade for Children Papers

National Association for the Advancement of Colored People Papers

National Child Labor Committee Papers

National Consumer's League Papers

Simon E. Sobeloff Papers

SELECTED NEWSPAPERS AND PERIODICALS

Birmingham (Ala.) News

Boston Evening Post

Brownies' Book

Chicago Defender

The Child (Children after 1954)

The Citizen

The Crisis

Jackson (Miss.) Clarion-Ledger

Journal of Educational Sociology
 (*Sociology of Education*, after 1963)

Journal of Educational Research

Kindergarten and First Grade Magazine

Intercultural Education News

Interracial Bulletin for Children

Liberty Bell

Life

Little Rock Arkansas Gazette

Look

Memphis (Tenn.) Commercial Appeal

The Nation

National Education Association Journal

National Parent-Teacher

Negro Digest

New Republic

New South Notes

Newsweek

New York Herald Tribune

New York Post

New York Times

New York University Law Review

Norfolk (Va.) Journal and Guide

Phylon

Saturday Evening Post

School Life

Science and Society

Slave's Friend

Sociology and Social Research

Survey Graphic

Time

BOOKS, ARTICLES, ESSAYS, DISSERTATIONS, PAPERS, AND FILMS

Abbott, Grace. "A Message to Colored Mothers." *The Crisis*, October 1932, 311–12, 332.

Adamic, Louis. "Will Racism Lead to World War III?" *Negro Digest*, September 1947, 8–13.

Adams, Edward L., Jr., William B. Dreffin, Robert B. Kamm, and Dyckman W. Vermilye. "Attitudes with Regard to Minority Groups of a Sampling of University

Men Students from the Upper Socioeconomic Level." *Journal of Educational Sociology* 21 (February 1948): 328–38.

Adams, Faith. "A Question to Democracy." *The Nation*, 10 November 1920. Reprinted in *Burning All Illusions: Writings from "The Nation" on Race, 1866–2002*, edited by Paula Giddings, 16–17. New York: Thunder Mouth/Nation, 2002.

Agee, James, and Walker Evans. *Let Us Now Praise Famous Men*. Boston: Houghton Mifflin, 1941.

"An Alabaman's Great Speech Lays the Blame." *Life*, 27 September 1963, 44B–C.

Alexander, Carlena. "Wandering Negro Boys." *The Crisis*, May 1933, 107, 118.

Allen, Lewis. "Strange Fruit." New York: Marks Music, 1939.

Alpenfels, Ethel J. "The Price of Prejudice." *National Parent-Teacher* 42 (February 1948): 4–6.

Alpern, Hymen. "The Role of the High Schools in Improving Intercultural Relations." *Journal of Educational Sociology* 16 (February 1943): 363–67.

Amende, Kathaleen. "Silence and the Frustration of Broken Promises: Anne Moody's Struggle with the Lynching of Emmett Till." In *Emmett Till in Literary Memory and Imagination*, edited by Harriet Pollack and Christopher Metress, 128–42. Baton Rouge: Louisiana State University Press, 2008.

Anderson, Nels. "Highlights of the Migrant Problem Today." In *National Conference of Social Work*, 109–17. N.p., 1940.

Annual Report of the American Anti-Slavery Society for the Year Ending May 1, 1859. New York: American Anti-Slavery Society, 1860.

Answers for Action: Schools in the South. Atlanta: Southern Regional Council, 1954.

The Anti-Slavery Alphabet. Philadelphia: Merrihew and Thompson, 1847.

Ariès, Philippe. *Centuries of Childhood: A Social History of Family Life*. Translated by Robert Baldick. New York: Knopf, 1962.

Armor, David J. *Forced Justice: School Desegregation and the Law*. New York: Oxford University Press, 1995.

Arter, Rhetta M. "The Effects of Prejudice on Children." *Children* 6 (September–October 1959): 185–89.

"As Others See Us: World Opinion on the School Crisis." *Little Rock Arkansas Gazette*, September 1957.

"Aspects of the Till Case Still Haunt Us." *New South Notes*, November 1955, 12.

"Auspice." "To the Editor of the Gazette." *Little Rock Arkansas Gazette*, 18 September 1963.

Austin, Joe, and Michael Nevi Willard, eds. *Generations of Youth: Youth Cultures and History in Twentieth-Century America*. New York: New York University Press, 1998.

Badger, Anthony J. *The New Deal: The Depression Years, 1933–1940*. New York: Macmillan, 1989.

Bagdikian, Ben H. "Negro Youth's New March on Dixie." *Saturday Evening Post*, 8 September 1962, 15–19.

Baker, R. Scott. *Paradoxes of Desegregation: African American Struggles for Educational Equity in Charleston, South Carolina, 1926–1972*. Columbia: University of South Carolina Press, 2006.

Baker, Russell. "Capital Is Occupied by a Gentle Army." *New York Times*, 29 August 1963. Reprinted in *Voices in Our Blood: America's Best on the Civil Rights Movement*, edited by Jon Meacham, 288–92. New York: Random House, 2003.

Baldwin, James. "Fifth Avenue, Uptown." *Esquire*, July 1960. Reprinted in *Smiling through the Apocalypse: Esquire's History of the Sixties*, edited by Harold Hayes, 643–50. New York: McCall, 1969.

———. *Notes of a Native Son*. New York: Dial, 1963.

Balien, Preston. "I Attended the NSL Conference." *The Crisis*, March 1934, 67–68.

"Baltimore Youth." *The Crisis*, April 1933, 89.

Banfield, Beryle, and Geraldine L. Wilson. "The Black Experience through White Eyes—The Same Old Story Once Again." *Interracial Bulletin for Children* 14, no. 5 (1983): 4–13.

Bardaglio, Peter W. *Reconstructing the Household: Families, Sex, and the Law in the Nineteenth-Century South*. Chapel Hill: University of North Carolina Press, 1995.

Bates, Daisy. *The Long Shadow of Little Rock*. New York: McKay, 1962.

Bateson, Gregory, and Margaret Mead. *Balinese Character: A Photographic Analysis*. New York: New York Academy of Sciences, 1942.

"The Battle of Nashville." *Time*, 23 September 1957, 14–16.

Beals, Melba Pattillo. *Warriors Don't Cry: A Searing Memoir of the Battle to Integrate Little Rock's Central High*. New York: Pocket, 1994.

"Beautiful Child Contest." *The Crisis*, April 1940, 99.

Becker, John. *The Negro in American Life*. New York: Messner, 1944.

Beim, Lorrain, and Jerrold Beim. *Two Is a Team*. New York: Harcourt, Brace, 1945.

Belfrage, Sally. *Freedom Summer*. New York: Viking, 1965.

Bell, Derrik A., Jr. "*Brown v. Board of Education* and the Interest-Convergence Dilemma." *Harvard Law Review* 93, no. 3 (January 1980): 518–33.

Bell, Howard M. *Youth Tell Their Story: A Study of the Conditions and Attitudes of Young People in Maryland between the Ages of 16 and 24*. Washington, D.C.: American Council on Education, 1938.

Bell, Inge Powell. *CORE and the Strategy of Nonviolence*. New York: Random House, 1968.

Benedict, Agnes E. "Young Nomads." *Survey*, 15 December 1926, 376–77.

Benedict, Ruth. *Patterns of Culture*. Boston: Houghton Mifflin, 1959.

Benjamin, Harold R., and Floyde Brooker. "UNESCO." *School Life*, October 1946, 9–10, 31.

Bettelheim, Bruno, and Morris Janowitz. *Social Change and the Dynamics of Prejudice: Including Dynamics of Prejudice*. 1950; New York: Free Press of Glencoe, 1964.

Bishop, L. K. "Character for a New-Built World." *National Parent-Teacher* 41 (February 1947): 27–29.

Blake, John. *Children of the Movement: The Sons and Daughters of Martin Luther King Jr., Malcolm X, Elijah Muhammad, George Wallace, Andrew Young, Bob Moses, James Chaney, Elaine Brown, and Others Reveal How the Civil Rights Movement Tested and Transformed Their Families*. Chicago: Hill, 2004.

Blanshard, Paul. "Negro Delinquency in New York." *Journal of Educational Sociology* 16 (October 1942): 115–23.

Block, Jim. "The Politics of Modern Childhood: American Socialization and the Crisis of Individualism." In *The Politics of Childhood: International Perspectives, Contemporary Developments*, edited by James Goddard, Sally McNamee, Adrian James, and Allison James, 32–49. New York: Palgrave Macmillan, 2005.

Bloom, John. "Rolling with the Punches: Boxing, Youth Culture, and Ethnic Identity at Federal Indian Boarding Schools during the 1930s." In *Generations of Youth: Youth Cultures and History in Twentieth-Century America*, edited by Joe Austin and Michael Nevi Willard, 65–80. New York: New York University Press, 1998.

Blumberg, Rhoda Louis. *Civil Rights: The 1960s Freedom Struggle*. Rev. ed. Boston: Twayne, 1991.

Bond, Horace Mann. *The Education of the Negro in the American Social Order*. New York: Prentice-Hall, 1934.

Bond, James. "The Education of the Bond Family." *The Crisis*, April 1927, 41.

Bond, Julian. "The Media and the Movement: Looking Back from the Southern Front." In *Media, Culture, and the Modern African American Freedom Struggle*, edited by Brian Ward, 16–40. Gainesville: University Press of Florida, 2001.

Bontemps, Arna. *Sad-Faced Boy*. Boston: Houghton Mifflin, 1937.

———. *You Can't Pet a Possum*. New York: Morrow, 1934.

Bontemps, Arna, and Langston Hughes. *Popo and Fifina: Children of Haiti*. New York: Macmillan, 1932.

Borgwardt, Elizabeth. *A New Deal for the World: America's Vision for Human Rights*. Cambridge: Belknap Press of Harvard University Press, 2005.

Bourdieu, Pierre. *Outline of a Theory of Practice*. Translated by Richard Nice. Cambridge: Cambridge University Press, 1977.

"A Boy Goes Home." *Newsweek*, 12 September 1955, 32.

Boyle, Kevin. *Arc of Justice: A Saga of Race, Civil Rights, and Murder in the Jazz Age*. New York: Holt, 2004.

"Boys and Girls of Detroit." *The Crisis*, October 1924, 272–74.

Bradley, Louise. "Afraid to Walk Alone at Night." *Birmingham News*, 29 September 1957.

Bragg, Susan. "Marketing the 'Modern' Negro: Race, Gender, and the Culture of Activism in the NAACP, 1909–1941." Ph.D. diss., University of Washington, 2007.

Brameld, Theodore. "Educational Costs." In *Discrimination and National Welfare: A Series of Addresses and Discussions*, edited by Robert M. MacIver, 37–48. 1949; Port Washington, N.Y.: Kennikat, 1969.

Branch, Taylor. *Parting the Waters: America in the King Years, 1954–1963*. New York: Simon and Schuster, 1988.

Bremner, Robert H., ed. *Children and Youth in America: A Documentary Reader*. 3 vols. Cambridge: Harvard University Press, 1970–74.

Brown, Mrs. I. M. "Call to Negroes to Turn a Deaf Ear." *Birmingham News*, 28 September 1957.

Brown, Tony N., and Chase L. Lesane-Brown. "Race Socialization Messages across Time." *Social Psychology Quarterly* 69, no. 2 (June 2006): 201–12.

Brownmiller, Susan. *Against Our Will: Men, Women, and Rape*. New York: Simon and
Schuster, 1975.

Brundage, W. Fitzhugh. *Lynching in the New South: Georgia and Virginia, 1880–1930*.
Urbana: University of Illinois Press, 1993.

Buck, Pearl S. "Save the Children, for What?" *Journal of Educational Sociology* 17
(December 1943): 195–99.

Burgum, Edwin Berry. "The Promise of Democracy and the Fiction of Richard
Wright." *Science and Society* 7 (Winter 1943): 338–52.

Burrell, Anna Porter. "American Education, the Contribution to 'The Dignity and
Worth of the Individual.'" *Journal of Educational Sociology* 21 (April 1948): 442–53.

Butler, Mrs. H. R. "Forward with the White House Conference." *The Crisis*, November
1930, 374–75.

Cahn, Edmond. "Jurisprudence." *New York University Law Review* 30 (January 1955):
150–69.

Caliver, Ambrose. "Certain Significant Developments in the Education of Negroes
during the Past Generation." *Journal of Negro History* 35 (April 1950): 111–34.

———. "The Negro Child in the World Chaos." *Journal of Educational Sociology* 17
(December 1943): 230–37.

———. "Project for the Adult Education of Negroes." *School Life*, November 1948,
4–5.

———. "Secondary Schools for Negroes." *School Life*, July 1940, 308–9, 320.

Caliver, Ambrose, and Joseph H. Douglass. "The Education of Negroes: Some Factors
Relating to Its Quality." *School Life*, June 1954, 134–35.

Caliver, Ambrose, and Theresa Wilkins. "Education of Negroes: Successful Transition
from Segregated to Unsegregated Schools." *School Life*, April 1954, 101, 111–12.

Carbine, Patricia. "An Arkansas Junior Pointed the Way." *Look*, 9 December 1958,
24–25.

Carson, Clayborne. *In Struggle: SNCC and the Black Awakening of the 1960s*.
Cambridge: Harvard University Press, 1981.

Carstens, C. C. "Child Labor." *Child Welfare League of America Bulletin*, February 1937, 4.

Carter, Hodding. "Segregation's Way in One Southern Town." *New York Times
Magazine*, 5 April 1953, 34.

Carter, Robert L. *A Matter of Law: A Memoir of Struggle in the Cause of Equal Rights*.
New York: New Press, 2005.

Cavallo, Dominick. *Muscles and Morals: Organized Playgrounds and Urban Reform,
1880–1920*. Philadelphia: University of Pennsylvania Press, 1981.

Chafe, William H. *Civilities and Civil Rights: Greensboro, North Carolina, and the Black
Struggle for Freedom*. New York: Oxford University Press, 1980.

Chamberlain, John. "Our Jobless Youth: A Warning." *Survey Graphic* 28 (October
1939): 578–82.

Chambers, M. M. "Culture Conflicts and the Welfare of Youth." *Journal of Educational
Sociology* 12 (April 1939): 463–69.

———. *Youth-Serving Organizations*. 2nd ed. Washington, D.C.: American Council
on Education, 1941.

"Charge Two Men in Kidnaping." *Jackson Clarion-Ledger*, 30 August 1955.

Chein, Isidor, and Leo Laks. "Attitudes and the Educational Process." *Journal of Educational Sociology* 19 (February 1946): 365–75.

"Child Labor: Child Labor in Sugar Beets." *The Child*, May 1937, 17.

Children's Bureau Commission on Children in Wartime. "A Children's Charter in Wartime." *The Child*, April 1942, 245–48.

The Child's Anti-Slavery Book: Containing a Few Words about American Slave Children and Stories of Slave Life. New York: Carlton and Porter, 1859.

"Child-Welfare Services in Rural Areas." *The Child*, May 1938, 156.

Chisholm, Ann J. "Letter to the Editor." *Look*, 6 March 1956, 12.

"Chronica Regiae Coloniensis Continuatio Prima, s.a. 1213, MGH, SS, XXIV, 17–18." In *The Crusades: A Documentary Survey*, edited by James Brundage, 213. Milwaukee: Marquette University Press, 1962.

"City Leaders Express Grief, Shock over Church Bombing." *Birmingham News*, 16 September 1963.

"City's People All Victims, Mostly Innocent." *Birmingham News*, 18 September 1963.

Clapp, Elizabeth J. *Mothers of All Children: Women Reformers and the Rise of Juvenile Courts in Progressive Era America*. University Park: Pennsylvania State University Press, 1988.

Clark, Ann Nolan. *Secret of the Andes*. New York: Viking, 1952.

Clark, Kenneth B., and Mamie P. Clark. "Race Prejudice and Children." *The Child*, March 1953, 113–15.

———. "Racial Identification and Preference in Negro Children." In *Readings in Social Psychology*, 3rd ed., edited by Eleanor E. Maccoby, Theodore M. Newcomb, and Eugene L. Hartley, 602–11. New York: Holt, 1958.

Coggins, Frank. "I Hate Negroes." *Negro Digest*, September 1946, 71–73.

Cohen, Robert. *When the Old Left Was Young: Student Radicals and America's First Mass Student Movement, 1929–1941*. New York: Oxford University Press, 1993.

Cohen, Ronald D. "Child-Saving and Progressivism, 1885–1915." In *American Childhood: A Research Guide and Historical Handbook*, edited by Joseph M. Hawes and N. Ray Hiner, 273–310. Westport, Conn.: Greenwood, 1985.

Coles, Robert. "Children and Racial Demonstrations." *American Scholar* 34 (Winter 1964–65): 78–92.

———. "On Courage." *Contemporary Psychoanalysis* 1 (Spring 1965): 85–98.

———. *The Political Life of Children*. Boston: Atlantic Monthly Press, 1986.

———. "Reconsideration: J. D. Salinger." *New Republic*, 28 April 1973, 30–32.

———. "Serpents and Doves: Non-Violent Youth in the South." In *Youth: Change and Challenge*, edited by Erik H. Erikson, 188–216. New York: Basic Books, 1963.

Colin, Mattie Smith, and Robert Elliott. "Mother Waits in Vain for Her 'Bo.'" *Chicago Defender*, 10 September 1955. Reprinted in *The Lynching of Emmett Till: A Narrative History*, edited by Christopher Metress, 30–31. Charlottesville: University of Virginia Press, 2002.

College Courses in Race Relations: An Effort to Meet the Challenge of the Southern Situation. Atlanta: Conference on Education and Race Relations, 1939.

Collier-Thomas, Bettye, and V. P. Franklin. *My Soul Is a Witness: A Chronology of the Civil Rights Era, 1954–1965.* New York: Holt, 2000.

Collins, Henry Hill, Jr. *America's Own Refugees: Our 4,000,000 Homeless Migrants.* Princeton: Princeton University Press, 1941.

Collins, James. "Taking the Lead: Dorothy Williams, the NAACP Youth Councils, and Civil Rights Protests in Pittsburgh, 1961–1964." *Journal of African American History* 88 (Spring 2003): 126–37.

"Conference on Children in a Democracy Called by the President." *The Child,* February 1939, 171.

Cope, Graeme. "A Thorn in the Side?: The Mother's League of Central High School and the Little Rock Desegregation Crisis of 1957." *Arkansas Historical Quarterly* 57 (Summer 1998): 160–90.

Cothran, Tilman C. "Integration and Educational Standards." *New South Notes,* May 1956, 12.

Cottle, Thomas J. *Time's Children: Impressions of Youth.* Boston: Little, Brown, 1967.

Cox, Alice. "The Rainey Affair: A History of the Academic Freedom Controversy at the University of Texas, 1938–1946." Ph.D. diss., University of Denver, 1970.

Cravens, Hamilton. "Child-Saving in the Age of Professionalism, 1915–1930." In *American Childhood: A Research Guide and Historical Handbook,* edited by Joseph M. Hawes and N. Ray Hiner, 415–88. Westport, Conn.: Greenwood, 1985.

Crawford, Vickie L., Jacqueline Anne Rouse, and Barbara Woods, eds. *Women in the Civil Rights Movement: Trailblazers and Torchbearers, 1941–1965.* Brooklyn, N.Y.: Carlson, 1990.

Cremin, Lawrence A. *American Education: The Colonial Experience, 1607–1783.* New York: Harper and Row, 1971.

Crespino, Joseph. *In Search of Another Country: Mississippi and the Conservative Counterrevolution.* Princeton: Princeton University Press, 2007.

"Crisis in Education." *Life,* 25 March 1958, 25–35.

Curriculum in Intergroup Relations: Case Studies in Instruction. Washington, D.C.: American Council on Education, 1949.

Curtis, Clara K. *Fighters for Freedom.* Rochester, N.Y.: privately printed, 1933.

Dabney, Virginius. "Virginia's 'Peaceable, Honorable Stand.'" *Life,* 22 September 1958, 51–52, 55–56.

Dalfiume, Richard M. "The 'Forgotten' Years of the Negro Revolution." *Journal of American History* 55 (June 1968): 90–106.

The Darkies ABCs. New York: International Art, n.d.

Davie, Maurice R. "Minorities: A Challenge to American Democracy." *Journal of Educational Sociology* 12 (April 1939): 451–56.

Davis, Allison, and John Dollard. *Children of Bondage: The Personality Development of Negro Youth in the Urban South.* Washington, D.C.: American Council on Education, 1940.

Davis, Allison, Burleigh B. Gardner, and Mary R. Gardner. *Deep South: A Social Anthropological Study of Caste and Class.* Chicago: University of Chicago Press, 1941.

Davis, Annie Lee. "Attitudes toward Minority Groups: Their Effects on Social Services for Unmarried Mothers." *The Child*, December 1948, 82–85.

Davis, Townsend. *Weary Feet, Rested Souls: A Guided History of the Civil Rights Movement*. New York: Norton, 1998.

Dawson, Howard A. "The Federal Government and Education." *Journal of Educational Sociology* 12 (December 1938): 226–43.

"The Day a Church Became a Tomb." *Birmingham News*, 16 September 1963.

"Death in Mississippi." *Commonweal*, 23 September 1955, 603–4.

"Declaration of the National Anti-Slavery Convention." In *First Annual Report of the American Anti-Slavery Society*. New York: American Anti-Slavery Society, 1834. Reprinted as "Declaration of the American Anti-Slavery Society." In *The Negro in American History*, vol. 3, *Slaves and Masters, 1567–1854*, edited by Mortimer J. Adler, 264–69. Chicago: William Benton/Encyclopedia Britannica, 1969.

Deloney, E. "What Negro Youth Expects from National Defense." *The Crisis*, August 1941, 253–54.

Delvin, Rachel. "*Linda Brown v. Board*: Girls and the Fight against Segregation in the American South." Paper presented at the Society for the History of Children and Youth Conference, Norrkoping, Sweden, June 2007.

Demos, John, and Virginia Demos. "Adolescence in Historical Perspective." *Journal of Marriage and the Family* 31 (November 1969): 632–38.

"Designed to Inflame." *Jackson Daily News*, 2 September 1955. Reprinted in *The Lynching of Emmett Till: A Narrative History*, edited by Christopher Metress, 19–20. Charlottesville: University of Virginia Press, 2002.

Dhonau, Jerry. "Negro Girl Turned Back, Ignores Hooting Crowd." *Little Rock Arkansas Gazette*, 5 September 1957.

Dhonau, Jerry, and Terrence Roberts. "Negro Says Most Students Received Him 'Pretty Well.'" *Little Rock Arkansas Gazette*, 26 September 1957.

Dillard, Mrs. W. O. "Children Are Being Harmed." *Birmingham News*, 28 September 1957.

Dittmer, John. *Local People: The Struggle for Civil Rights in Mississippi*. Urbana: University of Illinois Press, 1994.

Dodson, Dan W. "Social Action and Education." *Journal of Educational Sociology* 23 (February 1950): 345–51.

Douglass, Harl R. *Secondary Education for Youth in Modern America*. Washington, D.C.: American Council on Education, 1937.

Du Bois, Rachel Davis. "Building Tolerant Attitudes in High-School Students." *The Crisis*, October 1931, 334, 336.

———. "Sharing Culture Values." *Journal of Educational Sociology* 12 (April 1939): 482–86.

Du Bois, W. E. B. "As The Crow Flies." *Brownies' Book*, January 1920, 23.

———. *Black Reconstruction: An Essay toward a History of the Part Which Black Folk Played in the Attempt to Reconstruct Democracy in America, 1860–1880*. New York: Harcourt, Brace, 1935.

―――. *Darkwater: Voices from Within the Veil.* New York: Harcourt, Brace, and Howe, 1920.

―――. "Is the NAACP Lying Down on Its Job?" *The Crisis*, October 1931, 343, 354.

―――. "Our Baby Pictures." *The Crisis*, October 1914, 298.

―――. *The Philadelphia Negro: A Social Study.* 1899; New York: Blom, 1967.

―――. Postscript. *The Crisis*, January 1933, 20–22.

―――. *The Souls of Black Folk.* 1903; New York: Blue Heron, 1953.

―――. "Woofterism." *The Crisis*, March 1931, 81–83.

Dudziak, Mary L. "Brown as a Cold War Case." *Journal of American History* 91 (June 2004): 32–42.

―――. *Cold War Civil Rights: Race and the Image of American Democracy.* Princeton: Princeton University Press, 2000.

"The Editor Sez." *Arkansas Faith*, December 1955, 19.

Edwards, Newton. *Equal Educational Opportunity for Youth: A National Responsibility.* Washington, D.C.: American Council on Education, 1939.

Egerton, John. *Speak Now against the Day: The Generation before the Civil Rights Movement in the South.* New York: Knopf, 1994.

"Eighth Graders Examine Their Attitudes." *Journal of Educational Sociology* 16 (February 1943): 348–63.

Eliot, Martha M. "Furthering Individual Well-Being through Social Welfare." *The Child*, October 1952, 19–23.

Ellison, Ralph. *Invisible Man.* 1947; New York: Random House, 1952.

Ellsworth, Jeanne. "Women, Children, and Charity in Migrant Labor Camps, 1919–1939." Ph.D. diss., State University of New York–Buffalo, 1992.

Embree, Edwin R. "Native Son." *Negro Digest*, March 1944, 53–60.

Emery, Jane. "Can You Meet the Challenge?" *The Tiger*, 19 September 1957, ⟨http://www.centralhigh57.org/the_tiger.htm⟩. 30 August 2007.

Erikson, Eric H., ed. *Youth: Change and Challenge.* New York: Basic Books, 1963.

―――. "Youth: Fidelity and Diversity." In *Youth: Change and Challenge*, edited by Erik H. Erikson, 1–23. New York: Basic Books, 1963.

Evans, Eva Knox. *All about Us.* 1947; New York: Golden Press, 1965.

Evans, Medford. "As New as Childhood, and as Old as Truth." *The Citizen*, July–August 1965, 6–7, 15.

Evans, Sarah. *Personal Politics: The Roots of Women's Liberation in the Civil Rights Movement and the New Left.* New York: Vintage, 1980.

Everett, Arthur. "Till Nearly Missed His Fatal Journey to Land of Cotton." *Jackson Clarion-Ledger*, 19 September 1955.

Ewin, Oscar R. "An Opportunity and a Responsibility for America." *School Life*, March 1951, 82–83.

A Fair Chance for a Healthy Personality. Washington, D.C.: Mid-Century White House Conference on Children and Youth, 1950.

Fairclough, Adam, *Better Day Coming: Blacks and Equality, 1890–2000.* New York: Penguin, 2001.

―――. *To Redeem the Soul of America: The Southern Christian Leadership Conference and Martin Luther King, Jr.* Athens: University of Georgia Press, 1987.

Farmer, Mary J. "'Because They Are Women': Gender and the Virginia Freedmen's Bureau's 'War on Dependency.'" In *The Freedmen's Bureau and Reconstruction: Reconsiderations*, edited by Paul A. Cimbala and Randall M. Miller, 161–92. New York: Fordham University Press, 1999.

Fass, Paula S. *The Damned and the Beautiful: American Youth in the 1920s.* New York: Oxford University Press, 1977.

Fass, Paula S., and Mary Ann Mason, eds. *Childhood in America.* New York: New York University Press, 2000.

Feldstein, Ruth. "'I Wanted the Whole World to See': Race, Gender, and Constructions of Motherhood in the Death of Emmett Till." In *Not June Cleaver: Women and Gender in Postwar America, 1945–1960*, edited by Joanne Meyerowitz, 263–303. Philadelphia: Temple University Press, 1994.

Felix, Robert H. "The Teacher's Role in Mental Health Defense." *School Life*, January 1949, 1–3, 14.

Ferguson, Charles W. "Public-Spirited Youth." *National Parent-Teacher* 45 (February 1951): 4–6.

Fields, Barbara Jeanne. *Slavery and Freedom on the Middle Ground: Maryland during the Nineteenth Century.* New Haven: Yale University Press, 1985.

Findlay, James F. *Church People in the Struggle: The National Council of Churches and the Black Freedom Movement, 1950–1970.* New York: Oxford University Press, 1993.

Fisher, Dorothy Canfield. Introduction to *Native Son*, by Richard Wright, ix–xi. New York: Harper, 1940.

Fitch, Florence Mary. "Thumbs Down on Prejudice." *National Parent-Teacher* 33 (February 1949): 21–23.

"Five Point Action Program of the Citizens' Council." *The Citizen*, July–August 1963, 12.

Florant, Lyonel. "Youth Exhibits a New Spirit." *The Crisis*, August 1936, 237–38, 253–54.

Floyd, Silas Xavier. *Floyd's Flowers; or, Duty and Beauty for Colored Children: Being One Hundred Short Stories Gleaned from the Storehouse of Human Knowledge and Experience.* Atlanta: Hertel, Jenkins, 1905.

Fluke, Richard Paul. "Planters, Apprenticeship, and Forced Labor: The Black Family under Pressure in Post-Emancipation Maryland." *Agricultural History* 62 (Fall 1988): 57–74.

Foleno, Louis A. *A Critical Review of Selected Literature on College Student Unrest in the United States, 1968–1970.* San Francisco: Mellen Research University Press, 1992.

"For 14 Hours Terror Held Sway in City." *Birmingham News*, 16 September 1963.

Ford, Nick Aaron. "A Teacher Looks at Integration." *Phylon* 15 (3rd Qtr. 1954): 261–66.

Forman, James. *The Making of Black Revolutionaries.* New York: Macmillan, 1972.

Foster, Gerald Anthony, and Vonita White Foster. *Silent Trumpets of Justice: Integration's Failure in Prince Edward County.* Hampton, Va.: U.B. and U.S. Communications Systems, 1993.

Four Little Girls. Directed by Spike Lee. New York: HBO Films, 1997.

Frank, Lawrence K. "Childhood and Youth." In *Recent Trends in the United States: Report of the President's Research Committee on Social Trends*, 751–800. New York: McGraw-Hill, 1933.

Franklin, Jimmie Lewis. *Journey toward Hope: A History of Blacks in Oklahoma*. Norman: University of Oklahoma Press, 1982.

Franklin, V. P. "Patterns of Student Activism at Historically Black Universities in the United States and South Africa, 1960–1970." *Journal of African American History* 88 (Spring 2003): 204–17.

Fraser, James. "Black Publishing for Black Children: The Experience of the Sixties and the Seventies." *Library Journal* 97 (15 November 1973): 19–24.

Frazier, E. Franklin. *Negro Youth at the Crossways: Their Personality Development in the Middle States*. Washington, D.C.: American Council on Education, 1940.

Frost, S. E., Jr. "A Protocol for an Effective Democratic Education." *Journal of Educational Sociology* 20 (February 1947): 341–44.

Frystak, Shannon L. "Elite White Female Activism and Civil Rights in New Orleans." In *Throwing Off the Cloak of Privilege: White Southern Women Activists in the Civil Rights Era*, edited by Gail S. Murray, 184–203. Gainesville: University Press of Florida, 2004.

Fuller, R. G. "Child Labor on the Farm." *Good Housekeeping*, October 1922, 58–59, 150–56.

Gaillard, Frye. *The Dream Long Deferred*. Chapel Hill: University of North Carolina Press, 1988.

Gaines, Kevin K. *Uplifting the Race: Black Leadership, Politics, and Culture in the Twentieth Century*. Chapel Hill: University of North Carolina Press, 1996.

Gaither, Thomas. "Orangeburg: Behind the Carolina Stockade." In *Sit Ins: The Students Report*, compiled and edited by Jim Peck, 9–11. New York: Congress of Racial Equality, 1960.

Gardner, Katherine. "Changing Racial Attitudes." *The Crisis*, October 1931, 336.

Garner, Elvira. *Ezekiel*. New York: Holt, 1937.

———. *Ezekiel Travels*. New York: Holt, 1938.

———. *Way Down in Tennessee*. New York: Messner, 1941.

Garrow, David J. *Protest at Selma: Martin Luther King, Jr., and the Voting Rights Act of 1965*. New Haven: Yale University Press, 1978.

Gates, Henry Louis, Jr. *Colored People: A Memoir*. New York: Knopf, 1994.

Gates, Lorraine. "Power from the Pedestal: The Women's Emergency Committee and the Little Rock School Crisis." *Arkansas Historical Quarterly* 55 (Spring 1996): 39–57.

Gates, Maurice. "Negro Students Challenge Social Forces." *The Crisis*, August 1935, 232–33, 251.

Gates, Robbins L. *The Making of Massive Resistance: Virginia's Politics of Public School Desegregation, 1954–1956*. Chapel Hill: University of North Carolina Press, 1964.

Gavins, Raymond. "The NAACP in North Carolina during the Age of Segregation." In *New Directions in Civil Rights Studies*, edited by Armstead L. Robinson and Patricia Sullivan, 105–25. Charlottesville: University Press of Virginia, 1991.

Giddings, Paula J. *When and Where I Enter: The Impact of Black Women on Race and Sex in America*. New York: Morrow, 1984.

Gilbert, James Burkhart. *A Cycle of Outrage: America's Reaction to the Juvenile Delinquent in the 1950s*. New York: Oxford University Press, 1986.

Gillespie, James M., and Gordon W. Allport. *Youth's Outlook on the Future: A Cross-National Study*. Garden City, N.Y.: Doubleday, 1955.

"Give These Youngsters a Chance." *The Crisis*, November 1935, back cover.

"Give These Youngsters a Chance." *The Crisis*, December 1935, 355.

Gleason, Arthur. "Raising Children to Move Crops." *Hearst's International*, March 1924, 90–91, 125–27.

Goff, Regina Mary. *Problems and Emotional Difficulties of Negro Children: As Studied in Selected Communities and Attributed by Parents and Children to the Fact That They Are Negro*. New York: Bureau of Publications, Teachers College, Columbia University, 1949.

Goluboff, Risa L. *The Lost Promise of Civil Rights*. Cambridge: Harvard University Press, 2007.

Gonzalez, Gilbert G. *Chicano Education in the Era of Segregation*. Philadelphia: Balch Institute Press, 1990.

Goodman, James. *Stories of Scottsboro*. New York: Vintage, 1995.

Goodwin, Jeff, James M. Jasper, and Francesca Polletta, eds. *Passionate Politics: Emotions and Social Movements*. Chicago: University of Chicago Press, 2001.

Goodykoontz, Bess. "Life, Liberty, and Happiness for Children—Now." *School Life*, January 1942, 101–4.

Gordon, Clyde. "Letter to the Editor." *Jackson Clarion-Ledger*, 4 September 1955.

Gordon, Linda. *Heroes of Their Own Lives: Politics and Family Violence, Boston 1880–1960*. New York: Viking, 1988.

———. "Putting Children First: Women, Maternalism, and Welfare in the Early Twentieth Century." In *U.S. History as Women's History: New Feminist Essays*, edited by Linda K. Kerber, Alice Kessler-Harris, and Kathryn Kish Sklar, 63–86. Chapel Hill: University of North Carolina Press, 1995.

Graham, Gael. *Young Activists: American High School Students in the Age of Protest*. De Kalb: Northern Illinois University Press, 2006.

Grant, Joanne. *Ella Baker: Freedom Bound*. New York: Wiley, 1998.

Grant, Julia. *Raising Baby by the Book: The Education of American Mothers*. New Haven: Yale University Press, 1998.

Green, Eugene. "The Political Socialization of Black Inner-City Children." In *The Seeds of Politics: Youth and Politics in America*, edited by Anthony M. Orum, 180–94. Englewood Cliffs, N.J.: Prentice-Hall, 1972.

Green, Laurie Beth. "Rejecting Mammy: Ideological Struggles and Grassroots Organizing in the Urban South in the Era of Brown." Paper presented at the Organization of American Historians Annual Conference, Boston, 2004.

Greenberg, Jack. *Crusaders in the Courts: How a Dedicated Band of Lawyers Fought for the Civil Rights Revolution*. New York: Basic Books, 1994.

Greene, Christina. *Our Separate Ways: Women and the Black Freedom Movement in Durham, North Carolina*. Chapel Hill: University of North Carolina Press, 2005.

Greenstein, Fred I. *Children and Politics*. New Haven: Yale University Press, 1965.

Greenwood, Janette Thomas. *Bittersweet Legacy: The Black and White "Better Classes" in Charlotte, 1850–1910*. Chapel Hill: University of North Carolina Press, 1994.

Guinier, Lani. "From Racial Liberalism to Racial Literacy: *Brown v. Board of Education* and the Interest-Divergence Dilemma." *Journal of American History* 91 (June 2004): 92–118.

Gunter, James. "Wives Serious, Children Romp as Trial Begins." *Memphis Commercial Appeal*, 20 September 1955.

Hahamovitch, Cindy. *The Fruits of Their Labor: Atlantic Coast Farm Workers and the Making of Migrant Poverty, 1870–1945*. Chapel Hill: University of North Carolina Press, 1997.

Haines, Herbert H. *Black Radicals and the Civil Rights Movement, 1954–1970*. Knoxville: University of Tennessee Press, 1988.

Halberstam, David. *The Children*. New York: Random House, 1998.

Hale, Grace Elizabeth. *Making Whiteness: The Culture of Segregation in the South, 1890–1940*. New York: Pantheon, 1998.

Hall, G. Stanley. *Adolescence: Its Psychology and Its Relations to Physiology, Anthropology, Sociology, Sex, Crime, Religion, and Education*. New York: Appleton, 1904.

Hall, Jacquelyn Dowd. "The Long Civil Rights Movement and the Political Uses of the Past." *Journal of American History* 91 (March 2005): 1233–63.

———. *Revolt against Chivalry: Jessie Daniel Ames and the Women's Campaign against Lynching*. New York: Columbia University Press, 1979.

Hall, Louisa J. "Birth in the Slave's Hut." *Liberty Bell*, 1 January 1849, 42–44.

Halligan, Alice M. "A Community's Total War against Prejudice." *Journal of Educational Sociology* 16 (February 1943): 374–80.

Hampton, Henry, Steve Fayer, with Sarah Flynn, eds. *Voices of Freedom: An Oral History of the Civil Rights Movement from the 1950s through the 1980s*. New York: Bantam Books, 1990.

"The Hands at the Fuse in Birmingham Tragedy." *Little Rock Arkansas Gazette*, 17 September 1963.

Hansberry, Lorraine. *The Movement: Documentary of a Struggle for Equality*. New York: Simon and Schuster, 1964.

Harlow, S. Ralph. "Youth Takes a Hand in Mississippi." *The Crisis*, August 1932, 251.

Harold, Christine, and Kevin Michael DeLuca. "Behold the Corpse: Violent Images and the Case of Emmett Till." *Rhetoric and Public Affairs* 8 (Summer 2005): 263–86.

Harris, Fredrick C. "It Takes a Tragedy to Arouse Them: Collective Memory and Collective Action during the Civil Rights Movement." *Social Movement Studies* 5 (May 2006): 19–43.

Harris, Violet Joyce. "*The Brownies' Book*: Challenge to the Selective Tradition in Children's Literature." Ph.D. diss., University of Georgia, 1986.

Hartley, Eugene. *Problems in Prejudice*. Morningside Heights, N.Y.: Kings Crown, 1946.

Hartman, Andrew. *Education and the Cold War: The Battle for the American School.* New York: Palgrave Macmillan, 2008.

Hawes, Joseph M. *Children between the Wars: American Childhood, 1920–1940.* New York: Twayne, 1997.

Haynes, George Edmund. "Clinical Methods in Interracial and Intercultural Relations." *Journal of Educational Sociology* 19 (January 1946): 316–25.

Hendrickson, Paul. "Mississippi Haunting." *Rhetoric and Public Affairs* 8 (Summer 2005): 177–88.

Herman, Ellen. *The Romance of American Psychology: Political Culture in the Age of Experts.* Berkeley: University of California Press, 1995.

Hine, Darlene Clark. "Rape and the Inner Lives of Black Women in the Middle West: Preliminary Thoughts on the Culture of Dissemblance." In *Unequal Sisters: A Multicultural Reader in U.S. Women's History*, edited by Ellen Carol Du Bois and Vickie L. Ruiz, 292–97. New York: Routledge, 1990.

Hine, Darlene Clark, William C. Hine, and Stanley Harrold. *The African-American Odyssey.* 3rd ed. Upper Saddle River, N.J.: Pearson Education, 2006.

Hine, Darlene Clark, Wilma King, and Linda Reed, eds. *"We Specialize in the Wholly Impossible": A Reader in Black Women's History.* Brooklyn, N.Y.: Carlson, 1995.

Hine, William. "Civil Rights and Campus Wrongs: South Carolina State College Students' Protests, 1955–1968." *South Carolina Historical Magazine* 4 (October 1996): 310–33.

Hirsch, Carl. "50,000 Mourn at Bier of Lynched Negro Child." *Daily Worker*, 10 September 1955. Reprinted in *The Lynching of Emmett Till: A Narrative History*, edited by Christopher Metress, 31–34. Charlottesville: University of Virginia Press, 2002.

Hoffschwelle, Mary S. *The Rosenwald Schools of the American South.* Gainesville: University Press of Florida, 2006.

Hogan, Inez. *Nicodemus and His Little Sister.* New York: Dutton, 1932.

"Homer P. Rainey." *Current Biography*, edited by Anna Rothe, 497–99. New York: Wilson, 1946.

Honey, Michael K. *Southern Labor and Black Civil Rights: Organizing Memphis Workers.* Urbana: University of Illinois Press, 1993.

Houck, Davis W. "Killing Emmett." *Rhetoric and Public Affairs* 8 (Summer 2005): 225–62.

Howard, John R. *The Shifting Wind: The Supreme Court and Civil Rights from Reconstruction to Brown.* Albany: State University of New York Press, 1999.

"How Democratic Is Your School?" *School Life*, June 1949, 2–3.

Hrabowski, Freeman A., III. "The Role of Youth in the Civil Rights Movement: Reflections on Birmingham." Unpublished manuscript, in author's possession.

Hughes, Langston. "Cowards from the Colleges." *The Crisis*, August 1934, 226–28.

———. *Fight for Freedom: The Story of the NAACP.* New York: Norton, 1962.

Hughes, Langston, and Milton Meltzer. *A Pictorial History of the Negro in America.* Rev. ed. New York: Crown, 1963.

Huie, William Bradford. "The Shocking Story of Approved Killing in Mississippi."
Look, 24 January 1956, 46–50.
———. Three Lives for Mississippi. New York: WCC Books, 1965.
———. Wolf Whistle and Other Stories. New York: Signet, 1959.
Hulbert, Ann. Raising America: Experts, Parents, and a Century of Advice about Children.
New York: Knopf, 2003.
Hunter, Tera W. To 'Joy My Freedom: Southern Black Women's Lives and Labors after the
Civil War. Cambridge: Harvard University Press, 1997.
Illick, Joseph E. American Childhoods. Philadelphia: University of Pennsylvania Press,
2002.
"Integration: Letting George Do It." Newsweek, 23 September 1963, 33–34.
Jackson, John, Charles Maudlin, and Zannie Lee Murphy Jr. National Park Service
Interview. N.d. NPSSM-07. ⟨http://www.nps.gov.hfc/av/semo/docs/⟩. 26 July 2007.
Jackson, John P. Social Scientists for Social Justice: Making the Case against Segregation.
New York: New York University Press, 2001.
Jackson, Walter A. Gunnar Myrdal and America's Conscience: Social Engineering and
Racial Liberalism, 1938–1987. Chapel Hill: University of North Carolina Press, 1990.
Jacobs, Harriet. Incidents in the Life of a Slave Girl, Written by Herself. Edited by Jean
Fagan Yellin. Cambridge: Harvard University Press, 2000.
Jenkins, Martin D. "Gifted Negro Children." The Crisis, November 1936, 330–31.
Jensen, Noma. "Intolerance on the Juvenile Level." The Crisis, December 1945, 353–54.
Johns, Major. "Baton Rouge: Higher Education — Southern Style." In Sit Ins: The
Students Report, compiled and edited by Jim Peck, 12–14. New York: Congress of
Racial Equality, 1960.
Johnson, A. E. Clarence and Corinne; or, God's Way. Introduction by Hortense J.
Spillers. New York: Oxford University Press, 1988.
Johnson, Charles S. Growing Up in the Black Belt: Negro Youth in the Rural South.
Washington, D.C.: American Council on Education, 1941.
Johnson, Edward A. A School History of the Negro Race in America, from 1619 to 1890:
With a Short Introduction as to the Origin of the Race; Also a Short Sketch of Liberia.
Chicago: Conkey, 1897.
Johnson, Jim. "Let's Build a Private School at Hoxie." Arkansas Faith, December 1955, 12.
Jonas, Gilbert. Freedom's Sword: The NAACP and the Struggle against Racism in America,
1909–1969. New York: Routledge, 2005.
Jones, Juanita DaLomb. "He Who Perpetrates (My Day as a Picket for Freedom)."
Phylon 24 (Fall 1963): 290–99.
"The Junior Crisis." The Crisis, October 1929, 348.
"Jury Deliberations Expected to Begin Today in Till Case." Jackson Clarion-Ledger, 23
September 1955.
Kaestle, Carl F. Pillars of the Republic: Common Schools and American Society, 1780–
1860. New York: Hill and Wang, 1983.
Kaestle, Carl F., and Maris A. Vinovskis. Education and Social Change in Nineteenth-
Century Massachusetts. New York: Cambridge University Press, 1980.

Kamp, Joseph P. *Lawless Tyranny: An American Conspiracy against We, the People*. New Fairfield, Conn.: Headlines, 1966.

Karcher, Carolyn. *The First Woman of the Republic: A Cultural Biography of Lydia Maria Child*. Durham: Duke University Press, 1994.

Keesecker, Ward W. "Supreme Court Decisions Affecting Education." *School Life*, February 1949, 4–7.

Kelley, Robin D. G. *Hammer and Hoe: Alabama Communists during the Great Depression*. Chapel Hill: University of North Carolina Press, 1990.

———. *Race Rebels: Culture, Politics, and the Black Working Class*. New York: Free Press, 1994.

———. "The Riddle of the Zoot: Malcolm Little and Black Cultural Politics during World War II." In *Generations of Youth: Youth Cultures and History in Twentieth-Century America*, edited by Joe Austin and Michael Nevi Willard, 136–56. New York: New York University Press, 1998.

Kempton, Murray. "The Baby Sitter." *New York Post*, 20 September 1955. Reprinted in *The Lynching of Emmett Till: A Narrative History*, edited by Christopher Metress, 53–55. Charlottesville: University of Virginia Press, 2002.

———. "He Went All the Way." *New York Post*, 2 September 1955. Reprinted in *Voices in Our Blood: America's Best on the Civil Rights Movement*, edited by Jon Meacham, 111–13. New York: Random House, 2001.

———. "Next Day." *New York Post*, 12 September 1957. Reprinted in *Voices in Our Blood: America's Best on the Civil Rights Movement*, edited by Jon Meacham, 115–16. New York: Random House, 2001.

———. "Upon Such a Day." *New York Post*, 10 September 1957. Reprinted in *Voices in Our Blood: America's Best on the Civil Rights Movement*, edited by Jon Meacham, 113–15. New York: Random House, 2001.

Keniston, Kenneth. "Social Change and Youth in America." In *The Challenge of Youth*, edited by Erik H. Erikson, 191–222. New York: Anchor, 1965.

———. *Young Radicals: Notes on Committed Youth*. New York: Harcourt, Brace, and World, 1968.

Kennedy, John F. "The Negro and the American Promise." *Congressional Record*, 88th Cong., 1st sess., June 11, 1963, 10965–66.

Kett, Joseph F. *Rites of Passage: Adolescence in America, 1790 to the Present*. New York: Basic Books, 1977.

Key, Ellen. *The Century of the Child*. New York: Putnam, 1909.

Key, V. O. *Public Opinion and American Democracy*. New York: Free Press, 1962.

Kilpatrick, James Jackson. *The Southern Case for School Segregation*. New York: Crowell-Collier, 1962.

Kilpatrick, W. H., W. J. Stone, and S. G. Cole. "A Frame of Reference for Intercultural Education." *Journal of Educational Sociology* 22 (May 1949): 555–72.

King, Martin Luther, Jr. "Eulogy for the Young Victims of the Sixteenth Street Baptist Church Bombing, Delivered at the Sixth Avenue Baptist Church." Birmingham, Ala., September 18, 1963. ⟨http://www.stanford.edu/group/King/speeches/pub/ Eulogy_for_the_martyred_children.html⟩ 11 May 2007.

———. "I Have a Dream—Address at March on Washington." Washington D.C., 28 August 1963. ⟨http://www.stanford.edu/group/King/publications/speeches/address_at_march_on_washington.pdf⟩. 31 August 2007.

———. "Letter from Birmingham Jail." Birmingham, Ala., April 16, 1963. ⟨http://www.stanford.edu/group/King/popular_requests/frequentdocs/birmingham.pdf⟩ 11 May 2007.

———. *Stride toward Freedom: The Montgomery Story*. New York: Harper, 1958.

King, Mary. *Freedom Song: A Personal Story of the Civil Rights Movement*. New York: Morrow, 1987.

King, Wilma. *African American Childhoods: Historical Perspectives from Slavery to Civil Rights*. New York: Palgrave Macmillan, 2005.

———. *Stolen Childhood: Slave Youth in Nineteenth-Century America*. Bloomington: Indiana University Press, 1995.

Kinky Kids. New York: Ulman, 1908.

Kirby, John B. *Black Americans in the Roosevelt Era: Liberalism and Race*. Knoxville: University of Tennessee Press, 1980.

Kirp, David L. *Just Schools: The Idea of Racial Equality in American Education*. Berkeley: University of California Press, 1982.

Klarman, Michael J. *From Jim Crow to Civil Rights: The Supreme Court and the Struggle for Racial Equality*. New York: Oxford University Press, 2004.

Klineberg, Otto. "An Experimental Study of Speed and Other Factors in 'Racial' Differences." *Archives of Psychology* 93 (1928): 109–23.

Kluger, Richard. *Simple Justice: The History of Brown v. Board of Education and Black America's Struggle for Racial Equality*. Rev. ed. New York: Vintage, 2004.

Knebel, Fletcher. "Dixie's New Rebels." *Look*, 9 December 1958, 19–23.

Kolb, J. H., and Edmund de Schweinitz Brunner. "Rural Life." In *Recent Social Trends in the United States: Report of the President's Committee on Social Trends*, edited by President's Research Committee on Social Trends, 497–552. New York: McGraw-Hill, 1933.

Korstad, Robert Rodgers. *Civil Rights Unionism: Tobacco Workers and the Struggle for Democracy in the Mid–Twentieth Century South*. Chapel Hill: University of North Carolina Press, 2003.

Kotlowitz, Alex. *There Are No Children Here: The Story of Two Boys Growing Up in the Other America*. New York: Doubleday, 1991.

Kozol, Jonathan. *Amazing Grace: Lives of Children and the Conscience of a Nation*. New York: Crown, 1995.

Kozol, Wendy. *Life's America: Family and Nation in Postwar Photojournalism*. Philadelphia: Temple University Press, 1994.

Krumgold, Joseph. . . . *And Now Miguel*. New York: Crowell, 1953.

———. *Onion John*. New York: Crowell, 1959.

Ladd-Taylor, Molly. *Mother-Work: Women, Child Welfare, and the State, 1890–1930*. Urbana: University of Illinois Press, 1994.

———. *Raising a Baby the Government Way: Mothers' Letters to the Children's Bureau, 1915–1932*. New Brunswick, N.J.: Rutgers University Press, 1986.

Ladner, Joyce. "The South: Old-New Land." *New York Times*, 17 May 1979.

Lamb, Robert K. "Migration." In *Social Work Year Book 1943*, edited by Russel H. Kurtz, 333–39. New York: Sage, 1943.

Landphair, Juliette Lee. "'For the Good of the Community': Reform Activism and Public Schools in New Orleans, 1920–1960." Ph.D. diss., University of Virginia, 1999.

Lane, Howard A. "An Education-Centered Community Can Care for Children." *Journal of Educational Sociology* 20 (January 1947): 272–80.

"Largest Branch of Jr. NAACP Transfers to Senior Branch." *Detroit Independent*, 1 November 1924.

Lasch, Christopher. *Haven in a Heartless World: The Family Besieged*. New York: Basic Books, 1977.

Lassiter, Matthew D., and Andrew B. Lewis, eds. *The Moderates' Dilemma: Massive Resistance to School Desegregation in Virginia*. Charlottesville: University Press of Virginia, 1998.

Lau, Peter F. *Democracy Rising: South Carolina and the Fight for Black Equality since 1865*. Lexington: University Press of Kentucky, 2006.

———. "From the Periphery to the Center: Clarendon County, South Carolina, *Brown*, and the Struggle for Democracy and Equality in America." In *From the Grassroots to the Supreme Court: Brown v. Board of Education and American Democracy*, edited by Peter F. Lau, 105–28. Durham: Duke University Press, 2004.

"The Law: The Tension of Change." *Time*, 19 September 1955, 23–27.

"The Law: Trial by Jury." *Time*, 3 October 1955, 18–19.

Lawrence, Edward A. "National Youth Program." *The Crisis*, September 1936, 281–82.

Laws, Agnes J. "How Youthport Shall Be Conducted and What It Shall Aim to Do." *The Crisis*, January 1930, 26.

Lawson, Steven F., ed. *To Secure These Rights: The Report of President Harry S. Truman's Committee on Civil Rights*. 1947; Boston: Bedford/St. Martin's, 2004.

Lenroot, Katharine F. "American Childhood Challenges American Democracy." *The Child* 5 (July 1940): 3–8.

———. "Children in a Free Society." *The Child* 13 (July 1948): 2–5.

Lenski, Lois. *Judy's Journey*. Philadelphia: Lippincott, 1947.

———. *Strawberry Girl*. Philadelphia: Lippincott, 1945.

Lentz, Richard. *Symbols, the News Magazines, and Martin Luther King*. Baton Rouge: Louisiana State University Press, 1990.

Lewis, David Levering. *W. E. B. Du Bois: Biography of a Race, 1868–1919*. New York: Holt, 1993.

Lewis, John, with Michael D'Orso. *Walking with the Wind: A Memoir of the Movement*. New York: Simon and Schuster, 1998.

Light, Ken. *Delta Time*. Washington, D.C.: Smithsonian Institution Press, 1995.

Lindenmeyer, Kriste. *The Greatest Generation Grows Up: American Childhood in the 1930s*. Chicago: Dee, 2005.

———. *A Right to Childhood: The U.S. Children's Bureau and Child Welfare, 1912–1946*. Urbana: University of Illinois Press, 1997.

Liss, Julia E. "Diasporic Identities: The Science and Politics of Race in the Work of
Franz Boas and W. E. B. Du Bois, 1894–1919." *Cultural Anthropology* 13 (May 1998):
127–66.

Lomax, Louis E. "The Negro Revolt against the Negro Leaders." *Harper's Magazine*,
June 1960. Reprinted in *Voices in Our Blood: America's Best on the Civil Rights
Movement*, edited by Jon Meacham, 268–80. New York: Random House, 2003.

Lomax, Louis E., et al. *Mississippi Eyewitness: The Three Civil Rights Workers, How They
Were Murdered: The Exclusive Story by "Ramparts" Magazine*. Menlo Park, Calif.:
Keating, 1964.

"The London Convention." *Liberty Bell*, 1 January 1841, 88–98.

"A Look at the World's Week: Desegregation in Galveston." *Life*, 18 April 1960, 28.

Lott, Eric. *Love and Theft: Blackface Minstrelsy and the American Working Class*. New
York: Oxford University Press, 1993.

"Louisiana Argues Issue." *New York Times*, 7 November 1954.

Lumpkin, Katharine DuPre. *The Making of a Southerner*. New York: Knopf, 1947.

Lumpkin, Katharine DuPre, and Dorothy Wolff Douglas. *Child Workers in America*.
2nd ed. New York: International, 1937.

Lundberg, Emma O. "Security for Children in Post-War Years: Objectives of State and
Community Action." *The Child* 8 (July 1943): 8–12.

Luper, Clara. *Behold the Walls*. Oklahoma City: Wire, 1979.

Lyles, John. "To Upset the City Fathers: The Neighborhood Organized Workers and
the Politics of Civility in Mobile, Alabama, 1968." Master's thesis, University of
South Alabama, forthcoming.

Lynd, Robert S., and Helen Merrell Lynd. *Middletown: A Study in American Culture*.
New York: Harcourt, Brace, and World, 1956.

Lystad, Mary. *From Dr. Mather to Dr. Seuss: 200 Years of American Books for Children*.
Cambridge, Mass.: Schenkman, 1980.

MacCann, Donnarae, and Gloria Woodard, eds. *The Black American in Books for
Children: Readings in Racism*. Metuchen, N.J.: Scarecrow, 1985.

Mackenzie, Catherine. "How to Keep Your Child Free from Prejudice." *Negro Digest*,
May 1945, 79–80.

MacLeod, Anne Scott, ed. *American Childhood: Essays on Children's Literature of the
Nineteenth and Twentieth Centuries*. Athens: University of Georgia Press, 1996.

Macleod, David I. *The Age of the Child: Children in America, 1880–1920*. New York:
Twayne, 1998.

————. *Building Character in the American Boy: The Boy Scouts, YMCA, and Their
Forerunners, 1870–1920*. Madison: University of Wisconsin Press, 1983.

Maddox, James J. "The Farm Security Administration in Southern Communities." In
Proceedings of the National Conference of Social Work, 109–18. New York: Columbia
University Press, 1942.

Madigan, Mark J., ed. *Keeping Fires Night and Day: Selected Letters of Dorothy Canfield
Fisher*. Columbia: University of Missouri Press, 1993.

Markowitz, Gerald, and David Rosner. *Children, Race, and Power: Kenneth and Mamie
Clark's Northside Center*. Charlottesville: University Press of Virginia, 1996.

Marshall, Dominique. "Herbert Hoover, Children's Rights, and the Construction of the International Order, 1914–1950." Paper presented at the Society for the History of Children and Youth Conference, Norrkoping, Sweden, June 2007.

———. "Humanitarian Sympathy for Children in Times of War and the History of Children's Rights, 1919–1959." In *Children and War: A Historical Anthology*, edited by James Alan Marten, 184–200. New York: New York University Press, 2002.

Marten, James Alan. *The Children's Civil War*. Chapel Hill: University of North Carolina Press, 1998.

———. *Lessons of War: The Civil War in Children's Magazines*. Wilmington, Del.: Scholarly Resources, 1999.

Martin, Waldo E., Jr. "'Stretching Out': Living and Remembering *Brown*, 1945–1970." In *From the Grassroots to the Supreme Court: Brown v. Board of Education and American Democracy*, edited by Peter F. Lau, 321–39. Durham: Duke University Press, 2004.

Martinez, Elizabeth, ed. *Letters from Mississippi: Reports from Civil Rights Volunteers and Poetry of the 1964 Freedom Summer*. Brookline, Mass.: Zephyr, 2007.

Marx, Karl. *Economic and Philosophic Manuscripts of 1844*. Moscow: Foreign Languages, 1961.

Mason, J. A. "Ambassadors in Blue Jeans." *National Parent-Teacher* 51 (November 1957): 8–10.

May, Elaine Tyler. *Homeward Bound: American Families in the Cold War Era*. New York: Basic Books, 1988.

McAdam, Doug. *Freedom Summer*. New York: Oxford University Press, 1988.

McCall, Bertha. "Migration and the Federal Government." In *National Conference of Social Work*, 132. N.p., 1940.

McGill, Nettie P. "Children Who Work on Farms." *National Education Association Journal* 13 (June 1924): 193–94.

McGrath, Earl James. "Citizenship Begins with Children." *School Life*, March 1951, 84–85.

McKean, Else. *Up Hill*. New York: Shady Hill, 1947.

McNeil, Genna Rae. "Before *Brown*: Reflections on Historical Context and Visions." *American University Law Review* 52 (August 2003): 1431–60.

———. *Groundwork: Charles Hamilton Houston and the Struggle for Civil Rights*. Philadelphia: University of Pennsylvania Press, 1983.

———. "Youth Initiative in the African American Struggle for Racial Justice and Constitutional Rights: The City-Wide Young People's Forum of Baltimore, 1931–1941." In *African Americans and the Living Constitution*, edited by John Hope Franklin and Genna Rae McNeil, 56–80. Washington, D.C.: Smithsonian Institution Press, 1995.

McWhorter, Diane. *Carry Me Home: Birmingham, Alabama, the Climatic Battle of the Civil Rights Revolution*. New York: Simon and Schuster, 2001.

McWilliams, Carey. *Factories in the Field: The Story of Migratory Farm Labor in California*. Boston: Little, Brown, 1939.

————. *Ill Fares the Land: Migrants and Migratory Labor in the United States*. Boston: Little, Brown, 1942.

Meier, August. "Toward a New Synthesis of Civil Rights History." In *New Directions in Civil Rights Studies*, edited by Armstead L. Robinson and Patricia Sullivan, 211–24. Charlottesville: University Press of Virginia, 1991.

Meier, August, and Elliott Rudwick. *Black Detroit and the Rise of the UAW*. New York: Oxford University Press, 1979.

————. *CORE: A Study in the Civil Rights Movement, 1942–1968*. New York: Oxford University Press, 1973.

————. "The Origins of Nonviolent Direct Action in Afro-American Protest: A Note on Historical Discontinuities." In *Along the Color Line: Explorations in the Black Experience*, edited by August Meier and Elliot Rudwick, 307–404. Urbana: University of Illinois Press, 1976.

Menefee, Selden Cowles. *Mexican Migratory Workers of South Texas*. Washington, D.C.: U.S. Government Printing Office, 1941.

Metress, Christopher, ed. *The Lynching of Emmett Till: A Documentary Narrative*. Charlottesville: University of Virginia Press, 2002.

————. "On That Third Day He Rose: Sacramental Memory and the Lynching of Emmett Till." In *Emmett Till in Literary Memory and Imagination*, edited by Harriet Pollack and Christopher Metress, 16–30. Baton Rouge: Louisiana State University Press, 2008.

————. "What Happened to Emmett Till?: Collective Memory and the Long Shadow of William Bradford Huie." Unpublished manuscript, in author's possession.

Meyer, Mrs. Eugene. "New Values in Education." *School Life*, February 1946, 14.

Mickenberg, Julia L. *Learning from the Left: Children's Literature, the Cold War, and Radical Politics in the United States*. New York: Oxford University Press, 2006.

Mighty Times: The Children's March. Directed by Robert Houston. Montgomery, Ala.: Southern Poverty Law Center, 2004.

Miller, Laura A. "Challenging the Segregationist Power Structure in Little Rock: The Women's Emergency Committee to Open Our Schools." In *Throwing Off the Cloak of Privilege: White Southern Women Activists in the Civil Rights Era*, edited by Gail S. Murray, 155–78. Gainesville: University Press of Florida, 2004.

Minehan, Thomas. *Boy and Girl Tramps of America*. New York: Grosset and Dunlap, 1934.

"Minister Had Sought Entry of Children." *Birmingham News*, 9 September 1957.

Mintz, Steven. *Huck's Raft: A History of American Childhood*. Cambridge: Harvard University Press, 2004.

Mintz, Steven, and Susan Kellogg. *Domestic Revolutions: A Social History of American Family Life*. New York: Free Press, 1988.

"Mississippi: The Place, the Acquittal." *Newsweek*, 3 October 1955, 24, 29–30.

Mitchell, L. Pearl. "Importance to NAACP." *The Crisis*, September 1936, 281–83.

Mitchell, Mary Niall. "'Rosebloom and Pure White,' or So It Seemed." *American Quarterly* 54 (September 2002): 369–410.

Mnookin, Robert H. *In the Interest of Children: Advocacy, Law Reform, and Public Policy*. New York: Freeman, 1985.

Modell, John. *Into One's Own: From Youth to Adulthood in the United States, 1920–1975*. Berkeley: University of California Press, 1989.

Moody, Anne. *Coming of Age in Mississippi*. New York: Dial, 1968.

Moon, Bucklin. *The High Cost of Prejudice*. 1947; Westport, Conn.: Negro Universities Press, 1970.

"A Morally Right Decision: An Arkansas School Board Does Some Searching and Negro Children Enter Desegregated Classes." *Life*, 25 July 1955, 29–31.

Morin, Relman. "Deceptive Calm Swirls around Desegregation at Little Rock." *Birmingham News*, 7 October 1957.

Morris, Aldon D. *The Origins of the Civil Rights Movement: Black Communities Organizing for Change*. New York: Free Press, 1984.

Morris, Willie. *North toward Home*. Boston: Houghton Mifflin, 1967. Excerpt reprinted in *Voices in Our Blood: America's Best on the Civil Rights Movement*, edited by Jon Meachem, 32–40. New York: Random House, 2003.

Morrison, Chester. "The Pattern of Compliance." *Look*, 3 April 1956, 42–45.

Moseley, Ray. "Negro Parents Take Insults, Pray for Children's Safety." *Little Rock Arkansas Gazette*, 29 September 1957.

Moses, Robert P., and Charles E. Cobb Jr. *Radical Equations: Math Literacy and Civil Rights*. Boston: Beacon, 2001.

"Muddy River Gives Up Body of Brutally Slain Negro Boy." *Memphis Commercial Appeal*, 1 September 1955. Reprinted in *The Lynching of Emmett Till: A Documentary Narrative*, edited by Christopher Metress, 16–19. Charlottesville: University of Virginia Press, 2002.

"Murder Trial of Deltans Expected Later in Month." *Jackson Clarion-Ledger*, 7 September 1955.

Murphy, Edgar Gardner. *The Problems of the Present South: A Discussion of Certain of the Educational, Industrial, and Political Issues in the Southern States*. New York: Macmillan, 1904.

Murray, Gail Schmunk. *American Children's Literature and the Construction of Childhood*. New York: Twayne, 1998.

Murrow, Edward R. *See It Now*, 25 March 1955. Included in *The Best of See It Now* (DVD), CBS, 1991.

Muse, Benjamin. *Virginia's Massive Resistance*. Bloomington: Indiana University Press, 1961.

Muse, Daphne. "Black Children's Literature: Rebirth of a Neglected Genre." *Black Scholar* 7 (December 1975): 11–15.

"'My God, You're Not Even Safe in Church.'" *Newsweek*, 30 September 1963, 20–23.

Myrdal, Gunnar. *An American Dilemma: The Negro Problem in American Democracy*. New York: Harper, 1944.

"N.A.A.C.P. Youth Council News." *The Crisis*, September 1937, 282–83.

NAACP Youth Councils: Building for Total Democracy; Crusade for Freedom. New York: National Association for the Advancement of Colored People, 1945.

Nasaw, David. *Children of the City: At Work and at Play*. Garden City, N.Y.: Anchor, 1985.

Natanson, Nicholas. *The Black Image in the New Deal: The Politics of FSA Photography*. Knoxville: University of Tennessee Press, 1992.

"Negro Describes Boy's Abduction." *Jackson Clarion-Ledger*, 2 September 1955.

Newlon, Jesse H. *Education for Democracy in Our Time*. New York: McGraw-Hill, 1939.

Newsome, Effie Lee. "The Bronze Legacy (To a Brown Boy)." *The Crisis*, October 1919, 265.

Nobles, Wade W., and Lawford L. Goddard. *Understanding the Black Family: A Guide for Scholarship and Research*. Oakland, Calif.: Institute for Advanced Study of Black Family Life and Culture, 1984.

Norrell, Robert J. "One Thing We Did Right: Reflections on the Movement." In *New Directions in Civil Rights Studies*, edited by Armstead L. Robinson and Patricia Sullivan, 65–80. Charlottesville: University Press of Virginia, 1991.

―――. *Reaping the Whirlwind: The Civil Rights Movement in Tuskegee*. New York: Knopf, 1985.

Norton, Donna E. *Through the Eyes of a Child: An Introduction to Children's Literature*. 3rd ed. New York: Macmillan, 1991.

Oettinger, Katherine Brownell. "Current Concerns of the Children's Bureau." *Children* 5 (July–August 1958): 123–28.

"Officers of Junior NAACP Surprise Their Leader." *Detroit Independent*, 20 September 1924.

Official Proceedings: Second All-Southern Negro Youth Conference. Richmond, Va.: Southern Negro Youth Congress, 1938.

Olson, Lynne. *Freedom's Daughters: The Unsung Heroines of the Civil Rights Movement from 1830–1970*. New York: Touchstone, 2002.

"Organized Labor Speaks on Behalf of Children." *The Child* 13 (January 1949): 98–100.

Orum, Anthony M. *Black Students in Protest: A Study of the Origins of the Black Student Movement*. Washington, D.C.: American Sociological Association, 1972.

―――. "Patterns of Protest: The Politics of Black Youth in the 1960s." In *The Seeds of Politics: Youth and Politics in America*, edited by Anthony M. Orum, 271–81. Englewood Cliffs, N.J.: Prentice-Hall, 1972.

Overstreet, Bonar W. "The High Art of Belonging: Childhood Is the Starting Point." *PTA* (September 1948): 22–24.

Ovington, Mary White. "Students Eager for Inter-Racial Forums." *The Crisis*, June 1934, 181.

Pahl, Jon. *Youth Ministry in Modern America, 1930 to Present*. Peabody, Mass.: Hendrickson, 2000.

Parks, Rosa, with Jim Haskins. *Rosa Parks: My Story*. New York: Dial, 1992.

Patterson, James T. *Brown v. Board of Education: A Civil Rights Milestone and Its Troubled Legacy*. New York: Oxford University Press, 2001.

Payne, Charles M. *I've Got the Light of Freedom: The Organizing Tradition and the Mississippi Freedom Struggle*. Berkeley: University of California Press, 1995.

———. "'The Whole United States Is Southern!': *Brown v. Board of Education* and the Mystification of Race." *Journal of American History* 91 (June 2004): 83–91.

Peeples, Edward J. "A Perspective of the Prince Edward County School Issue." Master's thesis, University of Pennsylvania, 1963.

———. *Prince Edward County: The Story without an End*. Report Prepared for the U.S. Commission on Civil Rights, Justice Department. 1963. ⟨http://www.library.vcu .edu/jbc/speccoll/peco3a.html⟩. 22 August 2007.

Pennington, James W. C. "The Life of a Slave Child." 1849. Excerpt reprinted in *Childhood in America*, edited by Paula S. Fass and Mary Ann Mason, 221–22. New York: New York University Press, 2000.

Perkins, Frances. "General Child Welfare: The White House Conference on Children in a Democracy." *The Child* 3 (April 1939): 237–40.

Petry, Ann. "My Most Humiliating Jim Crow Experience." *Negro Digest*, June 1946, 63–64.

Phillipson, Elma. "Follow-Up of 1950 White House Conference Enters a New State: National Committee Hands Torch to Other Groups." *The Child* 17 (April 1953): 130–33.

Platt, Anthony M. *The Child Savers: The Invention of Delinquency*. Chicago: University of Chicago Press, 1969.

Pollack, Harriet. "Grotesque Laughter, Unburied Bodies, and History: Shape-Shifting in Lewis Nordan's *Wolf Whistle*." In *Emmett Till in Literary Memory and Imagination*, edited by Harriet Pollack and Christopher Metress, 178–201. Baton Rouge: Louisiana State University Press, 2008.

Pollack, Harriet, and Christopher Metress. "The Emmett Till Case and Narrative[s]." In *Emmett Till in Literary Memory and Imagination*, edited by Harriet Pollack and Christopher Metress, 1–15. Baton Rouge: Louisiana State University Press, 2008.

Pollock, Linda A. *Forgotten Children: Parent-Child Relations from 1500 to 1900*. New York: Cambridge University Press, 1983.

Posey, E. R. "Negroes Enter, Then Suffer?" *Birmingham News*, 28 September 1957.

Powdermaker, Hortense. *After Freedom: A Cultural Study in the Deep South*. 1939; New York: Russell and Russell, 1968.

"The Press and Emmett Till." *New South* 10 (October 1955): 10–11.

Putnam, Carleton. "This Is the Problem!" *The Citizen*, November 1961, 13, 17.

Pye, Lucian W. "Political Culture." In *International Encyclopedia of the Social Sciences*, edited by David L. Sills, 12:218–25. New York: Macmillan/Free Press, 1968.

Raab, Earl, and Seymour M. Lipset. *Prejudice and Society*. New York: Anti-Defamation League of B'nai B'rith, 1963.

Radke, Marian, Helen G. Trager, and Hadassah Davis. "Social Perceptions and Attitudes of Children." *Genetic Psychology Monographs* 40 (1949): 327–447.

Rainey, Homer P. *How Fare American Youth?* New York: Appleton, 1937.

Rampersad, Arnold, ed. *Richard Wright: Early Works*. New York: Library of America, 1991.

Ransby, Barbara. *Ella Baker and the Black Freedom Movement: A Radical Democratic Vision*. Chapel Hill: University of North Carolina Press, 2003.

Raper, Arthur F. *Preface to Peasantry: A Tale of Two Black Belt Counties*. Chapel Hill: University of North Carolina Press, 1936.

Raper, Arthur F., and Ira De A. Reid. *Sharecroppers All*. Chapel Hill: University of North Carolina Press, 1941.

Ravitch, Diane. *Left Back: A Century of Failed School Reform*. New York: Simon and Schuster, 2000.

———. *The Troubled Crusade: American Education, 1945–1980*. New York: Basic Books, 1983.

Rayburn, Sam. "That Civilization May Survive." *School Life*, October 1945, 9–10.

Reagon, Bernice Johnson. "Ella's Song." Washington, D.C.: Songtalk, 2003.

The Real Story of Scottsboro. New York: Scottsboro Defense Committee, 1936.

Reavis, Dick J. *If White Kids Die*. Denton: University of North Texas Press, 2001.

Reeves, Ben. "'So What?' Is Town's Attitude toward Integration." *Louisville (Ky.) Courier-Journal*, 2 December 1955.

Reston, James. "I Have a Dream . . . ," *New York Times*, 29 August 1963. Reprinted in *Voices in Our Blood: America's Best on the Civil Rights Movement*, edited by Jon Meacham, 285–87. New York: Random House, 2003.

Reid, Ira De Augustine. *In a Minor Key: Negro Youth in Story and Fact*. Washington, D.C.: American Council on Education, 1940.

Rice, John Andrew. *I Came Out of the Eighteenth Century*. New York: Harper, 1942.

Richards, Johnetta Gladys. "The Southern Negro Youth Congress: A History." Ph.D. diss., University of Cincinnati, 1987.

Ritterhouse, Jennifer Lynn. *Growing Up Jim Crow: How Black and White Children Learned Race*. Chapel Hill: University of North Carolina Press, 2006.

Roberts, Gene, and Hank Klibanoff. *The Race Beat: The Press, the Civil Rights Struggle, and the Awakening of a Nation*. New York: Vintage, 2006.

Robertson, Charles. National Park Service Interview. N.d. NSSMP-26. ⟨http://www .nps.gov.hfc/av/semo/docs⟩. 26 July 2007.

Robinson, Armstead L., and Patricia Sullivan, eds. *New Directions in Civil Rights Studies*. Charlottesville: University Press of Virginia, 1991.

Robinson, Jo Ann Gibson. *The Montgomery Bus Boycott and the Women Who Started It: The Memoir of Jo Ann Gibson Robison*. Edited by David J. Garrow. Knoxville: University of Tennessee Press, 1987.

Robnett, Belinda. *How Long? How Long?: African-American Women in the Struggle for Civil Rights*. New York: Oxford University Press, 1997.

Rodgers, Richard, and Oscar Hammerstein II. "You've Got to Be Taught." *South Pacific*, 1958.

Roosevelt, Eleanor. "Why I Still Believe in the Youth Congress." *Liberty* 17 (20 April 1940): 30–32.

Roosevelt, Franklin D. "White House Conference on Children in a Democracy: From the Address of the President of the United States." *The Child* 3 (June 1939): 263.

Rosenberg, Jonathan. *How Far the Promised Land?: World Affairs and the American Civil Rights Movement from the First World War to Vietnam*. Princeton: Princeton University Press, 2006.

Rossinow, Doug. *The Politics of Authenticity: Liberalism, Christianity, and the New Left in America*. New York: Columbia University Press, 1998.

Roucek, Joseph S. "Future Steps in Cultural Pluralism." *Journal of Educational Sociology* 12 (April 1939): 499–504.

Rowan, Carl T. "The Cradle (of the Confederacy) Rocks." In *Go South to Sorrow*. New York: Random House, 1957. Reprinted in *Voices in Our Blood: America's Best on the Civil Rights Movement*, edited by Jon Meacham, 129–50. New York: Random House, 2003.

Rudolph, Frederick, ed. *Essays on Education in the Early Republic*. Cambridge: Belknap Press of Harvard University Press, 1965.

Runciman, Steven. *A History of the Crusades*. Vol. 3, *The Kingdom of Acre and the Later Crusades*. Cambridge: Cambridge University Press, 1951.

"Russians Push Scare Story about Their Missile Threat." *Little Rock Arkansas Gazette*, 1 September 1957.

Salinger, J. D. *The Catcher in the Rye*. Boston: Little, Brown, 1951.

Sallee, Shelley. *The Whiteness of Child Labor Reform in the New South*. Athens: University of Georgia Press, 2004.

Scheele, Leonard A. "The School and National Health." *Journal of Educational Sociology* 22 (September 1948): 31–36.

Schmidt, James D. *Free to Work: Labor Law, Emancipation, and Reconstruction, 1815–1880*. Athens: University of Georgia Press, 1998.

"School's Out; Nobody's Glad." *Life*, 29 September 1958, 38–40.

Schrum, Kelly. *Some Wore Bobby Sox: The Emergence of Teenage Girls' Culture, 1920–1945*. New York: Palgrave Macmillan, 2004.

Schuyler, Lorraine Gates. *The Weight of Their Votes: Southern Women and Political Leverage in the 1920s*. Chapel Hill: University of North Carolina Press, 2006.

Schwartz, Marie Jenkins. *Born in Bondage: Growing Up Enslaved in the Antebellum South*. Cambridge: Harvard University Press, 2000.

Schwellenbach, L. B. "Put Children First." *The Child* 10 (March 1946): 135–36.

Scott, Daryl Michael. *Contempt and Pity: Social Policy and the Image of the Damaged Black Psyche, 1880–1996*. Chapel Hill: University of North Carolina Press, 1997.

———. "Postwar Pluralism, *Brown v. Board of Education*, and the Origins of Multicultural Education." *Journal of American History* 91 (June 2004): 69–82.

Scott, Joan W. "The Evidence of Experience." *Critical Inquiry* 17 (Summer 1991): 773–92.

———. "Gender: A Useful Category of Historical Analysis." *American Historical Review* 91 (December 1986): 1053–75.

Scott, Rebecca. "The Battle over the Child: Child Apprenticeship and the Freedmen's Bureau in North Carolina." *Prologue* 10 (Summer 1978): 101–13.

Scottsboro, the Shame of America: The True Story and the True Meaning of This Famous Case. New York: Scottsboro Defense Committee, 1936.

"Selected Highlights in American Education—1953." *School Life*, January 1954, 59–61.

Selig, Diana. "Cultural Gifts: American Liberals, Childhood, and the Origins of Multiculturalism, 1924–1939." Ph.D. diss., University of California–Berkeley, 2001.

Sellers, Cleveland, with Robert Terrell. *The River of No Return: The Autobiography of a Black Militant and the Life and Death of SNCC.* New York: Morrow, 1973.

"Senators Call Bombing Tragic Blow to Racial Peace." *Birmingham News,* 16 September 1963.

Seuss, Dr. *Horton Hears a Who!* New York: Random House, 1954.

————. *If I Ran the Zoo.* New York: Random House, 1977.

————. *McElligot's Pool.* New York: Random House, 1947.

————. "What Was I Scared Of?" In *The Sneetches and Other Stories,* 42–65. New York: Random House, 1961.

————. *Yertle the Turtle and Other Stories.* New York: Random House, 1979.

"Shades of Hitler! Thought-Control for Children: Segregationists Say Burn Books." *Norfolk (Va.) Journal and Guide,* 30 May 1959.

Shane. Directed by George Stevens. Hollywood, Calif.: Paramount Pictures, 1953.

Shaw, Ethel Popel. *Personal Adventures in Race Relations.* New York: Woman's Press, 1946.

Shaw, Stephanie J. *What a Woman Ought to Be and Do: Black Professional Women Workers during the Jim Crow Era.* Chicago: University of Chicago Press, 1996.

Sherman, Mandel. "Is Education Inciting Race Hate?" *Negro Digest,* April 1945, 3–7.

Sinclair, Dean. "Equal in All Places: The Civil Rights Struggle in Baton Rouge, 1953–1963." *Louisiana History* 39 (Summer 1998): 347–66.

Sitkoff, Harvard. *A New Deal for Blacks: The Emergence of Civil Rights as a National Issue.* New York: Oxford University Press, 1978.

————. *The Struggle for Black Equality, 1954–1992.* Rev. ed. New York: Hill and Wang, 1993.

Smith, Katharine Capshaw. "Childhood, the Body, and Race Performance: Early Twentieth Century Etiquette Books for Black Children." *African American Review* 40 (Winter 2006): 795–811.

————. *Children's Literature of the Harlem Renaissance.* Bloomington: Indiana University Press, 2004.

Smith, Lillian E. "Georgia Primer, Condensed from the Forthcoming Book, *Strange Fruit.*" *Negro Digest,* September 1943, 7–11.

————. *Killers of the Dream.* New York: Norton, 1949.

————. *Strange Fruit.* 1944; San Diego: Harcourt Brace, 1992.

————. "Why I Wrote *Strange Fruit.*" *Negro Digest,* April 1945, 47–49.

Smith, Robert Collins. "Prince Edward County: Revisited and Revitalized." *Virginia Quarterly Review* 73 (Winter 1997): 1–27.

————. *They Closed Their Schools: Prince Edward County, Virginia, 1951–1964.* Chapel Hill: University of North Carolina Press, 1965.

Smith, Shawn Michelle. *American Archives: Gender, Race, and Class in Visual Culture.* Princeton: Princeton University Press, 1999.

————. *Photography on the Color Line: W. E. B. Du Bois, Race, and Visual Culture.* Durham: Duke University Press, 2004.

"The South Will Fight." *Arkansas Faith,* December 1955, 6–27.

Southern, David W. *Gunnar Myrdal and Black-White Relations: The Use and Abuse of an American Dilemma, 1944–1969.* Baton Rouge: Louisiana State University Press, 1987.

"South's Closed Schools Bring Dreary, Wasted Days: The Lost Class of 1959." *Life,* 3 November 1958, 21–27.

Spargo, John. *The Bitter Cry of the Children.* 9th ed. New York: Macmillan, 1916.

Sperber, Dan. "Anthropology and Psychology: Towards an Epidemiology of Representations." *Man* 20 (March 1985): 73–89.

Spigel, Lynn. *Make Room for TV: Television and the Family Ideal in Postwar America.* Chicago: University of Chicago Press, 1992.

Spock, Benjamin. "Development of Healthy Personalities." *School Life,* March 1951, 85–86, 92–93.

Sribnick, Ethan. "Marian Wright Edelman and the Creation of the Children's Defense Fund: Law and the Administrative State, 1964–1975." Unpublished manuscript, in author's possession.

"A Statement by the NAACP on the Scottsboro Case." *The Crisis,* March 1932, 82–83.

"State Papers Hit Slaying of Negro." *Jackson Clarion-Ledger,* 3 September 1955.

Stearns, Peter N. *Anxious Parents: A History of Modern Child Rearing in America.* New York: New York University Press, 2003.

Steinbeck, John. *Travels with Charley: In Search of America.* New York: Viking Press, 1962.

Stocking, George W., Jr. *Delimiting Anthropology: Occasional Essays and Reflections.* Madison: University of Wisconsin Press, 2001.

Stowe, Harriet Beecher. *Uncle Tom's Cabin.* 1851–52; New York: Bantam Books, 1981.

Streator, George. "Negro College Radicals." *The Crisis,* February 1934, 47.

Studebaker, John W. "Communism's Challenge to American Education." *School Life,* February 1948, 1–7.

———. "Education Moves Democracy Forward." *School Life,* November 1939, 35–37.

———. "The Education of Free Men in American Democracy." *School Life,* October 1941, 5–7.

"Students and Parents View School Problem." *Little Rock Arkansas Gazette,* 6 September 1957.

Sullivan, Neil Vincent. *Bound for Freedom: An Educator's Adventures in Prince Edward Country, Virginia.* Boston: Little, Brown, 1965.

Sullivan, Patricia. *Days of Hope: Race and Democracy in the New Deal Era.* Chapel Hill: University of North Carolina, 1996.

———. "Prelude to *Brown*: Education and the Struggle for Racial Justice during the NAACP's Formative Decades, 1909–1934." In *From the Grassroots to the Supreme Court: Brown v. Board of Education and American Democracy,* edited by Peter F. Lau, 154–72. Durham: Duke University Press, 2004.

———. "Southern Reformers, the New Deal and the Movement's Foundation." In *New Directions in Civil Rights Studies,* edited by Armstead L. Robinson and Patricia Sullivan, 81–104. Charlottesville: University Press of Virginia, 1991.

"The Supreme Court Rules on School Segregation." *School Life,* May 1954, 117–18.

Sutherland, Elizabeth, ed. *Letters from Mississippi.* New York: McGraw-Hill, 1965.

Sutherland, Robert L. *Color, Class, and Personality*. Washington, D.C.: American Council on Education, 1942.

Taxel, Joel. "Reclaiming the Voice of Resistance." In *The Politics of the Textbook*, edited by Michael W. Apple and Linda K. Christian-Smith, 78–111. New York: Routledge, 1991.

"Terror Reigns in Birmingham; Six Negro Children Are Killed." *Little Rock Arkansas Gazette*, 16 September 1963.

"This Is Freedom's Price—Shuttlesworth." *Birmingham News*, 9 September 1957.

Thompson, Kathleen, and Hilary Mac Austin, eds. *Children of the Depression*. Bloomington: Indiana University Press, 2001.

Thornton, J. Mills, III. "Municipal Politics and the Course of the Movement." In *New Directions in Civil Rights Studies*, edited by Armstead L. Robinson and Patricia Sullivan, 38–64. Charlottesville: University Press of Virginia, 1991.

"Three Boards of Education Speak Out." *Intercultural Education News* 8 (Spring 1947): 4–5.

Tiffin, Susan. *In Whose Best Interest?: Child Welfare Reform in the Progressive Era*. Westport, Conn.: Greenwood, 1982.

Till-Mobley, Mamie, and Christopher Benson. *Death of Innocence: The Story of the Hate Crime That Changed America*. New York: Random House, 2003.

"A Time of Testing." *Little Rock Arkansas Gazette*, 1 September 1957.

Tipton, James H. "'Mass Truancy' in Gary." *Intercultural Education News* 9 (Fall 1947): 1–2, 6.

Tobias, Channing H. "Implications of the Public School Segregation Cases." *The Crisis*, December 1953, 612–13.

Tobin, Maurice J. "Child Labor and the Law." *National Parent-Teacher* 44 (April 1950): 8–10.

Tuck, Stephen G. N. *Beyond Atlanta: The Struggle for Racial Equality in Georgia, 1940–1980*. Athens: University of Georgia Press, 2001.

Turner, Kara Miles. "'Liberating Lifescripts': Prince Edward County, Virginia, and the Roots of Brown v. Board of Education." In *From the Grassroots to the Supreme Court: Brown v. Board of Education and American Democracy*, edited by Peter F. Lau, 88–104. Durham: Duke University Press, 2004.

Tushnet, Mark V. *Making Civil Rights Law: Thurgood Marshall and the Supreme Court, 1936–1961*. New York: Oxford University Press, 1994.

Tuttle, William M., Jr. *Daddy's Gone to War: The Second World War in the Lives of America's Children*. New York: Oxford University Press, 1993.

Tyack, David, Robert Lowe, and Elisabeth Hansot. *Public Schools in Hard Times: The Great Depression and Recent Years*. Cambridge: Harvard University Press, 1984.

"Universal Declaration of Human Rights." *The Child* 13 (March 1949): 140–42.

Urbiel, Alexander. "The Making of Citizens: A History of Civic Education in Indianapolis, 1900–1950." Ph.D. diss., Indiana University, 1996.

U.S. Advisory Committee on Education. *Report of the Committee*. Washington, D.C.: U.S. Government Printing Office, 1938.

U.S. Children's Bureau. *Conclusions and Resolutions on Behalf of the Youth of the World*.

Introduction by Katharine F. Lenroot. Publication 315. Washington, D.C.: U.S. Government Printing Office, 1946.

———. *Controlling Juvenile Delinquency: A Community Program*. Publication 301. Washington, D.C.: U.S. Government Printing Office, 1943.

U.S. Committee on Economic Security. *Social Security in America: The Factual Background of the Social Security Act as Summarized from the Staff Reports to the Committee on Economic Security*. Washington, D.C.: U.S. Government Printing Office, 1937.

U.S. Office of Education. *How Democratic Is Your School?: Checklists on Democratic Practices for Secondary Schools*. Washington, D.C.: U.S. Office of Education, 1949.

Verba, Sidney. "Comparative Political Culture." In *Political Culture and Political Development*, edited by Lucian W. Pye and Sidney Verba, 512–60. Princeton: Princeton University Press, 1965.

Wakefield, Dan. "Justice in Sumner." *The Nation*, 1 October 1955, 284–85.

Wallace, Robert. "The Restraints: Open and Hidden." *Life*, 24 September 1956, 98–109, 111–12.

Washington, Booker T. *Up from Slavery: An Autobiography*. New York: Doubleday, Page, 1901.

Waskow, Arthur I. *From Race Riot to Sit-In, 1919 and the 1960s: A Study in the Connections between Conflict and Violence*. Gloucester, Mass.: Smith, 1975.

Webb, Sheyann, and Rachel Nelson West. *Selma, Lord, Selma: Girlhood Memories of the Civil-Rights Days*. Tuscaloosa: University of Alabama Press, 1980.

Weinraub, Bernard. "The Brilliancy of Black." *Esquire*, January 1967. Reprinted in *Voices in Our Blood: America's Best on the Civil Rights Movement*, edited by Jon Meacham, 352–66. New York: Random House, 2003. Also reprinted in *Smiling through the Apocalypse: Esquire's History of the Sixties*, edited by Harold Hayes, 669–84. New York: McCall, 1969.

Weiss, Nancy Pottishman. "The Mother-Child Dyad Revisited: Perceptions of Mothers and Children in Twentieth Century Child-Rearing Manuals." *Journal of Social Issues* 34 (Spring 1978): 31–42.

Weld, Theodore D. *American Slavery as It Is: Testimony of a Thousand Witnesses*. New York: American Anti-Slavery Society, 1839.

Welsh, David. "Valley of Fear." In *Mississippi Eyewitness: The Three Civil Rights Workers and How They Were Killed: The Exclusive Story by "Ramparts" Magazine*, 50–59. Menlo Park, Calif.: Keating, 1964.

"'Were Never into Meanness' Says Accused Men's Mother." *Memphis Commercial Appeal*, 2 September 1955. Reprinted in *The Lynching of Emmett Till: A Narrative History*, edited by Christopher Metress, 34–35. Charlottesville: University of Virginia Press, 2002.

"What Orval Hath Wrought." *Time*, 23 September 1957, 11–14.

Whitaker, Hugh Stephen. "A Case Study in Southern Justice: The Emmett Till Case." Master's thesis, Florida State University, 1963. Partially published in *Rhetoric and Public Affairs* 8 (Summer 2005): 189–224.

White, Deborah Gray. *Too Heavy a Load: Black Women in Defense of Themselves, 1894–1994*. New York: Norton, 1999.

White, E. B. "Letter from the South." *New Yorker*, 7 April 1956. Reprinted in *Voices in Our Blood: America's Best on the Civil Rights Movement*, edited by Jon Meacham, 161–66. New York: Random House, 2003.

White, Walter. "The Youth Council of the N.A.A.C.P." *The Crisis*, July 1937, 215.

Whitfield, Stephen J. *A Death in the Delta: The Story of Emmett Till*. New York: Free Press, 1988.

"Who's Responsible." *New Republic*, 28 September 1963, 3–4.

Wiegman, Robyn. "The Anatomy of Lynching." In *American Sexual Politics: Sex, Gender, and Race since the Civil War*, edited by John C. Fout and Maura Shaw Tantillo, 223–45. Chicago: University of Chicago Press, 1993.

Wilkerson, Doxey A. *Special Problems of Negro Education*. Staff Study 12. Washington, D.C.: U.S. Government Printing Office, 1939.

Wilkins, Roy. "At Youth for Integrated Schools." In *In Search of Democracy: The NAACP Writings of James Weldon Johnson, Walter White, and Roy Wilkins, 1920–1977*, edited by Sondra Kathryn Wilson, 387–90. New York: Oxford University Press, 1999.

Wilkinson, J. Harvie, III. *From Brown to Bakke: The Supreme Court and School Integration, 1954–1978*. New York: Oxford University Press, 1979.

Williams, Garth. *The Rabbits' Wedding*. New York: Harper, 1958.

Williams, Inez. "Letter to Youthport." *The Crisis*, February 1930, 62.

Williams, Juan. *Eyes on the Prize: America's Civil Rights Years, 1954–1965*. New York: Viking Penguin, 1987.

Williams, Maurice O. *Constructing the Black Masculine: Identity and Ideality in African-American Men's Literature and Culture, 1775–1995*. Durham: Duke University Press, 2002.

Williams, Vernon J., Jr. *From a Caste to a Minority: Changing Attitudes of American Sociologists toward Afro-Americans, 1896–1945*. New York: Greenwood, 1989.

———. *Rethinking Race: Franz Boas and His Contemporaries*. Lexington: University Press of Kentucky, 1996.

"Will She Live in Peace and Security?" *Survey Graphic*, January 1947, 119.

Wilson, Sondra Kathryn, ed. *In Search of Democracy: The NAACP Writings of James Weldon Johnson, Walter White, and Roy Wilkins, 1920–1977*. New York: Oxford University Press, 1999.

"Winners in *The Crisis* Beautiful Child Contest." *The Crisis*, September 1940, 286–87.

Winston, Henry. *Life Begins with Freedom*. New York: New Age, 1937.

Wolf, Eric. *Europe and the People without History*. Berkeley: University of California Press, 1982.

Woods, Allan J. "Letter to the Editor." *Newsweek*, 14 October 1963, 2.

Woodward, C. Vann. *The Strange Career of Jim Crow*. New York: Oxford University Press, 1955.

Woofter, T. J. "Possibilities of Future Migration." In *National Conference of Social Work*, 125. N.p., 1940.

————. *Southern Race Progress: The Wavering Color Line*. Washington, D.C.: Public Affairs Press, 1957.

————. "The Status of Racial and Ethnic Groups." In *Recent Social Trends in the United States: Report of the President's Research Committee on Social Trends*, 553–601. New York: McGraw-Hill, 1933.

Work Projects Administration. *Final Statistical Report of the Federal Emergency Relief Administration*. Washington, D.C.: U.S. Government Printing Office, 1942.

Wright, Richard. "Down by the Riverside." In *Uncle Tom's Children*. Reprinted in *Richard Wright: Early Works*, edited by Arnold Rampersad, 277–327. New York: Library of America, 1991.

————. "How 'Bigger' Was Born." In *Richard Wright: Early Works*, edited by Arnold Rampersad, 851–82. New York: Library of America, 1991.

————. *Native Son*. In *Richard Wright: Early Works*, edited by Arnold Rampersad, 443–882. New York: Library of America, 1991.

Yates, Elizabeth. *Amos Fortune: Free Man*. New York: Dutton, 1950.

————. *Rainbow around the World: The Story of UNICEF*. Indianapolis: Bobbs-Merrill, 1954.

Zangrando, Robert L. *The NAACP Crusade against Lynching, 1909–1950*. Philadelphia: Temple University Press, 1980.

Zeligs, Rose. "Children's Intergroup Concepts and Stereotypes." *Journal of Educational Sociology* 21 (October 1947): 113–26.

————. "Races and Nationalities Most and Least Liked by Children." *Journal of Educational Research* 48 (September 1954): 1–14.

————. "Racial Attitudes of Children as Expressed by Their Concepts of Race." *Sociology and Social Research* 21 (March 1937): 361–71.

Zelizer, Viviana A. *Pricing the Priceless Child: The Changing Social Value of Children*. New York: Basic Books, 1985.

Zellner, Bob. Interview by author. Birmingham, Alabama, 2 May 2008.

Zinn, Howard. "Finishing School for Pickets." *The Nation*, 6 August 1960, 71–73.

Zipes, Jack. "Second Thoughts on Socialization through Literature for Children." *Lion and the Unicorn* 5 (1982): 19–32.

Zipf, Karen L. "Reconstructing 'Free Woman': African-American Women, Apprenticeship, and Custody Rights during Reconstruction." *Journal of Women's History* 12 (Spring 2000): 8–31.

INDEX

categories, 17, 19; on baby photo-graphs, 19; and talented tenth, 19, 22; class biases of, 22, 28; on problems of African Americans, 28; on educa-tion, 40, 48, 49–50, 80, 83, 86, 269 (n. 59), 273 (n. 80); on color line, 51; on "twoness," 68, 220–21; on racism's effect on children, 73, 122; and Boas, 74; on "the Veil," 99, 122; and youth activism, 153; and children's literature, 157–58, 159, 295–96 (n. 13); European travel of, 202

Dudziak, Mary L., 261 (n. 6), 283 (nn. 68, 71)

Dunbar, Paul Laurence, 156

Eastland, James O., 124

Eastman Kodak, 172

Eckford, Elizabeth, 107, 127, 138

Economic justice, 3, 5, 12, 24, 43, 147, 231, 273 (n. 79)

Edelman, Marian Wright, 323 (n. 2)

Edmund Pettus Bridge, 131, 245

Education: universal education, 3, 44, 45, 47, 57, 273 (n. 76); and youth prob-lem, 9, 33, 38, 268 (n. 57); extending public schooling opportunities, 12, 270 (n. 65); African American par-ents' commitment to, 16–17, 121, 205; compulsory education laws, 23, 47, 272 (n. 75), 273 (n. 76); and rights of childhood, 27; and New Deal, 31; and American Youth Commission, 38, 39, 42–48, 49, 79, 80, 270 (n. 65), 270–71 (n. 69), 272–73 (n. 76); Du Bois on, 40; of rural youth, 42–47, 264 (n. 34), 270 (nn. 67, 68); revolutionary poten-tial of, 47–50, 273 (n. 78); and race relations, 48, 78–79; and political ideology, 57; and democracy, 78, 79–85, 89, 92, 93, 206, 283 (n. 68); and racial prejudice, 78–79, 85, 123, 279 (n. 51), 280 (n. 52), 283 (n. 72); youth activists' sacrificing of, 224–25.

See also *Brown v. Board of Education* (1954); Equal education

Eisenhower, Dwight D., 130

Eleanor Roosevelt Memorial Founda-tion, 310 (n. 16)

Elie, Lolis, 203, 232

Ellison, Ralph, 135, 302 (n. 48)

Ellsworth, Jeanne, 271 (n. 70)

Emergency War Conference, 184

Employment practices: equal employ-ment, 87; and youth activism, 172, 185, 187, 215; and collective experi-ences of racism, 233–34. *See also* Labor issues; Unemployment

Equal education: and youth problem, 3, 48, 164; and home and family ideals, 4; and discrepancies between black and white schools, 40, 45, 49, 80–82, 228, 231; and discrepancies between urban and rural schools, 43, 44, 45, 47, 80, 81–82, 228, 270 (nn. 67, 68); as national issue, 47, 63, 79–80, 81, 82, 83, 272 (n. 74); and national security, 79–80, 81, 82, 88, 111, 112; and NAACP, 88, 111–12, 120, 128, 273 (n. 79), 283 (n. 68); and children as agents of change, 113; and youth activism, 172, 185; and citizenship, 274 (n. 12)

Erikson, Erik, 277 (n. 36), 307 (n. 6)

Eugenics, 12, 21, 262 (n. 20)

Evans, Angie, 114

Evans, Eva Knox, 307 (n. 9)

Evers, Medgar, 189, 190, 306 (n. 61), 313 (n. 30), 316 (n. 45)

Evers, Myrlie, 94, 101, 102

Fairclough, Adam, 291 (n. 63), 298 (n. 28)

Farmer, James, 140–41, 142, 196–97, 308 (n. 12)

Farm Security Administration, 34, 46, 272 (n. 72)

Farm tenancy, 42, 43, 168

Racial justice, 3, 12, 13–14

Racial prejudice: Du Bois on, 15, 16; Lenroot on, 61–62; Roosevelt on, 62; and limitations of childhood ideals, 63; and personality-development research, 66–67, 179, 276 (n. 28); Lillian Smith on, 67–68; and juvenile delinquency, 71, 72, 179; research on, 71, 73–75, 88–89, 108, 112, 113–14, 116, 118, 123, 139, 198, 275 (n. 25), 277 (n. 36), 282 (n. 67), 320 (n. 65); and race relations, 73–74, 278 (n. 42); and education, 78–79, 85, 123, 279 (n. 51), 280 (n. 52), 283 (n. 72); adults compared with children, 114, 115–18, 119, 120, 144, 288 (n. 43); and youth problem, 179; children's lack of, 182; and youth activism, 195–96; effects of World War II on, 202; and rights of childhood, 282 (n. 67); and national security, 307 (n. 8)

Racial-progress strategy, 2, 15, 21–22

Racial socialization, 75, 130, 161, 278 (n. 44), 311 (n. 20), 312 (n. 28)

Racial uplift, 11, 14–15, 16, 20–24, 225

Racism: effects on African American youth, 3, 12–13, 14, 40, 41, 69, 72–73, 109, 134, 213, 237–38; effects on African American children, 4, 73, 91, 92, 93, 94, 102, 107–8, 109, 121–22, 134, 135, 137, 139, 141; stories and images of black children and youth challenging, 19, 107; childhood ideals challenging, 20, 106, 108; and Children's Crusade for Children, 59; and personality-development research, 67, 68, 69, 276 (nn. 28, 30); and popular culture, 67–68; effects on white Americans, 67–68, 69, 276 (n. 30); and juvenile delinquency, 72; Wright on, 72–73; as learned system of belief, 76, 279 (n. 46); Lillian Smith on, 77–78; and national security, 82–83, 88, 112, 276

(n. 30), 307 (n. 8); and children as agents of change, 90, 102; and Till murder, 94; portrayals of racists, 108, 286 (n. 33); and home and family ideals, 131; in public libraries and schools, 158; effects of World War II on, 182–83, 202; and youth activism, 183, 194, 215; and World War II, 193; structural nature of, 250; and segregationist point of view, 292 (n. 76)

Racist philosophies, 10, 12, 14, 21, 24, 26, 39, 43

Rainach, William, 125

Rainey, Homer P., 33, 42, 43, 79, 269 (n. 64)

Ravitch, Diane, 210, 280 (n. 52), 312 (n. 28)

Reagon, Bernice, 246, 323 (n. 79)

Reavis, Dick J., 293 (n. 82)

Recreation programs: federal funding for, 12; and youth subcultures, 31; and youth problem, 33, 37; for preventing juvenile delinquency, 37, 38; and loafing, 38, 268 (n. 57); and NAACP youth councils, 172, 180–81; national debate on, 180; Jim Crow practices restricting, 180–81; and youth activism, 184, 187, 233; and extracurricular activities, 229

Reed, William, 96

Reeves, Thomas, 227–28

Reid, Ira D., 40–41

Respectability, 15, 17, 19, 20–24, 25, 107, 225, 263 (n. 31)

Rice, John, 75, 86, 234

Riis, Jacob, 23

Ritterhouse, Jennifer Lynn, 278 (n. 44), 308 (n. 12), 315–16 (n. 43)

Roberts, Gene, 106, 286 (n. 29), 290 (n. 58), 292 (n. 76)

Roberts, Terrence, 113

Robertson, Charles, 233, 245

Robeson, Paul, 233

home and family ideals, 15; benefi-
cence of as justification for, 23, 26,
155; and abolitionist children's litera-
ture, 153–54; and Civil War children's
literature, 155; sentimental ideas on
childhood undermining, 263–64
(n. 34)
Smith, Carolyn, 221
Smith, Claude, 211, 232
Smith, Frank, 217, 240
Smith, George W., 99, 101
Smith, Jerome, 235
Smith, Katharine Capshaw, 159
Smith, Lillian, 67–70, 76–78, 86, 99, 279
(nn. 47, 50), 316 (n. 45)
Social Security Administration, 34, 275
(n. 22)
Sociology, 268 (n. 55)
Solomon, Fredric, 194
South: racialized judicial system of, 8;
child labor and child-welfare-related
reforms in, 23; conditions of African
American youth in, 41, 81; rural edu-
cation in, 43, 44, 47, 270 (n. 67), 271
(n. 69); racialized sociopolitical order
in, 48, 62; lynching in, 68; dual school
system in, 80, 83; and contested na-
ture of black childhood, 95; reaction
to Till murder, 97–99
Southern Christian Leadership Confer-
ence (SCLC), 134, 145, 222–23, 243,
291 (n. 63)
Southern Conference Education Fund,
137–38
Southern Negro Youth Congress, 166,
298 (n. 28)
Southern Regional Council, 89, 118, 205
Southern Student Human Relations
Project, 115
Soviet Union, 111
Spargo, John, 24, 263 (n. 29)
Spencer, Chuck, 113
Sperber, Dan, 294 (n. 95)
Spillers, Hortense J., 295 (n. 11)

Spingarn Medal, 188
Sputnik, 111
Sribnick, Ethan, 323 (n. 2)
Stanford University, 178
Steele brothers, 227
Steinbeck, John, 47, 103, 267 (n. 51)
Stereotypes: photographs of black
children countering, 17, 19, 20, 22,
262 (n. 20); Washington addressing,
22–23; poor black children under-
mining efforts at countering, 23; of
African American youth's educational
abilities, 43; children's adopting of,
59; and Till murder, 97; and defense
of segregation, 125; African Americans compared to animals, 126–27;
in children's literature, 156–57, 158;
and youth activism, 168, 172, 192; and
NAACP youth councils, 180, 181
Stern, Edith, 268 (n. 58)
Stoner, Peter, 199
Stowe, Harriet Beecher, 13
Strand, John, 200
Studebaker, John W., 266 (n. 47)
Student Non-Violent Coordinating Committee (SNCC): and effects of racism
on African American children, 4, 91,
122, 141; images of children used by,
91, 92, 142, 143, 249, 293 (n. 84); advertisements of, 142; and ideas about
childhood, 142, 143–44; and public
attention to riots, 143–44; and youth
activism, 152, 153, 189, 209, 214, 225,
242, 243, 306 (n. 61), 322 (n. 76), 323
(n. 77); organizing efforts of, 167, 234;
membership in, 223, 316 (n. 46)
Sullivan, Patricia, 269–70 (n. 64), 298
(n. 27)
Survey Graphic, 45, 272–73 (n. 76)
Sutherland, Robert L., 40, 41
Swan, Edward, 175

Taylor, Paul S., 45, 267 (n. 51)
Teenager: as term, 31, 265 (n. 44)

376

Watson, Barbara Jean, 144
Wayne State University, 178, 186–87
Wells, Lyn, 221, 236
Wertham, Fredric, 71, 72
Wesley, Charles H., 181
Wesley, Cynthia, 137
White, E. B., 308 (n. 11)
White, Walter, 163, 164, 173, 177
White Americans: liberals, 2, 117, 145, 192; and images of civil rights movement, 4; lack of support for economic justice, 5; northerners, 8, 146, 261 (n. 5); effects of racism on, 67–68, 69, 276 (n. 30); reaction to Till murder, 97–99; and childhood ideals, 145; backlash of, 147–48, 293 (n. 91); reaction to young white activists, 149, 294 (n. 96); limits of sentimentality of, 150. *See also* White southerners
White Citizens' Councils, 90, 125, 127, 188
White House Conference on Children and Youth (1950), 8, 66, 195–96, 280 (n. 53), 308 (n. 10)
White House Conference on Children in a Democracy (1940), 61, 62–64, 65, 79, 275 (n. 22), 276 (n. 27)
White House Conference on Dependent Children (1909), 22, 264 (n. 34)
White middle-class children: ideal conceptions of, 2, 8, 12, 14, 15, 16, 58, 96; opportunities of, 41; reaction to integration, 104
Whiteness: American childhood defined as, 59–60, 84, 274 (n. 16); as social construct, 295 (n. 10)
White racial degeneracy: fears of, 264 (n. 34)
White southerners: conceptions of African American children, 2, 10; on Scottsboro Boys case, 7, 9, 10, 97, 216 (n. 3); justification of Jim Crow, 12; denial of citizenship rights for blacks, 27; and improvement of

African American schooling, 48, 49; defense of segregation, 80, 123–30, 290 (n. 56); opposition to civil rights, 90, 102–3, 104–5, 114, 115–16; and Till murder, 95, 98–99, 100; and images of integration, 103–4, 106, 107, 108, 113; and church bombing, 138, 291–92 (n. 70); and children's literature, 155; and youth activism, 172, 192, 204; fears of youths as agents of change, 289 (n. 55)
White supremacy: Du Bois's challenging of, 16; Lillian Smith on, 68, 69; and Till murder, 95, 98, 102; blacks compared to children, 97; vulnerability of African Americans in face of, 101, 109, 138; press coverage of, 106, 107–8, 117, 118; violent manifestations of, 109, 112, 135, 144–45; Wilkins on, 117; and purity of white race, 125–26; defense of segregation, 127; and racial awareness, 129–30; and African Americans' home and family ideals, 131–32; brutality of, 141, 144; as threatening and harmful to children, 142, 148; broader assault on, 147; terrorist tactics of, 149; press reflecting views of, 286 (n. 28)
White womanhood: and Scottsboro Boys case, 7, 9, 10, 97, 261 (n. 3); and Till murder, 93, 95, 96–97, 99; and defense of segregation, 125; lynching as protection of, 172–73
Whitfield, Stephen, 102
Wilkins, Roy, 95, 111, 115, 117, 129, 186, 187, 232–33, 319 (n. 58)
Williams, Clarissa, 190, 199–200, 220
Williams, Ethel James, 112
Williams, Eugene, 9
Williams, Garth, 307 (n. 9)
Williams, Maurice, 147–48
Williams, Vernon J., Jr., 278 (n. 42)
Wolf, Eric, 267 (n. 48), 268 (n. 55)
Women: and child protection and wel-

DATE DUE
